FRONTIER

FRONTIER

Exploring the Top Ten Emerging
Markets of Tomorrow

Gavin Serkin

BLOOMBERG PRESS

Library of Congress Cataloging-in-Publication Data
Serkin, Gavin, 1971–
 Frontier : exploring the top ten emerging markets of tomorrow / Gavin Serkin.
  pages cm
 Includes bibliographical references and index.
 ISBN 978-1-118-82373-6 (cloth)
1. Investments, Foreign—Developing countries. 2. Investments—Developing countries. I. Title.
HG5993.S467 2015
332.67'3–dc23
                                                        2014041647

Cover Design: Wiley
Cover Image: Sky ©Shutterstock.com/Pakhnyushchy;
Landscape ©Shutterstock.com/Anton_Ivanov

Set in 11/13 Adobe Garamond Pro by Laserwords Private Ltd, Chennai, India
Printed in Great Britain by TJ International Ltd, Padstow, Cornwall, UK

For my parents, Tricia & Stanley, and the
memory of epic caravan journeys

&

My late father-in-law, Victor, who summed up
these hundred thousand words in three:
"What, another holiday?"

Contents

About the Author

Gavin Serkin has been writing about developing economies for the best part of two decades as the Editor of *Portfolio International* magazine and more recently as the head of the emerging markets international desk at Bloomberg News in London.

His work keeps him in touch with some of the biggest investors and world leaders, chairing conference panels on issues from African development and Chinese growth to Islamic finance.

Gavin led Bloomberg's coverage of the credit and derivatives markets from 2004 to 2008, winning the Society of American Business Editors & Writers' Best in Business Award and the Society of Professional Journalists' Deadline Club Award. His team's exposure of problems brewing in the little-understood world of collateralized debt obligations provided warnings of the subprime mortgages disaster about to unfold.

Gavin has a joint honors degree in Economics & International Relations. He lives by the sea in Whitstable, England, with his wife and son.

Disclaimer

Financial markets and conditions can change rapidly, therefore the views in this book shouldn't be taken as current statements of fact nor should reliance be placed on them when making investment decisions. They shouldn't be considered as advice or a recommendation to buy, sell or hold a particular investment. Opinions expressed by named individuals don't necessarily reflect the views of the companies that employ them. Some of the individuals or their employers may have dealt in the investments discussed. As such, the book contains information and opinion on investments that doesn't constitute independent research, and therefore isn't subject to the protections afforded to independent research.

Prologue

PHOTOGRAPHY BY GABRIEL ROTICH, A24 MEDIA

"One's destination is never a place but a new way of looking at things."
Henry Miller

Where's the best place in the world to put your money?
So far this decade, it's a country deemed so doomed it's listed
with the ten most fragile states; a place where modern-day slavery, violence
and the breakdown of law and order rank it among the three worst hellholes
on the planet.[1-4]

Between deadly attacks by the Taliban, strikes by US drones and the
secret missions to monitor Osama bin Laden, shares in Karachi soared,
extending 1000% gains this century.[5]

It's not just Pakistan.

In the face of terror and global economic shocks, some of the biggest
investment rewards are turning up in the most vulnerable of places. Assets
in impoverished, radicalized or seemingly impenetrable corners of the world
are often wildly discounted. Even a glimmer of hope for political stability or
improvement in the economy can spark a major rally (Table 0.1).

At one time such countries were looked upon as *exotic* by a few
investors while mostly dismissed as basket cases. Now they form a growing
investment universe known as the frontier markets – a gateway before the
more mainstream emerging and developed markets that have trillions of
dollars of investment funds competing to buy assets. While some rank as
frontier because they have restrictive investment laws or tiny markets, most
are poor or riven by conflict.

So how can investors tell which of these frontier markets will be the ones
to take off? What are the signs the smartest money managers look for?

Armed with a spreadsheet of the emerging market and frontier funds that
achieved some of the best returns for their categories in the past five and ten
years, I began ringing around. I put three questions to each of the investors:
Which frontier markets do you favor most for the *next* five to ten years?
When are you visiting these countries? And can I come along?

The result was a crazy schedule to fit with ten busy diaries, crisscrossing
from Africa to Asia, Europe and Latin America, returning to Asia and Africa,
then onto the Middle East, back to Asia before winding up once again in
Africa (Table 0.2).

TABLE 0.1   Plucky seven

Best performing primary equity indexes this decade

Index	Return
Karachi 100 index	176%
Dubai Financial Market	149%
Philippine SE Index	145%
Stock Exchange of Thailand	120%
OMX Copenhagen 20	95%
Qatar Exchange Index	92%
Nairobi All Share	92%

Best performing primary equity indexes this millennium

Index	Return
Mongolia Stock Exchange Top 20 Index	3207%
Montenegro Stock Exchange	1237%
Colombia Colcap Index	1113%
Karachi 100 Index	1028%
Qatar Exchange Index	894%
Peru Lima General Index	890%
Kazakhstan KASE Stock Exchange	689%

Note: Data compiled by Bloomberg as of December 2014. Table excludes Venezuela Stock Market Index and Lusaka Stock Exchange All Share Index because of restrictions on repatriating foreign-currency returns or data constraints. Base currency: US dollar. *(Function: WEIS GO).*

As the poorest continent, and consequently the region offering the fastest potential economic growth, Africa accounts for four of the ten countries selected by the investors. At the most basic, it's a story of populations being lifted from subsistence living, and starting to consume the goods and services that drive the cycle of wealth creation.

But as we hop from democracy to autocracy, communist to Islamic regime, there's another ideal too – that broader economic and social inclusion can ultimately help give people a political voice.

TABLE 0.2 The money managers and their pick of countries

Destination	Portfolio Manager Participating	Company & Assets in Emerging Markets	Emerging Market Funds	Performance & Peer Ranking
Kenya	Brett Rowley	TCW Group, California $11 billion	TCW Emerging Markets Income Fund	3rd highest total return among 278 US-registered global emerging market fixed income funds over 10 years at 175% (annualized 10.6%)
Myanmar	Howie Schwab	Driehaus Capital Management $3.5 billion	Driehaus Emerging Markets Growth Fund	6th highest total return among 638 US-registered emerging market equity funds over 10 years at 287% (annualized 14.5%)
Romania	Andras Szalkai	Raiffeisen Capital Management $2.5 billion	Raiffeisen Emerging Markets-Aktien	2nd highest total return among 467 European Union-registered global emerging market funds over 5 years at 221% (annualized 26.2%)
Argentina	Julian Adams	Adelante	Adelante Emerging Debt Fund	2nd highest total return among 33 offshore-domiciled global emerging market debt funds over 5 years until liquidation at 52% (annualized 8.8%)
Vietnam	Mark Mobius	Templeton Asset Management > $40 billion	Templeton Emerging Markets Investment Trust	2nd highest total return among 46 global emerging market investment trusts over 10 years at 360% (annualized 16.5%)
Nigeria	Kevin Daly	Aberdeen Asset Management $13 billion	Aberdeen Global Select Emerging Markets Bond Fund	35th highest total return among 3033 offshore emerging market funds over 5 years at 85% (annualized 13.1%)

Destination	Portfolio Manager Participating	Company & Assets in Emerging Markets	Emerging Market Funds	Performance & Peer Ranking
Egypt	Andrew Stobart	Baillie Gifford $12 billion	Baillie Gifford Emerging Markets Growth Fund	14th highest total return among 636 UK-registered global emerging market funds over 10 years at 301% (annualized 14.9%)
Saudi Arabia	Sean Taylor	Deutsche Asset & Wealth Management $10 billion	DWS Top Asien Fund	27th highest total return among 986 Asia Pacific equity funds over 10 years at 118% (annualized 8.1%)
Sri Lanka	Timothy Drinkall	Morgan Stanley $25 billion	Morgan Stanley Galaxy Frontier Emerging Markets Fund	21st highest total return among 2571 offshore-domiciled global emerging market funds over 5 years at 118% (annualized 16.9%)
Ghana	Derrick Irwin	Wells Fargo Asset Management $12.4 billion	Wells Fargo Advantage Emerging Markets Equity Fund	17th highest total return among 638 US-registered emerging market stock funds over 10 years at 253% (annualized 13.4%)

Source: Data compiled by Bloomberg as of June 2014

An English financier summed it up after his Vietnamese wife came off her scooter in a crater in the road. Imagine the stink you'd cause over these potholes in England, we mused. But that's the difference in frontier markets, he said. Because hardly anyone pays direct taxes, they don't feel the same right to complain. The more a country taxes or borrows from its citizens, the more accountable it needs to be. And not just for the state of roads but for healthcare, corruption, human rights.

Rather than a comprehensive study of each country – there are countless admirably detailed works[6] to choose from for each of the 10 – this book is intended as a more practical view of realities on the ground, first from my own experience and then from the perspective of the investor.

With a different top-performing money manager in each country, we observe a range of investment approaches and their application, drawing from interviews with government ministers, central bankers and corporate leaders. After each meeting, the investors provide their "bottom line" analysis of the potential, followed by the events or "triggers" that would make them buy or sell.

At the back of the book is a ranking from the money managers of all of the countries and the stocks and bonds highlighted, along with summary notes and conclusions. We'll be tracking the investments with updates on the latest news at www.frontierfunds.org and on Twitter at @frontierfunds.

But first, we start at the beginning, with a guide to what constitutes *frontier* from the grandfather of emerging market investing, Mark Mobius.

Endnotes

1. Anonymous (2014) Fragile States Index, Foreign Policy. Available at: http://www. foreignpolicy.com/fragile-states-2014.
2. Gedmin, J. (2013) The 2013 Legatum Prosperity Index, Legatum Institute, p. 50. Available at: http://media.prosperity.com/2013/pdf/publications/PI2013 Brochure_WEB.pdf.
3. Anonymous (2013) The Global Slavery Index 2013, Walk Free Foundation. Available at: http://www.globalslaveryindex.org/report/?download.
4. Lattimer, M. (2013) Peoples under threat 2013, Minority Rights Group International. Available at: http://www.minorityrights.org/11989/peoples-under-threat/ peoples-under-threat-2013.html.
5. Mangi, F., Patterson, M. (2012) Pakistan stocks best as violence ignored: Riskless returns, Bloomberg News. Available at: http://www.bloomberg.com/news/2012- 11-20/pakistan-stocks-best-as-violence-ignored-riskless-return.html.
6. For my recommended reading list, go to www.frontierfunds.org.

Introduction to Frontier

BY MARK MOBIUS

Mark Mobius began investing in developing countries over four decades ago. Now aged 78, he still spends over 250 days a year traveling to manage more than $40 billion of assets as the Executive Chairman of Templeton Emerging Markets Group. His Templeton Emerging Markets Investment Trust returned 360% in the past ten years, ranking No. 2 among peers.

Over the past 25 years we've seen emerging markets grow into a multi-trillion dollar asset class. But today, we have the opportunity to invest in a whole new set of emerging markets: the frontier markets.

It's widely recognized that these are the emerging markets showing even quicker growth. In the past decade, the ten fastest growing economies were all emerging markets – and eight of them were frontier.[1]

Frontier markets are geographically and economically diverse and are found all over the world – in Africa, Asia, Latin America and central and eastern Europe. The countries include Nigeria, Kenya, Egypt, Saudi Arabia, Bangladesh, Vietnam, Kazakhstan, Romania, Argentina and many more – over 40 in total.

These countries have been under-researched or ignored totally as they were too small and perceived as being too risky or difficult to enter because of foreign exchange restrictions and other investor barriers. Each month, tens of thousands of company research reports are produced in the United States by brokers, banks and other organizations. In Nigeria – one of the largest frontier markets – the number is in the hundreds. This comparative lack of information can be a plus for those investors willing to do original on-the-spot research.

In terms of their economies, frontier markets range from some of the world's most impoverished nations to wealthy Gulf oil producers. Most have in common a desire to introduce market mechanisms to boost economic growth and development.

So how do we define a frontier market?

As a subset of emerging markets, they share the same characteristics that generally result in faster economic growth. But frontier markets are typically less developed than emerging markets generally – they have smaller market capitalization and liquidity, and they tend to have a lower correlation with price movements in other emerging and developed markets. Since they are growing at an even quicker pace, this younger generation is destined to become tomorrow's more mature emerging markets.

The potential for further growth is striking. While frontier markets account for 24% of the world's land area and 22% of the global population, only 8% of international gross domestic product comes from these countries. That gap is being closed rapidly as they catch up in production and consumption. The International Monetary Fund projected that 10 of the 20 fastest-growing economies will be in sub-Saharan Africa by 2017, with two more in north Africa.[2]

Frontier markets are not only growing faster – they also have a number of characteristics that make them safer than imagined. They generally have lower debt and higher foreign-exchange cash piles in relation to their gross domestic product. Many also have enormous reserves of natural resources. Countries that are strong producers of commodities such as oil, iron ore, aluminum, copper, nickel, and platinum look especially interesting. Infrastructure development in emerging markets has led to a continued need for hard commodities – those extracted through mining – while demand for soft commodities such as sugar, cocoa and select grains has also increased.

Faster growth in the economies than the populations creates higher income per capita, fueling demand for consumer products. Mobile phone usage is just one example. While the number of subscribers per 100 people in Japan is 109 and 98 in the United States, in Nigeria it's much lower at 68, and in Bangladesh it's 64. But they're catching up fast as incomes increase and communication networks expand. This has led to a positive earnings growth outlook for consumer-related companies. We look for opportunities in a wide range of products from beer to automobiles and banking. We have seen how these countries are leaping the technology gap and going from no bank accounts to transferring money using mobile phones.

The demand for consumer goods and services goes hand in hand with a need for infrastructure – electricity, roads, airports and so forth. You can't have a cell phone without a way to charge it and you can't have an air conditioner without an electric outlet. Where the government is unable to quench the thirst for electricity, the people create their own. We found that almost every building in Lagos has its own diesel generation system. Sometimes the fuel ran out and we'd get stuck in the hotel elevator!

Frontier investments have historically had a low correlation to developed and emerging markets, as well as with other frontier nations. This is due in part to differences in the underlying industries and the distinct growth drivers in each country. It means that adding frontier markets as a component of a portfolio could actually help reduce overall volatility and provide a source of diversification (Tables 0.3 and 0.4).

Of all the frontier markets, the most diverse and fascinating area is Africa. Building on its storied history as the bedrock for humankind, Africa has become a continent of ample investment opportunity. All of Africa can be classified as frontier with the exception of South Africa – though even in that country the exposure to the rest of the continent means that many of the stocks qualify as frontier targets.

Africa is well known for its wealth of natural resources – oil, gas, metals, minerals and huge tracts of agricultural land. These riches have lured global investors, most notably from the big emerging markets – China, India and Brazil – as they seek raw materials for their own development. African

TABLE 0.3 Frontier universe

Country	MSCI Equity Index	JPMorgan Bond Index
Angola	-	NexGEM
Argentina	Frontier	NexGEM
Bahrain	Frontier	CEMBI
Bangladesh	Frontier	-
Belarus	-	NexGEM
Belize	-	NexGEM
Bolivia	-	NexGEM
Bulgaria	Frontier	EMBI Global
Cote D'Ivoire	-	NexGEM
Croatia	Frontier	EMBI Global
Dominican Republic	-	NexGEM
Ecuador	-	NexGEM
Egypt	Emerging	NexGEM
El Salvador	-	NexGEM
Estonia	Frontier	-
Gabon	-	NexGEM
Georgia	-	NexGEM
Ghana	-	NexGEM
Guatemala	-	NexGEM
Honduras	-	NexGEM
Iraq	-	NexGEM
Jamaica	-	NexGEM
Jordan	Frontier	NexGEM
Kazakhstan	Frontier	EMBI Global
Kenya	Frontier	EMBI Global
Kuwait	Frontier	CEMBI

Country	MSCI Equity Index	JPMorgan Bond Index
Lebanon	Frontier	EMBI Global
Lithuania	Frontier	EMBI Global
Mauritius	Frontier	-
Mongolia	-	NexGEM
Morocco	Frontier	EMBI Global
Myanmar	-	-
Nigeria	Frontier	NexGEM
Oman	Frontier	CEMBI
Pakistan	Frontier	NexGEM
Paraguay	-	NexGEM
Romania	Frontier	EMBI Global
Saudi Arabia	GCC Countries	CEMBI
Senegal	-	NexGEM
Serbia	Frontier	EMBI Global
Slovenia	Frontier	-
Sri Lanka	Frontier	NexGEM
Tanzania	-	NexGEM
Togo	Frontier	-
Tunisia	Frontier	EMBI Global
Ukraine	Frontier	EMBI Global
Vietnam	Frontier	NexGEM
Zambia	-	NexGEM

Note: Frontier investors typically consider those countries excluded from the more mainstream indexes used by managers of pension and mutual funds to guide holdings. Some of these countries are specifically grouped in frontier indexes such as the MSCI Frontier Markets Index for equities or JPMorgan's Next Generation Markets Index (NexGEM) for bonds.[3-4] Others are "too frontier" even for these indexes, like Saudi Arabia, which is only now taking its first steps to allow foreigners to buy shares, and Myanmar, just in the throes of creating a stock exchange.

Source: Data compiled by Bloomberg as of December 2014

TABLE 0.4   MSCI Frontier Markets Index

Breakdown By Country	%
Kuwait (7 members)	24.0
Nigeria (17 members)	15.4
Argentina (6 members)	8.5
Pakistan (15 members)	7.5
Morocco (9 members)	6.7
Kenya (5 members)	5.7
Oman (9 members)	4.9
Vietnam (13 members)	4.1
Kazakhstan (3 members)	3.7
Slovenia (4 members)	2.6
Romania (5 members)	2.6
Lebanon (4 members)	2.3
Bangladesh (4 members)	2.2
Sri Lanka (3 members)	2.1
Croatia (3 members)	1.7
Bahrain (3 members)	1.3
Mauritius (2 members)	1.3
Togo (1 member)	0.8
Jordan (3 members)	0.7
Tunisia (2 members)	0.6
Estonia (2 members)	0.4
Serbia (2 members)	0.3
Ukraine (2 members)	0.2
Bulgaria (2 members)	0.2
Lithuania (2 members)	0.2

Breakdown by Industry	%
Banks (44 members)	41.5
Telecommunication Services (14 members)	15.3
Energy (16 members)	11.3
Food Beverage & Tobacco (10 members)	9.3
Materials (15 members)	6.0
Real Estate (6 members)	4.6
Diversified Financials (4 members)	2.9
Pharmaceuticals, Biotechnology & Life Sciences (3 members)	2.8
Transportation (2 members)	2.3
Capital Goods (3 members)	1.5
Utilities (3 members)	0.8
Insurance (3 members)	0.6
Household & Personal Products (2 members)	0.6
Retailing (2 members)	0.4
Consumer Services (1 member)	0.1

Note: This table shows the countries and industries with the biggest representation in the MSCI Frontier Markets Index, with the number of companies, or "members," listed from each and the percentage overall weighting. *(Function: MXFM Index MEMB GO).*
Source: Data compiled by Bloomberg as of December 2014

countries, in return, have received vitally needed transport links, power stations, hospitals and schools, which is bringing into play another great African resource – a huge and youthful population. More than a billion strong and with a median age of just 20, the population of Africa is seeing its prospects and productivity transformed by education, mobility and access to capital resources.

The effects of this virtuous circle are evident. Kenya, with a new constitution following the serious political disturbances in 2007, is attractive for its significant natural assets – notably in agriculture – and as an entry point for much of the investment into Africa. A well-regulated telecoms market provides opportunities to invest in the mobile industry along with retailers and banks.

In north Africa, Egypt has one of the biggest economies of the continent, spanning banking, telecommunications and tourism, as well as trade with the Middle East and Europe – all represented on its stock market. Its large population of 81 million is young and relatively well educated. The country's wrenching political turmoil and accompanying economic dislocation has made a number of companies with appealing longer-term prospects attractively valued.

Beyond Africa, countries in central Asia and eastern Europe hold great potential. Kazakhstan, for example, a country rich in oil and other natural resources, is making significant investments in infrastructure development, while in Romania we see opportunities for growth in energy, agriculture and the consumer sectors.

Within Asia, the importance of Vietnam can't be overstated. With a population at around 90 million, it is often touted as the last big frontier. GDP growth is expected to accelerate to between 6–7% annually through to 2018.

Some investors perceive the additional growth in frontier markets to be available only at the cost of heightened risk because of political instability, low shareholder protection or corruption. While the risks in frontier markets are more salient, they're similar in scale to any other market, whether developed or emerging. The real difference is a lower degree of understanding and research on the part of the global investment community. A research-oriented model allows investors to better manage this information gap.

We are particularly cautious where capital controls and investor expropriation could become risks. But we think this risk is already priced into the valuations of frontier stocks, which often trade at discounts – sometimes wide discounts – to their emerging and developed peers.

Low liquidity and the small individual size of frontier markets are other factors that have discouraged investors. Certainly, patience is required to build positions, but it's worth noting that at the end of 2013 the total capitalization of frontier markets amounted to $1.6 trillion, including more than 7000 companies, and daily turnover averaged $2.5 billion. This is largely the result of governments selling state assets to the public through stock market listings while entrepreneurs are increasingly using the capital markets as a source of funding. This expansion of the frontier markets universe, in turn, is starting to bring in more investors.

That said, liquidity is still lower than in developed or emerging markets, which does carry risk in the event of fund redemptions, for example. But having fewer large investors also has some benefits. Less competition for stocks often allows positions to be accumulated at attractive valuations. Once purchased, the assets can command a premium as other investors seek to enter.

Frontier markets are sometimes seen as excessively dependent on commodities and natural resources. This criticism underplays the diversity. Some economies, notably Kenya and Ukraine, are oriented toward agriculture and domestic spending. Even those driven by oil, such as Nigeria and the Gulf states, have experienced rapid diversification as commodity earnings filter through the wider economy.

Investors cleaving closely to frontier market benchmarks might find themselves unintentionally having a heavy weighting toward one region, country or sector at the expense of others. We generally avoid this by investing without reference to benchmarks and build our portfolios from a ground-up, stock-specific perspective.

The fact that frontier markets aren't well known and not many investors are active in them (yet) means big opportunities are waiting to be found. There's a broad spectrum of information available at your fingertips. Companies' annual reports and websites as well as the wider internet can be very valuable tools. Dig deep – research the people behind the numbers, learn about the industry, look into competitors – you could learn valuable information.

Where practical, on-site examinations of operations and factories can yield critical additional insight. It's important to keep your eyes open as soon as you land in a country to form a complete picture. How crowded are the restaurants or hotels? How efficient is the public transportation? How modern is the airport? The small things can tell you a lot.

Endnotes

1. Data compiled from The Economist, International Monetary Fund shows fastest average annual GDP growth from 2003-2013 for: Angola (10.3%), China (10.2%), Ethiopia (9.5%), Myanmar (9.0%), Chad (8.5%), Cambodia (7.9%), Uzbekistan (7.7%), Rwanda (7.7%), India (7.4%), Mozambique (7.3%).
2. International Monetary Fund, World Economic Outlook (2014), for growth outlook for 2019 see pages 184–186. Available at: http://www.imf.org/external/Pubs/ft/weo/2014/01/pdf/text.pdf.
3. MSCI classifies 33 countries as Frontier Markets and includes 24 of these in the MSCI Frontier Markets Index. Saudi Arabia Index is not currently included in the MSCI Frontier Markets Index but is part of the MSCI Gulf Cooperation Council (GCC) Countries Index. MSCI considered moving Egypt from the Emerging Markets Index to the Frontier Markets Index in 2013, citing the country's shortage of foreign currency. More details available at: http://www.msci.com/products/indexes/country_and_regional/fm/.
4. JPMorgan's Next Generation Markets Index tracks dollar-denominated bonds issued by frontier-market governments. Members of NexGEM are also included in the EMBI Global, JPMorgan's broader grouping of emerging market bonds. The JPMorgan Corporate Emerging Market Bond Index, or CEMBI, groups dollar-denominated company debt. The table shows members of the CEMBI Broad index, which includes a wider universe of issuers. More details available at: https://www.jpmorgan.com/cm/cs?pagename=JPM_redesign/JPM_Content_C/Generic_Detail_Page_Template&cid=1320478263158.

CHAPTER 1

Kenya

PHOTOGRAPHY BY GABRIEL ROTICH, A24 MEDIA

1 — Mamboz

Jomo Kenyatta Airport feels like a war zone.

Armed cadets motion passengers from the plane to a beige-green bus marked National Youth Service. We sit cramped together, luggage on laps.

To our right, a steel wall barricades the main airport building gutted by fire.

Our driver, in a beret and green army fatigues, weaves through the pitch black before pulling up at a multi-story car park that's serving as the makeshift arrivals hall. Soldiers usher us to immigration gates where ticket machines stood a few months ago.

I head to "Foreign Visitors" until I feel a tug at my arm. "This officer is a friend of mine."

My impromptu guide jumps me through the "Kenyan Citizens" line and fires a meaningful nod at the olive-uniformed guard. He asks me the purpose of my visit but before I can say "business" my passport is stamped and I'm through.

My new-found friend sat next to me on the plane. He was a candidate in the 2013 election for a ward in Nakuru, Kenya's third largest city after Nairobi and Mombasa. He lost the election but became the assistant to the winning MP, a mate of his. As we wait half an hour in the four parking rows that make up baggage reclaim, he shows me one of his three mobile phones. He has private numbers for everyone who's anyone, right up to President Uhuru Kenyatta – "my cousin."

Two extended families have rotated Kenya's political leadership since the British colonialists withdrew in the 1960s. Jomo Kenyatta – the current president's father – was from the biggest tribe, the Kikuyus. After 15 years he gave way to Daniel Arap Moi, a Kalenjin. Moi's dictatorship lasted a quarter of a century before the presidency swung back to the Kikuyus in 2002 under Mwai Kibaki.

It was Kibaki's re-election at the end of 2007 and opposition claims of vote rigging that descended into clashes which killed over a thousand people and displaced half a million.[1] A national unity government hastily formed the next year made Kibaki the president and Raila Odinga prime minister. Kikuyu rule continued in 2013 with Uhuru's victory.

I wondered aloud what Moi was up to these days. "He's my next-door neighbor!"

As it turns out, the despot whose secret police tortured hundreds of political prisoners in waterlogged gallows[2] spends a pleasant retirement pottering around a sprawling farm, tending to his cattle.

As the politician's assistant's four matching suitcases arrive, I swap my mobile number for his three. By dawn I'm heading south from the capital to Kenya's largest national park, Tsavo West, and the hotel that began the safari industry. With me is cameraman Gabriel Rotich who's meant to be taping my journey, though, for reasons no one can explain, filming is banned in the nature reserve.

Tourism is Kenya's biggest source of foreign earnings after tea. It accounts for about 12.5% of the economy. I want to assess the impact from the spate of violent shocks – from the post-election clashes of 2008, to the electrical fault that destroyed Nairobi's main airport, to the horrific Westgate shopping mall siege and subsequent terror attacks by Somalia's al-Shabaab.[3]

The road runs 400 kilometers along the migratory corridor to Tsavo. Antelopes and zebras graze under purple leaf jacaranda trees. It is a breathtaking sight. Folklore has it colonialists gazing out and exclaiming "Look at Kenya" inspired the local name Lukenya, our safari driver Eric Mueke recounts as we pass through. He's ferried tourists along this route for a decade. The only thing that's changed is a drop in the number of visitors.

Eric was booked for a three-van convoy two weeks earlier. In the end only one was needed. America's official travel caution[4] in the aftermath of Westgate made it too expensive for some of the companies to get travel insurance. A few days before we arrived, a US divorce court stopped a mother traveling with her child to Kenya after her husband argued the country was a terrorist risk.[5]

The attacks rekindled the nation's reputation for violence after the battles of 2008. Most of Gabriel's friends in the Kalenjin region of Nakuru were caught up in the violence, defending a bridge from the advance of a Kikuyu gang. The scenes of tribal fighting stuck in the world headlines years on, with the International Criminal Court pursuing war crime charges against President Kenyatta and his Vice President, William Ruto.[6]

"It's not good for the tourist industry," says Eric. "The faint hearted won't come here."

While ethnicity continues to split political allegiance, cultural identity and language, there are other layers too. Eric, from the Kamba tribe, lives 200 kilometers from Gabriel in Machakos. Though both understand Swahili, Gabriel, as a younger man, mixes it with English in the dialect known as Sheng. The Swahili expression of surprise his parents would say – "ati?" – gets mixed with the English learned in school – "what?" – as "atiwhat?" A young guy relaxing will blend the Swahili "kuji" into "kujinice." Other phrases mix the vernacular. The most famous of Swahili phrases – "jambo" – or "hello" – becomes "mamboz."

Youths devised Sheng as a code their parents wouldn't understand.[7] In Gabriel's hometown, youngsters add a further twist by saying words backwards. Others use euphemisms. The Sheng word for a gun – "mguu wa kuku" – translates literally as the "leg of a chicken." Even Sheng-speaking youths in Nairobi sometimes can't understand each other because phrases differ between the neighborhoods.[8] Rap artists miss out on lucrative ad campaigns – the only way to make money in an industry rigged by pirating – because they can't speak Swahili.

We pass through the town of Sultan Hamud, named after the ruler of Zanzibar who visited a century ago.[9] Rain has loosened the red soil, bringing women out to plough the fields with wooden hoes. In the Maasai tradition of polygamy, the wives farm the land, take care of livestock, build the "manyatta" family mud hut, smear it with soil and cow dung, collect water and firewood, wash and cook.[10] And the husband? Well, he guards the family from attack.

It's a role not to be taken lightly. His teenage circumcision is a test of strength. One wince from the pain could forfeit his passage to Maasai warrior.[11,12] This, after all, is the region where scores of men were eaten alive by lions infamous ever since as the Man-Eaters of Tsavo. Their victims had been building the colonial-era railway from Nairobi to Mombasa.[13]

The track still runs parallel to the road, yet for the entire journey we don't see one train. It takes three times longer, explains Eric. It's hard to believe as we amble behind over-filled trucks while skirting the potholes and bony cows and goats feeding on freshly watered tufts of grass by the roadside.

I ask Eric and Gabriel why the trains run so slowly. They look at me like I've got two heads. How can they run any faster with all the animals walking by the track?

Any driver running down an animal here is liable for punitive fines. Landowners are ordered to look on when migrating beasts devour their crops. They can go to the government for compensation, but it's a long process that often doesn't pay the true value of the lost produce.

Running beside the road, smallholders offer oranges, tomatoes and onions. This is the town of Emali, which means wealthy, and it does seem like the townsfolk find every way possible to earn a few shillings. The huts here are brightly painted in green and white, advertising Wrigley's Spearmint Gum, or blue and yellow for Kensalt, whose refinery further south in Mombasa supplies three-quarters of Kenya's table salt.[14]

In the town of Makindu, meaning palm tree, we pass a majestic mosque neighboring a Sikh temple and then the "Loving Jesus Saloon." Religious tensions had been low in Kenya before the attacks from al-Shabaab stirred Muslim–Christian tension. Shortly after the Westgate attack, a Muslim cleric was shot dead in his car with three others in Mombasa. The shooting sparked deadly riots as a Protestant church was torched.[15]

Finally we enter Tsavo. Between the east and west national parks, its grassy plains stretch 21,000 square kilometers, about the expanse of New Jersey. The Kilaguni Safari Lodge opened here a year after independence from Britain. Photos in the dark-wood-beamed reception show Jomo Kenyatta looking out from the veranda as elephants group at the watering hole right in front. Half a century on, it looks just the same. Maasai giraffes, zebras and warthogs take their turn to wallow in the water.

Every room at the two-story lodge, now owned by the Aga Khan's Serena group, has the same incredible view – and every room is booked. Any drop-off from European and American tourists has been made up by Asians and Africans, says manager Henrietta Mwangola.

"The government has driven its marketing campaigns out to the Asian markets as well as the European markets," she says. "As a result of that there has been an increase in Asian tourists. We've been able to get an interesting blend."

Beyond terrorism and perceptions of violence, it's the slow transport network that's holding back tourism generally, she says. "I would just request for more to be done so that tourists are able to access their destinations in less time."

In front of us, plains stretch all the way to the snowy peak of Kilimanjaro in Tanzania. Wildebeest roam with hippos, baboons, buffalo, ostriches and yellow-billed storks. A leopard lounges by a stream watched from afar by a blue-necked helmeted guinea fowl. It's a picture of harmony.

"My grandmother used to leave beer out for these birds," says Eric. "The birds would drink thinking it was water. Then, when they were too drunk to fly, she would catch them and cook them for dinner. It's a very lean meat, very good."

Top Down Data

Country	Population	GDP on PPP Basis ($)	GDP/ Capita on PPP basis ($)	Inflation (% pa)	Unemployment (%)
Kenya	45,010,056	79,900,000,000	1800	5.8	40.0

Source: CIA World Factbook, December 2014

[1] Population data from 2014.
[2] GDP at purchasing power parity (PPP) exchange rates is the sum value of all goods and services produced in the country valued at prices prevailing in the USA, based on 2013 estimates.
[3] GDP per capita (PPP) divided by population, based on 2013 estimates.
[4] Inflation rate shows the annual percentage change in consumer prices in 2013.
[5] Unemployment rate shows the percentage of the labor force without jobs in 2008. The United Nations Development Program said unemployment was 12.7% in a 2013 report.

Endnotes

1. Anonymous (2008) UN: 600,000 displaced in Kenya unrest, Associated Press. Available at CBS News: http://www.cbsnews.com/news/un-600000-displaced-in-kenya-unrest/.
2. Greste, P. (2010) Kenya torture victims get compensation payment, BBC News Africa. Available at: http://www.bbc.co.uk/news/world-africa-10721384.
3. Malingha Doya, D. (2013) Westgate attack leaves Kenya needing premium on Eurobond sale, Bloomberg News. Available at: http://www.businessweek.com/news/2013-11-04/westgate-attack-leaves-kenya-needing-premium-on-eurobond-sale.
4. Travel Warning (2013) U.S. Department of State, Bureau for Consular Affairs. Available at: http://travel.state.gov/travel/cis_pa_tw/tw/tw_6025.html.
5. Kariuki, J. (2013) Kenya unsafe for U.S. child, rules court. Available at: http://mobile.nation.co.ke/News/Kenya-unsafe-for-US-child--rules-court/-/1950946/2043586/-/format/xhtml/-/qbkqh7z/-/index.html.
6. Anonymous (2013) Kenya's William Ruto loses ICC trial attendance ruling, BBC News Africa. Available at: http://www.bbc.co.uk/news/world-africa-24666472.
7. Dean, L. (2013) Street Talk: How the urban slang of nairobi slums is becoming the language of the people, slate. Available at: http://www.slate.com/articles/news_and_politics/roads/2013/11/sheng_is_becoming_a_kenyan_language_how_the_urban_slang_of_nairobi_slums.html.
8. Universitat Zurich, Countries where Swahili is spoken, The Swahili language. Available at: http://www.spw.uzh.ch/afrling/aliswahili/matini/aswi-21d-where-IsItSpoken.html.
9. Nyamai, F. (2013) Why was Ukambani town named after a sultan? Available at: http://mobile.nation.co.ke/lifestyle/Sultan-Hamud-Town/-/1950774/2020842/-/format/xhtml/-/7bdfa/-/index.html.
10. Nkoitoi (2005) The life of a maasai woman, opportunity fund for developing countries. Available at: http://www.ofdc.org/story.html.
11. Budgor, M. (2013) Kenya: My mission to become the first female Maasai warrior, *The Guardian*. Available at: http://www.theguardian.com/travel/2013/sep/06/kenya-first-female-maasai-warrior.
12. Maasai Ceremonies & Rituals, Maasai Association. Available at: www.maasai-association.org/ceremonies.html.
13. Patterson, J.H. (1907) *The Man-Eaters of Tsavo and Other East African Adventures*, Macmillan. Available at: https://archive.org/details/maneatersoftsavo00pattiala.
14. Kensalt Ltd. Available at: http://kensalt.com/about.html.
15. Vogt, H. (2013) Kenyan riots pivot on religious conflict, *Wall Street Journal*. Available at: http://online.wsj.com/news/articles/SB10001424052702303722604579115101433876649.

II — Can't Believe You're Going to Kenya

A round noon on a busy Saturday, Nairobi's most upscale shopping mall is stormed by masked men firing indiscriminately. In an 80-hour siege, the al-Shabaab Islamists kill 67 people, claiming retribution for Kenyan military operations across the border in Somalia.

Six weeks later, a 23-year-old gunman rampages through Los Angeles airport. He picks people at random: "Hey, are you TSA?" He kills a Transport Security Administration officer and wounds six more.

The next day, Brett Rowley, a 44-year-old father of four, takes a flight from LA to meet me in Nairobi.

"Friends said I can't believe you're going to Kenya after that mall attack," says Brett, who looks after African investments as part of a team managing more than $11 billion of emerging market bonds.

"I just said, look, we have crazy things that happen in Los Angeles, there are crazy things that happen in New York, and as it turned out my closest call was right at home. As long as I'm careful, I really don't have any concerns about coming to Kenya. It was a fantastically uneventful journey."

For all the tensions here, Kenya does feel welcoming, especially by comparison to some other African countries. The last time Brett visited Angola, his visa took a month to come through. His colleagues at TCW Group in California had their passports with the embassy for six weeks and still weren't processed in time for the trip. When Brett finally landed in Luanda, his Blackberry was stolen before he'd even made it through immigration.

In Kenya, Brett got his visa on arrival within ten minutes.

"Countries that actually want tourists and investors try and make it easy," says Brett. "In Angola or Nigeria, everyone assumes you're in oil or some kind of business to be paying a visit. But in Kenya, there's the idea that people might come because they want to see the country."

Brett flew here via London. The last direct flight from the USA left in the 1980s. Delta attempted a service in 2009 – Kenya's transport minister even flew to America for a seat on board ready for the prime minister's welcoming party in Nairobi – but on the eve of departure US Homeland Security denied approval because of "security vulnerabilities."[1]

The rebuild of the airport after the blaze in 2013 provides an opportunity to set things right – separating arriving and departing passengers, for example – opening the potential for US flights to resume.[2]

"It would be a tremendous boost," says Brett. "If the new terminal can address the previous safety issues, I don't see why US flights wouldn't come here."[3-6]

Fund Factbox

Company & Assets in Emerging Markets	Emerging Market Fund	Performance & Peer Ranking	Portfolio Manager: Brett Rowley
TCW Group (Trust Company of the West) $11 billion	TCW Emerging Markets Income Fund	3rd highest total return among 278 US-registered global emerging market fixed-income funds over 10 years at 175% (annualized 10.6%)	Managing Director for sovereign research, based in Los Angeles Joined in 1995. Returned to TCW in 2008 after a couple of years at global macro hedge fund Pantera Capital Management

Source: Data compiled by Bloomberg as of June 2014

Endnotes

1. Anonymous (2009) Kenya angered by US refusal to allow direct flights, voice of America. Available at: http://www.voanews.com/content/a-13-2009-06-03-voa26-68691802/356127.html.
2. Straziuso, J. (2014) Kenya airways aims for major expansion, Flights to USA, Associated Press. Available at: http://www.usatoday.com/story/todayinthesky/2014/01/29/kenya-airways-aims-for-big-expansion-flights-to-usa/5023311/.
3. Anonymous (2013) Timeline: Main attacks since 1998, AlJazeera. Available at: http://www.aljazeera.com/news/africa/2013/09/201392294643836478.html.
4. Madete, O. (2014) Thika Blasts Devastate Nairobi, Urban Perspective. Available at: http://www.upnairobi.com/dt_portfolio/thika-blasts-devastate-nairobi/.
5. Anonymous (2014) Kenya massacre: Somali extremists targeting Christians kill dozens at resort, NBC News. Available at: http://www.nbcnews.com/storyline/world-cup/kenya-massacre-somali-extremists-targeting-christians-kill-dozens-resort-n131846.
6. Karimi, F., Walker, B. (2014) Gunmen kill 22 in Ambush at Kenyan Coast, CNN. Available at: http://edition.cnn.com/2014/07/06/world/africa/kenya-attacks/.

III — Sleeping Serpent

Al-Shabaab was like a wounded buffalo,
and we in Kenya know that a wounded buffalo
is even more dangerous

Raila Odinga
Ex-Prime Minister, Opposition Leader

L ate in 2013, Kenya's Auditor General told the Parliament some money had gone missing from the government's coffers: $3.5 billion to be exact.

Edward Ouko said he had no way of knowing whether 303 billion shillings – a third of annual government expenditure – was incurred lawfully or not. In a 437-page report, he documented unauthorized expenses ranging from a monthly mobile phone bill for over $12,000 claimed by the late environment minister John Michuki to $90,000 for sundries including fresh flowers for the Ministry for Development of Northern Kenya & Other Arid Lands.[1]

The money – enough to build and stock a hospital in each of the nation's 47 counties – went missing at a time when Kenya was battling its worst drought in half a century, with nearly a quarter of the population at risk of starvation, fumed the country's oldest newspaper, the *Standard*.[2]

The media outrage lasted all of two days, says Mwalimu Mati, a lawyer who runs an anti-corruption watchdog in Nairobi. No one resigned.

In the UK, a scandal over MPs' expenses epitomized by a $3000 duck house sparked dozens of arrests and resignations, months of front-page articles, even a West End musical.

"Here this sort of thing is normal," says Mati, the founder of MARS Group or Media Analysis & Research Services. "We're used to corruption scandals in the order of a billion dollars as a matter of course."[3]

Grand-scale graft has been going on for as long as anyone can remember. One item in the auditor general's report is an $8 million payment on debt borrowed in 1970 for a fertilizer plant. The plant was never built. Yet the bill is still being paid almost half a century later.

At the MARS HQ that also serves as his home in a leafy and heavily guarded neighborhood of Nairobi, Mati is archiving evidence "in case at some point there might be a government that's serious about dealing with corruption." But he doesn't hold out much hope.

In the five decades since independence, Kenya has had only four presidents and all are inter-related. Uhuru Kenyatta is the son of the first president. The second, Daniel Arap Moi, was Jomo Kenyatta's vice president. The third, Mwai Kibaki, was Moi's vice president.

"It's actually one regime," says Mati.

Among the opposition leaders today, Raila Odinga, who contested against Uhuru for the presidency in 2013, is the son of the first vice president under Jomo Kenyatta. Musalia Mudavadi, who placed third in the 2013 vote, is the son of Moses Mudamba Mudavadi, who served as a minister under Moi and was married to one of his relatives. In 2002, Musalia Mudavadi was Uhuru Kenyatta's running mate.[4]

The nationalist politicians who led the independence movement and their descendants are in charge of politics, says Mati – "and it will stay like that for a very long time."

One reason is more than half of the country's wealth is in the hands of the political elite and their relatives, led by Uhuru, Kenya's richest man.[5] Uhuru's father amassed vast swathes of land in the 60s and 70s for a pittance under a British transfer scheme. The family estate spans half a million acres along with commercial banks, luxury hotels and dairies to boot. His media interests include *The People* newspaper, K24 TV and several radio stations.[6,7]

Kroll Associates, a corporate investigation and risk consultancy, chronicled almost $1 billion dollars transferred from the country's coffers to family-owned bank accounts and private estates by Moi during his presidency between 1978 and 2002.[8,9] His family own stakes in the *Standard* newspaper group, KTN TV and a Swahili-language radio station.[10] Odinga's wealth through oil, gas, real estate and media holdings may be over 7 billion shillings ($81 million).[11]

"It's a stable, predictable political system," says Mati. "They're the wealthiest, they're the ones who are able to mobilize, and there are no real ideological differences between them. The only things that change are the personalities."

The clubby world of elite politicians isn't reflected on the street. In 2002, the year Moi ceded to elections, a Gallup poll showed Kenyans were the most optimistic people in the world as democracy beckoned.[12] The euphoria turned to despair five years later with the deadly clashes pitting Kikuyu masses backing Mwai Kibaki against the Luos and Kalenjin behind Raila Odinga in the 2007 election.

The lack of substantive policy differences between the politicians feeds the impulse to vote along ethnic lines. Every election has been a dead heat with 45% for one tribal grouping and 45% for another. Victory comes down to who can "steal" the remaining 10%, says Mati.

That game gets played out in the electoral commission that's meant to oversee fairness in the polling stations and declare the results. The system breaks down because the commission is itself made up of political appointees.

"It's as if the players choose the referees," says Mati. "People don't trust any electoral commissions we've ever had."

In the polls of 2007 and 2013, the commission announced the result before the last votes were even counted.

For Kenyans, it's just another corruptible institution – like the police, education and transportation. Kenya ranks among the 20 worst countries for fatal road accidents partly because the driving test can be bought – and that's the way it's been for decades.[13,14]

"All Kenyans feel the pain of having to pay bribes to get medical attention, to get kids into schools, to get out of a jam with the police, to apply for national identification documents – the simplest services have become corrupted," says Mati. "They feel very frustrated but I just don't see them rallying in the political field."

Transparency International, the global watchdog where Mati previously worked as a lawyer, placed Kenya among the 40 most corrupt of 177 countries.[15] It's one reason 40% of Kenyans are living below the poverty line.[16]

The government has a grand plan to lift the nation's fortunes. The cross-party Vision 2030 manifesto promises to boost economic growth to at least 10% a year by investing in oil exploration and connecting Kenya's cities.[17] The remote and undeveloped Turkana region in Kenya's northwestern Rift Valley may hold 600 million barrels of crude deposits. London-listed Tullow Oil committed to exploration even as it scaled back its global program amid tumbling crude prices.

A new Nairobi to Mombasa railway line will speed up the connection between the capital and east Africa's biggest port from 2017, easing the pressure on roads. It's Kenya's most expensive infrastructure project since independence at a cost of over $5 billion. The wandering elephants, giraffes and buffalos of Tsavo will be kept at bay by a 1.8-meter reinforced concrete and metal mesh fence.[18]

Kenya hasn't laid a single piece of track since the British built the railway in 1902, despite taking 11 train-related loans. With billions of dollars being lent once again, anti-corruption activists like Mati are worried history will repeat itself. From the perspective of an investor bankrolling Kenya by buying its bonds, Brett is concerned about the risk of the country sinking into debt without putting the money to work effectively on improving infrastructure or other means to boost economic growth.

The rail project is already mired in allegations of inflated payments. The initial cost of the line at $3.8 billion looks high compared with a train track in

Ethiopia, members of the National Assembly's Public Investments Committee complained in an April 2014 report. The committee questioned why the government had awarded the contract without an open bidding process.

The company contracted is China Road & Bridge Corp. The World Bank in 2009 debarred the Chinese government-linked group and two years later its parent, China Communications Construction Company Ltd., from participating in its road and bridge projects until 2017, citing fraudulent practices relating to a road project in the Philippines.[19–22] CCCC has appealed. It said in a 2014 statement that there's no basis for allegations of corruption and that it maintains strict management systems. Meanwhile Kenya is pressing on to the next stage, with an even higher price tag of $13 billion for a jointly funded plan to extend the line to Uganda and Rwanda.

The Standard newspaper fretted that the rail project risks becoming a bigger corruption scandal than Goldenberg. In Kenya's most notorious scam to date, hundreds of millions of dollars were siphoned from the Treasury as fictitious incentive payments to a supposed gold exporter called Goldenberg International – despite the country having no commercial gold deposits. The payments were in full swing when Musalia Mudavadi became finance minister under Moi in 1993. It took more than a decade for the fraud to be probed by a Commission of Inquiry in 2006, which absolved Mudavadi of involvement.[23]

"It's very difficult to see this happening again," says Mudavadi. We catch up with him a ten-minute drive from his home at a bungalow that serves as the headquarters for his party – the United Democratic Forum. The opposition group was formed in 2012 when Mudavadi was still deputy prime minister in the Kibaki–Odinga coalition. He went on to lead the UDF at the 2013 presidential election.

In a brass-button navy blazer, the 54-year-old fits us in before a golf competition at his club.

"In terms of transparency, there has been tremendous improvement," he says. "I can tell you now, in this country it is extremely difficult to have transactions with public entities not being fully scrutinized."

He points to checks and balances like the Ethics & Corruption Commission, parliamentary watchdogs, the media and all of the reporting requirements prescribed by the revised constitution.

The constitution was rewritten in 2010 in response to the post-election violence. Among the biggest changes is the devolution of power to local regions. At a national level, however, the new rules make it as hard as ever to break the political mold. Any new party must, for example, have offices in at least 24 constituencies. "For new players, that's very difficult," says Mudavadi. "Expenditure is loaded on to the party."

But there's more to it than just the cost. Unlike Europe or America's political systems, Kenya's parties lack obvious defining traits of left and right, or other ideologies that might help draw in nationwide support.

It is hard to grasp substantive policy differences at election time, Mudavadi acknowledges.

"If you were to look at the manifestos of the three major contenders at the last election, to a great extent they were almost the same," he says. "Most of the issues were pegged around Vision 2030 – infrastructure, good economic management, governance and so forth. Looking at all the manifestos, basically they're talking about the same thing."

This affinity increased in the aftermath of the Westgate siege. Uhuru, elected only five months earlier, asked the opposition leader Odinga to address the international media. The slogan "we are one" ran in countless newspaper headlines.

While Mudavadi insists the UDF does clash with the government on specific issues, like which goods should carry VAT and regulation of the media, it would take a "lot of voter education" for Kenyan politics to evolve from its ethnic basis to policies. "Being able to decipher what's a policy that's good for the country or region – we're very weak on that, we have a lot of work to do in that regard."

One point both main opposition leaders criticized Uhuru for was his perceived attempt to escape trial at the International Criminal Court. The ICC repeatedly delayed his case as key prosecution witnesses withdrew on concern for their safety while the government blocked prosecutors from accessing Uhuru's bank statements for evidence.[24]

Yet when the ICC finally abandoned the case against Uhuru in late 2014, Odinga congratulated his "brother."

We meet with the former prime minister at a Nairobi hotel minutes after a press conference. Having lost his legal challenge to the election result, Odinga accepted the ruling and was now hoping to play a role as elder statesman in brokering closer economic ties with Kenya's neighbors, in particular Tanzania to the south.[25] Odinga offered to chair a Panel of Eminent Persons to mediate relations between the five members of the East African Community. All of the countries' presidents were reportedly willing to accept his diplomatic mission except one: Uhuru Kenyatta.[26]

Under the previous administration, Odinga had been forging closer links with the four other nations of the EAC, easing restrictions on work permits and cross-border tariffs and discussing joint transport projects with Uganda, Rwanda, Burundi and Tanzania, all helped along by oil and gas discoveries in the region.

But under Uhuru's government, Kenya narrowed its focus to Rwanda and Uganda, excluding Tanzania in a club dubbed the "coalition of the willing." While Tanzania has been slower to move forward on agreeing freedom of movement and land issues, some political analysts suspect the snub has more to do with the war in the Democratic Republic of Congo, which borders all three countries. Tanzanian troops are part of the United Nations' Force Intervention Brigade that's been fighting M23 rebels. Although Rwanda denies links to M23, Human Rights Watch accuses the government of direct support.[27] Tanzania hasn't won any favors with the Kenyan government either, after showing reluctance to back Uhuru's bid to defer the ICC case and in particular to have it transferred from The Hague to the Tanzanian city of Arusha.[28]

"Kenya stands to gain more with Tanzania in the East African Community than when it is out of it," says the 69-year-old Odinga. "For Kenya to access the central and southern African markets that we have tried to do for so long, we need to pass through Tanzania."

While the East African Community represents the opportunity for Kenya's economy, Somalia is the country's biggest foreign policy challenge. Westgate was one of several acts of reprisal for Kenya's invasion in the al-Shabaab stronghold of Kismayo in September 2012. Odinga as prime minister co-chaired the National Security Council meeting that resolved to attack the city in alliance with the Somali National Army following grenade assaults on bars and churches in Kenya by the al-Qaeda linked group.[29]

"We didn't go into Somalia blindly," says Odinga. "We were forced in because they fought Kenyans, they kidnapped and killed tourists."

"After we liberated Kismayo, al-Shabaab was like a wounded buffalo, and we in Kenya know that a wounded buffalo is even more dangerous. They were substantially weakened but not defeated, so we knew that it was a matter of when and not if, for them to carry out an attack like they did on Westgate."

Discussion Point: Fighting Corruption – Whose Side Are You On?

While Kenya's cliquey political system helps stabilize governance – with no wild card leaders threatening to lurch policy in a new direction – it also limits the odds of anyone tackling corruption head on or challenging the dominance of ethnicity at elections. With that in mind, I wondered whether the investor craving certainty is on the same side as the activist fighting corruption:

Brett: As a fixed-income investor you want stability and continuity, so you think about what kinds of things could be out there to destabilize the market that we haven't heard of yet – for example, how far back is the opposition willing to go and to what extent are they willing to destabilize financial markets to seek justice or payback for political dealings in the past?

Mwalimu: Redressing grievances was very possible in 2002 and 2007. When Kibaki won in 2002, that was a key pillar. But the purge quickly collapsed when the new government saw this as an opportunity – you know, you find a corruption cartel and instead of punishing them you just join them. And that I think, unfortunately, is what also would have happened to the Odinga side to an extent. There are no serious anti-corruption politicians now.

Gavin: To what extent are you misaligned in what you want to see from Kenya? We discussed this perceived lack of an effective opposition – no challenge to corruption – and for Mwalimu that's presumably a big problem. Yet for Brett, this helps strong government and stability.

Brett: Clearly over the longer term, improvement in transparency and reduced corruption helps to improve creditworthiness and boost bond prices. We want to see predictable, steady improvements rather than volatile swings in one direction or the other because as an investor, we have a base case scenario of what we think is going to happen, and then we shock it to the upside with potentially positive developments. We also factor in potential negative shocks and calculate a risk-adjusted return. If we think there's potentially more upside risk than downside, we'll go for it. If it's a binary outcome, we may sit on the sidelines.

Mwalimu: I don't want shock change as in a revolution, but I do want a revolution in the attitude of the government by re-emphasizing corruption as a national enemy and something that can steal development from the people. It increases the cost of doing business in Kenya if, for example, someone needs work permits and they're not available at the official fee, only for a 10% top-up. Corruption is no longer regarded as a priority issue, and yet it's the sleeping serpent in the house, it's the kind of thing that could trip up all of these great opportunities.

Investor Analysis: TCW's Brett Rowley on Policy

Bottom Line

- Odinga's willingness to accept the court's ruling that validated Kenyatta's **election** victory showed just how far Kenya has come since the election that ended in widespread protests and violence in 2008.
- Although some degree of implementation risks remain, Kenya has made tremendous progress with the new constitution and **devolution**.

Buy/Sell Triggers

• **Intra-regional trade** is set to increase as Kenya and other east African countries try to capitalize on recently discovered, commercially viable natural resources in Kenya, Tanzania and Mozambique. While there may be hiccups along the way, there are more benefits to be shared from greater cooperation than trying to compete with one another.
• Keeping a watch on government **expenditure** is critical as a holder of Kenyan bonds.
• We will also continue to monitor the security situation in Kenya. The **al-Shabaab** threat is unlikely to go away anytime soon, and an escalation in attacks in Kenya could significantly reduce tourist arrivals.

Endnotes

1. Report of the Auditor General On The Appropriation Accounts, Other Public Accounts And The Accounts Of The Funds Of The Republic Of Kenya For The Year 2011/2012, Office Of The Auditor General website. Available at: http://s3.marsgroupkenya.org/media/documents/2013/10/ca943d72f2aa99 49cf7ff168f4f79031.pdf.
2. Kiarie, L., Michira, M. (2013) Audit: Flowers, Tea and Airtime Top List in Missing Sh338b, Oct. 10, 2013, Standard Media. Available at: http://www.standardmedia.co.ke/mobile/?articleID=2000095274&st ory_title=audit-flowers-tea-and-airtime-top-list-in-missing-sh338b&pageNo=3.
3. Anonymous (2011) Lest we forget: The faces of impunity in Kenya, Kenya Human Rights Commission. Available at: file:///C:/Users/Traveler/Downloads/ LEST%20WE%20FORGET-The%20Faces%20of%20Impunity%20in%20 Kenya.pdf.
4. Nesoba, R. (2013) Profile: Musalia Mudavadi, BBC News Africa. Available at: http://www.bbc.co.uk/news/world-africa-21566741.
5. Nzioka, P., Namunane, B. (2014) Political families own half of private wealth, Nation Media Group. Available at: http://www.nation.co.ke/news/Kenyans-Wealth-Families-Politicians/-/1056/2215578/-/rw5iryz/-/index.html.
6. Nsehe, M. (2011) Kenya's richest man pursues presidential dream. Available at: http://www.forbes.com/sites/mfonobongnsehe/2011/11/21/kenyas-richest-man-pursues-presidential-dream/.
7. Mugera, S. (2013) Uhuru Kenyatta: Indicted President, BBC News Africa. Available at: http://www.bbc.co.uk/news/world-africa-21544245.

8. The Looting of Kenya under President Moi. Available at: http://wikileaks.org/wiki/The_looting_of_Kenya_under_President_Moi.
9. Wikileaks, KTM Report. Available at: http://wikileaks.org/wiki/KTM_report.
10. Anonymous (2013) Here is a list of Kenyan politicians (Raila, Uhuru, Ruto) and the media houses they own, *The Kenyan Daily Post*. Available at: http://www.kenyan-post.com/2013/07/here-is-list-of-kenyan-politicians.html.
11. Anonymous (2013) So how rich is Raila Amollo Odinga *Kenyan Daily Post*. Available at: http://www.kenyan-post.com/2013/01/so-how-rich-is-raila-amollo-odinga-if.html.
12. Githongo, J. (2010) Fear and loathing in Nairobi: The challenge of reconciliation in Kenya, Foreign Affairs. Available at: http://www.foreignaffairs.com/articles/66470/john-githongo/fear-and-loathing-in-nairobi.
13. Road Traffic Deaths Index 2009 Rankings, Global Status Report on Road Safety. Available at: http://www.photius.com/rankings/road_traffic_deaths_country_rankings_2009.html.
14. Bellamy, D. (2001) Money Talks for Kenyan Drivers, BBC News. Available at: http://news.bbc.co.uk/1/hi/world/africa/1230004.stm.
15. Transparency International (2013) Corruption Perceptions Index 2013. Available at: file:///C:/Users/Traveler/Downloads/2013_CPIBrochure_EN.pdf
16. The World Factbook (2012) Central Intelligence Agency. Available at: https://www.cia.gov/library/publications/the-world-factbook/geos/ke.html.
17. Doya, D.M. (2014) Kenya $5.2 Billion Rail to be Largest Post-Colonial Project, Bloomberg News. Available at: http://origin-www.bloomberg.com/apps/news?pid=conewsstory&tkr=EIBCZ:CH&sid=a6_9eSTmeD44.
18. Kibwage, J.K. (2014) ESIA Study Report for the Mombasa – Nairobi Standard Gauge Railway Project, on behalf of Africa Waste and Environment Management Centre (AWEMAC). Available at: http://www.marsgroupkenya.org/documents/documents/11353/#.UxAocmeGnIW.
19. Public Investments Committee: Special report on the procurement and financing of the construction of standard gauge railway from mombasa to Nairobi (Phase I), April 29, 2014.
20. World Bank Applies 2009 Debarment to China Communications Construction Company Limited for Fraud in Philippines Roads Project. Available at: http://www.worldbank.org/en/news/press-release/2011/07/29/world-bank-applies-2009-debarment-to-china-communications-construction-company-limited-for-fraud-in-philippines-roads-project.
21. Oirere, S. (2014) Corruption Allegations Swirl Around $3.8B Kenyan Rail Contract, *Engineering News Record*. Available at: http://enr.construction.com/infrastructure/transportation/2014/0217-Corruption-Allegations-Swirl-Around-38B-Kenyan-Rail-Contract.asp?page=2.

22. Kwayera, J. (2014) why rail project could be Kenya's biggest scandal yet, Standard Media. Available at: http://www.standardmedia.co.ke/business/article/2000101450/why-rail-project-could-be-kenya-s-biggest-scandal-yet?pageNo=1.

23. See (4).

24. Namunane, B., Opiyo, D. (2014) Blow for Uhuru as ICC rejects bid to stop trial, Daily Nation. Available at: http://www.nation.co.ke/news/Uhuru-loses-bid-to-terminate-ICC-case/-/1056/2264648/-/rik84n/-/index.html.

25. Anonymous (2013) Raila accepts Supreme Court verdict, Standard Digital. Available at: http://www.standardmedia.co.ke/?articleID=2000080475&story_title=Kenya-Raila-accepts-Supreme-Court-verdict.

26. Anonymous (2013) Tanzania, Uganda, Burundi, Rwanda, South Sudan Welcome Raila Odinga's Mediation but Uhuru Kenyatta Refuses, *Kenyan Daily Post*. Available at: http://www.kenyan-post.com/2013/11/tanzania-uganda-burundi-rwanda-south.html.

27. Human Rights Watch (2013) DR Congo: M23 Rebels Kill, Rape Civilians; New Evidence of Rwandan Support for M23. Available at: http://www.hrw.org/news/2013/07/22/dr-congo-m23-rebels-kill-rape-civilians.

28. Allison, S. (2013) Analysis: How did Tanzania become the loneliest kid on the East African Bloc? Available at: http://www.dailymaverick.co.za/article/2013-11-05-analysis-how-did-tanzania-become-the-loneliest-kid-on-the-east-african-bloc/#.Uzqe-vldUuc.

29. Chonghaile, C.N. (2012) Kenyan troops launch beach assault on Somali city of Kismayo, *The Guardian*. Available at: http://www.theguardian.com/world/2012/sep/28/kenyan-soldiers-capture-kismayo-somalia.

IV — Prowling Leopard

Njuguna Ndung'u grew up on a peasant smallholding in the Aberdare Mountains.

In the mornings as he walked from the coffee farm to school, hyenas and a leopard would prowl close by.

"I knew as long as I didn't make any sudden movements, the leopard wouldn't attack."

The 12th of 19 children in a polygamous two-mother family, Ndung'u was the first to go to university.

"My father used to tell me, the only way to escape poverty is a good education, so I thought I'll study and one day save enough money to buy a parcel of land to grow tea."

Ndung'u became a professor of economics and bought an 8-acre farm to plant tea for a hobby, before being appointed Kenya's central bank governor.

Sitting in his oak-paneled office in Haile Selassie Avenue, it's the lessons of the central highlands that retain the biggest hold on Ndung'u.

"You have to pull from where you are," he says. "The moment you're appointed governor of the central bank you're in public policy, and public policy in a nutshell is welfare improvement; poverty reduction in short."

His cornerstone has been financial inclusion: getting people however poor to save and borrow. The poorer the individual, the more important it is that they have secure ways to set aside what little they can for however limited a period of time. It's a way to maximize spending power and smooth consumption in good and bad times by providing the capacity to buy when the need is greatest or prices are lowest.

The tricky part was getting financial services out to remote farming communities with small, irregular flows of income at a low enough cost to be profitable for the bank while paying enough interest to prevent savings being eaten away by inflation.

The year was 2006. The worst drought in living memory was causing hunger and malnutrition in Kenya's northeast.[1,2] In the west of the country, a freshman Democrat senator from Illinois named Barack Obama visited his grandmother's village and warned that Kenya's "reassertion of ethnic identity as the basis for politics" was not a good sign.[3] In Nairobi and Mombasa, Kenyans were starting to use their mobile phones to pay for shopping and send money to relatives.

To get cash to a mother in need far away in the countryside, the family bread winner in the city would have to pay a bus driver to carry their money. Mobile phones brought a cheaper and safer solution. Users would buy airtime and then transfer the credit to the person they owed money or to their family to redeem for cash.[4] In a country where far more people have access to a phone than a bank account, airtime credits started growing rapidly.

Kenya's biggest network provider, Safaricom, realized the opportunity and adapted the system in March 2007 to create the world's first SMS-based mobile money, or in abbreviated Swahili: M-Pesa.

Banks were appalled. They lobbied for the central bank to ban the system, citing the risk of fraud. Instead, Ndung'u encouraged M-Pesa's development, telling banks it would help them in the long run by strengthening the financial system and bringing more Kenyans into the formal economy.

As financial inclusion doubled to 67%[5] by 2013, banks went from opposing the system to pursuing tie-ups to turn Safaricom's subscribers into savers and borrowers.

"For financial inclusion, this has been the winning formula to reach the poor and those in geographically disadvantaged regions, away from financial services points," says Ndung'u.

It's also made Safaricom the most valuable member of Kenya's stock exchange, accounting for 24% of the Nairobi All-Share Index with a market capitalization of $6.1 billion (Table 1.1).

We head to the company's sleek headquarters in the Westlands business district, close to the ruins of the Westgate mall. The day's financial papers are dotted about on glass coffee tables, with Chief Executive Officer Bob Collymore grinning from every front page. The company has just reported its best quarterly earnings since listing in 2008. A quadrupling of the shares from the beginning of 2012 has sent the price to over 20 times annual earnings, among the highest valuations of its peer group (Table 1.2).[6]

"One of the tricks about Safaricom," says Collymore, in his spacious office, "is this understanding of the micro nature of the economy. I didn't understand that coming from the UK, but my team understood that."

Kenyans can take out loans of just 100 shillings – $1.24 – from M-Kesho, a mobile account Safaricom set up with Equity Bank, Kenya's second largest lender. They can deposit a single shilling – 1 cent – in an M-Shwari savings account, created with Commercial Bank of Africa.

M-Pesa's green and red logo can be seen in every village across Kenya, transforming shacks and mud huts into formal financial transaction points. The handful of payments through M-Pesa every month to family or friends multiplies to 300 transactions per second from over 11 million subscribers.

The system is being upgraded on projections for twice that amount. Coca-Cola, Diageo and Unilever have started using M-Pesa, partly to minimize the risk of robberies by reducing the amount of cash held with delivery drivers and outlets. Transactions are developing from person-to-person transfers to settling rent, school fees, traffic fines - or buying a bottle of Coke.

TABLE 1.1   Nairobi All-Share Index

Company	% Index Weight
1. **Safaricom Ltd**	**24.1**
2. East African Breweries Ltd	10.5
3. Equity Bank Ltd	8.1
4. Kenya Commercial Bank Ltd	7.6
5. Standard Chartered Bank Kenya Ltd	4.5
6. Barclays Bank of Kenya Ltd	4.0
7. Co-operative Bank of Kenya Ltd	4.0
8. British American Tobacco Kenya Ltd	3.9
9. Bamburi Cement Co Ltd	2.5
10. Nation Media Group Ltd	2.4
11. Diamond Trust Bank Kenya Ltd	2.4
12. I&M Holdings Ltd-New	2.2
13. British-American Investments Co Kenya Ltd	2.2
14. CFC Stanbic Holdings Ltd	2.1
15. ARM Cement Ltd	1.9
16. NIC Bank Ltd	1.8
17. Centum Investment Co Ltd	1.8
18. Umeme Ltd	1.7
19. Kenya Power & Lighting Ltd	1.3
20. Jubilee Holdings Ltd	1.2

Note: The index has 62 members in total. The % index weight is calculated from Bloomberg data as of December 2014. (*Function: NSEASI Equity MEMB GO*).

Kenyan Shares in MSCI Frontier Markets Index

Safaricom Ltd

East African Breweries Ltd

Equity Bank Ltd

Kenya Commercial Bank Ltd

Co-operative Bank of Kenya Ltd

Source: Data compiled by Bloomberg as of December 2014

TABLE 1.2   Relative Value: Safaricom vs. Peers

Name	P/E
Average	12.7
Safaricom Ltd	24.2
MTN Group Ltd	14.9
Oman Telecommunications Co	10.1
Bezeq The Israeli Telecom Co	9.1
National Mobile Telecom	11.2
Bahrain Telecom Co	11.9
Cellcom Israel Ltd	9.1
Mobile Telecommunications Co	11.0
Saudi Telecom Co	11.0
Emirates Telecom Corporation Global	10.8
Ooredoo QSC	14.7
Maroc Telecom	38.5
Etihad Etisalat Co	20.0
Telecom Egypt	8.9

Source: Data compiled by Bloomberg as of December 2014. (*Function: SAFCOM KN Equity RV GO*)

While M-Pesa provides a safer route for money transfers than entrusting the bus driver, it isn't cheap. Charges start at 30%, or 3 shillings to transfer between 10 and 50 shillings. Withdrawing 50 to 100 shillings from a cash dispenser costs 10 shillings.[7]

The cost of a loan through the M-Shwari service was 7.5% a month in 2014. That would mean the customer paying back twice the amount borrowed over a year – though the loans are purposely only for 30 days.

It's a lucrative strategy for Safaricom. The rate M-Shwari pays out to savers is between 2% and 5% a year.[8] Loans are typically around $10, with the risk of nonpayment underwritten entirely by the bank. The service had 2.5 million accounts within months of its launch in 2013.

"I don't ever want to be lending money to buy a car, that's not our business," says Collymore. "But I do want to lend for emergencies."

For Ndung'u, M-Pesa is a start. The next challenge is the third of the population that remains financially excluded – and that demands policies to lift millions out of poverty through economic growth.[9]

Ndung'u began pushing for growth in the aftermath of the ethnic violence of 2008 and the global financial crisis. He repeatedly reduced borrowing costs to stimulate activity in the economy. Initially the central bank's scope to decrease interest rates was helped by inflation slowing to a record low. But even when prices started creeping higher in 2011, Ndung'u kept on going with the rate cuts. Lending soared as benchmark government borrowing rates dropped way below inflation to 2%.[10]

To Ndung'u – who wrote his PhD thesis on controlling inflation – the best way to absorb rising prices was to expand the economy – to increase the opportunities for spending and investment. After all, inflation was out of his hands – the result of droughts lifting food prices and rising global energy costs.

For investors, however, cutting interest rates at a time of accelerating inflation was the sign of a central bank governor losing the plot. They sold the shilling for currencies benefiting from rising interest rates, causing the exchange rate to depreciate the most worldwide. That fanned inflation further by making imported food, fuel and other goods even more expensive. The reaction forced Ndung'u to finally hike interest rates from 5.75 to 18% by the end of 2011 as inflation peaked at 19.7%.

While the shilling soon strengthened again and inflation returned to single digits in 2012, Ndung'u took the wrath of parliamentarians who attempted to fire him through a censure motion. A Reuters poll ranked him Africa's worst policymaker of the year.[11] Then, two years later, Kenya's anti-graft agency filed a case accusing him of abuse of office through involvement in a tender to install security software at the bank.

Ndung'u denied being involved in the tender process. He's equally emphatic that his approach to fighting inflation was right.

"Many years ago we used to ask, can you trust the central bank? Is he a conservative central bank governor, in the sense that he's going to do what he said he's going to do?" says Ndung'u. "The conservative central banker was very targeted to fighting inflation."

But in the modern world, where inflation is imported through events beyond the influence of domestic policies, central bankers don't have the same anchor to pull prices down, he argues. In the Horn of Africa, the most important inflationary factor is rain, as shortages of food drive up prices and dams without enough water to generate electricity force people to use power generators that run on petroleum. That pushes up fuel prices, adding to production costs across the economy.

The best defense central bankers are left with is a strict pre-commitment to target inflation at a set level. For Kenya, the level is 5%, plus or minus 2.5 percentage points. In 2012, inflation dropped to 3.2% and remained in single digits through 2013 and 2014 (Figures 1.1–1.3).

"You have to train the market," says Ndung'u, "because the market is very unforgiving if you don't do the right thing."

FIGURE 1.1   Interest rates by Ndung'u

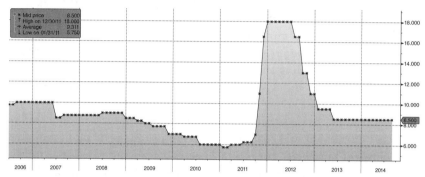

Source: Data compiled by Bloomberg. (*Function: KEIRCBR Index GP GO*).

FIGURE 1.2   Depreciation: Shillings Per Dollar

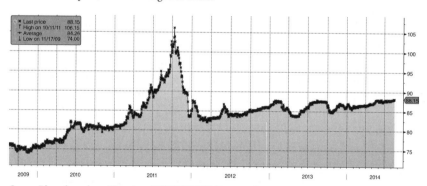

Source: Bloomberg data. (*Function: USDKES BGN Currency GP GO*).

FIGURE 1.3   Rise and fall of inflation

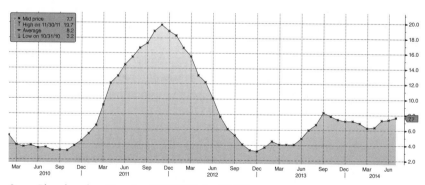

Source: Bloomberg data. (*Function: KNPRIYY Index GP GO*).

My Kenya: Central Bank's Njuguna Ndung'u

- Ultimately, for inflation targeting to work, east Africa needs **three buffers**: food security, petroleum and foreign-currency reserves. The central banks in the region are responsible only for the last one. The crisis of 2011 provides a good illustration.
- The government, through Vision 2030, had developed a stimulus policy for the economy. It meant **domestic consumption** rising, but most of this demand was being satisfied through imports. That widened the current account deficit to 13% of GDP – a crisis level for exchange-rate stability.
- The Vision 2030 infrastructure projects meant spending more **foreign currency** than Kenya could generate in the short run, adding further to the current account deficit.
- The **drought** effect came simultaneously, causing heavy imports of food as prices rose dramatically.
- **Energy prices** increased, with fuel consistently above $100 a barrel. The pass-through effect for the economy is magnified to the tune of 1.5 times.
- The global financial crisis meant everyone was **rushing for dollar** denominated assets. All African economies with a floating exchange rate and open capital account suffered.
- All these factors caused an exchange-rate depreciation and inflation **spiral**. Sudden and drastic monetary policy tightening was needed, not only in Kenya but all the East African Community countries.

Investor's Notebook: Safaricom's Bob Collymore

Politics

Corruption has to be fixed. If you tackle that problem, many of the other issues will sort themselves out. Infrastructure is needed, but you're not going to fix the roads until you fix corruption. The road outside this office gets destroyed whenever the rain comes because there's too little tarmac laid. Why? Because someone has stolen the money.

Business direction

In Kenya, the news comes on at 7 o'clock and 9 o'clock, but people don't want that. They want immediacy. On-demand media is where we see the business heading without a shadow of a doubt. We could be playing relatively prominently in that space – the application and delivery of content to tablets, phones or TVs; aggregating content from media platforms like YouTube.

Products

The cheapest smart phone handsets are $65; we expect the cost to fall to $55. That will help penetration of the market. Suppliers are Huawei, Tecno and Nokia. If you're on a low income, you want a phone that will last you five years; Nokia phones just keep on going until you can't even read the numbers on the keypad.

Stocks Box: Safaricom

Company & Trading Platform	Description	Average Annual Return	Price–Earnings Ratio	Price–Book Ratio/ NAV	Return on Equity	Gross Dividend Yield	Market Value ($m)	Top Holders %
Safaricom Nairobi Stock Exchange	Kenya's biggest listed stock & No.1 provider of mobile services incl. M-Pesa mobile money	36% since listed 2008	24.2	6.1	26.8%	3.4%	6,129	Vodafone 39.9% State 35.0% Free float 25.1%

Source: Data compiled by Bloomberg as of December 2014

Investor Analysis: TCW's Brett Rowley on Safaricom

Bottom Line

• We **own** some Safaricom stock, it's one that we have liked for a while. M-Pesa has been phenomenal both for the company and the country.

Buy/Sell Triggers

• My main focus is the next step. They're moving forward with M-Pesa, not just stagnating because it's been such a great success. They're **partnering up with banks** so they can take deposits and lend. It will be interesting to see how these relationships develop.

• Bob Collymore is clearly looking at what's going on in other telecoms around the world. I was impressed with how quickly he answered the question on **expanding to other media**. It was a very definitive "yes." They have a captive audience and they'll get content deals with channels. It could be another growth leg.

Investor Analysis: TCW's Brett Rowley on the Central Bank

Bottom Line

• Ndung'u has been a real champion of **financial inclusion**. It's not just words for him. M-Pesa has been a game changer. He was critical in letting this new idea take shape.
• I was impressed that right after the **Westgate** attack the currency appreciated, which was a sign of the confidence investors have. Kenya sold infrastructure bonds that week.

Buy/Sell Triggers

• I do have a concern that history could **repeat** itself, that the central bank won't tighten monetary policy when needed.
• Although Kenya's newly discovered natural resources should boost the country's exports over the medium term, investment to exploit these resources requires substantial capital goods imports. This suggests that Kenya's current account **deficit** is likely to remain elevated in the near term. That could put downward pressure on the shilling.

Endnotes

1. Wax, E. (2006) In Kenya, 'Why does this keep happening?' *Washington Post*. Available at: http://www.washingtonpost.com/wp-dyn/content/article/2006/01/07/AR2006010701024.html.
2. Pflanz, M. (2006) Two-year drought brings Kenya to brink of famine, *The Telegraph*. Available at: http://www.telegraph.co.uk/news/worldnews/africaandindianocean/kenya/1509478/Two-year-drought-brings-Kenya-to-brink-of-famine.html.

3. Gettleman, J. (2006) Obama gets a warm welcome in Kenya, *New York Times.* Available at: http://www.nytimes.com/2006/08/26/world/africa/26obama.html?_r=0.
4. Greeley, B., Ombok, E. (2011) In Kenya, securing cash on a cell phone, Bloomberg Businessweek. Available at: http://www.businessweek.com/magazine/in-kenya-securing-cash-on-a-cell-phone-09082011.html.
5. Figures cited by Ndung'u; also FSD Kenya (2013) FinAccess National Survey 2013: Profiling Developments in Financial Access & Usage in Kenya. Available at: http://www.fsdkenya.org/finaccess/documents/13-10-31_FinAccess_2013_Report.pdf.
6. Share price at 12.7 shillings as of Aug. 15, 2014, rising from 2.95 at the beginning of 2012. Data from Bloomberg.
7. M-Pesa Tariff FAQs, Safaricom. Available at: http://www.safaricom.co.ke/personal/m-pesa/m-pesa-services-tariffs/tariffs/tariff-faqs.
8. M-Shwari FAQs, Safaricom. Available at: http://www.safaricom.co.ke/personal/m-pesa/m-shwari/m-shwari-faqs.
9. The World Factbook (2012) Central Intelligence Agency. Available at: https://www.cia.gov/library/publications/the-world-factbook/geos/ke.html.
10. Borrowing costs based on three-month Treasury bill rates, according to data compiled by Bloomberg.
11. Anonymous (2012) Profile – Kenya's Central Banker Governor Njuguna Ndung'u, Reuters. Available at: http://www.reuters.com/article/2012/06/19/kenya-cenbank-idUSCENBANKKE20120619.

V — Clinker

The thinly tarmacked roads that vex Bob Collymore in the business district of Nairobi aren't typical. Most have no tarmac at all.

Dusty tracks connect towns and villages housing people in the same round mud huts and wooden shacks their ancestors built before them. Paved roads and concrete homes are still an aspiration.

Despite purchases of cement rising by over 60% in the past five years, Kenyans use only a third of the quantity for each South African and a fifth of the amount by Egyptians. With the IMF predicting Kenya's economy will grow by at least 6% a year through this decade, a boost in construction seems a logical bet.[1–3]

The trend in developing countries is for cement use to increase at almost twice the pace of economic growth, says Pradeep Paunrana, the chief executive officer of Athi River Mining, Kenya's biggest cement maker after Bamburi Cement. For Kenya, that's amounted to an increase of 14% a year since 1999.

"The biggest mistake of my career," says Paunrana, who took over running ARM from his father, "was underestimating the demand for cement in this region. Had we believed in those numbers – that it was possible to grow at 14% every year for the next 14 years – we would have taken some different steps to build capacity, but we missed that."

Kenya's demand for cement could double again by 2020, Paunrana says. Currently most goes to Nairobi for homes. Commercial construction such as warehouses makes up around 15% and government contracts slightly less, he says. With the government's Vision 2030 agenda, the state segment could grow rapidly.

Infrastructure projects like the Nairobi to Mombasa railway will not only increase use but should also create major cost savings to boost the economy. Using his own business as an example, Paunrana estimates a good train system would cut his cost to transport a ton of cement from Mombasa to Nairobi from $45 to $15. The saving across the economy from an efficient transport system may be equivalent to 10% of GDP, he says.

Paunrana is busy adding plants to grow his production capacity. He plans to spend $250 million building a factory to make clinker, the main cement ingredient, and a further $50 million on other expansion projects. Although ARM has shares listed on the exchange, the $300 million will probably come from the debt market. Paunrana is looking at a sale of Eurobonds, a type of IOU issued to international investors that can be bought and sold on financial markets. It's a relatively unusual step for a Kenyan company.

Whereas in most emerging markets, the amount of shares investors can buy is dwarfed by a mountain of tradable debt securities, or bonds, in Kenya, the situation has been the reverse.[4-7] While Nigeria has targeted international investors with Eurobonds since 2011, Kenya delayed tapping the market until 2014. Companies waiting for the government to set a benchmark rate so they could start borrowing in the bond market turned to banks for loans instead.[8]

Things are changing rapidly though with Kenya's inaugural Eurobond firing the starting gun for corporate borrowers. The Nairobi Stock Exchange has said it expects the amount of bonds sold by companies to reach the equivalent of 40% of GDP by 2023, compared with less than 2% now. That would open up a whole new market for investors like Brett.[9]

"The faster we develop the credit markets," says Paunrana, "the faster we can build capacity."

TABLE 1.3 Relative value: ARM Cement vs. Bamburi

Name	Market Value ($m)	Earnings Per Share (1 Year)	Price–Earnings Ratio	Return on Equity(%)	Dividend Yield(%)
ARM Cement	472	9.3%	28.4	18.0%	0.7%
Bamburi Cement	624	–21.5%	19.6	9.8%	9.7%
Peer Group Average	-	–7.7%	18.1	12.2%	3.1%

Source: Bloomberg data as of December 2014. (*Function: ARML KN Equity RV GO*)

Investor Analysis: Brett Rowley on Kenya's Bond Market

Bottom Line

- We've noticed in several countries that when the government comes out with a benchmark bond sale it sets the tone for **companies to issue** bonds.
- One thing that would help to get investors like me on board is to make the amount **big enough** to be included in the main indexes used by bond fund managers. Without inclusion in these indexes, the bonds can become illiquid, meaning it takes longer to find a buyer when you want to exit the investment.[10]
- Another issue is where the bonds are **registered**. As a US-based investor, it's much easier to buy bonds that have so-called 144a authorization from the Securities & Exchange Commission in Washington. Buying bonds that have only the European "Reg S" approval requires additional hurdles.

- Bonds that have a credit **rating** assigned to signal the level of risk are a good place to start. The rating agencies are another pair of eyes that look at the issuer's credit fundamentals.
- **Local-currency bonds** governed by domestic regulations can offer better value than international bonds as the yield tends to be a little higher. Some impose withholding and/ or capital gains taxes, so we evaluate our expected returns on an after-tax basis.

Bond Box: Kenyan Government Bonds

Security & Trading Platform	Asset Description	Maturity/Amount Outstanding	Average Annual Price Change	Coupon/ Annual Interest	Yield
Sovereign Eurobonds Euroclear/ Clearstream	Kenyan sovereign debt Dollars	2019 + 2024 Largest is 2024 maturity with $2 billion	N/A	6.875% on 2024 bond	5.9%
Infrastructure Bonds Nairobi Securities Exchange	Kenyan sovereign debt Local Currency	2018–2025 Biggest of the 6 bonds matures in 2025 with 36.9b shillings ($410m) outstanding	N/A	12.5% on 2021 bond	11.7%

Source: Data compiled by Bloomberg as of December 2014

Investment Pipeline: Kenyan Bonds

Security/Trading Platform	Issuer Description	Issuer Comments
ARM Cement Inaugural corporate Eurobond	Kenya's second biggest cement maker after Lafarge's Bamburi	Managing Director Pradeep Paunrana: ARM Cement plans to sell $300 million of Eurobonds to boost capacity. "The faster we develop the credit markets, the faster we can build capacity."

Investor Analysis: TCW's Brett Rowley on ARM Holdings ▬▬

Bottom Line

- As the country develops its infrastructure there will be a lot of **demand** for cement – many people still live in mud huts beyond the center of Nairobi, and roads are unpaved.
- ARM has a good capital expenditure plan. We would definitely consider **buying** if they come to the Eurobond market.

Stocks Box: ARM Cement

Company & Trading Platform	Description	Average Annual Return	Price–Earnings Ratio	Price–Book Ratio/ NAV	Return on Equity	Gross Dividend Yield	Market Value ($m)	Top Holders %
ARM Cement Nairobi Stock Exchange	Kenya's second biggest cement maker after Lafarge's Bamburi	48.1% since listed 1997	28.4	4.7	18.0%	0.7%	472	Amanat 27.7% Paunrana 18.1% Free float 48.4%

Source: Data compiled by Bloomberg as of December 2014

Endnotes

1. Ombok, E. (2014) ARM Cement awaiting directors' approval for South African plant, Bloomberg News. Available at: http://www.bloomberg.com/news/2014-01-02/arm-cement-awaiting-directors-approval-for-south-african-plant.html.
2. Cement consumption per capita was 103 kilograms in 2013, according to data from ARM.
3. Emerging Market and Developing Economies: Real GDP (Annual % change), IMF, World Economic Outlook, p. 186. Available at: http://www.imf.org/external/Pubs/ft/weo/2014/01/pdf/text.pdf.

4. Kenya's total outstanding government bonds totaled 1.15 trillion shillings ($13.12bn) in April 2014, before the sale of Eurobonds: Ndung'u, N. (2014) Expansion of the Kenyan Bond Market, African Financial Markets Initiative. Available at: http://www.africanbondmarkets.org/en/news-events/african-bond-market-review/article/expansion-of-the-kenyan-bond-market-52164/.

5. Kenyan bonds listed on Bloomberg totaled 14 billion shillings ($160 million) as of June 2014, before the government's inaugural Eurobond sale. Bloomberg function: SRCH GO.

6. The government issued 252.2 billion shillings of bonds in 2013, according to data provided by the Capital Markets Authority's Statistical Report. Available at: http://tinyurl.com/ozmek97.

7. Total amount of Kenyan equities on the Nairobi Securities Exchange All Share Index as of June 2014 was 2.12 trillion shillings ($23.9 billion), according to data compiled by Bloomberg: NSEASI Index DES.

8. Gachiri, J. (2014) Treasury delay in Eurobond issue to hurt companies, *Business Daily*. Available at: http://www.businessdailyafrica.com/Treasury-delay-in-Eurobond-issue-to-hurt-companies/-/539552/2220296/-/b3kxu1z/-/index.html.

9. Ombok, E. (2014) Kenya Bourse plans derivatives, REITs to boost market value, Bloomberg News. Available at: http://www.bloomberg.com/news/2014-02-19/kenya-bourse-plans-derivatives-reits-to-boost-market-value.html.

10. Bonds must be at least $500 million to be included in the JPMorgan EMBI Global and CEMBI indexes. The CEMBI Broad Index includes bonds of at least $300 million.

CHAPTER 2

Myanmar

45

1 – Halcyon Days

From Kenya's militarized airport, arriving in Myanmar feels disarmingly serene.

Immigration officers in pristine white uniforms smile amiably from booths advertising Samsung air sanitizers.

The sense of calm crystallizes as I turn on my mobile and realize I won't get a single text or call. Most foreign network providers are still waiting for a signal. Locally there are only six million phones for nearly sixty million people.[1] I'm missing the cacophony of voices announcing they've arrived, the urgent catch-ups on a day's missed meetings. Putting my mobile in my backpack, the noise in my own head switches off.

On the road, there's something else. The beep-beep of south Asian driving is a constant. But there's no buzz of scooters. Motorcycles are banned from Yangon in the interests of security, safety and quietude.[2]

And then there are the monks.

Wrapped in maroon robes with matching parasols, they emanate tranquility. Identical with shaven heads but in pink are nuns. Most of the country's 50 million Buddhists join their ranks several times in their lives. There are over half a million at any one time. Their monasteries and golden pagodas are everywhere.[3,4]

This halcyon aura makes it all the harder to comprehend the upsurge of violence here. I check in at Traders, the swanky Shangri-La hotel frequented by the international business elite. Three weeks earlier, a bomb went off in a ninth floor room, injuring an American woman staying with her two children. It followed a series of explosions in hotels around the country the previous week that killed three and injured ten.[5] While no group claimed responsibility, security officials blamed ethnic Karens from the southeastern border region with Thailand. A guerilla army there is defending what could be the region's largest gold deposits from companies cooking up mining contracts with the government.[6]

At the opposite end of the country in the northwestern state of Rakhine, ethno-religious tensions have flared since 2012 when Buddhist vigilantes claiming revenge for the rape and murder of a Burman woman intercepted a bus and beat ten Muslims onboard to death. The local Rohingya Muslims are denied citizenship and face a two-child restriction on the official view they're really Bengalis. The US has led international rebuke of President Thein Sein's government for failing to protect them.[7–10]

In the east, on the border with China, the Shan states have been fighting a separatist war since Burmese independence from Britain in 1948. The Shan are the biggest ethnic group after the majority Burmans, at around a tenth of the population.

In a sop to the ethnic groups, Burma's military rulers renamed the country Myanmar in 1989, though linguists say the two words mean the same thing. America and Britain have mostly stuck to calling the country Burma in sympathy with the democracy movement led by Aung San Suu Kyi, which refused to recognize changes made by an illegitimate government.[11,12]

It was her release from 15 years of house detention along with comrade Tin Oo and the promise of free elections that convinced the USA and Europe to relax economic sanctions against the country in 2012, ending half a century of isolation since the rise of the dictator Ne Win.

Segregation from the West has kept the traditional way of life intact here. Just as they have for two millennia, women and children paint their faces with circles or stripe patterns of *thanaka*, a yellowy white paste made from ground bark that cools the skin and protects it from the sun.[13] Men wear a *longyi*, an ankle-length sarong.

In other ways it's a thoroughly modern place. My mobile flickers back to life with the hotel wi-fi but I realize I left the charger in Nairobi, so my first task is to hunt down an iPhone plug in just about the only country Apple doesn't export to. It takes all of five minutes. It's an ugly thick cable that prompts a message warning it's unauthorized, but it does the job.

Like just about everywhere here, the phone shop only takes cash, so I cross the street to a bank. Between the cashiers is a ten-foot stack of kyats (pronounced chats).

With my $100 bill replaced by a thick wad of notes, I head to the Shwedagon Pagoda, the gold-domed temple that's Myanmar's international emblem. A bus jolts to a halt beside me, the conductor hanging off, shouting out the places he's heading. In Kenya, I was warned against taking the *matatu* minibuses because of the risk of getting robbed by passengers often in cahoots with the driver. I jump on and reach for my pocket to pay the fare but an elderly man thrusts a 50 kyat (5 cents) note on my behalf. "Our guest," he says, waving away my protest.

I get off at the Thone Htat Monastic School, just before the road climbs to the temple. Shaven-headed child monks, called novices, run about stacking wood, watering plants and scrubbing down a white board ready for a lesson, maroon robes knotted around their legs to make baggy shorts.

The street leading to the Shwedagon is lined with stalls. Some squeeze juice from sugar cane through a mangle with a jingling bell, others sell a mix of hardened tobacco with spice and rose powder wrapped in betel leaf. Like old American chewing tobacco, it goes between the lower lip and front teeth, staining the local smile a chocolate brown. Conversations are hard to understand with a betel-sucking Burman before he hawks and spits the brown liquid residue.

Pagodas are a haven: no shoes, no spitting. A woman introduces herself as Lily Lwin and offers to be my guide. She knows every inch from the Buddhas to the five-ton gold dome and its jewel-clustered peak. Lily asks my date of birth and looks it up in a pocket calendar going back a century. She beams, delighted. At the octagonal pagoda people go to one of eight shrines according to the day they were born, but Wednesday babies get two.

Lily and her little red calendar have seen visitors come and go since 1996. The last couple of years have been the busiest.

"We have so much beauty to show," she says, "it makes me very proud. It's good to see people returning."

Top Down Data

Country	Population	GDP on PPP Basis ($)	GDP/ Capita on PPP ($)	Inflation (%)	Unemployment (%)
Myanmar	55,746,253	111,100,000,000	1700	5.7	5.2
Kenya	45,010,056	79,900,000,000	1800	5.8	40.0

Source: CIA World Factbook, December 2014

[1] Population data from 2014.
[2] GDP at purchasing power parity (PPP) exchange rates is the sum value of all goods and services produced in the country valued at prices prevailing in the USA, based on 2013 estimates.
[3] GDP per capita (PPP) divided by population, based on 2013 estimates.
[4] Inflation rate shows the annual percentage change in consumer prices in 2013.
[5] Unemployment rate shows the percentage of the labor force without jobs in 2013. Kenya data from 2008. Myanmar from 2013.

Endnotes

1. Myanmar had 6 million phones for a population of 56 million in 2013 for a mobile penetration of 11%, among the lowest in the world, according to Myanmar Marketing Research & Development Co. in Yangon.
2. No byline (2013) Smuggled motorcycles fuel a burgeoning black market. Available at: http://m.bangkokpost.com/topstories/329431.

3. Gray, D.D. (2007) For monks in Myanmar an uphill battle. Available at: http://www.nbcnews.com/id/21020964/#.Uz7_kvldUuc.
4. Arrowsmith, R. (2013) Being a monk in Myanmar: Personal transformation in a changing country. Available at: http://edition.cnn.com/2013/10/14/world/asia/myanmar-buddhist-monk-retreat-experience/.
5. Weng, L. (2013) Burma police say Karen businessmen plotted bombings. Available at: http://www.irrawaddy.org/burma/burma-police-say-karen-businessmen-plotted-bombings.html.
6. Winn, P. (2012) Guerilla economics in Myanmar's 'Black Zone.' Available at: http://www.globalpost.com/dispatch/news/regions/asia-pacific/myanmar/120809/economy-karen-state-burma?page=0,0.
7. Harvey, G. (2014) Myanmar: The worsening plight of the Rohingya. Available at: http://thediplomat.com/2014/03/myanmar-the-worsening-plight-of-the-rohingya/.
8. Harf, M. (2014) United States Concern Over Events in Rakhine State: Press Statement. Available at: http://www.state.gov/r/pa/prs/ps/2014/04/224342.htm.
9. UN News Centre (2014) Myanmar: UN warns hundreds of thousands affected by aid disruption in Rakhine state. Available at: http://www.un.org/apps/news/story.asp/story.asp?NewsID=47486&Cr=myanmar&Cr1=#.Uz8mgPldUuc.
10. BBC News Asia (2013) Aung San Suu Kyi condemns Rohingya 'Two Child Policy'. Available at: http://www.bbc.co.uk/news/world-asia-22681192.
11. Roughneen, S. (2012) Is it 'Burma' or 'Myanmar'? U.S. officials start shifting, *The Christian Science Monitor*. Available at: http://www.csmonitor.com/World/Global-News/2012/0122/Is-it-Burma-or-Myanmar-US-officials-start-shifting.
12. Scrivener, L. (2007) The Burma question, *The Star*. Available at: http://www.thestar.com/news/insight/2007/10/06/the_burma_question.html.
13. Moe, J. (2008) Thanaka stands the tests of time, Mizzima News. Available at: http://www.bnionline.net/index.php/feature/mizzima/4971-thanaka-withstands-the-tests-of-time.html.

II – Uncle

A long the Shwedagon Road from the pagoda, the statues of Buddha give
way to Burma's political idol.

Aung San Suu Kyi smiles from books, badges and baseball caps at
stalls lining the approach to the headquarters of the National League for
Democracy.

Inside they're preparing for government.

A dozen desks with red plastic chairs and battered filing cabinets mark
beginnings of shadow ministries. One group is planning an education curric-
ulum to introduce concepts of democracy and parliament to children whose
parents have known only dictatorship. At another table sits a 75-year-old
man jailed for seven years in the 90s for writing a song the government didn't
like. He hands me a leaflet showing an artist's impression of a three-story
HIV/AIDS clinic planned for Yangon.

Behind him, a narrow creaking staircase climbs to the NLD's meeting
room.

Every space is crammed with boxes of Aung San Suu Kyi merchandise –
an essential source of party funding.

Tacked on a thin plywood wall is the red NLD flag with its white star
and yellow fighting peacock. Beside it, a life-sized golden bust of "the Lady."
Rested against her is a framed photo showing Barack Obama with Suu Kyi
one side and on the other, General Thura Tin Oo, the party's founder and
now – at 87 years old – its patron.

Tin Oo was 19 when he joined the army under the command of General
Aung San – Suu Kyi's father.

"We served our country in our younger days," he says, sitting at the head
of the party's long board table, "for the restoration of liberty and democracy
– for our cause."

A year later, in 1947, Aung San negotiated Britain's withdrawal from
Burma. Within months he was assassinated by a political rival.

During the succession of communist insurgencies that followed –
culminating in the dictator Ne Win seizing power from 1962 – Tin Oo
rose through the military ranks. By 1976, he was viewed as a potential
challenger to Ne Win and was dismissed from the army on corruption
charges and then jailed for withholding information on an assassination
plot against the ruler.

On release in 1980, he became a monk, studied law and then joined the
cause for democracy. By that time Burma's economy was sinking into Least

Developed Country status[1] as Ne Win blocked all foreign trade. His policy mix, born out of paranoia and superstition, included wiping out countless savings by replacing the largest denomination notes with new 45 and 90 kyat bills. Ne Win wanted those numbers because they're divisible by nine and their numerals add up to nine – and nine was his lucky number.[2]

Ne Win stepped down in July 1988 and a month later, on the 8th of the 8th, 1988, in what became known as the 8888 Uprising – another auspicious number – Burma's student-led protest movement demanded democracy. Tin Oo founded the NLD with Suu Kyi and the former newspaper editor, Win Tin. They would spend most of the next two decades between prison and house detention.

Suu Kyi's call for "reconciliation, not retribution" for the wrongs of the military is embodied by Tin Oo.[3] "I don't think I, or any individual, has the right to say I forgive or not forgive," the Nobel laureate said of her captors shortly after being released from house detention and 23 years of exile from her husband and two sons in 2012.[4]

It was under Tin Oo's tenure as army commander-in-chief that soldiers opened fire, killing striking workers and protesting students in 1974.[5-7]

"I had to face up to the harm I did to people," Tin Oo told three thousand delegates at a civil society forum in Yangon in early 2014. "Admitting one's errors is painful, but it is an important step for reconciliation. We cannot let our ego overtake the welfare of future generations."[8]

Dressed in the party's salmon-pink uniform shirt and blue-green longyi, Tin Oo nowadays runs the party headquarters while Suu Kyi as an MP is 400 kilometers north in the political capital Naypyitaw.

Midway through our meeting two American women enter the headquarters looking for "Uncle." They hug his frail frame, present a box of dates and reminisce of their antics as political activists when they'd feed the guard dogs to break through in the days of the house arrests. They ask after "Aunty." Daw Suu Kyi is "very busy now," he says, smiling. "Always busy."

While Tin Oo sees the "light for the way to betterment" in the current political transition, there are three big issues that must be resolved.

The first, he says tapping his fingers on the white cloth to punctuate his speech, is the rule of law. It's the starting point Suu Kyi references when asked for her stance on the ethnic conflicts in Rakhine or the Karen region: enforce basic laws and soldiers are suddenly accountable.

"We do not yet enjoy the rule of law because the judiciary is not independent," says Tin Oo. "The judges have been appointed. They must be elected based on independent, prestigious experience."

The second priority is amending the constitution to rescind those clauses that hand a quarter of parliamentary seats to the military and bar anyone with a foreign spouse or children from becoming president. Suu Kyi's late husband was British, as are her two sons.

The 25% of parliamentary seats granted to the army happens to be just enough to block any changes to the constitution, which require at least 75% support.

"We are going to change the constitution," says Tin Oo. "It must not be meant for one person or one group but it must serve us all together."

Finally, the government needs to resolve the armed conflicts in the ethnic regions through the devolution of power from Yangon.

"Many people don't like to hear federalism because they think it means a split of the union," taps Tin Oo. To him, it means equal status for all nationalities and self-determination. It requires that business deals in the Karen gold-mining areas and any other region must be transparent and inclusive – "not the secret military man and the businessman" deals that inevitably cause resentment.

I put to Tin Oo a concern we heard constantly from business executives – that the NLD is inexperienced in matters of the economy. Even those proclaiming themselves democracy supporters saw the best outcome being a continuation of rule under President Thein Sein with Suu Kyi as his deputy.

Suu Kyi, with a degree in politics, philosophy and economics from Oxford University, "very much understands how to run the economy," replies Tin Oo. Beyond demanding business transparency, NLD economic policies range from improving infrastructure to reducing the reliance on China.[9]

"Every day," says Tin Oo, "the lights go off for half an hour, one hour even. There was a very huge forum recently, a very prestigious forum, with businessmen from the USA, the EU, Japan and other countries, but they are hesitant to make big business in Burma because our country's infrastructure is so bad. This is the time we're going to improve the infrastructure of this country and then the big businesses will come in."

The NLD will push for better terms from China on infrastructure projects, says Tin Oo.

"Whenever they've got anything that needs money they approach China, and the people don't like it," he says. "These people are getting too much in the way of concessions. If they carry on like that, the growth of the country will get worse and worse."

Fund Factbox

Company & Assets in Emerging Markets	Emerging Market Fund	Performance & Peer Ranking	Portfolio Manager: Howie Schwab
Driehaus Capital Management $3.5 billion	Driehaus Emerging Markets Growth Fund	6th highest total return among 638 US-registered emerging market stock funds over 10 years at 287% (annualized 14.5%)	Howie joined Driehaus in 2001, initially focusing on investment in smaller capitalization companies before running the emerging markets group from 2007 The 35-year-old lives in Chicago with his new wife and two dogs. Committed conservationists, they honeymooned in an elephant camp in Kenya

Source: Data compiled by Bloomberg as of June 2014

Investor Analysis: Driehaus's Howie Schwab on the Political Outlook

Bottom Line

- The big negative surprise was the concern **Aung San Suu Kyi** lacks a convincing economic plan. Her ability as a government leader rather than a protest figurehead has to be tested.
- One of the more compelling arguments we heard for the change of direction toward democracy was the military and politicians foresaw that without opening up to the West, **China** would overwhelm the country and its de facto takeover would become inevitable. A stronger China hungry for the resources that Burma has – natural gas, minerals – would have compromised the military and political establishment. The country may end up being a significant piece in the USA–China chess game. That's important to watch.

Buy/Sell Triggers

- The **experts and technocrats** around Suu Kyi will be among the biggest positive or negative drivers.
- With so many reforms needed, the volume of work risks causing a **policy paralysis.**

Endnotes

1. The Least Developed Countries: Historical Background, United Nations. Available at: http://www.un.org/events/ldc3/prepcom/history.htm.
2. Chirot, D. (1994) Modern Tyrants. New York: Free Press. Available at: http://books.google.co.uk/books?id=e-kVgozyE8gC&pg=PA336&lpg=PA336&dq=chirot+modern+tyrants+ne+win+45+90+kyat&source=bl&ots=90t0EsvgQ1&sig=NwW3r9lIo6t8ocVffcYcoq15sas&hl=en&sa=X&ei=akwVVODkKILeavzjgqgE&redir_esc=y#v=onepage&q=chirot%20modern%20tyrants%20ne%20win%2045%2090%20kyat&f=false.
3. YouTube (2012) "Reconciliation, Not Retribution" says Aung San Suu Kyi in her first press conference in Europe, International Labour Organization. Available at: https://www.youtube.com/watch?v=ctCg1iGJkjU.
4. Uy, V. (2012) Suu Kyi on democracy, forgiveness and revolution, InterAksyon. Available at: http://www.interaksyon.com/article/28284/suu-kyi-on-democracy-forgiveness-and-revolution.
5. Burma Labour Solidarity Organization (2004) A Review of Labour Law in Burma. Available at: http://www.seaca.net/viewArticle.php?aID=17.
6. Soe-Win, H. (2008) Peace eludes U Thant. Available at: http://www.asiantribune.com/?q=node/11810.
7. Alternative Asean Network on Burma (2000) Ten Years On: A Parliament Denied: Burma's Struggle to Convene the People's Parliament, Altsean-Burma.
8. Tin Oo (2014) Speech at the Opening of the ASEAN Civil Society Conference/ASEAN Peoples Forum.
9. Anonymous (2014) Aung San Suu Kyi to be awarded Honorary Degree, University of Oxford. Available at: www.ox.ac.uk/media/news_stories/2012/120524.html.

III – Yoma

Howie's only Burmese investment trades 2500 kilometers away on the Singapore Stock Exchange. Yoma Strategic Holdings is by far the biggest listed Myanmar business. It spans agriculture, transport, the auto industry and real estate. Among its portfolio is Star City, a waterfront development planned to house over 30,000 people along with golf courses, hotels and industrial sites.

The company has made founder, Serge Pun, the richest Burman never to appear on US or European sanctions lists for connections to the military.

Pun left Burma when he was 12. His father, a Chinese-born banker, settled the family in Beijing in 1965. The Cultural Revolution followed and young Pun was packed off with the Red Guards for re-education.

At the age of 20, he left for Hong Kong with 5 HK dollars in his pocket. He got a job selling air sanitizers. It was his pitch to a real estate office that brought his first break. The owner, Elmar Busch, hired him on the spot.

Returning to Burma in the early 90s, Pun started out with a 500-acre gated community in the west of Yangon. His empire quickly expanded into banking but then hit the rocks. In the fallout from a nationwide run on deposits in 2003, Yoma Bank was barred from conducting regular banking business for nearly a decade.

In the last few years, Yoma has become a proxy for money flowing back into the country. In 2011, as President Thein Sein took the first steps toward democratic government and liberalizing the economy, the stock doubled. It quadrupled in 2012 as the USA and Europe responded by easing sanctions and Yoma won back its full banking license. Four decades after Busch hired him in Hong Kong, Pun returned the favor by appointing Busch to run his real estate division.

While Driehaus owns Yoma in its Emerging Markets Small Cap fund, Howie sold the stock from his main portfolio in 2013. The shares had started getting too expensive as the company's valuation jumped from 33 times its annual earnings in September 2012 to 68 times a year later.

The stock flat-lined as Yoma lost in its bid for a telecoms license to Norway's Telenor and Ooredoo QSC of Qatar, reducing its price–earnings ratio to below 40 by late 2014.

"Myanmar has been the darling of the market," says Pun, sinking into a comfortable white Jacquard armchair at his office in Yangon. "Some of that euphoria has come off. We've come to see more sensible expectations."

But foreign investors need to keep a longer term perspective, he says. What's significant about the government reforms afoot is that they resemble the political liberalization of Mikhail Gorbachev's "glasnost" with its focus on eliminating corruption and trying to enforce rule of law. This sets Myanmar apart from countries like Vietnam and Cambodia, which adopted Deng Xiaoping's more limited model of economic reforms for China.

The changes won't yield results right away. Wiping out corruption at the lowest levels of government, for example, first requires that officials are paid enough to live. It will probably take three presidential terms – 15 years – for these policies to take root, says Pun. But if they're even partially successful, Myanmar will emerge as a country with the low corruption and rule of law of Singapore but with far bigger economic resources.

For now, tourism is the "low hanging fruit" in the economy for Pun. While visitors to Myanmar tripled from 300,000 in 2012 to a million in 2013, that number pales next to neighboring Cambodia, which took in 3 million. That's the level the Burmese government targeted reaching by the end of its term in 2015 – yet Thailand receives around 18 million.

"We have snow-capped mountains, skiing, tropical islands, highlands, serene lakes, hiking, we have such a diverse tourism resource," says Pun, who took his company name from the Burmese for mountain range. "These are exponential growth numbers, and they're conservative projections, so it's a no-brainer to go into tourism."

Along with hotels, Pun is running planes to take tourists from the Himalayas between China and India in Myanmar's north to its southern-most reaches just above Phuket in Thailand. He started flights between Yangon and the capital, Naypyitaw, in 2012 as a separate business from his main holding company.

Property development brings in most of Yoma's revenue. Rent in three office towers built in Yangon in the 90s – the Sakura Tower, FMI Centre and Centrepoint Towers – climbed from $22 per square foot in 2011 to around $100 by 2013. That topped downtown Manhattan at under $75. Tenants include Standard Chartered, PricewaterhouseCoopers, Coca-Cola and Nestlé.[1]

Prices are rallying because there's only a tenth of the office space needed, according to Pun. Until demand is met, prices won't fall. "Most companies are carrying on from private homes because there are no offices available." The same shortage applies in residential housing, he says.

But Pun doesn't predict gains for all property in Myanmar. The rally in industrial land prices looks unsustainable. "That works in a very different mold. When industrial land is so inflated, it doesn't make sense to build a factory here, so the demand disappears. This is a sector that's going to be hurt."

Stocks Box: Yoma Strategic

Company & Trading Platform	Description	Average Annual Return	Price–Earnings Ratio	Price–Book Ratio/ NAV	Return on Equity	Gross Dividend Yield	Market Value ($m)	Top Holders %
Yoma Strategic Singapore Exchange	Biggest listed Myanmar business. Spans property, transport, autos, agriculture	166% from 2011, when reforms paved way for sanctions easing	38.9	2.2	4.5%	N/A	703	Serge Pun 37.3% Aberdeen 7.1% Free float 62.1%

Source: Data compiled by Bloomberg as of December 2014

Investor's Notebook: Banks – Yoma Bank, Special Advisor to CEO, Hal Bosher

Growth Outlook
Myanmar's banking landscape is modernizing fast. Currently, the equivalent of 5% of GDP is in the financial sector. In the UK, Canada and the USA, it's north of 100%, so our growth multiples are exponential. If we have a robust financial system where people are comfortable putting in a deposit overnight then the opportunity is huge.

Investor's Notebook: Banks – KBZ Bank Deputy Chairman U Than Lwin & Senior Managing Director U Than Cho

Company Brief
The biggest among 22 privately owned banks in Myanmar.

Foreign Partners
Japanese are best placed to form joint ventures, helped by financial support from their government to Myanmar.

Central Bank

The central bank should be fully restructured from top to bottom. Despite reform, it's still conservative. They need a better salary scale to attract bankers with experience because most have gone to private banks or abroad. They need to hire either very old or very young people who received a more open education that is conducive for capacity building.

Investor's Notebook: City Mart, Ronald Lee

Company Brief

Founded in 1996 by family members, City Mart owns 15 supermarkets, five hypermarkets (increasing to 10) and a bakery chain. It also has an independent food distribution network, including a premium channel to deliver confectionery and frozen food to restaurants, hotels and caterers.

Competitors

Orange supermarkets, Capital hypermarkets and the "mom & pop" stores that account for 90% of retailing in Myanmar.

Growth Outlook

Some second-tier towns are almost untouched by modern retail including those on Indian, Chinese and Thai trade routes; loyalty cards and credit cards offer strong growth potential; there may be less emphasis on food, more on goods such as bicycles.

Revenue

The company's own brand is City Value, which provides higher-quality non-food items such as tissue paper. It currently makes a very small contribution to revenue at 1–2% of sales.

Personal Brief

Project director for the real-estate development arm of City Mart Holding Co.

Investor Analysis: Driehaus's Howie Schwab on Yoma vs. City Mart

Bottom Line

- In a lot of countries **corruption** is expected as just a part of doing business, so I've been impressed by how many people here are taking a stand against corruption.
- As it's the go-to **proxy** for the country, my investment view on Yoma would be at least as impacted by the macro outlook for the country as for the company itself.
- **Tourism** is a compelling business for Myanmar, with English spoken as the second language, the natural beauty of the country, and the fact that all of the hotels are going to be brand new and modern. The biggest challenge is that the overall cost isn't necessarily cheaper than Phuket, although it's somewhat cheaper than Bali.
- Yoma's **corporate structure** is a bit fuzzy. FMI, the Burmese holding company, is different from Yoma Strategic Holdings, which is the capital-raising company in Singapore. It has a bit of the VIE, or Variable Interest Entity structure, that was introduced for Chinese shares listed in America to comply with China's restrictions on foreign ownership. It basically means shareholders have less direct financial interest in the revenue and earnings stream, and don't actually have a claim on the assets of the company.
- City Mart is the company we want to buy. It's No. 1 out of the retailers in terms of quality, service and penetration. There's a **nascent consumerism**: people want to spend. Mostly that's still in the street stalls and informal sector. Formal retail outlets only account for 10% of overall spending, which all adds up to massive potential. Fast-moving consumer goods (FMCG) companies will follow well-established regional roadmaps to quickly penetrate the Burmese market and bring brands to the consumer.
- What stood out at City Mart was how it evolved its **distribution network** as an independent platform, creating the potential to benefit from the Coca-Colas and the Nestlés looking for distribution and expertise.
- They speak the **language of the markets**. The investor relations manager understands KPIs (Key Performance Indicators), management incentives, bonus structures for individual employees – they understand how modern retail works. These guys should have no problem getting seed capital. They're talking with private equity firms and presumably will prepare for a listing in the next five years.

Buy/Sell Triggers

- Pun is smart and his **execution of strategy** has been superb, but it's difficult to determine how much of that was about being in the right place at the right time to acquire a significant land bank. Going forward, the challenge is putting all of your trust in one man. There is a board of directors but it seems like he's calling all the shots. When you're dealing with independently wealthy individuals as majority owners, you have to balance the risk that presents in terms of how their ego might color business decisions, like getting into the airline industry.

- At the right **valuation**, Yoma makes sense as a way to capture the Burmese growth story. Given the varied parts of the business, investors may choose to evaluate Yoma by weighing up what its units would be worth individually if the company was broken up. The so-called sum of the parts, or SOTP, approach would make the company attractive at around 0.6 Singapore dollars, or a P/E ratio up to around 45.

- City Mart looks more interesting than Yoma. It's not as dependent on a single transaction and what may be significantly overpriced real estate, or on certain relationships and strategic contacts. It's not going to be distracted by a bump in politics. It will evolve with the economy to move up the **value chain** – selling Häagan Dazs ice cream rather than boxes of tissues. Its own private label goods in time will become cheaper products than the international brands, rather than higher quality.

- We'll definitely watch to see if City Mart ever becomes public. The listing would be in Singapore or Hong Kong; to list in Burma would be a mistake. My biggest concern would be that it's **family owned**, which makes it less predictable. The high cost of living here also limits how much discretionary income is left over for consumers, which means pushing aspirational brands may be challenging.

- The **property** market has clearly got ahead of itself. You see a significant gap between ultra-wealthy and the rest of the population, and that's creating this two-speed economy where a small serviced executive apartment fetches the same price as in Singapore. This is something to watch: if tourists and companies are put off coming here because of the costs, it could slow development. It could also foment social unrest in the same way that China is experiencing.

Endnotes

1. Vallikappen, S., Thakur, P. (2013) Yangon more expensive than NYC sparking boom: Real Estate, Bloomberg News. Available at: http://www.bloomberg.com/news/2013-07-29/yangon-more-expensive-than-nyc-sparking-boom-real-estate.html.

IV – Son

Toe Naing Mann hands us two business cards. One says he's the Chairman of RedLink, Myanmar's largest telecommunications group. The other says he's the Advisor to the Speaker of Pyithu Hluttaw.

Pyithu Hluttaw is Myanmar's lower house of parliament. The Speaker is his dad, General Shwe Mann.

"I always refer to my father as my boss," says the 35-year-old.

Before the transition toward civilian rule in 2011, Shwe Mann was the army's joint chief of staff and the No. 3 in the military government council that ran the country for two decades under Senior General Than Shwe.

Chairman Toe says he began advising on a voluntary basis.

"I was trying to serve him," he says. "My father became the Speaker of the Lower House. We had no experience of that. We didn't know how to implement or how to organize a parliament, so I tried to find out how to make resolutions, plenary sessions, commissions, committees."

Now he's on his father's parliamentary payroll, but he refutes my suggestion of nepotism.

"Why has the Speaker appointed his son as Advisor? Why? We have 46 commissioners in our commission but the rest of the guys are very busy. I'm the only one who lives with the Speaker, so we don't need to negotiate or make appointments every time."

Chairman Toe is the general's younger son. A year older is Aung Thet Mann. He's also done well, creating a construction-to-fertilizers company that's owned by Myanmar's wealthiest businessman, Tay Za.[1] The tycoon is on America's sanctions list of Specially Designated Persons with links to the military, as is Aung Thet Mann.[2]

Toe's wife, Zay Zin Latt, is also on the US list as the daughter of Khin Shwe, a property magnate and member of the upper house of parliament.[3]

Toe isn't on the sanctions list. Rather than benefiting from his father's position, he insists he's had to wind down some of his business activities to focus on his political role.

"I have to serve my boss as my comrade," he says. "I had four companies, I had to shut three. I can't take care of all these companies. We lost a lot of money. Sometimes I don't know whether my communication company can survive or not."

Suddenly the chairman stands up, complaining of back pain. He damaged his spinal cord in the army in 2006, he explains. He left two years later and set up RedLink in 2009. He lights a cigarette, looking out at the construction site for office expansion below.

"I have lived with the military for more than 30 years. I know all the leaders, every man. I listen to them – what's their ideology, their vision."

"Currently, the military is very sensitive, they are very angry. They think they can't get any credit from the democratization. You have to understand the military tolerance. We need democratization to happen step by step."

During the adjustment process, the military should keep its 25% of the parliamentary seats, he says.

"If we can create political stability in 2015 to 2020, then we can say, 'okay military, what are you doing in parliament with this 25%?' If everybody asks, they will be shy, and they will step down. It's a transition. Don't interfere until after the election."

While military connections run through many of Myanmar's biggest companies, two are directly owned by the army: Myanmar Economic Corp., or MEC, with interests ranging from steel and cement plants to banks and insurance; and Union of Myanmar Economic Holding Ltd (UMEHL), which spans gems, tourism, real estate, transportation and metals.

"All of the Myanmar soldiers have their shares in UMEHL," says Toe. "I have also, I'm maybe around the $2000 mark, not very much."

"If you tell a general, you have to shut down your MEC, you have to shut down your UMEHL, how about his feelings? We need to give them appropriate time to step down from the business sector."

* * *

Former Silicon Valley investor Daniel Michener worked as a consultant to RedLink soon after the US lifted sanctions.

"I'm probably the only American who's served in an executive capacity in any Myanmar company," says Michener. "I've been here pretty much since the gates opened."

Michener shares Chairman Toe's view that the military can't be flushed out of the economy too quickly.

"I don't see the military thing as necessarily bad," says Michener. "It's just reality. The people who have had money here are the former military officers and people related to them. There wasn't a private sector entrepreneurial class, it just didn't exist, and if there were people who had money, they mostly went to the UK or Singapore."

"People would always say things about RedLink – U Toe Naing Mann owns it so it's a government proxy. It doesn't operate like that at all. I don't see Thura U Shwe Mann exerting influence over his son. I think the days of overt corruption for the most part are gone."

"That doesn't mean it doesn't happen. You're still visiting ministers and bringing them bottles of nice Scotch and trying to curry favor."

Transparency International ranks Myanmar as the 21st worst country for corruption of 177 worldwide. Still, that's an improvement from 2012 when it was in the bottom five with Sudan, Afghanistan, North Korea and Somalia. The World Bank's International Finance Corp. groups it among the eight worst for ease of doing business.[4]

Getting companies to open their books to the level needed by international investors is a struggle, says Michener.

"People feel that you're trying to pry when all you're doing is due diligence. They've had so much control over their businesses historically that this transparency thing, they know they need to do it but it also means giving up power."

Another reason is tax. "People do statutory audits and none of them are right because they're designed for the tax inspector, and so they'll do things like pull revenues out," says Michener. "I heard a story today that someone went to the tax authorities and they said you can't report this much, you'll mess it up for everybody else, so you can't look at the numbers and trust them right now."

The lack of transparency can make it hard to identify whether a person on the sanctions list is involved in a company.

"Until they make that transition, I think you're going to have trouble raising capital."

My Myanmar: Daniel Michener, CEO, Burst Networks

The Big Idea

We're working on a way to provide low-cost broadband internet access nationwide. We have designed a network that doesn't rely on the underdeveloped (and in some instances non-existent) power grid and at the same time will provide street lighting to neighborhoods and cities. Wi-fi access points would be on LED street lights that are powered by solar energy with a battery back-up.

Funding

We're initially focused on developing a wireless educational and healthcare platform that benefits the country in both urban and rural areas. If we get the go-ahead from the government, we have many large funding sources interested in supporting the project.

Telecoms

There's still not a great deal of coverage here even to send a text. The network doesn't always go to the point you think it will because it was built for the military, so it might have fiber going into a jungle, which isn't doing anything.

Yangon

This town, when I look at the skeleton of it, is a high-quality city. It's green, they've got broad avenues, park areas, they have among the most colonial buildings in all of Asia, so with a little spit and chewing gum you can fix this place up. It will be nice in five or ten years.

Companies

Most of the biggest are conglomerates sprawling over several sectors. They lack focus. It's like someone hit the piñata and the candy's all over the ground and everyone's grabbing it.

Management

This is very different from the West. Everyone reports directly to the chairman. A friend of mine is a CEO but he had to get permission from the chairman just to buy umbrellas – that's how flat the structure is.

Labor Market

For locals, the wages here are almost embarrassingly low. My driver was making about $150 a month; I've spent more money on a night on the town. It will all start increasing when they get some skilled jobs and plants here, but right now they have a distinct labor cost advantage over most of the other countries.

Recruiting

They don't do things like on-campus interviews, so I'm not convinced they're looking in all the right places. They put ads in newspapers but they don't say 'salary commensurate with experience,' they say you're going to get 400 bucks. You don't always attract the best candidates doing that. There's a lot of learning companies can do to recruit better.

Raising Finance

Don't get local money because not that many people have funds here and, if they do, they may be on a sanctions list or an unsavory character that will cause you problems down the road. The money comes primarily from Singapore, China, Korea and Japan. Americans and Europeans are going to be slow to put money in.

Investor Analysis: Driehaus's Howie Schwab on Telecoms ▬▬▬

Bottom Line

- **Telecoms** represent a big opportunity. Only two or three years ago it cost up to $4000 for a SIM card, now it's $1.50. While mobile phone ownership is near 100% or even more in many countries, here it's still only a fraction of the population that has a phone.
- This is a big **consumerism driver** in itself, as increased mobile phone ownership will make people feel wealthier and more connected for services like mobile banking and e-commerce.

Buy/ Sell Triggers

- A silver lining from being ostracized from the rest of the world for decades is the ability to leapfrog **technology**. This area is probably the nearest-term opportunity. You're coming from such a low base that the growth in customers is huge.

Endnotes

1. Tay Za Financial Network (2008) U.S. Department of the Treasury, Office of Foreign Assets Control. Available at: http://www.treasury.gov/resource-center/sanctions/Documents/tayza_02062008.pdf.
2. Specially Designated Nationals and Blocked Persons List (2014) Office of Foreign Assets Control. Available at: http://www.treasury.gov/ofac/downloads/t11sdn.pdf.
3. Szep, J. Marshall, A.R.C. (2012) An image makeover for Myanmar Inc., Reuters. Available at: http://articles.chicagotribune.com/2012-04-12/news/sns-rt-us-myanmar-cronies-imagebre83b0yu-20120412_1_myanmar-aung-san-suu-kyi-trade-sanctions/4.
4. Anonymous (2014) Ease of Doing Business, IFC. Available at: http://www.doing-business.org/data/exploreeconomies/myanmar.

V – Gaung Baung

It's 4.30 in the morning and Yangon is already buzzing as we head to the main bus station at the northern edge of the city.

Taxi drivers pick up three or four newspapers at a time from dozens laid on the ground by a street vendor. The media multiplied after the government ended a half-century of censorship. The *Yangon Times* shows a candle-lit protest over rising electricity prices. Less than half of the population has power in their homes, and even for those lucky ones, long blackouts are the daily routine. The *New Light of Myanmar*, the government-run newspaper dubbed Dim Light on Myanmar, celebrates the "Sustainable Development of the Country" on its front page.

At the sprawling bus terminal maroon-draped monks wander between queueing passengers. They hold bowls to collect food for the day. Shopkeepers and families leave plates of uncooked rice outside for them. I hand a novice some fruit I took for the journey.

We're heading in a straight line north to Naypyitaw. Midway on the four-hour trip we stop at a service station for breakfast. The Traders hotel has packed me some sandwiches and four boiled eggs. I offer some to my local journalist colleague but the eggs stay untouched in their shell. I suggest we give them to the two skinny monks waiting with their alms bowls at the entrance. Spooning in chopsticks full of fried egg and rice, Kyaw Thu shakes his head. You give before you eat, never the leftovers. This demarcates the honor of donating from begging.

The two-lane road from Yangon gives way to a 20-lane highway at Naypyitaw. Each car has its own carriageway, yet drivers still honk at every vehicle they pass, ignoring the "No Horn" signs.

An area of paddy fields until a decade ago, Naypyitaw has the soulless feel of a city dreamt up by the military. The centerpiece is an exact replica of Yangon's golden Shwedagon pagoda only a foot shorter.[1] A neatly manicured park with a fake waterfall and huge fountain is the entertainment highlight; at night it spurts water in approximate rhythm to blaring pop videos on a giant screen behind.

The biggest tourist pull is a family of white elephants miserably cooped up in an enclosure by the pagoda. They would have seemed an appropriate idiom only a few years ago. But now the city is starting to fill up – with the arrival of its most famous resident, Aung San Suu Kyi, and 43 other National League for Democracy MPs since the election in 2012.

The parliament area is a maze of 20 identical white buildings with maroon tiered roofs. We head first to the Ministry of Finance.

Dr Maung Maung Thein, the minister responsible for capital markets and insurance, is sat at his desk watching SkyNet News. He's glued to yesterday's debate in the upper house of parliament, the Amyotha Hluttaw. Rows of men are dressed in identical white collarless shirts and the napkin-type head wrap, or gaung baung, with its tongue sticking out the side. The standout is an MP in the back row in a gaung baung of bear fur with white tusks, a traditional style of the Chin region.[2,3] Then there's the military's quarter of seats – all in green uniform, never speaking, only voting.

"My turn's coming up," Maung Maung Thein says grinning, turning up the volume. "You see my image there? Second from extreme right."

An MP in a white gaung baung – the most common style here, traditional to the Burmese or Mon – reads a speech from a sheet of paper without looking up. The camera flicks to the Speaker seated on a wooden podium facing the MPs, and then to Maung Maung Thein.

"That's me!" He points to himself in a light green gaung baung and blue longyi.

The debate is focused on the President's decision to draw 1.5 million kyats ($1558) as a monthly salary rather than his full 5 million-kyat entitlement.

The Speaker, wearing all black, has argued that the President must take his full salary by law. "We can set the president's salary at 3 million, 4 million or 5 million kyat a month and he has to accept it because if he does not, he is in breach of the law."[4]

"I said 'No!'" Maung Maung Thein says, laughing his head off, and translating as the broadcast finishes. "The law in essence tells you what to do or what not to do: Do not kill – that falls into the 'what not to do' law. You can take less than what has been fixed. It's not breaking the law."

The President got away with his pay cut and the debate won him glowing headlines.

With his 15 minutes over, Maung Maung Thein turns to a less clear-cut issue he's grappling with: how to open a stock exchange now when none of the companies we've met plan listing for several years.

"They have some skepticism about it," says Maung Maung Thein. "That's quite natural because we have to start it from scratch, from ground zero, and the time limitation is very short. But we will just start, just set up the beginning of the beginning, not the whole market, the perfect market."

The Yangon Stock Exchange will be capitalized initially with 32 billion kyats ($33 million) and based in a building owned by the central bank, near the Sule Pagoda in the city center. Daiwa, Japan's second-largest brokerage,

which has been working with the government since the late 90s on the Myanmar Securities Exchange, is a partner in the new bourse.

Along with the government's local-currency bonds moving across from
the securities exchange, Maung Maung Thein expects three or four companies to list shares immediately. They include Asia Green Development Bank,
a Yangon-based lender with 29 branches.[5] "We're talking with other groups
as well. We're going to sign some commitments."

While it might take 10 or 20 years to develop the stock exchange, it's
essential to make a start, says Maung Maung Thein. "Without the stock
exchange, companies can't raise capital, and one of the ingredients for an
open economy is there must be a market to raise capital."

Along with the exchange, Maung Maung Thein wants to help companies
raise money in the international market for bonds and syndicated loans. He's
considering approaching global institutions like the World Bank's International Finance Corp. for a loan to the Finance Ministry that could be passed
on to companies. The central bank is busy creating a credit bureau to assess
the risk of potential corporate borrowers.

* * *

Investment Pipeline: Yangon Stock Exchange

Security/ Trading Platform	Issuer Description	Issuer Comments
Yangon Stock Exchange	Plans for opening stock exchange following easing of trade sanctions	Deputy Finance Minister Maung Maung Thein: Exchange opening in 2015, initially capitalized with 32 billion kyats ($33 million). Three or four companies are to list shares immediately including Asia Green Development Bank, a Yangon-based lender with 29 branches. Government local-currency bonds to move across from the securities exchange

My Myanmar: Yangon Stock Exchange
Serge Pun, Founder of Yoma Strategic Holdings

The one good thing about having military people as your leaders is they say, "I want this," and they'll get it. It doesn't have to be perfect, it doesn't have to be well thought out, but it will be there. It will happen in a very immature, incomplete way. I see a lot of half-baked IPOs happening for the sake of having a lot of IPOs to make a party.

There aren't actually that many companies that qualify to list. Fortunately we qualify because we were incorporated in 1992. We've consistently made dividend payments in bad or good times. The measure that's used here is dividends as a percentage of par value. It doesn't matter if your shares are trading at 10,000, it goes back to the par value (original face value). Every year we've paid 35 to 250%.

Mark Mobius, Executive Chairman, Templeton Emerging Markets Group

The real hope is that the government gets companies to privatize. They can still keep control but let's say they sell 20–30% – then you've got big companies that could be very liquid. I think the IMF and World Bank will push them in that direction. The other way to do it is to say any company that's listed gets a 10 or 20% discount on its income tax, or profit tax. The main reason people don't want to list is because they're cheating on their taxes and by listing they have to be transparent. That's the reality.

Daniel Michener, CEO, Burst Networks

It's going to take longer than they think. They're trying to get it up and running in 2015. I don't see operationally how you do that. I don't see how you get volume in the market to support IPOs. At best it will be 2017, probably 2020, before they have the breadth to support IPOs.

* * *

Across a pentagonal concrete expanse from the Finance Ministry, in an identical white building, is the Commission on Legal Affairs and Special Issues. It's the same body with oversight of law reform that Toe Naing Mann sits on. We meet with four members of the commission. Our conversation flips from energy policy to tourism, agriculture, human rights, corruption, ethnic tensions and the rule of law. The commissioners are meeting today with Bill Clinton and later with Catherine Ashton and Isabel Durant from the European Union for discussions on energy, infrastructure, development aid and civil society.[6]

Many business executives told us they're concerned the government is pushing in too many directions to get anything done. So what's the priority?

"The first thing we need," says Aye Aye Mu, a commission member who joins us half an hour late in her rush between meetings, "is poverty alleviation for the farmers. The next is to upgrade our education system and the third is health. If people's children can't study or they're not healthy, we can't convince them that the system works."

Farmers need to move from subsistence agriculture to large-scale contracts in the way they have in neighboring Thailand. The European Union can help to improve education.

After these three objectives, the next on Aye Aye Mu's list is the rule of law – the No. 1 priority for Aung San Suu Kyi and Tin Oo.

"This is the merry-go-round," says Aye Aye Mu. "Political reform – economy reform." If people aren't earning enough to live they will seek bribes.

"For the rule of law, first we need to fight against corruption. If you don't need to pay anything under the table in the police station or for judges, that will be very good for the rule of law. But reducing corruption also depends on improving the economy."

And where do the ethnic conflicts rank on the list of priorities to tackle? That's already well in hand. "We are at a very good stage of reconciliation," she says.

The government began discussions with representatives from 18 armed rebel groups in late 2013 aimed at achieving an umbrella peace accord.[7,8] "During the last 20 to 30 years, we have never seen everyone at the one table sitting together and talking openly."

* * *

A 15-minute drive from the air-conditioned grandeur of the parliament we enter a chalet park where MPs from some of the poorer constituencies stay. On the bare concrete floor of his one-room home, washing hanging beside his bed, Aye Maung sits in a deckchair wearing a white T-shirt and grey longyi. His constituency is in Rakhine – a 600-kilometer strip on the Bay of Bengal edged with white sands and palm trees.

Long before the Mongol, Portuguese and British empires, Rakhine was a separate kingdom from Burma called Arakan. It has been ruled by the Buddhist Arakanese and at times by Muslims, known as Rohingyas, who called the state Rohang.[9]

Tensions mounted as large groups of Rohingyas fled north across the Chittagong Hills into Bangladesh during times of persecution and subsequently returned to the region, some agitating for an Islamic state.

The Burmese government responded by insisting all Rohingyas are Bengali immigrants, refusing Burmese citizenship even for those whose families had lived for centuries in the country.

Violence erupted in 2012 when the rape and murder of a Buddhist woman triggered a bloody reprisal by vigilantes who killed 10 Muslims on a bus. That sparked rioting by hundreds of Rohingyas after Friday prayers, hurling rocks and torching Buddhist homes and buildings.[10] At least 140,000 people have been displaced.

In an area lacking adequate water, sanitation, food and medical services, the US State Department complained that government delays to travel permits and attacks on aid stations have hampered humanitarian efforts.[11] More than 86,000 fled by boat, the UN High Commissioner for Refugees estimated in 2014.[12]

Aye Maung, a Buddhist, leads the Rakhine Nationalities Development Party with six seats in the upper house and eight in the Pyithu Hluttaw. He also chairs the Citizens' Fundamental Rights, Democracy & Human Rights Commission, set up to investigate the ethnic clashes. For him, it's clear who's to blame.

He leans forward, speaking softly in short sentences, listening intently to Kyaw Thu's translation and watching our reaction to make sure his words register.

"There's a hidden political agenda behind this," he says. "The Bengalis want a separate state and administration. When the country moved to democracy, they took advantage."

According to Aye Maung, the more the international community focuses on the region, the greater the risk of the tensions escalating. "The conflict usually starts when a delegation or a head of state visits. They're trying to get political benefit from this."

I ask about the progress in the ethnic reconciliation talks championed by Aye Aye Mu and the government.

"If the Bengali can stop their ambition of becoming an ethnic people under the name of Rohingya and become an ethnicity, if they can cooperate with us to have citizenship in the proper way, everything will be okay. If not," says Aye Maung, "the conflict is not started by us."

A few months after our meeting, in the Malaysian capital Kuala Lumpur, two men on a motorbike fire bullets at a car carrying Aye Maung and the president of the Arakan League for Democracy, Aye Thar Aung. Both survive.[13]

Endnotes

1. Roughneen, S. (2013) Naypyidaw's synthetic Shwedagon shimmers, but in solitude. Available at: http://www.irrawaddy.org/z_naypyidaw/naypyidaws-synthetic-shwedagon-shimmers-solitude.html.
2. Myanmar Burma, Wondering about those interesting looking hats? Available at: http://www.myanmarburma.com/blog/739/wondering-about-those-interestinglooking-hats.
3. Freedom Travel. Available at: http://www.freedomtravelmyanmar.com/myanmar-tribes.htm.
4. Mizzima (2013) Upper House speaker, deputy minister clash over president's salary sacrifice. Available at: http://www.mizzima.com/mizzima-news/politics/item/10563-upper-house-speaker-deputy-minister-clash-over-president-s-salary-sacrifice/10563-upper-house-speaker-deputy-minister-clash-over-president-s-salary-sacrifice.
5. Onomitsu, G. (2013) Daiwa to advise Asia Green Development Bank for Myanmar listing, Bloomberg News.
6. EU–Myanmar Taskforce (2013) Second Media Advisory. Available at: http://eeas.europa.eu/myanmar/docs/media_advisory_myanmar.pdf.
7. Kachin News (2013) Burma's armed ethnic groups sign nationwide ceasefire pledge in Laiza. Available at: http://www.kachinnews.com/news/2592-burma-s-armed-ethnic-groups-sign-nation-wide-ceasefire-pledge-in-laiza.html.
8. Shibani Mahtani (2013) Peace talks between Myanmar, ethnic rebels fall short. Available at: http://online.wsj.com/news/articles/SB10001424052702304672404579181442173910768.
9. Arakanese (2013) Available at: http://www.britannica.com/EBchecked/topic/31967/Arakanese.
10. Petty, M. (2012) Four killed as Rohingya Muslims riot in Myanmar: government. Reuters. Available at: http://www.reuters.com/article/2012/06/08/us-myanmar-violence-idUSBRE85714E20120608.
11. Harf, M. (2014) United States Concern Over Events in Rakhine State. Available at: http://www.state.gov/r/pa/prs/ps/2014/04/224342.htm.
12. Anonymous (2014) UN agency concerned about reported abuse as thousands continue to flee Myanmar, UN News Centre. Available at: http://www.un.org/apps/news/story.asp?NewsID=48003#.VBVzvfldUuc.
13. Prakash, G. (2014) Police say attack on Myanmar national linked to Rakhine riots, *Malay Mail*. Available at: http://www.themalaymailonline.com/malaysia/article/police-say-attack-on-myanmar-national-linked-to-rakhine-riots#sthash.6lmP7SgS.dpuf.

VI – Monk of Mandalay

Bloomin' idol made o' mud –
Wot they called the Great Gawd Budd –
Plucky lot she cared for idols when I kissed 'er where she stud!
On the road to Mandalay...
When the mist was on the rice-fields an' the sun was droppin' slow,
She'd git 'er little banjo an' she'd sing "Kulla-lo-lo!

Rudyard Kipling, Mandalay – 1890

B y nightfall I'm back on the bus for the road to Mandalay.
Where Rudyard Kipling's green-capped maiden sang "kulla-lo-lo," a video screen above my head blasts a talent show with karaoke lyrics. After two hours there's short relief as we pull into a halfway house. A panpipes interpretation of "Oh Danny Boy" plays on repeat in the restaurant.

I already ate in Naypyitaw but the guy who was next to me on the bus won't hear of me missing dinner here. He calls the waiter with the kissing sound used for a cat. Like the old man on the bus in Yangon, there's no way he's letting his "guest" pay. The food is Chinese as are the shop signs the further we head north toward the border, the road becoming smoother and wider.

We pass through the lakeside town of Meiktila. It was here one dawn in March 2013 that a Buddhist mob massacred scores of Muslims. On the wreckage of shops, rioters painted three numbers: 969.[1]

I check into the Pacific Hotel right by Mandalay's bus station. The bell boy shows me my room and then hunkers down on the floor outside. Below is a two-lane roundabout where motorbikes, some ferrying monks on the back seat, shoot in every direction, narrowly skirting people and bicycles. I drift off to the tooting and revving, missing the tranquility of bike-less Yangon.

Mandalay has the layout of an American city, with straight-line horizontal roads numbered 1st to 50th Street while 51st to 88th run vertically. It helps as I hire a motorbike the next day with a rider who speaks no English.

I point on the map to 80th Street for the Mandalay Palace, the last bastion of Burma's monarchy. Its multi-tiered roofs, the all-important display of the inhabitants' importance, are unlovingly reconstructed in corrugated iron. The army, or Tatmadaw, check the tourists coming and going beneath a giant billboard warning: "Tatmadaw and the People Cooperate and Crush All Those Harming the Union."

Close by on 82nd Street is the Mahamuni Pagoda. It turns out there's a stricter code of Buddhism here. The knee-length shorts I wore at the Shwedagon in Yangon are too short for the monks of Mandalay. I'm ushered to a longyi stall where I obligingly step into the wide waist and pull it to my hips. I let the stallholder tie it in the local style. With shoes off and longyi on I head to the giant gold Buddha shrine. And at that moment the longyi falls to my ankles. Children giggle as my driver quickly binds a sturdier knot.

As the authority of Myanmar's military wanes, monks have the biggest influence on how people think and vote – especially beyond the commercial and political centers of Yangon and Naypyitaw. One monk in particular is amassing a big following.

The Masoeyein Monastery, near the broad Irrawaddy River, is set out like a campus with a dozen or so two-story buildings. Monks shrouded in maroon or orange drift about reading Buddhist canons or clean and sweep for karma.

On the approach to the middle building, all harmony is shattered. Pinned to the wall are photos of dead bodies – a woman in a makeshift coffin, another with a red gash from her ear to her neck, a man with his stomach sliced open, intestines spilling out. To the side, larger than life, Aung San Suu Kyi waves from a vinyl hoarding, the fighting peacock above her head.

Ashin Wirathu is dressed in orange but he's instantly recognizable from his picture in a maroon robe on the cover of *Time* magazine with its headline: The Face of Buddhist Terror.

Wirathu caught the attention of the world media when his sermons went out on YouTube early in March 2013. "Do not let your money go to your enemy by spending at Muslim shops," Wirathu tells his followers. With a soft voice and passive face, he urges them to stop their children from marrying Muslims lest they become a "threat to your country and destroy our religion." Muslims, he says, "would snatch us away from our land." [2]

It's not just words with Wirathu. So that followers know where and where not to spend, Buddhist shops and cabs are given stickers with the numeric symbols for religious virtue: 969.

As is expected in the monastic order, Wirathu sits at his desk while his guests – they've included the president, Aung San Suu Kyi and the Dalai Lama – sit below him on the floor. Behind his chair on a jade-blue painted wall are five framed photographs of himself and a calendar with pictures of Suu Kyi. Twenty books are piled in front of him.

A disciple videos the meeting, part of Wirathu's rules of engagement since finding himself on the cover of *Time*. The French ambassador visited recently but objected to being filmed; he left 15 minutes later, says Wirathu.

Every few minutes, followers come to pay homage. They kneel and bow. Wirathu gives them DVDs of his teachings and the message of 969.

He pours himself a cup of tea from a pot. His voice emits no emotion save for a dismissive laugh when presented with the accusation that he's fueling violence against Muslims.

"The root causes are on both sides," Wirathu begins evenly. "The root cause is that Muslims raped and acted in group violence even though they knew there would be conflict. The second thing is that, instead of taking legal action against the offender, the Burmese responded by attacking other people who did not commit the crimes."

In the town of Meiktila, says Wirathu, Muslims killed a monk and beheaded the Buddha image before the Burmans responded.

According to eye witness accounts in international media reports, the killing in Meiktila was sparked by an argument over a hairclip. Aye Aye Naing, a 45-year-old Buddhist, went with her husband and sister to pawn her gold clip at New Waint Sein, a Muslim-owned shop.

The Buddhist version of events is that after workers studied the gold, it came back damaged and the shop owner halved the price he was prepared to offer to 50,000 kyats ($52). The woman called the owner unreasonable. He slapped her. When Aye Aye Naing's husband remonstrated, he was pulled outside and beaten by three staff.

As police arrived and detained both parties, an angry crowd started shouting anti-Muslim slogans, hurling stones and wrecking the shop.

Four Muslim men responded. They attacked a monk on the back of a motorbike with swords. Then they doused him with fuel and set him alight. A Buddhist mechanic who witnessed the murder ran to the market shouting "a monk has been killed." In the hours that followed Muslim homes, shops, a mosque and an orphanage burnt to the ground.[3]

"When a person is always bullying you," says Wirathu, "to what extent can you tolerate it? The victim tolerates it ninety nine times but the hundredth time, he can no longer."

"All the monks have this kind of resentful feeling, but it hadn't yet exploded. How and when does it explode? In a case like in Meiktila, when a monk with an alms bowl is killed."

The international community, Wirathu complains, "only questions why we responded like that to the hundredth incident. They don't know how the people suffered the other ninety nine times."

Violence is against Buddhist principles, he says, and bad for the nation and religion. Wirathu claims he always preaches for the public to know that. For evidence he shows a pamphlet that reads: "969 Denounces Killing, 969

Does Not Accept Terrorism." He denies calling himself the Buddhist Bin Laden.

He says he's participated in interfaith discussions at the Myanmar Peace Center and wants to work with Muslim leaders. One Muslim from Yangon who visited him four times for discussions stopped after receiving threats on Facebook while his house was stoned.

"If the Islamic leaders talk with me today, the conflict will be stopped today. If they discuss tomorrow, it will stop tomorrow. It's because I know the root cause of the conflicts in detail."

It isn't the first time Wirathu has been accused of fueling violence. In 2003, he was sentenced to 25 years in jail for inciting religious conflict. Thein Sein released him in 2012 under an amnesty. A year later the government blocked *Time* magazine's issue from sale in Myanmar. The President denounced the report for undermining the trust being built between faiths.[4]

"We religious groups warned the government about the hate speech before the conflicts happened," says Nyunt Maung Shein, President of the Islamic Religious Affairs Council. "'Please take action, President' – we wrote three times. They did not take action."

Nyunt Maung Shein is from the town of Meiktila. He lost several of his family in the rampage. The violence, he says, was professionally orchestrated, with stimulant drugs fed to the attackers.

"People with red eyes came into the houses holding swords. They killed elderly, youngsters, pregnant women, people in wheelchairs. Then that group went out and another group came in and looted," he says. Finally they burned down the houses and mosques.

"It's obvious that people who were trained did this," he says. "I told the generals and ministers that this is highly organized. They also know it, but why don't they acknowledge this? The government has a duty and a responsibility."

While the official death toll in Meiktila was 32, Shein says 86 were killed. Four were his relatives. Their killer was jailed for just seven years, says Shein.

"We can forgive," he says, "but it's very difficult to forget. I am over 70 years old, we will not forget."

Meiktila has 14 mosques. Only a handful have reopened and they're all far from where people live. When Shein complained that they were being denied the right to worship, the President ordered government ministers to re-open the mosques, he says. Yet still they remain shut. "They don't honor the President's words."

Shein says he too is engaged in interfaith dialogue. But resolving the conflict will take more than talks between leaders.

"We have to go to the conflict area and persuade the people." The task is made harder, he says, because only 3 to 5% of people are educated. There are state schools but no students.

"They don't know why they should study when in the economy there is only fishing, no other business," says Shein. "The economy is really bad. This is one of the factors in today's problems. In this situation, foreign investment won't come. Why? There is not tranquility."

Investor Analysis: Driehaus's Howie Schwab on Myanmar

Bottom Line

- The ethnic conflicts represent the biggest risk in **disrupting investment**. With so many ethnic groups, it's a huge challenge. We'll be watching this closely. Logically it should be a matter of reaching out to ethnic regions economically and from a security standpoint – through legal ownership rights, sharing of the fruits of the economy, educating the populations to participate in the economic success. In reality it's never that simple. Ethnic rifts can change dramatically without rhyme or reason.
- Suppression by the military has cemented a communal feel. However, religiously affiliated rifts are threatening rural advancement and pose a severe threat to economic and social **stability**.
- The situation is highly flammable, but overall my impression is there are **more positives than negatives** about this country from an investment perspective.
- There's an overwhelming feeling of optimism here, that things are moving forward. People generally are kindhearted and there's this communal sense that helps the **anti-corruption** effort. There's not the aggression you sometimes feel in, say, China or Nigeria.
- I'm off to Indonesia next. That country is at the other end of the cycle we're just seeing take off here. It has the traffic pollution and problems from credit growth. Here that whole **cycle of credit** spurring economic growth has yet to kick in. I'd rather be here than in Indonesia's smog.

Endnotes

1. Szep, J. (2013) Buddhist monks incite Muslim killings in Myanmar, Reuters. Available at: http://www.reuters.com/article/2013/04/08/us-myanmar-violence-specialreport-idUSBRE9370AP20130408.
2. YouTube (2013) Anti Muslim Monk Wirathu talks about Meiktila before riot. Available at: https://www.youtube.com/watch?v=N7irUgGsFYw.
3. BBC News Asia (2013) Burma riots: Muslim gold shop workers jailed. Available at: http://www.bbc.co.uk/news/world-asia-22124346.
4. VOA News (2013) Burma bans *Time* magazine labeling monk as 'Face of Terror'. Available at: http://www.voanews.com/content/burma-bans-time-story-labeling-monk-as-face-of-terror/1689130.html.

CHAPTER 3

Romania

I – Ro-man-ee-a!

B ucharest doesn't feel *frontier*.
     At the Henri Coandă Airport, named after the jet plane inventor, a carpeted bridge leads to the terminal building. Thirty identical black and white Adidas bags rotate at baggage reclaim, heralding the arrival of the Greek national team for the World Cup run-offs. Outside, familiar corporate names top glass and steel towers. Wide highways lined with linden trees are packed with BMWs, Saabs and Dacias – the car produced here by Renault since communist times for export to Germany and beyond.

Most often seen as yellow taxis, the Dacias take their name from the kingdom before the Roman Empire gave the country its modern-day identity and Latin tongue. The sounds of *Bucuresti* are more like *Roma* a thousand kilometers west than the Slavic nations bordering to the north and east. Visually the city is a steal from Paris, with a slightly smaller Arc de Triomphe, a broader and longer Champs Élysées and names like Piata Charles de Gaulle binding French and Latin influences that survived communism.

This is my third trip to Romania. I first came as a child in the early 80s to a drab Black Sea resort near the port of Constanta. My memories are of a man haggling to buy an old polo shirt my Dad was wearing as we left one of the foreigner-only *Comturist* shops, and the suspicion that a student in swimming trunks and long gray socks who befriended us on the beach was Securitate. Nicolae Ceausescu's secret police were recruiting thousands at the time. Children would spy on parents, teachers and friends at school and at the hundreds of orphanages spawned by a ban on contraception.[1,2]

The era casts a long shadow over modern Bucharest, quite literally. On a hill at the center of the city is the People's House – the world's most extensive and expensive civilian government building – with underground parking for 20,000 cars, and 3500 tons of crystal decorating its 480 chandeliers. Ceausescu destroyed historic churches, synagogues and tens of thousands of homes to clear the way and had 8000 workers and 7000 soldiers dedicated to the project every day for much of the 80s. Meanwhile bread, cooking oil, sugar, coffee and corn were rationed to repay $10 billion of debt run up with Western banks.[3,4]

Ceausescu never got to see his palace completed. The last dictator standing after the striking shipyard workers of Gdansk triggered a wave of uprisings across Eastern Europe, Ceausescu and his wife Elena were executed by a military firing squad on Christmas Day 1989.[5]

It was this colossus that was my base when I returned to Romania in 2002 for a showcase European intergovernmental conference. Across Bucharest's old town in Revolution Square, the walls of buildings were still marked with bullet holes. There was a sense of rectitude as people recounted memories of the most violent of the Eastern Bloc uprisings and optimism as the European Union's commitment to Romanian membership unleashed a tiger economy.

Returning now, more than a decade on, some of the pock marks of history are cemented over. European integration moving up another gear has newspapers dreading an influx of rich Brits or Germans buying up their farmland and recruiting their doctors – an antithesis to the fear in the UK press of Romanian immigrants taking jobs and benefit payments.[6]

Walking around, it seems easier to find people with a kind word for Ceausescu than for today's leaders – whether it's older Romanians missing the certainty of a job or young couples delaying having children because they're unable to afford a home of their own.

Romania's runaway economic growth ground to a halt in 2009 with a recession that dragged on for two years amid austerity measures fostered by the International Monetary Fund as part of its package of bailout loans. Policies targeted cutting the government's budget deficit from as much as 9% of gross domestic product to little over 2%, one of the most drastic reductions in the EU. Romanians were hit as public sector wages plunged 25% while the cost of living soared, with a 5% hike in VAT and a depreciating currency increasing the cost of imported food. Unemployment jumped by up to 50% in 2012 as foreign investment plunged 83%.[7]

Public resentment brought down the government of Emil Boc that year as Victor Ponta became the third prime minister in the space of six months.[8] Ponta immediately locked horns with President Traian Basescu, attempting to have him impeached. The situation had German Chancellor Angela Merkel fretting over the future of democracy in Romania as the currency, the leu, sank to a record low.

As in other countries, the worsening economy stoked concern that borrowers wouldn't be able to repay their debts. However, Romania had the added headache that people had been taking out loans in foreign currencies to get a lower rate of interest. The cost of repaying the debt in Swiss francs, euros and dollars threatened to rocket with the currency weakening.

By 2013, Romanians were in arrears on more than a fifth of all credit, the sixth-worst rate in the World Bank's data from 99 countries.[9,10]

"The financial crisis really hurt us," says Ionut Gheorghe, who calls himself Johnny to the foreign business people he drives around in his black Dacia. "You know, when you're not used to a lot and then in a few short years you have more than you can imagine, and then after another few years they take it back, the feeling – well it's like a party finishing."

In the near-freezing evening, opposite a giant construction site for a new "Mega Mall," Bucharest's Arena Nationale is packed to capacity for the game with Greece. Over 50,000 flag-waving soccer fans with patriotic blue, yellow and red striped faces are in defiant mood. Romania lost 3:1 in Athens a couple of days earlier and needs at least a two-goal advantage tonight for a chance of making it to the World Cup. The fact that the nation hasn't got through in 16 years counts for nothing.

The bar stops serving alcohol before the half-time break. It's probably just as well as the mood darkens in the second half. Romania is tying 1:1 but only by virtue of an own goal from the Greeks. Impassioned chants of "Ro-Man-Ee-A!" give way to demands for the coach to resign. A Facebook image of him as the accident-prone Mr Bean character is doing the rounds.

A few months later in the political arena, Basescu's maximum term expires. Ponta stands for the presidency. He has a 10-point lead in the first round of voting. Then, within two weeks, the electorate turns on him. Two million Romanians switch sides to elect ethnic German Klaus Iohannis, angered by corruption scandals in Ponta's party and poor management of voting abroad. It's an unforgiving crowd.

Top Down Data

Country	Population	GDP on PPP Basis ($)	GDP/ Capita on PPP ($)	Inflation (% pa)	Unemployment (%)
Romania	21,729,871	288,500,000,000	14,400	3.2	7.3
Myanmar	55,746,253	111,100,000,000	1700	5.7	5.2
Kenya	45,010,056	79,900,000,000	1800	5.8	40.0

Source: CIA World Factbook, December 2014
[1] Population data from July 2014 estimates.
[2] GDP at purchasing power parity (PPP) exchange rates is the sum value of all goods and services produced in the country valued at prices prevailing in the USA, based on 2013 estimates.
[3] GDP per capita (PPP) divided by population, based on 2013 estimates.
[4] Inflation rate shows the annual percentage change in consumer prices in 2013.
[5] Unemployment rate shows the percentage of the labor force without jobs in 2013, except for Kenya (2008).

Fund Factbox

Company & Assets in Emerging Markets	Emerging Market Fund	Performance & Peer Ranking	Portfolio Manager: Andras Szalkai
Raiffeisen Capital Management $2.5 billion	Raiffeisen Emerging Markets-Aktien	2nd highest total return among 467 European Union-registered global emerging market funds over 5 years at 221% (annualized 26.2%)	Raiffeisen Capital Management set up one of the first eastern European equity funds 20 years ago Andras was an analyst at OTP Bank and Erste in his native Hungary before moving to Austria as a fund manager for Vontobel and later to Sweden with East Capital. He joined Raiffeisen in Vienna in 2011 as fund manager for emerging Europe ex-Turkey, Russia

Source: Data compiled by Bloomberg as of June 2014

My Romania: Andras Szalkai

- I know Romania from my childhood. I was at a **wedding in Transylvania** and it was a big adventure – the roads were terrible. My father said he'll never return because the car was ruined. I started to look from a different perspective when I joined Raiffeisen. At the time, Romania was still in bad shape, but then suddenly something happened – the government decided it wanted to start in the capital markets.
- With **European frontier markets**, the point isn't that they're under-developed economically. The point is their stock exchanges are small or the liquidity is poor, or some kind of regulation isn't on the level of other markets. Right now, Romania has only a few listed stocks. Even if you go to Kenya or Nigeria, you can easily invest $10 million a day. In Romania, you can't. As a result, Romania only accounts for around 2% of the frontier markets universe.
- If the government's program of privatizing state-owned companies continues, Romania will become an **emerging market**, but it will take another two or three years at least.

Endnotes

1. McLaughlin, D. (2006) Ceausescu regime used children as police spies, *The Guardian*. Available at: http://www.theguardian.com/world/2006/jul/22/main-section.international1.
2. Anonymous (1990) Romania's Orphans: A Legacy of Repression, Human Rights Watch. Available at: http://www.hrw.org/reports/1990/12/01/romanias-orphans-legacy-repression.
3. Cowell, A. (1989) Upheaval in the East: Ceausescu's legacy; In a dictator's palace, lavish echoes of power, AP. Available at: http://www.nytimes.com/1989/12/31/world/upheaval-east-ceausescu-s-legacy-dictator-s-palace-lavish-echoes-power.html.
4. World Record Academy. Available at: http://www.worldrecordacademy.com/biggest/largest_administrative_building_world_record_set_by_the_Palace_of_the_Romanian_Parliament_80185.htm.
5. Ceausescu.org. Nicolae Ceausescu. Available at: http://www.ceausescu.org/ceausescu_texts/ceausescu_chronology.htm.
6. Fontanella-Khan, J. (2014) Romanians despair that wealthy Britain is taking all their doctors, *Financial Times*. Available at: http://www.ft.com/cms/s/0/f4c0b734-7c70-11e3-b514-00144feabdc0.html#axzz2zz9AaoxW.
7. Antena 3 (2013) Five years under economic crisis. What happened to the Romanian economy during this time. Available at: http://www.antena3.ro/en/romania/five-years-under-economic-crisis-what-happened-to-the-romanian-economy-during-this-time-228157.html.
8. Romania Profile (2014) BBC News Europe. Available at: http://www.bbc.co.uk/news/world-europe-17776265.
9. Bank nonperforming loans to total gross loans (%), The World Bank. Available at: http://data.worldbank.org/indicator/FB.AST.NPER.ZS.
10. Savu, I. (2013) Romania braces for 'shock' on bad loans after bank probe, Bloomberg News. Available at: http://www.bloomberg.com/news/2013-12-05/romania-braces-for-shock-on-bad-loans-after-bank-probe.html.

II – Systematization

Some of those uprooted for Ceausescu's palace and monolithic tower blocks have finally been receiving compensation.[1–3]

Paying cash to the victims of "systematization" – Ceausescu's North Korea-inspired policy to eradicate "irrational" villages and vast swathes of towns and cities – would have bankrupted Romania. So instead the government opted to pay using state assets.

Shares of national companies were bundled into an investment fund that was then floated on the stock exchange and portioned out to the cash value of claims by thousands of so-called restituents.

The job of managing the fund – Fondul Proprietatea – was put out to tender in 2010 and awarded to Franklin Templeton with a mandate to maximize shareholder profits. Most of the original restituents cashed out early on in 2011 as the stock price halved. By the time the shares doubled in 2013, individual Romanians were holding less than a quarter. Foreign fund managers were the main buyers, taking a 59% stake.

Andras Szalkai at Raiffeisen Capital Management was among them. He bought the shares in 2013, his biggest position in the Romanian market. The Fondul Proprietatea annual investor forum where we meet has become a fixture in his diary.

While lawsuits continue between Bucharest and the European Court of Human Rights for many who missed out or were undercompensated,[4] the restitution fund has taken on a momentum of its own. Fondul Proprietatea has become Romania's biggest non-banking stock (Table 3.1). With a value of $4.6 billion it's also the largest investment fund of its kind on any stock exchange worldwide.[5]

TABLE 3.1 Bucharest BET Index: Fondul Proprietatea has biggest weighting

	Name	% Index Weight
1	Fondul Proprietatea SA/Fund	21.5
2	OMV Petrom SA	18.1
3	Banca Transilvania	15.5
4	Romgaz SA	15.4
5	BRD-Groupe Société Générale	8.9
6	Electrica	7.8
7	Transgaz SA Medias	5.8
8	Transelectrica SA	4.2
9	Nuclearelectrica	1.7
10	SC Bursa DE Valori Bucuresti SA (Stock Exchange operator)	1.0

Source: Data compiled by Bloomberg as of December 2014. *(Function: BET Index MEMB GO)*

Fondul's broad range of holdings, from energy producers to banks and airports, means much of its own stock performance comes down to investor confidence in the overall economy. But it's also about squeezing value out of the 66 companies. That process begins with seeking a seat on the management board and then pushing to weed out waste or malpractice – like unauthorized payments, the appointment of family members, expenditure on unconvincing projects or supply contracts on preferential terms (Table 3.2).

Fondul's board members "take a lot of punishment," says Mark Mobius, chairing the investor conference at the Radisson Blu hotel in the center of Bucharest. "You can imagine the kind of disputes that arise when somebody goes on the board of a company that has absolutely no corporate governance and raises questions."

Pressure is applied first in the boardroom and then in the courts and government ministries.

"At the end of the day you're forcing these managements to face the music and stop doing improper things," says Mobius.

Other times it's about trying to align the interests of managers and employees with those of the companies' stakeholders. Among Fondul's 20 biggest investments is Transelectrica, the power grid operator. Fondul is working with the Finance Ministry to introduce "phantom share option schemes" to compensate Transelectrica's managers as if they were holding their own shares.

If all goes to plan, the managers will be waking up, checking the share price and making time to meet investors to promote the company, says Grzegorz Konieczny, Fondul's chief executive officer. "That's always been the trouble with state-controlled companies, that they didn't want to meet investors."

"Hopefully after this first share option plan we'll be able to copy and paste to some other companies."

Most of the companies in the Fondul portfolio, however, have yet to sell shares. Among those Fondul hopes will come to the market next are Bucharest Airports and Constanta Ports.[6,7]

```
┌─────────────────────────────────────────────────────────────────────────┐
│ Stocks Box: Fondul Proprietatea                                           │
│                                                                           │
```

Company & Trading Platform	Description	Average Annual Return	Price–Earnings Ratio	Price–Book Ratio/ NAV	Return on Equity	Gross Dividend Yield	Market Value ($m)	Top Holders %
Fondul Proprietatea Bucharest Stock Exchange	Romania's restitution fund has become the country's most traded stock & the world's largest closed-end investment fund	40% since listed 2011	N/A	24% discount to NAV	N/A	5.4%	3,530	Manchester Securities 15.4% Baillie Gifford Overseas 1.4% ING Int'l 0.7%

Source: Data compiled by Bloomberg as of December 2014

TABLE 3.2   Fondul Proprietatea: largest holdings by net asset value

Company	Status	Majority	% Stake	NAV (EUR m)	% of Fondul NAV
OMV Petrom	Listed	OMV	19.0%	1147.0	34.4
Hidroelectrica	IPO Expected 2015	State	19.9%	477.2	14.3
Romgaz	Listed	State	10.0%	314.5	9.4
ENEL Distributie Banat	Unlisted	Enel Group	24.1%	130.0	3.9
ENEL Distributie Muntenia	Unlisted	Enel Group	12.0%	107.2	3.2
GDF Suez Energy Romania	Unlisted	GDF Suez	12.0%	91.7	2.8
ENEL Distributie Dobrogea	Unlisted	Enel Group	24.1%	85.9	2.6
E.ON Moldova Distributie SA	Unlisted	E.ON Group	22.0%	78.3	2.4

Source: Fondul Proprietatea data as of Sept. 30, 2014

My Romania: IMF's Guillermo Tolosa

Watching Fondul's progress closely is the International Monetary Fund, which has made 20 billion euros ($28 billion) of loans available to Romania on the understanding it's moving toward opening up the economy through state asset sales among other policies. Guillermo Tolosa is the IMF's resident representative.

- Romania's **vulnerabilities** include large financing needs, with most public debt coming due in short maturities, and government expenditure that isn't growth enhancing, including an inefficient public healthcare system.
- Policies helping stability include Romania's adoption of the **fiscal compact** that commits EU governments to cut their budget deficit to below 3% of GDP.
- Romania has preserved or strengthened its **comparative advantage**. Wages continue to be among the lowest in Europe. This helps to explain why unemployment has been lower, minimizing the risk of social unrest. The exchange rate, in contrast with other European countries, remains in line with the country's fundamentals, so we would not expect sharp movements that would undermine macro-economic stability.[8]

Investor Analysis: Raiffeisen's Andras Szalkai on Fondul Proprietatea

Bottom Line

- It's a special animal as a fund that also trades on the stock exchange. It is the most **liquid** stock in the country with 3–5 million euros traded every day.
- It's a good way of getting **stakes** in the biggest state-owned companies.
- Templeton have done brilliant job in **promoting** and bringing these companies to the market.

Buy/Sell Triggers

- The rally in the shares has increased the value of Fondul Proprietatea to a level where it's approaching the amount its assets are worth. While the shares had been trading 30% below the **net asset value**, that discount has shrunk. As we get closer to 20% it's on the edge whether you really want to be there.
- Fondul is very **biased to energy**. It would be interesting to see some new investment areas. We're hearing so much about agriculture, for example, but there's no company listed on the Romanian exchange doing agricultural business.

Endnotes

1. Sen, A., Johung, J. Landscapes of mobility: Culture, politics, and placemaking, Ashgate.
2. Manolescu, I. Erasing the Identity of the Past: Effects of the "Systematization" Process in Nicolae Ceausescu's Communist Romania, Universitatea Bucureşti. Available at: http://phantasma.lett.ubbcluj.ro/?p=944&lang=en.
3. Johnson, M. (2013) *Season Forgotten*, AuthorHouse.
4. Ilie, L. (2013) Fight to get back homes is legacy of Romania's communist past, Reuters. Available at: http://mobile.reuters.com/article/Davos2012/idUSL6N0E 449L20130528?irpc=934.
5. Butcher, D. (2014) U.S. Charge D'Affaires Duane Butcher's Remarks at Bucharest Stock Exchange for Three Year Anniversary of Fondul Proprietatea Listing. Available at: Romania.usembassy.gov/policy/charge/pr-01222014.html.
6. Chirileasa, A. (2014) Romania's Fondul Proprietatea sells stake in Transelectrica for Eur 48.5 Mln, Romania Insider. Available at: http://www.romania-insider.com/romanias-fondul-proprietatea-sells-stake-in-transelectrica-for-eur-48-5-mln/126949/.
7. Anonymous (2014) Fondul Proprietatea Announces Sale Agreement For A 5 Percent Stake In Romgaz, Govnet. Available at: http://www.govnet.ro/Financial/Economics/Fondul-Proprietatea-announces-sale-agreement-for-a-5-percent-stake-in-Romgaz.
8. Romanian unemployment was the eighth lowest in the EU at a seasonally adjusted rate of 7.3% as of May 2014, according to the Statistics Portal. Available at: http://www.statista.com/statistics/268830/unemployment-rate-in-eu-countries/.

III – Brown Envelopes

In the Ceausescu-era apartment blocks, some things haven't changed.
Once a month, the building administrator divides up the heating bill by the number of inhabitants. The amount apportioned is marked on a chart in the hallway. Residents pay the administrator, probably with the same lei notes they received in their wage packet.

"This country loves cash," says Tomas Spurny, the head of Romania's biggest bank by assets, burying his head in his hands. "I know of several large companies with hundreds of employees. When it's time to pay the staff, a car comes to a restaurant, all the employees are sitting around, they throw the envelopes out of the window – that's how they pay people."

Romania has the lowest rate of banking penetration, or financial inclusion, in the European Union after Lithuania.[1] It's one of the biggest problems for the banking industry, says Spurny.

Spurny was hired from Hungary in 2012 to rescue Banca Comerciala Romana from a surge in delinquent loans. Under pressure from Austrian owner Erste Group to reduce BCR's costs to the level of its revenue, he fired around a fifth of his workforce and closed a hundred of 660 branches.

"The psychological impact is heavy," he says. The bank ran a survey of its staff. Unsurprisingly, less than a third felt safe in their job.

"If you made all of this illegal so that condominiums have to have a bank account and you have to settle your dues through the bank account, the banking business in this country would grow immediately," he says. "This isn't rocket science, it's just things that are absolutely ordinary."

The global financial crisis sent over 21% of all credit into arrears in Romania by 2013 – more than twice the proportion in Spain.[2] Even though most of the country's banks are owned by EU institutions, being outside of the Eurozone left Romania's industry without the support of the European Central Bank's cheap financing.

BCR reported a loss of more than a billion lei, or over $300 million, as bad debt mounted in 2012.[3,4]

As part of his restructuring plan, Spurny undertook to improve credit controls. The bank adopted a rigid formula for deciding which companies it should lend money to by grading them on a scale of 1 to 10. Those scoring 1 to 5 – or in the top two of four quartiles – would be potentially eligible for loans.

The trouble was every other bank applied similar guidelines. They ended up chasing the same group of borrowers, squeezing the margin they could charge over their own costs of funding even in the 3 to 5 credit rating bracket.

"You have an incredibly intense fight for the second quartile," says Spurny. "Everyone wants good credits, so there is pressure on margins."

At the other end of the ratings scale, a huge part of the market has been neglected. "No one wants to touch it, and there you have a big debate about whether banks are fulfilling their mission, about social responsibility. This is really the debate behind the scenes, and it's very unpleasant."

BCR returned to profit in 2013. To grow its corporate lending business without taking on riskier borrowers, BCR has been pushing into trade finance for smaller companies. A supplier of windscreen wipers, for example, might have to wait five months for an invoice to be paid under 150-day business terms from a car producer like Dacia. For a fee, BCR would step in and pay the windscreen wiper company immediately and go to Dacia in five months for its money. Because the funds are coming from a creditworthy name like Dacia, BCR is able to provide better terms to the windscreen wiper producer than it could on a regular loan.

"We're trying to create more working capital and a supply chain financing culture in the network," says Spurny.

BRD Groupe, Romania's second-largest bank, saw its non-performing loans reach nearly a quarter of all debt. The company, which is controlled by Paris-based Société Générale, is also focusing on small and medium-sized enterprises, and especially those involved in international supply chains.[5]

But it's not just banks that BRD is competing against for business, says Claudiu Cercel, the deputy CEO. Non-bank providers are also muscling in on the core business of bill payments.

"There are a lot of companies now offering possibilities for customers to pay utility bills using terminals in malls or on the internet," he says. "That's eating up fee generation."

Stocks Box: Romania's Banks

Company & Trading Platform	Description	Average Annual Return	Price–Earnings Ratio	Price–Book Ratio/ NAV	Return on Equity	Gross Dividend Yield	Market Value ($m)	Top Holders %
BRD-Groupe Bucharest Stock Exchange	Romania's second-largest bank. Nearly 1/4 of debt was non-performing at height of banking crisis	34.5% since listed 2001	N/A	1.1	–7.0%	N/A	1595	Société Generálé 60.2% SIF3 4.6% Free float 39.8%
Erste Group Bank Vienna Stock Exchange	Austria's biggest lender owns Banca Comerciala Romana (BCR), Romania's biggest bank by assets	16.6% since 2001	N/A	0.9	–17.0%	0.9%	11,640	Erste Osterreichisch 20.7% Caixabank 9.1% Free float 75.2%

Source: Data compiled by Bloomberg as of December 2014

Investor Analysis: Andras Szalkai on Romanian Banks

Bottom Line

- If you want to invest in the local economy, the banks are the only way to play. It's not a perfect story but compared to other regions it's **getting better** and there is a potential for a positive surprise from the economy.
- When I was here last, they had just appointed Spurny to restructure BCR. It was a **big mess** but he was sure he would make it work. Erste shares traded at 15 euros then and almost doubled a year later. I sold at 24 in early 2013 as I was worried the price had gone too far.

- BRD was in big trouble with its **non-performing loans**. They made a lot of foreign-currency loans. The NPLs were highest from smaller companies, especially those related to real estate.

<u>Buy/Sell Triggers</u>

- BCR's **legacy** bad loan portfolio may be a drag on profitability.
- I'm okay with keeping my BRD position, but to increase I need to see more **proof** that business really is getting better.

Endnotes

1. World Bank (2013) Domestic credit provided by financial sector (% of GDP). Available at: http://data.worldbank.org/indicator/FS.AST.DOMS.GD.ZS?order=wbapi_data_value_2012+wbapi_data_value+wbapi_data_value-last&sort=asc.
2. Bank nonperforming loans to total gross loans (%), The World Bank. Available at: http://data.worldbank.org/indicator/FB.AST.NPER.ZS.
3. Sava, I. (2013) Erste's Romanian BCR unit posts 2012 net loss on bad-loan costs, Bloomberg News. Available at: http://www.bloomberg.com/news/2013-02-28/erste-s-romanian-bcr-unit-posts-2012-net-loss-on-bad-loan-costs.html.
4. Anonymous (2014) BCR Group reports nearly 600 million Lei in 2013 net profit, Act Media. Available at: http://actmedia.eu/financial-and-banking/bcr-group-reports-nearly-600-million-lei-in-2013-net-profit/50891.
5. Marinas, R. (2014) Romanian Bank BRD's profit nearly doubles in first half, Bloomberg News. Available at: http://www.reuters.com/article/2014/08/01/romania-brd-idUSL6N0Q71WV20140801.

IV – Mega Mall

A few months before crashing real estate prices dragged the world toward financial meltdown in 2007, South African Martin Slabbert and a few gung ho friends had the idea to start a property company. They jacked in highly paid consultancy jobs at Deloitte and began buying.

One of their first investments was a retail unit 200 kilometers north of Bucharest in Brasov. It wasn't long before the main tenant, a white-goods store, went bankrupt, halting lease payments.

Undeterred, they bought an adjacent plot of land and built a strip mall. The aim was to create enough stores to pull in customers as they did their weekly shop at the Carrefour hypermarket next door.

It worked. Fashion stores Deichman, C&A, Takko and New Yorker moved in, bumping revenue to a level where the property became profitable.

Emboldened, they scoured further. A four-hour drive east near the border with Moldova, the Armonia center in Braila was heading for insolvency. As footfall at the 45 million-euro outlet dropped to a couple of thousand, its developer Red Management concluded retail prices were out of reach for the local population, among the poorest in the country.[1,2]

Slabbert and co. didn't agree. They bought a mall just down the road for 63 million euros from another developer destined for bankruptcy.[3] Then they spent a further 7 million euros building a leisure extension, including a ten-screen cinema and the town's first ice rink.

"People thought we were mad," says Slabbert. "It's not a wealthy part of the world, and from a financial perspective – the rent that the leisure extension generated – it made no sense, but we knew we needed to add a significant leisure component to turn it into a regional shopping center."

With KFC and fashion stores like H&M and C&A moving in, the number of shoppers tripled to 15,000.

While most of the big developers in the country collapsed from 2009, Slabbert's company – New Europe Property Investments, or NEPI – has tripled in price to a market value of $1.5 billion.

It was buying groceries at his local corner shop in Bucharest that convinced Slabbert to create NEPI.

"I remember as a child in South Africa waking up one day and realizing that in the places where there used to be independents, there were now formal shops, and then came the big hypermarkets and shopping centers and convenience stores."

"Arriving here in 2005, I could see you were starting to get the same thing happening, it was visually very clear."

The potential for big chain stores was helped by the European Union's commitment to Romanian membership, creating legal stability.

He resigned with two colleagues from Deloitte and the trio started NEPI with backing from a group of investors Slabbert knew from Johannesburg. By the time the financial crisis hit Romania, the group was fully invested.

"In 2007, nobody expected things to get particularly bad," says Slabbert, sitting in a small glass-walled conference room. "The debt markets started showing some worrying signs, but everyone assumed it would be over by the end of the summer."

Romania's economy was still pumping at the fastest pace in the EU in 2008.[6] It was a year later that eastern European markets collapsed amid concern about their dependency on western Europe for exports and the banking system.

"We were good at dealing with risk and issues before they became larger issues," says Slabbert. Outside our conference room people are just starting to leave the office at 7 pm. "I've been personally involved in lots of turnaround situations and one of the lessons I've learned is you take action when you see trouble on the horizon. We work out what's the best we can do in our circumstances, and sometimes that means investing more money."

NEPI is slowly starting to look at the surrounding countries including Slovakia and Serbia for investments. "We wouldn't want to have a wide range of countries. We want to have substance, management on the ground," says Slabbert.

NEPI's business model is all about benefiting as incomes converge with EU levels. Romanians are the lowest earners in the EU with Bulgarians at an average $14,400.[7] As you head northwest toward Germany, incomes start rising, with Hungarians making $19,800, Slovaks on $24,700 and Czechs at $26,300.[8]

"Romania in ten years will be at similar spend levels to Slovakia," says Slabbert. "And then we're going to be very happy with the retail developments we have today. It quickly turns."

One of Romania's highest income regions is Gorj county on the way to the western border with Serbia, where NEPI is building the Targu Jiu Shopping City. Triple the size at 70,000 square meters is its Mega Mall construction in eastern Bucharest, opposite the Arena Nationale stadium.

NEPI generally favors malls over offices and regional cities over Bucharest. Tourist developments aren't on the shopping list. "I don't think Romania has a particular advantage when it comes to tourism," says Slabbert. "If you see the Romanian Black sea coast, it's pretty ugly; it's much prettier in Bulgaria."

Industry Factbox: Real Estate

- Romanian **farmland** prices soared 40% a year in the decade to 2012, twice the global average, to around $6500 a hectare – still lower than Polish land at $7816.[4]
- The lower prices are attracting buyers, especially from the **Middle East and China**, according to Tomas Spurny at BCR.
- Prices for prime **city center** real estate at around EU2370 in Romania compare with EU3100 per square meter in Poland, according to Global Property Guide Research.[5]
- Romania's property market was given a fillip by the central bank's policy of guaranteeing **mortgages** denominated in the local currency. Without the need to cover the risk of default, banks were able to slash lending rates in 2013 to less than half the 15% levels of 2009.

Stocks Box: NEPI

Company & Trading Platform	Description	Average Annual Return	Price–Earnings Ratio	Price–Book Ratio/ NAV	Return on Equity	Gross Dividend Yield	Market Value ($m)	Top Holders %
New Europe Property Investments Johannesburg Stock Exchange	Developer of mostly Romanian shopping malls & office blocks	35.2% since shares issued 2009	N/A	~2 (based on co. data)	N/A	4.4%	1,840	Resilient Property 9.6% Fortress Income 7.6%

Source: Data compiled by Bloomberg as of December 2014

- **Established** in 2007 by Martin Slabbert as CEO, Victor Semionov as Finance Director and investment from Resilient Property Income Fund, a Johannesburg-listed property company.
- NEPI operates as a developer and investor/property **manager**; nothing is outsourced.
- Net income from the property assets is distributed twice a year as **dividends** in a similar way to a Real Estate Investment Trust, or REIT.
- Development is aimed primarily at generating **income**.
- **Employs** around 150 staff for the property management side of the business.

Investor Analysis: Andras Szalkai on NEPI ━━━━━━

Bottom Line

- It's a strange animal, a **South African** company investing its money in Romania. It is listed in London and Bucharest as well but most of the investors are South African.
- They report **success** after success, and yet we know the property market has been in trouble. Everybody talks about so much pain in real estate but these guys just keep making money.
- There are no **consumer** companies on the Bucharest Stock Exchange, so that makes NEPI interesting, given it operates shopping malls.
- In terms of its **valuation**, the stock is trading at around twice its net asset value. This is a level I would normally never touch because I can buy companies in eastern Europe at 0.5 or 0.6 times the book value – but these companies aren't paying dividends. NEPI pushes for shareholder returns. They don't even try to justify the share price based on book value, they focus much more on cash revenue. Most companies also don't distribute the money they earn straight to shareholders, so you look at the price–earnings ratio. Here, maybe that's not so relevant.

Buy/Sell Triggers

- **Dividend yield** is an important factor to watch. The stock was yielding little over 4% in 2014, while three years before the yield was close to 6%.
- While NEPI is a special case, the Romanian real estate market needs to show signs of a **rebound** in general. The market has been in bad shape.

Endnotes

1. Moga, C. (2009) Armonia center of Braila closes for at least six months, Ziarul Financiar. Available at: http://www.zf.ro/zf-english/armonia-center-of-braila-closes-for-at-least-six-months-4685424/.
2. Anonymous (2012) Bankrupt shopping centre Armonia in Braila to be auctioned, PMR. Available at: http://www.ceeretail.com/news/119705/bankrupt-shopping-centre-armonia-in-braila-to-be-auctioned.
3. Newsroom (2013) Another Romanian mall enters insolvency, Business Review. Available at: http://business-review.eu/featured/another-romanian-mall-enters-insolvency/.
4. Goldhill, O. (2014) British farmland prices rising faster than prime London property, *The Telegraph*. Available at: http://www.telegraph.co.uk/finance/newsby-sector/constructionandproperty/10744112/British-farmland-prices-rising-faster-than-prime-London-property.html.
5. Europe: Square Metre Prices, Premier City Centre, Global Property Guide Research. Available at: http://www.globalpropertyguide.com/Europe/square-meter-prices.
6. GDP Growth (Annual %) The World Bank. Available at: http://data.worldbank.org/indicator/NY.GDP.MKTP.KD.ZG/countries/RO-EU?display=graph.
7. Anonymous (2014) GDP per capita, consumption per capita and price level indices, Eurostat. Available at: http://epp.eurostat.ec.europa.eu/statistics_explained/index.php/GDP_per_capita,_consumption_per_capita_and_price_level_indices.
8. CIA (2013) GDP – per capita (PPP) compares GDP on a purchasing power parity basis divided by population as of 1 July for the same year, World Factbook, Central Intelligence Agency. Available at: https://www.cia.gov/library/publications/the-world-factbook/rankorder/2004rank.html.

V – Drac-ul-a

Foreigners know only two things about Romania, three at most, complains Johnny, the driver of the black Dacia: Ceausescu, Dracula and Gheorghe Hagi.

"We have a beautiful country – it's one of the few in Europe that has mountains, plains and is next to a sea, we have the delta of the Danube which is unique, but people come here only for Dracula," he fumes, raising his palms from the leather steering wheel to heaven. "OK – it's a castle!"

Hagi, known locally as Regele – the King – is adored as Romanian football's top goal scorer. As for Dracula, "everybody goes to Bran Castle and everybody leaves disappointed," says Johnny. "You see small rooms, like Dracula was a midget."

The next morning I'm boarding a flight with Andras and 30 other investors and analysts, heading northeast – to the heart of Transylvania.

We touch down in an area of rolling green fields, forests and wooden shuttered bungalows. Six centuries ago this was the kingdom of Wallachia, ruled over by Vlad II. As a member of a Christian knights' fraternity called the Order of the Dragon, Vlad had his coins stamped with its emblem – a dragon on a cross – so he became known as Vlad the Dragon. The Romanian for dragon, and also the devil, is "drac"; "ul" is the definitive article. When the throne passed to his son, Vlad III became the son of the devil: Dracula.

The prince lived up to his name and added another: Vlad Tepes, or Vlad the Impaler, after his favored method of execution – plunging a stake through the body.

In Sibiu, where we touch down – a city of stepped cobbled streets connecting medieval church spires and piatas – ten thousand people were impaled in 1460.[1,2] Vlad speared Ottoman Turks along with maidens who lost their virginity, adulterous wives and unchaste widows.[3]

For Ceausescu, Dracula was a national hero. He ordered postage stamps commemorating a "leader of the struggle of the Romanian people."[4] His playboy son, Nicu Ceausescu, inherited control of Sibiu as the local Communist Party chief. It became one of the Securitate's top recruitment posts, with 830 informers including 170 children in 1989.[5] In the uprising that year, Nicu ordered troops to fire on anti-government demonstrators, killing around 90. At his trial, Nicu pleaded he made the order to use force because he was drunk.[6]

Since the reign of Dracula and the Ceausescus, Sibiu's fortunes have improved. In 2007, the EU named the town Europe's Capital of Culture for the dynamism created from integrating Romania's largest German community with Hungarian, Roma, Slovak, Ukrainian and ethnic Romanian populations.[7] Its industry includes the country's largest stock exchange after Bucharest, the Sibex.[8]

So popular was its mayor, he defeated Ponta to become President Klaus Iohannis.

From Sibiu, we travel by coach to the town of Medias. It's less than 40 kilometers from the okra-yellow townhouse still standing in Sighisoara where Dracula was born.

But this busload of foreigners didn't come here for Dracula. They're more interested in the green rolling hills around us, or rather what's beneath them. A little over a century ago, geologists drilling hundreds of meters down for potassium salts instead hit on methane gas.

By 1917 Romania became the only country in Europe to light its towns with natural gas and the first to export the energy internationally in 1959 in an agreement with Hungary.

The producer extracting the gas from the ground is Romgaz. A couple of weeks before we arrived, the government sold a 15% stake in the company on the stock exchange. It raised over half a billion dollars. This is the first opportunity for most of the investors to see exactly what they bought.

After three hours traveling by plane and bus, we finally arrive. Thirty money managers and analysts from the world's financial metropolises are handed blue helmets and red ear protectors. We troop out and gaze across the gas fields.

Basically, we're looking at grass.

The gas is invisible. Not even a hazy blur of vapors is detectable in the gleaming winter sun. It has no smell, no sensation at all.

In the vast green plain stretched out in front of us are three small steel enclosures. At the center of each is a ladder and pipes going deep underground. These are the wells. There are 310 dotted across the area.

The gas from the wells ultimately collects in giant yellow and gray pipes looping at right angles up, across and then down to a compressor station. Without the ear protectors the noise from the station would be literally deafening. After compression the gas is piped 6 kilometers from here to a dehydration station to reduce the water content before flowing into the national grid.

That's where the work of Romgaz ends and Transgaz begins, transporting the gas through its network of pipes to every corner of Romania. The government sold 15% of Transgaz on the stock exchange in 2013, a year after the electricity grid, Transelectrica. The sales have made energy along with banks the core component of the stock exchange.

After our tour of the production site, a visit to a museum documenting a hundred years of gas and a two-hour meeting quizzing Romgaz executives at the headquarters in Medias, I ask Andras what he gleaned.

Stocks Box: Romanian Energy

Company & Trading Platform	Description	Average Annual Return	Price–Earnings Ratio	Price–Book Ratio/NAV	Return on Equity	Gross Dividend Yield	Market Value ($m)	Top Holders %
OMV Petrom Bucharest Stock Exchange	Romania's largest oil producer	39.1% since listed 2001	6.6	0.9	13.5%	7.4%	6642	OMV AG 51.0% State 20.6% Fondul Proprieta-tea 19.0% Free float 28.4%
Romgaz Bucharest Stock Exchange	Romania's largest natural-gas producer	N/A Listed 2013	13.1	1.4	10.7	7.6%	3676	State 70.0% Fondul Proprieta-tea 10.0% Free float 30.0%
Trans-electrica Bucharest Stock Exchange	Romania's power grid operator	–0.6% since listed 2006	10.2	0.8	8.1%	7.7%	592	State 58.7% Fondul Proprieta-tea 13.5% Free float 41.3%
Nuclear-electrica Bucharest Stock Exchange	Romania's nuclear energy producer	N/A	4.8	0.3	5.4%	15.3%	624	Ministerul Economiei 81.3% Fondul Proprieta-tea 9.7% Free Float 18.7%

Source: Data compiled by Bloomberg as of December 2014

He looks around him. "I don't understand," he says finally, "how come the largest gas company in Romania is located in a tiny city in the middle of nowhere?"

Medias, with its winding narrow lanes, gothic churches and the Bazna Salt spa, has a population of less than 60,000.[9]

"And another company, Transgaz, which is responsible for transporting all over the country and delivering to Europe, is also here. These are giant companies. How can they attract managers to live in this town?"

"Right," says Marius Dan, an investor relations manager from Franklin Templeton, based in Bucharest. "But think about it, the managers here are the sons of the people who have been there for 50 years. It's a generational thing."

"But should I take that as a positive or negative?" asks Andras. "At least I know they're very experienced in the technicalities. On the other hand, how can they cope with these investor relations demands, with young people in the markets who are analyzing their company?"

"Most of the time, the important thing is not that you're a super producer of gas but how you make a presentation. If you can't present yourself then you cause value destruction because investors won't believe your story."

Back in Bucharest, we call in on yet another energy company, Nuclearelectrica. Romania's biggest producer of nuclear fuel listed 10% of its stock in 2013.

We arrive at the address and search everywhere for a sign with the company's name before finding an entrance tucked down a side street. Inside are bare beige walls with no pictures; the blinds are down, blocking the winter sun.

I wonder whether the nuclear company is trying to be anonymous to avoid attracting protesters.

Not at all, says Mihai Darie, an adviser to the CEO at the time of our meeting who was later appointed chief financial officer. "This is the HQ but it's purely an office building."

The nuclear plants are east from here near the Black Sea and to the west in Pitesti. The company plans two more units in the next ten years to meet its projections for rising demand as coal-fired power stations need updating and nuclear becomes key to meeting European de-carbonization targets. There's an opportunity to export to Turkey where the price is almost double Romania's if a submarine cable could be laid, says Darie.

"In Romania, regular people aren't against nuclear energy. It's not like Austria or Germany."

Investor's Notebook: Romanian Power ━━━━━

- Romanian oil producer OMV Petrom and America's ExxonMobil discovered 42–84 billion cubic meters of **gas in the Black Sea** at the Domino 1 well. The reserve is five times Romania's annual gas consumption of around 12–13 billion cubic meters. Advanced technology is needed to gauge the full potential of the area.[10]
- Electricity is supplied under two systems: the **regulated** market and the competitive market. In the regulated market, the government sets the tariffs. Romania has an obligation to the EU to liberalize the market because cheaper tariffs amount to an energy subsidy for industry. The industrial market was de-regulated in 2014. Full liberalization is scheduled for the end of 2017.
- Romania's biggest IPO to date was the power distributor **Electrica** in 2014, topping Romgaz in 2013.[11]
- **Hidroelectrica** has been in technical insolvency proceedings since 2012 to resolve financial problems the new management blames partly on contracts to sell energy at discounted rates to certain parties. The government plans an IPO once the insolvency proceedings are concluded.

Investment Pipeline: Hidroelectrica

Security/Trading Platform	Issuer Description	Issuer comments
Hidroelectrica Bucharest Stock Exchange	Hydropower provider in technical insolvency since 2012, a process engineered to get rid of unprofitable contracts. IPO planned once insolvency concludes.	Romania may sell shares in the second half of 2015, Energy Minister Razvan Nicolescu said (Bloomberg, September 2014)

Portfolio Structuring: Andras Szalkai's Investing Criteria

At the moment, our people are very focused on dividends. It's interesting because all of these state-owned companies have a legal obligation to pay a minimum 50% of profits as dividends, but they're actually paying more, something around 80–90% – that's true for Nuclearelectrica and Romgaz. The most important reason is the state, as the biggest shareholder, needs money, and the state, as the biggest shareholder, decides what kind of dividends it gets.

Dividend yield = Annual payout to shareholders expressed as a percentage of the share price

Investor Analysis: Andras Szalkai on Romanian Power

<u>Bottom Line</u>

- The Black Sea gas project is big for Romania. This is one of the last countries in Europe that's almost self-sufficient in energy. It's not impossible we could be looking at the **next Norway** some day.
- **Hidroelectrica** is a crazy story. This is the second largest water utility in Europe, it has a huge hydropower plant in the Danube, but had a lot of mismanagement and gave out long-term contracts to some buyers of electricity below the market price, so the company didn't make any profit for years. When Templeton came to Fondul they forced the management to change, but it was such a tough job that they realized to really cancel all of these old contracts they had to bring the company to bankruptcy. This kind of stuff happens, this is why Romania is a frontier market.
- **Nuclearelectrica** is more than 80% state-owned. You need a certain amount of shares trading in the market for liquidity. The government doesn't want to continue with further privatization of the company so this won't be as interesting. Romania is also one of the key places for wind energy and there are a lot of solar projects, so why build a nuclear power plant? I think in ten years' time this connection will be built to Turkey, but it will take time.

<u>Buy/Sell Triggers</u>

- The **dividend** is the most important valuation measure for Romgaz. As an investor in a relatively small company, I have in my head the rationale that if I can't sell the asset because it's too illiquid, I can at least show I'm getting a higher return from the dividends. With trust built up, people will move on from this very simple way of assessment but for now this is the market driver.
- The **pricing** for Nuclearelectrica shares has to be lower. The valuation after the IPO was 14 times annual earnings, compared with 8 times for Romgaz and 7 times for Petrom.
- Hidroelectrica is the **jewel of the jewels**. It's clean energy. At the end of the day, which energy source has a future? With nuclear, that's always going to be a question. Hidroelectrica provides very cheap electricity generation and it's very profitable. I'm very, very excited by Hidro; I'm waiting for this to come to market.

Endnotes

1. Jenkins, M. (2010) *Vampire Forensics: Uncovering the Origins of an Enduring Legend*, National Geographic Society. Available at: http://books.google.com/books?id=4hyqLBwxyPMC&pg=PA60&lpg=PA60&dq=sibiu+1460+impaled&source=bl&ots=JzKtHl2FKl&sig=Uh-RudUDDaVr4ZLIcxqAlUukBCA&hl=en&sa=X&ei=NO5PU7mkNeme7AanooEQ&ved=0CDAQ6AEwAQ.
2. Transylvania Tours. Available at: http://www.transylvania-tours.com/transylvania/vlad.htm.
3. Sprott, C. Why do Romanians think Vlad the Impaler was a Good Guy? Sprott's Gateway. Available at: http://sprott.physics.wisc.edu/pickover/vlad.html.
4. Anonymous (1978) Ceausescu calls Dracula a hero, AP. Available at: http://news.google.com/newspapers?nid=1734&dat=19780414&id=tOkbAAAAIBAJ&sjid=mVEEAAAAIBAJ&pg=2445,4077646.
5. McLaughlin, D. (2006) Ceausescu regime used children as police spies, *The Guardian*. Available at: http://www.theguardian.com/world/2006/jul/22/mainsection.international1.
6. Anonymous (1990) Nicu Ceausescu guilty, gets 20 years: Romania: The deposed dictator's son is convicted of instigation to murder in the bloody December revolt, *LA Times*. Available at: http://articles.latimes.com/1990-09-21/news/mn-923_1_nicu-ceausescu.
7. Anonymous (2007) Luxembourg and Sibiu: 2007 European Capitals of Culture, European Parliament. Available at: http://www.europarl.europa.eu/sides/getDoc.do?pubRef=-//EP//TEXT+IM-PRESS+20070125STO02408+0+DOC+XML+V0//EN.
8. Sibiu Stock Exchange website. Available at: www.sibex.ro.
9. Romania Tourism. Available at: http://www.romaniatourism.com/medias.html.
10. Khan, M., Chestney, N. (2013) Analysis: Black Sea gas bonanza remains elusive, Reuters. Available at: http://www.reuters.com/article/2013/10/24/us-blacksea-gas-analysis-idUSBRE99N0PK20131024
11. Anonymous (2014) Electrica IPO Raises EUR 444 Mln, Business Review. Available at: http://business-review.eu/featured/electrica-ipo-raises-eur-444-mln-66455.

VI – Crossroads

Being on the crossroads means you have potential.

Ludwik Sobolewski
Director General, Bucharest Stock Exchange
Former Chairman, Warsaw Stock Exchange

Ludwik Sobolewski is Romania's fourth stock exchange chief in five years. The last two were fired.[1-4] He already knows what that feels like.

In 2013, he was sacked from his role earning half a million dollars as the head of the Warsaw Stock Exchange.

The 49-year-old's fall from grace began in a romantic liaison with his former assistant. Ex-model Anna Szarek, 20 years his junior, was starring in a Polish comic movie about a holiday gone wrong in Egypt. Sobolewski asked an employee if he knew any investors who might be interested in providing finance. When the employee sent emails about the project to companies including a few on the exchange's NewConnect trading platform, Sobolewski was accused of abusing his position and creating a conflict of interests.[5]

A soft-spoken man with half-rimmed spectacles and close-cropped receding fair hair, Sobolewski was offered the chance to resign quietly. He refused, insisting his interest in the movie was during his free time, that he hadn't contravened any rules and the risk of a conflict of interest had been properly managed. So Treasury Minister Mikolaj Budzanowski dismissed him, calling his behavior "unethical" and "shameful."[6] Three months later, the minister himself was fired by the premier for failing to properly supervise state-owned companies.[7]

During his seven years at the helm, Sobolewski transformed Poland's parochial bourse into the fastest-growing market in Europe by luring companies from the Czech Republic to Lithuania to list while expanding trading from equities to bonds.[8]

His departure marked the start of a retreat[9] in Polish shares in 2013 as the government encouraged pension savers to pull money out of the private retirement funds that were the bedrock of the stock market and transfer to state-run funds.[10] The policy caused Fondul Proprietatea to abandon its plans for a secondary listing in Warsaw, eyeing London as a possibility instead.

While stocks slumped across eastern Europe through 2013 and 2014, Romania's equity index has surged, helped by the government listing state energy companies. The Bucharest exchange, with 13 billion euros of traded assets,[11] should almost double to reach the level of Prague by 2016, Sobolewski says.

"When investors look at the map of central and eastern Europe, they'll see two vibrant financial centers and stock markets: Warsaw, which will still be more advanced, and Bucharest," he says. "I don't see another candidate in the region. This is why I wouldn't accept any other proposal from the region and, yes, I had another one."

"Romania still has a chance to make its capital markets an engine for growth. Once we have capital markets, it will be another reason for investors to be here, to take positions in Romania."

Like Martin Slabbert at NEPI, Sobolewski recognizes a trait in Romania from his native country.

"Romania is on the crossroads," he says. "This is something I argued with regard to Poland, which is between east and west. It's the same for Romania."

"This is a nation in the center of Europe with Slavonic influences, but it's culturally different. The Latin links are very strong – it's a Western country by this standard – and yet its history is marked by very strong diversity, with Russian, Austro-Hungarian and Ottoman influences. If something is on the crossroads it may be in a position to do things better. Being on the crossroads means you have potential."

While Sobolewski lives during the week in Bucharest, weekends are spent back in Warsaw – with Anna Szarek. She's put her movie career on hold to study psychology.

Stocks Box: ETFs

Exchange Traded Funds offer a way to buy a country's stock exchange without picking the individual shares:

Security/ Trading Platform	Issuer Description	Annual Return	Top 10 Index Holdings	
ETF BET Tradeville	Open-end ETF incorporated in Romania seeking to track the performance of the Bucharest Stock Exchange Trading (BET) Index by matching equity holdings	25.2% in 2013, first full year	Fondul Proprietatea SA/Fund	21.5%
			OMV Petrom SA	18.1%
			Banca Transilvania	15.5%
			Societatea Nationala de Gaze	15.4%
			BRD-Groupe	8.9%
			Electrica SA	7.8%
			Transgaz SA Medias	5.8%
			Transelectrica SA	4.2%
			Societatea Nationala Nuclear	1.7%
			SC Bursa DE Valori Bucuresti	1.0%

Source: Data compiled by Bloomberg as of December 2014

Bond Box: Romanian Eurobonds

Security & Trading Platform	Asset Description	Maturity/Amount Outstanding	Average Annual Price Change	Coupon/ Interest	Yield
Romanian Government Eurobonds Euroclear/ Clearstream	Sovereign Dollars/ Euros	2015 – 2044 Most traded of the bonds matures 2024 with $1.5b outstanding	6.7% on bond due 2022 issued in 2012	6.75%	3.5%

Source: Data compiled by Bloomberg as of December 2014

Investor Analysis: Raiffeisen's Andras Szalkai on Romania

Bottom Line

• This is a good time to come into the stock market. We're at the start of something. Part of Romania's program with the IMF is designed to stimulate financial markets. There will be **lots of listings** on the stock exchange.
• **Barriers** to investing on the stock exchange mean many investors will say, "I'm sorry, you're a good company – cheap, interesting – but I gave up on this after a week." Opening a broker account, for example, requires signed documents from the main shareholder or owner of the investment; in other markets this isn't required. Trading and settlement costs are 3–5 times higher than in standard Western markets.

Buy/Sell Triggers

• There are **two big game changers** in Romania. One is the positive catalyst of Fondul. The second is the huge gas deposit in the Black Sea – there are some hints that what they have found so far is just the beginning.
• I hope that within five years the exchange will **expand**. I want to see not only energy here but other companies as well.
• Though I do see the commitment from the politicians, we have to be constantly reviewing positions and watching the **politics**.

Endnotes

1. Rizea, R. (2009) Anca Dumitru becomes new Stock Exchange general manager, Hot News.Ro. Available at: http://m.hotnews.ro/stire/5335251.
2. Anonymous (2010) Bucharest Stock Exchange appoints broker Valentin Ionescu on general manager position, *Daily News*. Available at: http://www.romania-insider.com/bucharest-stock-exchange-appoints-broker-valentin-ionescu-on-general-manager-position/8638/.
3. Chirileasa, C. (2012) Bucharest Stock Exchange chooses Romanian Victor Cionga at its helm, *Daily News*. Available at: http://www.romania-insider.com/bucharest-stock-exchange-chooses-romanian-victor-cionga-at-its-helm/61072/.
4. Anonymous (2013) Bucharest Bourse names new CEO, SeeNews.
5. Tokarz, C. (2013) No. Never. I do not understand, Bloomberg Businessweek Poland. Available at: http://www.bloombergbusinessweek.pl/artykul/976803.html?p=3.
6. Cienski, J. (2013) 'Pharaoh's Curse' costs WSE chief his job, *Financial Times*. Available at: http://www.ft.com/cms/s/0/e3fe5394-60c8-11e2-b85b-00144feab49a.html#axzz2zDNRkss7.
7. Anonymous (2013) Polish Minister fired over Gazprom deal, Reuters. Available at: http://www.themoscowtimes.com/business/article/polish-minister-fired-over-gazprom-deal/478957.html.
8. Kozlowski, P., Gomez, J.M. (2011) Warsaw pushes debt trading on fastest-growing Europe market, Bloomberg News.
9. Bloomberg data (2013) WIG20 Index GP Graph from Jan. 17, 2013, through June 2013.
10. Bujnicki, P. (2014) Warsaw IPO boom at risk as Poles ditch funds for state pensions, Bloomberg News.
11. Bursa De Valori Bucuresti (2013) Market Capitalisation Sep 2013, IR Update, Business Overview presentation.

CHAPTER 4

Argentina

I – Arbolitos

Traveling from Bucharest via Barcelona to Buenos Aires gives a feeling of faded Latin glory, and nowhere more so than in Argentina – swinging with the world's ten wealthiest nations a century ago before its drift into progressively crazier economic policies.[1-3]

The lunacy hits before you even step foot in the country. This is the only immigration form where I have to state the model of mobile phone I possess and its accessories. I faithfully declare my iPhone 5 and accompanying charger, though no one asks for the form at customs.

When it comes to buying pesos, I have a choice: swap $100 legally for 550 pesos or get a thousand on the street. It's hard to avoid falling into crime.

In Calle Florida, the main shopping street in Buenos Aires, an official currency kiosk is void of customers. Within 5 meters a woman waves a calculator, calling "cambio, cambio." Locals nickname them arbolitos or "little trees" – they're as much a part of the city's landscape as the tangueros dancing on street corners.

A teenage arbolito spots me at one of the bright yellow tourist information booths helpfully dotted around the city. He shows me his maxi calculator and punches in 950. I shake my head, "mil." He presses AC, keys in 980 and beckons me to a dress shop. He's the broker; the woman with the dresses is the dealer with a stash of greenbacks under the counter.

Walking out, the arbolito tells me how he loves British culture – he's seeing the English 80s pop band Depeche Mode tonight and he's a big fan of Monty Python. Around us, the Union Jack is a la mode on T-shirts and handbags – surprising for a nation whose populist president has been whipping up the idea of kicking the Brits out of the Falkland or Malvinas Islands.

It's Saturday morning and the shops are packed with people spending money like it's going out of style – which, in Argentina, of course, it is.

The peso is crashing. Everyone's been through this enough times to recognize the signs. The gulf between the official exchange rate and the arbolitos' is the credibility gap driving Argentines to spend their pesos any way they can.

Over the decades, currencies have been repeatedly created, inflated and disbanded. A hundred *pesos moneda nacional* were replaced by a single *peso ley* in the 70s, then 10,000 peso leys by one *peso Argentino*, 1,000 peso Argentinos by an *austral* and 10,000 australes by a *peso convertible*.[4] By the early 90s as inflation hit 20,000%, a single peso convertible – or ARS as the "Argie spot" is suitably known in the language of currency traders – equated to 10 trillion of the pesos used two decades earlier to buy a cup of coffee.[5]

President Carlos Menem's economy minister, Domingo Cavallo, broke the pattern for a few years, restoring confidence by making the peso convertible one for one to the US dollar and limiting the notes it printed to the amount of dollars held in reserve. The peso's exchange rate peg survived intact through the Mexican "tequila" crisis, Asia's economic flu and the Russian debt default of the 90s. But the currency's strait jacket could only buy so much time without accompanying steps to cut spending and borrowing. By the end of the decade, Argentine farmers were struggling to compete against Brazilian exporters benefiting from a plunge in the real.

When President Fernando de la Rua came to power in 1999, Argentina's recession had depleted the government's coffers to the point where it risked running out of funds to support the dollar peg. Having shoveled in billions of dollars in support, the IMF finally threw in the towel at the end of 2001, causing Argentina to renege on $95 billion of debt. A rare decade of currency stability ended with the peso sliding from 1 to 3.8 per dollar as the economy shrank 11%.[6,7]

While Néstor Kirchner – becoming Argentina's fourth president in two years in 2003 – managed to keep a lid on the peso as the economy recovered, rising government spending during his wife Cristina Fernandez de Kirchner's presidency eroded the reserve of dollars. In 2011, as the currency weakened further, a newly re-elected Fernandez attempted to smother the foreign-exchange market by restricting it to those needing dollars to travel abroad or pay for imports.

To the wealthier, it was an invitation to scam the system. Trips overseas jumped 13% the next year as Argentines flew to New York or took the hour-long boat trip across the Rio de la Plata to Uruguay to withdraw cash on their credit cards. To a dollar-hungry Argentine, getting the official exchange rate using their plastic abroad beat receiving half that amount from arbolitos, even with a 20% transaction tax. The most popular purchases were those goods hardest to find back home because of import restrictions – like Apple laptops and iPhones, fetching triple the price in Buenos Aires compared to New York.[8]

Other Argentines were getting rid of depreciating pesos by buying Chinese goods on the internet or German cars. One economist in our run of meetings said he'd treated himself to a new motor with a loan in pesos at 20% interest. Seeing inflation at 30% and a likely 50% devaluation in the peso, he was laughing all the way to the bank. A commodities trader was finding inner peace at a Buddhist retreat when "the ARS fell out of bed" in early 2014. He'd bought a stack of soybeans with borrowed pesos. The soybeans were gaining on Chinese demand as the peso tumbled.

By the time the government got around to closing some of the foreign-purchase loopholes by slapping a 35% tax on international credit-card transactions and 50% on purchases abroad,[9] backed by controls like my immigration card, the roads were chock-a-block with German cars. Next, Argentines turned to local produce. Prices for yogurt to flat-screen TVs – already in hot demand ahead of the World Cup – were jumping 20% in a week and fast food chains were running out of imported ketchup. As supermarkets responded by jacking up prices, La Campora, the ruling Peronist party's youth organization linked to Fernandez's son Maximo,[10] patrolled the aisles to check for breaches in cost-controlled items like medicine and put up placards calling the owners "robbers" in the battle against hyperinflation.[11,12]

Walking a couple of blocks east from Florida through the narrow City of London-style streets of the financial district, construction workers are on overtime. Bold, angled towers are popping up behind the facade of historic walls left as an architectural nod to the rich heritage. The banks here have been reaping big profits from all the high-interest loans to the countless car buyers and soybean speculators. Their cash, however, has also been trapped inside the country as foreign-exchange rules have restricted the payment of dividends to overseas owners and shareholders. Property has become the last outpost in the defense against wealth erosion by inflation and devaluation.

Out toward the Atlantic is the smart waterfront barrio of Puerto Madero. The area has withstood successive crises. Just as Argentina was on the brink of the world's biggest debt default in December 2001, developers unveiled the Puente de la Mujer, or Women's Bridge. The white modernist outstretched leg of a tango dancer pivots to let ships pass. On the canal bank the streets, all with women's names, group pricey restaurants with fine Argentine steaks, the uber cool Hotel Faena and skyscraper offices such as YPF, the oil producer that was unceremoniously seized from Spain's Repsol in 2012.

Across the water is La Casa Rosada, the pink palace where Juan Domingo and Evita Peron addressed the masses from the famous balcony and set the country on the "third position" between communism and capitalism – encapsulating high social spending and protectionist economic policies.[13]

In front, where the crowds gathered on the Plaza de Mayo, a group of grandmothers has met every Thursday afternoon since the overthrow of the last of the Peron governments in an army coup in 1976. In the so-called Dirty War that followed, the military junta killed at least 10,000 Peronistas and abducted hundreds of their babies for adoption by couples in the army.

Their grandmothers – las abuelas – urge people now in their late 30s and 40s to get their DNA tested to check their parents aren't their abductors.

Since the military regime crumbled with the Falklands defeat, most of the subsequent governments have been elected on a Peronist platform. But Fernandez lurched politics far to the left of her predecessors – Carlos Menem and her late husband. Her own brand of Kirchnerismo has made social inclusion the central tenet of policy, with generous utility subsidies to cut the cost of living for households.

Yet many here don't hold a house. On the Avenida de Mayo running from la Casa Rosada to the Congress, smartly dressed families enjoy a Sunday lunch as a band plays. Next door, children aged 2 and 5 with muddied bare feet and dirty clothes play a clapping game while their mother sleeps in the doorway of a shuttered shop. A few yards along, three toddlers sit near the roadside, their washing hanging from iron railings, possessions in a pram, waiting for their parents to return with bread pilfered from the restaurants for lunch.

There were more homeless families two or three years ago, says Pablo, a bar owner in the colorful, artisan barrio of Palermo Viejo. Pablo's Peronista parents were booted out of the country in the 70s when he was three, fleeing to England. He moved back, from Brighton to Buenos Aires, in the year of Fernandez's landslide re-election in 2011.

Her policies aren't so crazy to Pablo. "You don't want to sell dollars to locals because it means their money will just go abroad," he says, mixing English and Spanish as he talks to me and his wife while pouring from a brown liter bottle of Quilmes at a table outside. Seizing YPF from Repsol reversed the legacy of foreigners taking over Argentine assets through the 90s, he says. And her Malvinas rhetoric? Well, that's just "flag waving."

Most Argentines are more critical. "Of all the stupid policies in Argentina over the decades, invading the Falkland Islands was the stupidest of all," says Lucha, a drama student who part-times as a city tour guide. "We don't need this being resurrected."

To illustrate the second craziest she leads a route past mothers begging on the steps of the Catedral Metropolitana to the beautiful mosaic floored interior. A couple of years earlier, all of these hundreds of thousands of tiny tiles were individually broken off and cleaned. "They had nothing better to do," she says, shaking her head.

Top Down Data

Country	Population	GDP on PPP Basis ($)	GDP/ Capita on PPP ($)	Inflation (% pa)	Unemployment (%)
Argentina	43,024,374	771,000,000,000	18,600	20.8	7.5
Romania	21,729,871	288,500,000,000	14,400	3.2	7.3
Myanmar	55,746,253	111,100,000,000	1700	5.7	5.2
Kenya	45,010,056	79,900,000,000	1800	5.8	40.0

Source: CIA World Factbook, December 2014

[1] Population data from July 2014 estimates.
[2] GDP at purchasing power parity (PPP) exchange rates is the sum value of all goods and services produced in the country valued at prices prevailing in the USA, based on 2013 estimates.
[3] GDP per capita (PPP) divided by population, based on 2013 estimates.
[4] Inflation rate shows the annual percentage change in consumer prices in 2013.
[5] Unemployment shows the percentage of the labor force without jobs in 2013, except for Kenya (2008).

Country Factbox: Argentina

In 1900, Argentine incomes were 75% of the level in the USA. By 1950, they were half. By 2000, they were down to less than a third
Tyler Cowen & Alex Tabarrok, Modern Principles: Macroeconomics, Worth Publishers (2010)

Investor's Notebook: Deutsche Bank's Gustavo Canonero, Head of Emerging Markets Economic Research

The **Kirchner plan** was to take advantage of the depreciated currency to give a massive competitive lift to business, which is a decent policy proposition. But to sustain that competitive edge, you need inflation in check to keep the wage bill down. It wasn't compatible with the big public sector spending, money printing and interventionist bias deterring investment. One clear example was the subsidies, with the government spending almost 5% of GDP on energy and transportation, while production declined and the energy surplus became an increasing deficit.

Endnotes

1. Cowen, T., Tabarrock, A. (2010) *Modern Principles: Macroeconomics*, Worth Publishers. Available at: file:///C:/Users/Traveler/Downloads/Cowen%20CH06%20 (21).pdf.
2. Glaeser, E. (2009) What happened to Argentina? Economix. Available at: http:// economix.blogs.nytimes.com/2009/10/06/what-happened-to-argentina/.
3. (2013) GDP – per capita (PPP) compares GDP on a purchasing power parity basis divided by population as of 1 July for the same year, The World Factbook. Available at: https://www.cia.gov/library/publications/the-world-factbook/ rankorder/2004rank.html.
4. Helft, D., Raszewski, E. (2005) Argentine inflation held in April near 22-month high, Bloomberg News. Available at: http://www.bloomberg.com/apps/news?pi d=newsarchive&sid=aNm9cSHXjiQo&refer=latin_america.
5. Baer, W., Miles, W.R. (2001) *Foreign Direct Investment in Latin America: Its Changing Nature at the Turn of the Century*, Haworth Press.
6. Hornbeck, J.F. (2002) The Argentine Financial Crisis: A Chronology of Events, CRS Report for Congress. Available at: http://fpc.state.gov/documents/organization/8040.pdf.
7. Timeline: Argentina's road to ruin, *Washington Post*. Available at: http://www. washingtonpost.com/wp-srv/business/articles/argentinatimeline.html.
8. H.C. (2013) Argentina's dollar tourists: A vacation from inflation, *Economist*. Available at: http://www.economist.com/blogs/americasview/2013/05/ argentinas-dollar-tourists.
9. Gilbert, J., Rathbone, J. P. (2014) Argentina restricts internet shopping to curb capital flight, *Financial Times*. Available at: http://www.ft.com/cms/ s/0/6850567e-8387-11e3-aa65-0014feab7de.html#axzz2zz9AaoxW.
10. The Economist (2014) The CFK psychodrama. Available at: http://www.economist.com/news/americas/21600680-argentinas-president-weakened-and-isolated-still-powerful-cfk-psychodrama.
11. Parks, K., Turner, T. (2014) Argentina eases currency rules to stem crisis, *Wall Street Journal*. Available at: http://online.wsj.com/news/articles/SB2000142405 27023034482045793402831997902 64.
12. Anonymous (2014) Argentina struggling again with inflation, DW. Available at: http://www.dw.de/argentina-struggling-again-with-inflation/a-17429229.
13. Zanatta, L. (2006) The rise and fall of the third position. Bolivia, Perón and the Cold War, 1943–1954. Available at: http://socialsciences.scielo.org/pdf/s_rde/ v1nse/scs_a04.pdf.

II – Del Fin Del Mundo

In this world in the future we're not talking about 6 to 7 billion people;
we should imagine at least 15 to 20 billion.
But not only with an income of around $1000 per capita in poor
countries; we must imagine an income of $10,000 to $20,000.

Eduardo Eurnekian
Argentina's richest self-made billionaire

Down the road from Pablo's bar in Palermo, across a run-down railway
track, is the discrete two-story headquarters of Eduardo Eurnekian.

The son of Armenian immigrants, Eurnekian followed his parents into
the textile business, supplying the sports brand Puma, until international
trade agreements in the 80s left the company unable to compete with cheaper
foreign competition.

So he switched tack entirely, placing a bet on the growth of mass media
and advertising. He bought a bunch of cable TV startups to bring the likes of
CNN and the BBC to Argentina. And from there, he built a media empire
with the country's first news channel – CVN – along with the America TV
network, the financial daily *El Cronista*, four radio stations and Argentina's
biggest cable broadcaster by subscribers.

The investments paid off in the mid-90s as President Menem's free-market policies and the stability from Economy Minister Cavallo's currency peg
lured US cable operators looking to expand. He made $600 million selling
Cablevision to Denver-based Tele-Communications International.

Eurnekian used the money to jump into his third industry. He clubbed
together with the operator of Milan airport and a ground-services group
in New York for a three-decade concession to run 33 mostly unprofitable
Argentine airports. From there he built up to become the world's biggest private airports operator, with over 50 licenses and around $2 billion in annual
sales from Brazil to Italy and Armenia.[1-3]

From running the main airport in his ancestral land, Eurnekian developed
Armenian businesses from banking to the postal service to orchards and
vineyards. In Argentina, he used the financial meltdown in 2001 to amass
250,000 acres of farmland, producing cotton, oilseeds, grains and wine.[4]
Interests in computer chips, oil, gas, wind and biofuels have made Corporacion
America the most diversified holding company in Argentina and Eurnekian
the country's richest self-made billionaire.

In his executive dining room with leather couches and big modern art, the 81-year-old reflects on business over a bottle of reserve red from his bodega.

"This is a good wine," he says quietly, almost a mumble. "But there are many good wines."

He inspects the label. It's uncluttered, understated. An upside-down elongated triangle is the only image. It's words that are designed to stimulate the imagination: Del Fin Del Mundo, Patagonia – The End of the World.

In the lobby of the Sheraton, a bottle retails at $80. It's not the top of the hotel's range but close.

"It's the wrapping," says Eurnekian. "That's the marketing part."

It's a parable for where Argentina needs to be.

"The Chinese go for the French wine because the French give that added value," he says. "The same goes for technology from America. We sell beef but the Italians sell the Parma ham. It costs three to four times more than the simple ham in Argentina. That's the difference of marketing. Nobody buys a product from a country that doesn't capture the imagination of the buyer. We must know how to market our products, that is the future."

He draws a second lesson from a half-century spent building up and exiting industries.

"Many times friends ask me, what can I invest my money in? Here's the problem: I won't be at hand when it's time to leave."

Timing in Argentina requires reading the politics. "Good policies" improve economic efficiency but often at the cost of unpopular sacrifices, while bad policies ultimately self-destruct.

It's the reason for the ten-year cycle of government as populism ultimately becomes unsustainable, demanding a switch to spur greater efficiency. It's that process that shaped the Menem–Cavallo free-market reforms of the 90s which then gave way to the populist Kirchner administrations from 2003.

Now the pendulum is swinging back to liberal policies. The turning point was when Fernandez ousted Guillermo Moreno in November 2013. Moreno was appointed interior commerce minister by Nestor Kirchner to help bring inflation down. As the government stuck to insisting inflation was half the rate perceived by independent economists, Moreno started slapping fines on analysts who published higher numbers. Famed for his intimidating style, he once showed up for a meeting at a unit of Grupo Clarin, Argentina's largest media group, wearing boxing gloves to show he would fight the company. After his ousting, Clarin shares surged 16% in a week.

Appointing Axel Kicillof the new economy minister and Jorge Capitanich cabinet chief in the same week showed a rare acknowledgment that the economy needed fixing.[5]

Fernandez made the changes after a five-week absence for surgery to remove a blood clot close to her brain and a weakened position politically from mid-term parliamentary elections.

"Until then, the government did nothing," says Eurnekian. "Then came a government presenting a plan."

Sitting to his right, Eurnekian's nephew Hugo takes up the theme. Hugo runs the oil, gas, biofuels and wind farms businesses. He sees less of a pendulum, more of a continuum.

"In his life," says Hugo, looking to his uncle, "he's seen many different things. In my life, you've had the 90s, which was a very clear period of free commerce and openness, and ultimately society demonized this concept, and then another period began, which is this period, and that was the opposite – a closed market, very regulated."

"What I feel is that our society is learning and evolving – that everything isn't black or white – the free or the regulated market. What we're seeing now is the start of absorbing all these lessons and changing again."

"I say this perhaps due to my youth whereas he's seen this ten times before and doesn't see an evolving curve."

The old man – never married, with no children, who's parceled his empire into units run by his four nephews – is looking for action, not words. The starting point is freeing up access to dollars to fix the distortions created in the economy. Next is to prune the branches of government by replacing blanket energy price caps that don't help those most in need with subsidies properly directed at the poor.[6]

"We must close the gap between the more humble and those who win more," says the elder Eurnekian. "In countries more advanced – in England or the US – the difference between an operator and a technician is not as large as it is here. We have to shrink this."

The final step is to nurture efficiency through smarter industrial competition. With this, Argentina will create a "dynamic society," he says. "Today you have 40 million people awaiting a solution from above."

Eduardo's emphasis on efficiency and smarter industrial competition speaks to his most ambitious endeavor yet.

Much of the processed soya, beef and wine that Argentina ships from the Atlantic port of Buenos Aires to China takes a 5000-kilometer week-long trip south to the cone of Patagonia and across the Strait of Magellan to the Pacific Ocean. From Rio de Janeiro or Uruguay the journey is farther still. The alternative is a 12,000-kilometer voyage north to the Panama Canal. By road, it's a grueling drive across the Cristo Redentor Pass, traversing the mountains at a 3200-meter altitude. Trucks get stranded as snow shuts the road for a month or two every year.

Eurnekian's solution? Blast a hole through the Andes.

More specifically, he wants to cut a 52-kilometer tunnel and 33 secondary tunnels totaling 20 kilometers and then build 205 kilometers of rail track to link Mendoza in Argentina with Santiago in Chile. The route would be 700 meters lower than the Cristo Redentor Pass, ensuring it can open in all seasons.

The challenge isn't the technology, says Eurnekian, after all it's shorter than the 57-kilometer Gotthard Base Tunnel going through the Swiss Alps. But that's in Switzerland, the world's 15th wealthiest nation with an average income near $50,000. Argentina is a middle-income country at $19,000.

So Eurnekian proposes making the project entirely privately funded. Corporacion America would commit upwards of $3 billion. It's leading a consortium grouping Empresas Navieras and Contrera Hermanos of Chile with Japan's Mitsubishi and Geodata of Italy. Feasibility studies alone have so far run to $25 million.[7,8]

Both Chile and Argentina have declared the project of national interest and will invite bids for a public tender, says Eurnekian.

The route would cut the time to transport goods from the South Atlantic to the Pacific to just 24 hours, he says. "It's all about competitive efficiency."

It's becoming his mantra. The reason, he stresses, is this will be an increasingly vital concept, and not just for Argentina.

"In this world in the future we're not talking about 6 to 7 billion people; we should imagine at least 15 to 20 billion. But not only with an income of around $1000 per capita in poor countries; we must imagine an income of $10,000 to $20,000."

Among the largest nations, China's average income is just approaching this level at $10,000 while Indonesians earn around $5000 and Indians $4000. Most Africans are below $2000.

"Do you know what a China with $20,000 per capita income by the end of the century will look like? Or even India and Indonesia – half of humankind? Enormous amounts of goods will have to be moved around the world. That's why transportation – air travel, freight – will increase."

Survival in the new order will require efficiency or resources. Eurnekian splits the world into three categories. The first contains countries like the USA, Germany and the Nordics that can borrow cheaply in their own currency and are mostly efficient. The second consists of the four or five major oil producers – Saudi Arabia, Kuwait, Qatar, the Emirates – nations that until recently at least have had no compulsion to become efficient because of their wealth. Then there are the rest of the countries that "don't know how they'll reach the end of the month." These are the ones that really are in competition. "They can't afford not to be efficient," says Eurnekian. "They have no choice."

Company Factbox: The Eurnekians & Corporacion America

- Eduardo Eurnekian is the wealthiest Argentine after Carlos and Alejandro **Bulgheroni**, who inherited the Bridas Corp. oil and gas company from their father.[9]

- Corporacion America's **value** could be anywhere from $15 billion, according to Eurnekian. He plans to issue shares in the energy, airports and technology businesses on the New York Stock Exchange.[10]

- **Martin Eurnekian,** the eldest of the nephews, runs the airport operations including businesses in Uruguay, Peru, Ecuador, Italy and Armenia. Aeropuertos Argentina 2000 SA, which operates 33 airports in the country, sold $300 million of ten-year dollar-denominated bonds in 2010. The price has rallied, halving the yield from a peak of 18% in 2012 (Figure 4.1).

- **Hugo Eurnekian** manages the energy businesses, spanning oil and gas under Compañia General de Combustibles along with biofuels through Unitec Bio and wind farms in Uruguay under the name of Parque Eolico Crapé. The oil business includes five fields in Argentina and two in Venezuela, with a total 37.7 million barrels of proven reserves.[10] Corporacion America is financing its wind farms with a loan of $176 million from lenders led by the Inter-American Development Bank, paying interest at 7% a year for 18-year debt.[11]

- **Matias Gainza Eurnekian** heads the semiconductor business including the Unitec Blue factory south of Buenos Aires that makes credit card microchips, mobile GSM cards and public transport smartcards. Eurnekian entered Brazil in 2014, buying a 33.3% stake in SIX Semicondutores SA from Eike Batista, once Brazil's richest person. The company, a partnership with IBM and the development bank BNDES, was rebranded Unitec do Brasil and headed by Matias. It will supply the Argentine Unitec with silicon wafers to replace imports from France and South Korea.[12]

- **Jorge Del Aguila Eurnekian** is in charge of the agribusiness including Bodega Del Fin Del Mundo and Bodega Armavir in Armenia, along with a cotton-producing estate in Chaco, Argentina.

- Half a dozen other **heirs** to the Eurnekian empire are being trained in real estate, finance, communications and public works divisions.

FIGURE 4.1   Aeropuertos Argentina 2000 bonds: Prices have returned to above par value, or 100 cents on the dollar

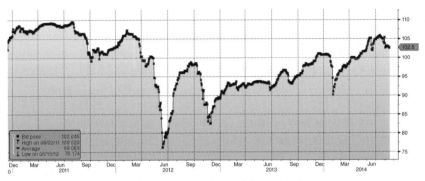

Source: Data compiled by Bloomberg. *(Function: EI515884 Corp GP GO).*

Bond Box: Aeropuertos Argentina 2000

Security & Trading Platform	Asset Description	Maturity/ Amount Outstanding	Average Annual Price Change	Coupon/ Interest	Yield
Aeropuertos Argentina 2000 corporate bonds	Corporate	2020	–1% since issued in 2010	10.75%	8.6%
EuroMTF/Frankfurt/ Luxembourg	Dollars	$300m			

Source: Data compiled by Bloomberg as of December 2014

Investment Pipeline: Corporacion America

Security/Trading Platform	Issuer Description	Issuer Comments
Corporacion America NY Stock Exchange	World's biggest private airports operator by number of licenses; most diversified holding company in Argentina. Seeking to build tunnel through the Andes	Corporacion America founder Eduardo Eurnekian plans to issue shares in his energy, airports and technology businesses on the New York Stock Exchange. The value could be anywhere from $15 billion

Investor Analysis: Julian Adams on Corporacion America ▬▬▬

<u>Bottom Line</u>

- Eurnekian's big message was there's change afoot, that Argentina's turn is coming around again. In the markets we tend to look at six to 12 months, but he's looking in decades, and the next decade will be more moderate, conformist and orthodox economically. Now is the time to **ramp up** business.

- He's a **big picture** ideas person – a tunnel through the mountain to Chile to get access to ports on the Pacific. At the time I thought it was pretty crackpot, but it makes sense. It would also create a big shift in society. An Argentine friend was telling me there's too much power in Buenos Aires, and the reason is that it's the main port. Families make money out of their position as the gateway to the world. If there's another route out, they lose some of that power to Mendoza.

- The **Chinese are coming**. Industrial & Commercial Bank of China (ICBC), the biggest Chinese lender, has been expanding with the purchase of Standard Bank Argentina in 2012. They're building up. It's a similar strategic alliance to the one China is creating in Venezuela's economy. Venezuela basically receives financing in exchange for oil. In Argentina, it's soy.

Endnotes

1. Spinetto, J.P., Cancel, D. (2014) Argentine billionaire plans New York IPO for airports to oil, Bloomberg News. Available at: http://washpost.bloomberg.com/Story?docId=1376-N4LVUG6JIJVW01-65CHTOAFA0R7Q52H-82TUIQ8B36.
2. Friedland, J. (1998) Argentine Visionary Hopes To Become a Tourism King. Available at: http://www.cilicia.com/armo22_eduardo_eurnekian.html.
3. Eduardo Eurnekian, World's Rich People. Available at: http://www.worldsrichpeople.com/eduardo-eurnekian.html.
4. Gonzalez, P. (2013) Billionaire plots to beat Chevron to largest Latin shale, Bloomberg News. Available at: http://www.bloomberg.com/news/2013-04-29/billionaire-plots-to-beat-chevron-to-largest-latin-shale-energy.html.
5. Gonzalez, P. (2013) Argentine Secretary Moreno ousted as Kicillof power rises, Bloomberg News. Available at: http://www.bloomberg.com/news/2013-11-20/argentine-trade-secretary-moreno-ousted-as-kicillof-power-rises.html.

6. Anonymous (2014) Subsidies in the Argentine Economy Totaled an Estimated 4.9% of GDP in 2013. Available at: http://en.mercopress.com/2014/02/11/subsidies-in-the-argentine-economy-totaled-an-estimated-4.9-of-gdp-in-2013.

7. Rathbone, J.P. (2013) Consortium pursues grand plan of tunnel through Andes, *Financial Times*. Available at: http://www.ft.com/cms/s/0/d0af9b7c-3ff2-11e3-a890-00144feabdc0.html#axzz30LzPYmmn.

8. Bustos, E. (2012) Eurnekian's vision: "Latin America needs to become connected," Latin Trade. Available at: http://latintrade.com/2012/02/eurnekian%E2%80%99s-vision.

9. Forbes (2014) Eduardo Eurnekian. Available at: http://www.forbes.com/profile/eduardo-eurnekian/.

10. Spinetto, J.P., Cancel, D. (2014) Billionaire Eurnekian plans New York share sale next year, Bloomberg News. Available at: http://www.bloomberg.com/news/2014-04-27/billionaire-eurnekian-plans-new-york-share-sale-next-year.html.

11. Gonzalez, P. (2014) Corporacion America gets $176 million loan to build wind farm, Bloomberg News.

12. Turner, T. (2014) Brazilian microchip firm sees sales at $1.7 billion in 2016, *Wall Street Journal*. Available at: http://online.wsj.com/article/BT-CO-20140508-720311.html.

III – Vaca Muerta

The End of the World is getting more crowded.

In the Patagonian province of Neuquen, where Eurnekian opened the region's first winery,[1] multi-billion dollar companies are moving in.

They're not here for Malbec or the Pinot Noir. They're sampling shale.

Argentine oil company YPF first hit on deposits in 2011 in the area stretching from Neuquen called Vaca Muerta – the Dead Cow. Its reserves place Argentina second only to China for technically recoverable shale gas and fourth in the world for shale oil.[2,3] The discovery offers a chance for Argentina to escape its cycle of widening deficits.

As recently as 2010, Argentina was a net exporter of oil and gas. By 2013, it was importing over $6 billion.[4]

One reason was artificially cheap energy prices boosting consumption. Householders paying less than a quarter of the amount it cost to supply them with electricity in 2013 increased their usage by a third.[5] State spending on subsidies rose by the same proportion, pushing the government's primary budget to its widest shortfall in 21 years.[6]

Just as energy demand was peaking, domestic supply was on the wane, sending the current account to its biggest deficit since 2000 as fuel imports soared.

The President blamed Repsol. The Spanish oil producer had bought a controlling stake in YPF in the 90s during Menem's privatization wave. To have the country's biggest company in foreign hands was anathema to Fernandez, who complained it was draining Argentina's oil profits and failing to invest in exploration and production. Repsol had pushed YPF to pay 90% of its net income to itself and other shareholders as dividends. While the government repeatedly voted against this, it carried little weight with just 0.2% of the shares.[7]

Repsol had reason to be leery of adding to its investment in Argentina. Since 2007, the government had capped the maximum price for exports at $42 a barrel, keeping the difference between that amount and the actual price paid by foreign buyers as a tax. YPF's output dropped by a third in 2011 while fuel imports doubled.

The next year, as oil and gas production slumped to 32 million cubic meters from 46.5 million a decade earlier, Fernandez seized Repsol's stake to run YPF "professionally."

But rather than boost energy production and the economy, the sudden expropriation scared off foreign investors. Spain denounced Argentina's "hostile" move and the IMF warned it would complicate negotiations for relief on the $9 billion the country owed governments grouped under the Paris Club. Repsol sued for $10 billion and kept international energy companies out of Vaca Muerta by threatening legal action against anyone partnering with YPF.

By the end of 2012, the nationalized YPF was looking at scaling back its $37 billion investment program after returning empty handed from investor meetings in the USA and Britain.[8]

Fernandez began the next year by deepening the country's isolation, sending an open letter to British Prime Minister David Cameron calling for the UK to hand over the Falkland Islands, another potentially lucrative area for oil.[9] Meanwhile the peso's depreciation gathered pace as central bank reserves to support the currency dwindled.

And then the government began to change tack. First, in a bid to lure companies to Vaca Muerta, Fernandez overhauled export duties so oil companies could receive an increased price of $70 a barrel. Six months later, in July, the government permitted those investing over $1 billion to export 20% of their output tax-free. A day after the announcement, Chevron, the world's second-biggest oil company, agreed to invest $1.24 billion in Vaca Muerta through a joint venture with YPF.[10] Argentina's benchmark Merval share index doubled in the next seven months (Figure 4.2).

Taking the reins of government as cabinet chief, Jorge Capitanich and economy minister Axel Kicillof immediately drove toward a deal for Repsol to receive $5 billion compensation in the form of bonds in return for dropping any further legal claims over YPF.[11]

"At this point you started to feel Kirchnerismo was signing off and it was time to think seriously about investing while it was still cheap," says Gustavo Canonero, Deutsche Bank's head of emerging-markets economic research.

FIGURE 4.2 Stock market rally: Signs of economic revival buoyed the Merval index

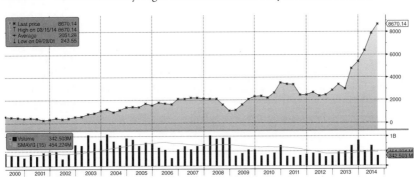

Source: Data compiled by Bloomberg. *(Function: MERVAL Index GP GO).*

The change was just as dramatic for electricity companies. Blackouts were becoming more and more frequent as the power distribution networks struggled to keep pace with demand boosted by cheap prices. Fernandez had responded by threatening to withdraw the companies' concessions and forcing them to compensate customers, nine out of ten of whom were already receiving subsidized energy.

The bonds of Edenor, the biggest of Argentina's electricity distributors, and the main power transporter, Cia Transporte Energia, were trading at less than half their face value through 2012 and much of 2013. The yield, reflecting their cost to borrow, jumped above 20% (Figure 4.3).

Then Capitanich and Kicillof suddenly started cutting household subsidies on natural gas and water in a bid to halve the burden on the budget from up to 5% of GDP. Shares in Edenor, or Empresa Distribuidora y Comercializadora Norte, soared fivefold in ten months by April 2014 and bond yields dropped by 5 percentage points on renewed prospects for the industry to become profitable.

With the legal threat from Repsol removed and oil prices more aligned to global market rates, Chevron committed to cover a 395-square-kilometer area of Vaca Muerta with YPF. The project involves drilling 1500 wells with an expected yield of 50,000 barrels of oil a day and 3 million cubic meters of gas. This field, the largest in Argentina, is just the beginning. The entire span of Vaca Muerta stretches 13,000 square kilometers.

FIGURE 4.3   Electric bond rally: Recovery in Edenor's 2022 bond price

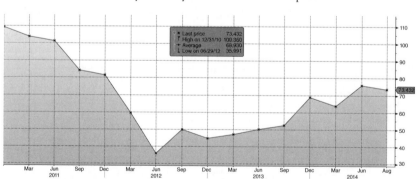

Source: Data compiled by Bloomberg. *(Function: EI439837 Corp GP GO).*

Among the investors, Eurnekian signed a preliminary deal with YPF to invest $500 million in non-shale conventional drilling in Vaca Muerta and agreed a $200 million acquisition of oil producer Cia. General de Combustibles SA, which has a stake in the region's gas pipelines.[12]

A third of the area falls within the province of Neuquen. It's negotiated separate deals to develop eight areas under Gas & Petroleo del Neuquen SA with the likes of Shell and Exxon.[13] Drilling has continued, undeterred by the downturn in oil prices.

As the Texan oil giant Exxon began excavating land untouched for millennia, it dug up more than dead cows. Beneath the earth were the remains of Sauropods, among the biggest dinosaurs.[14]

Stocks Box: YPF & Edenor

Company & Trading Platform	Description	Average Annual Return	Price–Earnings Ratio	Price–Book Ratio/ NAV	Return on Equity	Gross Dividend Yield	Market Value ($m)	Top Holders %
YPF Sociedad Anonima New York Stock Exchange	Biggest Argentine company; oil producer exploring world's 2nd largest deposits of shale gas and 4th largest of shale oil.	19.9% from 2002, after default by Argentina	N/A	N/A	N/A	0.4%	13,154	Grupo Financiero 5.7% Mason Capital 4.0% Lazard 4.0%
Empresa Distribuidora y Comercializa-dora Norte (Edenor) Buenos Aires Stock Exchange	Distributes & sells electricity in north-east of greater Buenos Aires	40.7% since offering 2007	N/A	N/A	N/A	N/A	795	Admin Nacional Seguridad 55.0% Pampa Energia SA 4.4% Free float 38.5%

Source: Data compiled by Bloomberg as of December 2014

Stocks Box: ETFs

Security/ Trading Platform	Issuer	Average Annual Return	Top 10 Index Holdings	
Global X FTSE Argentina 20 ETF	ETF incorporated in the US. The fund seeks to track the performance of the FTSE Argentina 20 Index	−2.1% since inception in 2011	Tenaris SA	18.6%
			MercadoLibre Inc	16.5%
			YPF SA	9.6%
New York Stock Exchange			Banco Macro SA	5.6%
			Grupo Financiero Galicia SA	5.4%
			Telecom Argentina	5.2%
			Arcos Dorados Holdings Inc	4.1%
			BBVA Banco Frances SA	3.9%
			Pampa Energia SA	3.0%
			Petrobras Argentina SA	2.8%

Source: Data compiled by Bloomberg as of December 2014

Investor Analysis: Adelante's Julian Adams on the Energy Sector

<u>Bottom Line</u>

- The **era is over** for subsidized utilities. The budget and balance of payments have reached a level where the government can no longer afford them. A friend has a four-bedroom flat in Buenos Aires, he pays 70 pesos ($8.70) a month for his gas bill – he just leaves the heating on.
- The **policy shifts** have been positive, particularly the removal of internal trade minister Guillermo Moreno, the formation of a new cabinet and the resolution of the Repsol issue with YPF.
- Part of the reason for bringing in Capitanich was Fernandez's realization that there was no **succession path** for her legacy. Capitanich was viewed as an able technocrat, so the idea was to empower him. The change was

dramatic – even in the way the government communicates all the time. He holds a press briefing every day at 8 am, even if there's nothing to say – they talk about football.

- Capitanich knew the first thing was to sort out **Repsol**. No one was going to invest in the energy industry when the government had just seized the state oil company.

- The **power distribution companies'** bonds had been trading at a price that anticipated their complete demise – people really thought they were going bust. But they weren't going bust because they had very little debt, and then suddenly you had the government changing course. The market went nuts.

<u>Buy/Sell Trigger</u>

- Argentina right now has a structural energy deficit which it's covering with imports, but it can **transform** its fortunes with shale, so this is a key area to watch even with the collapse in energy prices.

Endnotes

1. Wines of Argentina. Available at: http://www.winesofargentina.org/bodegas/B/647/.
2. Gonzalez, P. (2014) Argentina oil province to tout shale joint ventures in Houston, Bloomberg News.
3. Haskel, D. (2014) Argentine congress backs plan to pay $5B to Spanish oil firm for confiscated assets, Bloomberg News.
4. Spinetto, J.P., Cancel, D. (2014) Argentine billionaire plans New York IPO for airports to oil, Bloomberg News.
5. Background briefing from industry executive, November 2013.
6. Krauss, C. (2011) Argentina hopes for a big payoff in its shale oil field discovery, *New York Times*. Available at: http://www.nytimes.com/2011/07/05/business/global/05shale.html?pagewanted=all&_r=0.
7. Orihuela, R. (2012) Argentina seizes oil producer YPF, as Repsol gets ousted, Bloomberg News. Available at: http://www.bloomberg.com/news/2012-04-16/argentina-to-send-bill-to-congress-for-control-of-51-of-ypf-1-.html.
8. Gonzalez, P. (2012) YPF said to hasten bond sale as shale partners prove elusive, Bloomberg News.

9. Donaldson, K. (2013) Cameron rebuffs Argentine leader's call to hand over Falklands, Bloomberg News.

10. Porzecanski, K. (2013) YPF isolation ending as shift lures investment: Argentina credit, Bloomberg News.

11. Cancel, D. (2014) Repsol deal to open Argentine energy investment, Capitanich says, Bloomberg News. Available at: http://www.bloomberg.com/news/2014-04-23/repsol-deal-to-open-argentine-energy-investment-capitanich-says.html.

12. Gonzalez, P. (2013) Billionaire plots to beat Chevron to largest Latin shale: Energy, Bloomberg News.

13. Gonzalez, P. (2014) Argentina oil province to tout shale joint ventures in Houston, Bloomberg News.

14. Sebastian, S. (2014) Hunt for shale gas becomes a dinosaur dig, *Houston Chronicle*. Available at: http://www.houstonchronicle.com/business/energy/article/Hunt-for-shale-gas-becomes-a-dinosaur-dig-5316455.php.

IV – Adelante

A five-minute walk from the neon bustle of London's Piccadilly is a cobblestone alley housing Burberry, a French Bistro and Julian Adams' office.

An elevator the size of a phone box runs to a fourth floor suite where a PA sorts out the coffee, wi-fi and appointments between analysis of the bond markets. This is investing at its most boutique.

Julian, 52, started out in emerging markets when they were still known as less developed countries in the 80s, trading LDC debt for firms in London and then Paris. In the 90s he worked with Mark Coombs at ANZ before the management buyout that created Ashmore and made Coombs a billionaire. Then he set up Aberdeen Asset Management's first emerging market debt fund, a business that has grown into today's $13 billion behemoth.

In 2003 it was Julian's turn to lead a management buyout. When Aberdeen was scaling back after losses on interlinked funds known as split-capital investment trusts, Julian took on its Guernsey-based emerging market debt fund with former colleague Paul Luke. In four years, they built the fund from $50 million to $500 million. It was bought by Threadneedle Asset Management in 2007 – just before the global financial crisis. The fund lost 90% of its assets by early 2009.

Julian re-purchased the depleted fund that year to form Adelante. After outperforming peers through 2012, Julian handed investors their money back. A big driver behind the portfolio's gains was about to reverse. The US Federal Reserve reducing American borrowing costs to almost zero had the effect of bringing down interest rates around the world, lowering the yields on emerging market bonds and boosting their price. On top of that, the Fed's easy credit policy known as quantitative easing was creating abundant cash waiting to be invested.

As America's economy recovered, the Fed prepared to wind down the policy. "It seemed like a good time to take a break and sit out of the market for a couple of years," says Julian. The benchmark index for emerging market bonds, which almost doubled between 2008 and 2012, had its first losing year in 2013 since the financial crisis began.

Julian describes Adelante now as an exotic investment club, investing money of his own and for a few friends and clients. Its Spanish name – meaning going forward – reflects a bias to Latin America.

Being boutique allows Julian to look at the less explored, higher yielding reaches of the market. While larger fund managers tend to buy the most widely held bonds with billions of dollars outstanding because they're quicker and cheaper to sell when the time comes to exit, the relative popularity can come at a cost of lower yields. Julian bought bonds of Buenos Aires province

for example. Along with the extra yield, he took a view they'd be better insu-
lated than federal government debt as the risks started mounting of another
sovereign default in 2014.[1]

Rather than any shortage of funds to pay bondholders, Argentina's
default this time around was triggered by a lawsuit from a group of creditors who'd refused to accept Argentina's settlement offer after the debt
restructuring in 2001. While most investors had agreed to take 70%
losses on the $95 billion they were owed, a few hedge funds led by Paul
Singer's Elliott Management Corp. held out for full repayment instead.
The billionaire pursued the government through courts in the USA, the
jurisdiction in which their bonds were issued.

After a decade-long battle the turning point came when a New York
judge blocked Argentina from paying its bondholders until Singer and the
rest of the so-called holdouts received $1.5 billion.[2] Fernandez argued she
couldn't pay these "vultures" as that could trigger legal demands by more
bondholders for up to $120 billion.

While the president insisted Argentina hadn't defaulted – that its efforts
to pay creditors had been blocked by the US court – the net result was the
same on the streets of Buenos Aires. As central bank reserves dwindled amid
a loss of confidence, the peso sank to new lows. Against an official exchange
rate of 8 pesos per dollar, the credibility gap widened to 14 pesos from the
arbolitos on Calle Florida.

Fund Factbox

Company & Assets in Emerging Markets	Emerging Market Fund	Performance & Peer Ranking	Portfolio Manager: Julian Adams
Adelante Asset Management	Adelante Emerging Debt Fund	2nd highest total return among 33 offshore-domiciled global emerging market debt funds over 5 years until liquidation at 52% (annualized 8.8%)	Built Convivo with Paul Luke from $50 million of assets bought from Aberdeen Asset Management to $500 million, and sold the funds on to Threadneedle Asset Management in 2007. Re-purchased amid the global financial crisis in 2009 to form Adelante

Source: Data compiled by Bloomberg as of June 2014

Bond Box: Argentine Republic, Buenos Aires

Security Trading Platform	Asset Description	Maturity/Amount Outstanding	Average Annual Price Change	Coupon/ Interest	Yield
Argentine Republic	Sovereign	2033	12.0%	7.82%	9.6%
Euroclear/ Clearstream	Euros	EU2.3b			
Province of Buenos Aires	Municipal	2015–2035	–1.6% on bonds due 2015 since issued in 2010	11.75%	14.3%
Euroclear/ Clearstream	Dollars/Euros	Most traded of the bonds matures 2015 with $1.05b outstanding			

Source: Data compiled by Bloomberg as of December 2014

Investor's Notebook: Carlos Calderon, Independent Prop Trader

- The people have demanded a substantially different model to the Kirchner set-up. Quite how it plays out is detail. The important point is that because of its difficulty in borrowing, Argentina has a **low level of dollar debt**. Total public sector borrowing is equivalent to about half of GDP, of which foreign-currency debt held by the private sector is only 18%, a low level by international standards.
- The **growth potential** of the country is huge as there has been no real investment for the past decade in infrastructure, energy or agriculture – soy is like Argentina's crude oil.

Investor Analysis: Adelante's Julian Adams on Argentina

Bottom Line

- Optimism is supported by the idea that all the bad things have taken place. The **confrontational style** that radicalized the country into pro-government and enemy camps encapsulated by the rhetoric of the president and the internal trade minister Moreno has become unacceptable to the public.

- Argentina has experienced capital flight and **disinvestment** for the past decade, so if you have a half sensible government with orthodox and balanced economic policies then you should get a big return of capital, creating an investment-driven recovery.
- The low debt level would make it easy for Argentina to tap the capital markets and the bonds should trade with a low and very **affordable interest rate**.
- The government was almost heading in that direction in mid-2014 but then Fernandez blew it and turned the other way. **Capital flows** can come back very quickly.

<u>Buy/Sell Triggers</u>

- The real challenge is to stop the hemorrhage of **dollar reserves** in defense of the currency. Once they tackle that we have a new investment paradigm.

Endnotes

1. While the federal government's discount bonds due 2033 fell 10% in the two weeks following the default in late July 2014, Buenos Aires bond prices climbed slightly higher, according to data compiled by Bloomberg.
2. Porzecanski, K., Russo, C. (2014) Soros's Argentine bond bet revealed in lawsuit in London, Bloomberg News. Available at: http://www.bloomberg.com/news/2014-08-26/soros-s-bond-bet-revealed-in-lawsuit-in-london-argentina-credit.html.

CHAPTER 5

Vietnam

I – Confucius

Yamaha, Honda and Sym rule Vietnam's streets – 37 million motorbikes for a population of 90 million. There's no parallel in the world.[1]

They swarm like wasps in every space, disregarding traffic lights and pedestrian crossings, riding on the wrong side of the road, on pavements, even into shops.

The lack of order on the road applies equally to the most visible part of Vietnam's $171 billion economy.[2] Ho Chi Minh City, or Saigon, is one giant market. Every house has a stall or café outside. The few spaces between parked bikes are cluttered with tables and tiny red plastic stools that level your knees to your elbows.[3]

Vietnam ushered in private enterprise in 1986 with its version of Deng Xiaoping's opening up, known here as Doi Moi, or renovation. Amidst the market bustle on every street flies the Communist Party red flag with yellow star, along with posters, banners and statues of the Vietnam War leader Ho Chi Minh.

"This isn't the communism I studied in the classroom," says Andy Ho, the chief investment officer of Vietnam's biggest money manager, VinaCapital. "People are free to build hotels, sell coffee, buy a car, and most people are free to say what they want – as long as you don't become disruptive."

While commerce is overwhelmingly private and informal, big industry is firmly under the state's control in a system riddled with corruption. The Confucian sense of obligation to the family distorts into nepotism. The country's largest shipbuilder was driven to the brink of bankruptcy after its former chairman appointed his son and relatives to multiple roles.[4] Prime Minister Nguyen Tan Dung (pronounced "zhung") apologized in 2012 for "weaknesses of the government in leadership and management." As part of a crackdown, two former executives at Vietnam National Shipping Lines were sentenced to death for embezzlement the following year.[5]

Yet Dung's own family has come under scrutiny. His son-in-law was awarded a contract to bring McDonalds to Vietnam.[6] His daughter chaired Viet Capital Bank.

And corruption is only getting worse. Among those people who had contact with the police in 2010, nearly half paid a bribe. Three years later, the proportion increased to 64%. Vietnamese are the least likely to refuse to pay up in all of southeast Asia and the least willing to report corruption, according to Transparency International.[7]

While the state media profiles the corporate executives officially fallen from grace, other coverage is heavily sanitized. In a window to the complicated world of relations with neighboring China – Vietnam's former colonial master and biggest trading partner – a prominent story in *Vietnam News* warns parents not to buy toys without a government safety stamp.[8] By the seventh paragraph, it becomes apparent we're really talking about Chinese imports. Japan is consistently the ally, providing a trillion-yen package of development funds for highways, ports and climate change response.

Vietnam has warmed to Japan along with America, the European Union and Russia amid Chinese encroachment on disputed waters around the Paracel and Spratly Islands in the South China Sea.[9] When China placed an oil rig in the area in May 2014, Japan pledged support for Vietnam.[10] Demonstrations against China were initially tolerated by Vietnam's authorities before they morphed into two days of deadly rioting.[11,12]

While criticism has been permitted against Dung – including a high-profile call for his resignation from the floor of the National Assembly in 2012 – activists challenging the one-party state or sensitive issues have been beaten and jailed. Three founder members of the Free Journalists' Club have been serving prison sentences of up to 12 years after writing about human rights abuses, corruption and foreign policy. The mother of one of the trio set herself on fire in protest.

At his home on a bank of the Saigon River, Dominic Scriven, the co-founder of Dragon Capital, keeps a collection of brightly colored communist propaganda paintings alongside darker expressionist art.

The man described as Mr Vietnam by the *Sunday Times* in London was one of the first foreign investors here back in 1994 and has built the country's second-biggest fund management company after VinaCapital with about $1 billion of assets. Away from the hubbub of motorbikes and street stalls, farmers chug by his garden on boats piled with grass foraged for their cows as industrial vessels deliver aggregates and timber.

"I'm particularly interested in self-portraits," says Dominic, pony-tailed with a blue short-sleeved shirt patterned with suns and dragons, as he paces in flip-flops along a row of 50 or so angst-ridden images in a corridor of his house. "It's one of the ways Vietnam shows its history."

One haunting image is by an artist called Hanh. He's holding a cup of coffee and looking out. Behind him is a blurred woman.

"I had a Vietnamese friend living in the US and she was obsessed with this painting," says Dominic. "She had known of this bloke when she was growing up in the States called Uncle Hanh. She happened to be in the Louvre one day and there was a group of Vietnamese, and one was called Hanh. They got talking and he said he'd been in love with this woman. It turned out the lady in the painting was my friend's mother."

The woman had fled with her family to America as the communist Viet Cong forces swept south after the US retreat in 1975.

"She'd left without any communication, which is something you often hear about that time," says Dominic. "It was chaotic, tumultuous – everyone's got a story of some sort."

Another self-portrait shows an artist looking to one side. His crewcut hair is painted red with the yellow star of the flag. Where he's looking are the words: "However sharp the sword, it can't cut anyone in the mirror. In the mirror I reflect on my art – and how about you?"

Under the rules of self-expression, religious gatherings are tolerated so long as the community is registered and approved. Human Rights Watch points to repression in the central highlands near Cambodia and Laos of a 300,000 strong group of Dega protestants, which the authorities assert isn't a legitimate religion but the cover for an independence movement.[13,14] Around 40% of Vietnamese worship local spirits and gods, 16% are Buddhist and 8% Christians – mostly Catholic.[15,16]

In Saigon's version of the Notre Dame cathedral, built by the French during colonial rule in the 1800s, the pews are packed for a Sunday evening mass. People stand at the back and side entrances and a couple of hundred more are outside on parked motorbikes watching. Everyone here, young and old, knows the words and sings on cue.

Opposite the red brick cathedral in a park area, youngsters sit in circles jamming on guitars to Western and local pop songs. Stallholders offer chilled coconuts with their green skin cut for an elegant white shell. Further along is the People's Committee. The institution is flanked on both sides by stores emblazoned with the fashion brands Hugo Boss and Ralph Lauren in glittering white light.

It's another of the contradictions. In some ways, an absence of everyday rules and structures makes life feel less restricted here than in Europe or America. Entire families cram on a single scooter with various livestock on their laps, weaving along the roads. Pedestrians must step out in their path to have a chance of crossing the road. And yet there are remarkably few accidents for the number of bikes. The World Health Organization estimates Vietnam has 16 road deaths per 100,000 people a year, a better record than average and half the level in South Africa.[17] Amid the constant braking and tooting, no one so much as tuts in frustration.

"It's a sense of harmony," says Andy Ho, who returned to his native Vietnam twenty years ago from the USA. "People respect the natural flow of the city. We understand how it works here instinctively. If someone refuses to adhere to the flow they upset that harmony, and that's when what looks like chaos *becomes* chaos."

Top Down Data

Country	Population	GDP on PPP Basis ($)	GDP/ Capita on PPP ($)	Inflation (%)	Unemployment (%)
Vietnam	93,421,835	358,900,000,000	4,000	6.8	1.3
Argentina	43,024,374	771,000,000,000	18,600	20.8	7.5
Romania	21,729,871	288,500,000,000	14,400	3.2	7.3
Myanmar	55,746,253	111,100,000,000	1700	5.7	5.2
Kenya	45,010,056	79,900,000,000	1800	5.8	40.0

Source: CIA World Factbook, December 2014

[1] Population data from July 2014 estimates.
[2] GDP at purchasing power parity (PPP) exchange rates is the sum value of all goods and services produced in the country valued at prices prevailing in the USA, based on 2013 estimates.
[3] GDP per capita (PPP) divided by population, based on 2013 estimates.
[4] Inflation rate shows the annual percentage change in consumer prices in 2013.
[5] Unemployment rate shows the percentage of the labor force without jobs in 2013, except for Kenya (2008).

Bond Box: Socialist Republic of Vietnam

Security & Trading Platform	Asset Description	Maturity/Amount Outstanding	Average Annual Price Change	Coupon/ Interest	Yield
Socialist Republic of Vietnam Singapore Exchange/ Stuttgart	Sovereign Dollars	2016–2028 Among the most traded matures 2020 with $1b outstanding	2.4% on bonds due 2020 since issued in 2010	6.75%	4.0%

Source: Data compiled by Bloomberg as of December 2014

Stocks Box: ETFs

Security/Trading Platform	Issuer Description	Average Annual Return	Top 10 Index Holdings	
Market Vectors Vietnam ETF New York Stock Exchange	ETF incorporated in the USA aiming to replicate the price and yield performance of the Market Vectors Vietnam Index	−3.4% since inception in 2009	Masan Group Corp	8.8%
			Vingroup JSC	7.8%
			Bank for Foreign Trade	7.3%
			Saigon Thuong Tin	6.7%
			Gamuda Bhd	5.3%
			PetroVietnam Technical	5.2%
			Minor International	5.0%
			Charoen Pokphand Foods	4.6%
			Bao Viet Holdings	4.4%
			Petrovietnam Fertilizer	4.2%

Source: Data compiled by Bloomberg as of December 2014

Endnotes

1. Vietnam News Agency (2013), Speeding drivers need to think twice, Available at: http://en.vietnamplus.vn/Home/Speeding-drivers-need-to-think-twice/20137/36328.vnplus.
2. World Economic Outlook Database (2014) International Monetary Fund. Available at: http://www.imf.org/external/pubs/ft/weo/2014/01/weodata/weorept.aspx?sy=1980&ey=2013&scsm=1&ssd=1&sort=country&ds=.&br=1&c=582&s=NGDPD%2CNGDPDPC&grp=0&a=&pr.x=97&pr.y=17.
3. Food Export Association of the Midwest USA, data compiled 2011. Available at: http://www.foodexport.org/Resources/CountryProfileDetail.cfm?ItemNumber=1021.
4. Anonymous (2010) Nepotism caused shipbuilder to go under? Vietnam Breaking News. Available at: http://www.vietnambreakingnews.com/2010/07/nepotism-caused-shipbuilder-to-go-under/.
5. (2013) Vinalines' former executives sentenced to death in Vietnam trial, Bloomberg News. Available at: http://www.bloomberg.com/news/2013-12-16/vinalines-former-executives-sentenced-to-death-in-vietnam-trial.html.
6. Banyan (2013), McDonalds to Vietnam: Golden Arches, *The Economist*. Available at: http://www.economist.com/blogs/banyan/2013/08/mcdonalds-vietnam.

7. (2013) Global Corruption Barometer: Views & Experiences from Vietnamese Citizens, Transparency International. Available at: http://www.transparency.hu/uploads/docs/GCB2013_Report_Embargo.265.pdf.
8. (2013) Ministry cracks down on poor quality toys, *Vietnam News*. Available at: http://vietnamnews.vn/society/248543/ministry-cracks-down-on-poor-quality-toys.html.
9. Anonymous (2014) Vietnam prepares legal challenge against China, Premier says, Bloomberg News. Available at: http://www.bloomberg.com/news/2014-05-30/vietnam-has-prepared-evidence-against-china-in-sea-spat.html.
10. Karunungan, L. (2014) Anti-China riots spoil Vietnam dollar bond rally: Asean Credit, Bloomberg News. Available at: http://www.businessweek.com/news/2014-06-02/anti-china-riots-spoil-vietnam-dollar-bond-rally.
11. Anonymous (2014) Vietnam Government Cracks Down on Protesters, Pledges to Protect Foreign Investors, Vietnam Briefing. Available at: http://www.vietnam-briefing.com/news/vietnam-government-cracks-protestors-pledges-protect-foreign-investors.html/#sthash.i0GMjJs3.dpuf.
12. A reporter on the ground says loudspeakers were set up for protesters to speak and free bottles of water handed out at the initial demonstrations. The difference was "night and day" at the subsequent protests they cracked down on.
13. Human Rights Watch, World Report 2013. Available at: http://www.hrw.org/world-report/2013/country-chapters/vietnam?page=1.
14. Human Rights Watch: Montagnard Christians in Vietnam, A Case Study in Religious Repression. Available at: http://www.hrw.org/sites/default/files/reports/vietnam0311Web.pdf.
15. Dodd, J., Lewis, M., Emmons, R. (2003) *The Rough Guide to Vietnam*, p. 509.
16. Taylor, P (2004) *Goddess on the Rise: Pilgrimage and Popular Religion in Vietnam*, University of Hawaii Press.
17. Anonymous (2011) Road accidents around the world, survey of 178 countries, *The Guardian*. Available at: http://www.theguardian.com/global-development/poverty-matters/2011/may/11/most-dangerous-roads.

II - Aristotle

*If you go back to Aristotle, the ideal form of government was a benevolent
dictatorship, and communists have tried to achieve that.*

Mark Mobius
Executive Chairman
Templeton Emerging Markets Group

Mark Mobius is deep in conversation about events across the border in
Thailand when I meet him for breakfast.

Bangkok's stock market is sliding, wiping out a year's gain, as the government teeters on the brink of another military coup.

Wearing a yellow shirt with white trousers, white shoes, white sport socks
and a white watch, the 78-year-old is in a relaxed mood. He cut his exposure to Thailand a couple of days earlier, sensing the shares had become too
expensive.

"I'd rather be here than there," says Mark. "It's more stable."

It's a challenging notion. Franklin Templeton – the Wall Street jugger-
naut with the "first American," Benjamin Franklin, for its symbol – takes
comfort in the stability of a communist administration.

Mark's reference point starts two millennia ago.

"If you go back to Aristotle, the ideal form of government was a benevolent dictatorship, and communists have tried to achieve that."

"People living in democracies say it doesn't work because you don't have a
check and balance, but if you can create a system where there is strict adher-
ence to a high moral ethic – which is what the communists have tried to do
– it can work."

The apology by Vietnam's Premier in 2012 is a sign the Communist
Party is evolving and trying to reach that higher standard of ethics, says Mark.
"They've had to adjust to reality because the idealism of the past didn't quite
work."

Mark's approach is apolitical. He groups Vietnam with red China but
also with the United Arab Emirates and Singapore among one-party states.

"You're going to have some kind of restrictions imposed to keep a grip on
law and order," says Mark. "But if your stated objective is to do the best for
the people then, as you've seen in Singapore, you can do pretty good."

Singapore, with the world's highest concentration of millionaires, ranks alongside Scandinavian nations and New Zealand for the least corruption. Yet Vietnam is among the worst at 116th place, below Thailand, according to Transparency International.

"A lot of the countries in Africa are looking at the Singapore model and thinking maybe this is the way we ought to go."

Becoming "the Singapore of Africa" is the stated goal of Rwanda's government. It's spending $150 million of foreign bondholders' money to build a huge conference center. Meanwhile President Paul Kagame is accused of using the country's recovery from genocide as a cover for creeping autocracy, with opposition leaders jailed for causing "divisionism."[1]

On her first official visit to Singapore, Burmese opposition leader Aung San Suu Kyi wondered aloud "whether I don't want something more for our country." "Perhaps Singapore could learn from us a more relaxed way of life," she told journalists.

"You have to remember," says Mark, who has adopted Singapore as his home for the brief interludes between roving the planet, "we're taking only a small segment of each country. We're picking stocks. We make a decision in the context of the environment – political, economic, social."

The one key test Mark uses to gauge that environment is known as the misery index. It's a measure adding together the rate of inflation plus unemployment, the two biggest causes of public dissatisfaction. It gets at the same point as the test for potential negative shocks Brett Rowley of TCW applied to Kenya. The misery index is an indicator of possible political upheaval, "so you've got to keep an eye on that," says Mark.

The Arab Spring uprising of 2011 was sparked by the inability of people to afford rising food prices, igniting protests across the Middle East.

"That's another very good thing here," reflects Mark. "The Communist Party hasn't been interfering too much, allowing people to do their own thing, and that allows them to let off steam. Here you see it's very free in many, many ways. There are not many restrictions, as long as you don't challenge the party."

Unemployment, officially at least, has remained in the low single digits[2] in part because of the readiness of the Vietnamese to make money from stalls, cafés or trading. Inflation dropped from over 20% in 2011 to below 5% in 2014, cheering the misery index (Figure 5.1).[3]

FIGURE 5.1   The misery index, an indicator of possible upheaval, has plunged as inflation slowed

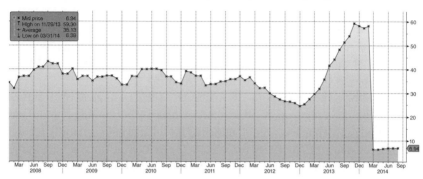

Source: Data compiled by Bloomberg. (*Function: MSRYVN Index GO*).

Vietnam first made an impression on Mark through a friend at the Massachusetts Institute of Technology in the 60s. On graduating, Mark's friend went back to Saigon, got married and took a government post. When the communists came down from the north in 1975, he was slung in a "re-education camp." He fled by boat with his family, but the boat capsized and his wife and children drowned. He was brought back to Vietnam a prisoner but managed to escape again, and this time made it to San Francisco. "He was such a nice person, I was very much drawn to the country," says Mark.

Nearly two decades later when the government announced plans to open the economy to foreign capital, Mark was among the first in.

"They took us to this beautiful art deco French bank building, and they said, this will be the stock exchange, so I said 'wow, let's start a Vietnam fund.' We raised $120 million, which was a hell of a lot of money in those days, and then we said 'OK, where's the stock exchange?'"

It was the early 90s. There was no stock exchange until 2000.[4]

In lieu of any tradable stocks, Mark's team put money into a tea-processing factory, the Metropole Hotel in Hanoi and an apartment complex with some Australian investors and the Vietnamese army, who controlled the land. His colleagues were still trying to dispose of some of the assets when we returned 20 years on.

He jokes about starting up a Myanmar fund ready for the exchange to open in Yangon. "We were too early," he says, "and it's a good lesson."

Franklin Templeton remains among the biggest investors in the stock market after VinaCapital and Dragon Capital, holding over $200 million, mostly through its $3 billion Templeton Frontier Markets Funds. Vietnam is among the three biggest investments in the portfolio along with Nigeria and Saudi Arabia, reflecting Mark's outlook for the most compelling economies over the next five to 10 years. It could overtake Nigeria and Saudi Arabia as the biggest position if the government lifts restrictions that limit foreign investors to a 49% stake in companies, or if more shares become available.

Mark relies on a group of 50 analysts from 18 offices dotted around the world for research and allocating funds. With two local analysts and another flown in from Singapore, we climb into a Mercedes van for a three-hour drive south to our first meeting.

After presenting gifts to his colleagues, Mark jumps in the front seat and buckles up, ignoring the universal disdain for seat belts here.

He's distracted still by events beyond the border. The Thai market is down 20% from its peak in 2013, but even after that plunge the shares are more expensive than Vietnam's, trading at prices equivalent to 14 times the companies' annual earnings, versus 13 times for Vietnam (Figure 5.2).

Mark phones Bangkok. The discussion strengthens his conviction that prices will come down further before they recover. He has in mind an entry point another 20% lower than the market's current level. It's a holiday in Thailand so nothing more can be done.

Mark's attention turns to another news item. He struggles to make the lettering large enough to read on his iPhone – one of the few concessions to age for a man who spends two-thirds of his life traveling and works out every day. Australia has reportedly just made a big oil discovery. Mark calls his regional analyst in Malaysia. It turns out the oil find isn't significant enough as yet to shake global crude prices.

FIGURE 5.2 Vietnam's stocks have historically traded at prices below regional peers

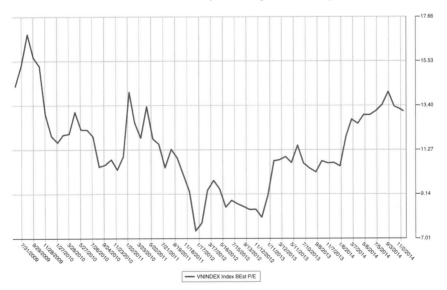

Source: Average Price-Earnings data compiled by Bloomberg. *(Function: VNINDEX Index GE GO).*

We're speeding out of Saigon. Our driver gives motorbikes free rein on the side of the road we should be on and we hog the middle. Looking up from his phone and seeing we're heading straight into the path of oncoming bikes, Mark waves his arm in front of the driver: "Slow down, we don't want anyone getting killed for this." He makes no impression as the driver carries on, hooting a warning every other second.

In the back seat is Mark's head of private equity for Asia, Richard Piliero. His job is to spot smaller companies yet to reach the stage of selling shares to buy a stake. Top of his shopping list are hoteliers and plastics manufacturers, both big growth areas. Each prospect is put through a suitability test that ranges from requiring at least 10% earnings growth a year to full openness and disclosure from management (see Mobius's Investing Criteria below).

Private equity is a way of putting money to work in countries where opportunities on the stock exchange are limited. It's appealing in Vietnam because of the foreign-ownership limits. The most popular shares are already at their 49% ceiling, making it difficult to buy any more without offering a big premium to convince other foreign holders to sell. The challenge is finding good stocks that aren't yet so appreciated they carry a premium.

One of those may be the company we're heading to next – a somewhat depressed drug maker.

My Vietnam: Mark Mobius

- Our experience in Vietnam began in 1994. Under the policy of **Doi Moi,** Vietnam had started decentralizing state management of the economy and introducing market principles while ending years of international isolation by normalizing relations with China in 1991, Japan in 1993 and the USA in 1995.
- The Templeton Vietnam **Opportunities Fund** raised $120 million ready for the opening of the stock market. The fund morphed into a regional fund in 1998 and then a global fund. Franklin Templeton Investments also built a local asset management presence by buying a 49% stake in Vietcombank Fund Management Co., while Templeton Asset Management Ltd opened a research office in Ho Chi Minh City.
- A further turning point came in the late 90s when President Clinton called on Vietnam to liberalize its trade and investment practices. A bilateral **trade agreement** with the USA followed in 2000, simplifying company registration requirements. That made a big difference as private businesses and foreign manufacturing investment returned to the country. The stock market opened the same year.
- Vietnam became the **World Trade Organization's** 150th member in 2007.

Fund Factbox

Company & Assets in Emerging Markets	Emerging Market Fund	Performance & Peer Ranking	Portfolio Manager: Mark Mobius
Templeton Asset Management Over $40 billion	Templeton Emerging Markets Investment Trust	2nd highest total return among 46 global emerging market investment trusts over 10 years at 360% (annualized 16.5%)	The nomadic 78-year-old investor joined Templeton in 1987 as president of the Templeton Emerging Markets Fund – now one of over 50 mutual funds he oversees. He was named one of the world's "50 Most Influential People" in 2011 by Bloomberg Markets Magazine

Source: Data compiled by Bloomberg as of June 2014

Portfolio Structuring: Mark Mobius's Investing Criteria

The following are some of the key measures Mark Mobius uses to assess investment opportunities.

<u>Numerical Ratios</u>

• **Earnings growth:** Revenue should be increasing by at least 10% a year.

• **Five-year forward price-to-earnings ratio:** The share price should be less than 10 times the estimated annual earnings per share:

$$\text{Forward P/E} = \frac{\text{Stock price per share}}{\text{Est. earnings per share}}$$

• **Price-to-cash flow:** The stock price should be less than 10 times the revenue stream, preferably less than 5 times:

$$\text{Price/CF} = \frac{\text{Stock price per share}}{\text{Cash flow per share}}$$

• **Return on equity:** Annual net income should be at least 20% of shareholder equity:

$$\text{ROE} = \frac{\text{Annual net income}}{\text{Shareholder equity}}$$

• **Return on invested capital:** Annual net income should be at least 20% of total common and preferred shares plus long-term debt:

$$\text{ROIC} = \frac{\text{Annual net income}}{\text{Total capital}}$$

- **Net profit margin:** Net income should be more than 10% of revenue:

$$\text{Net Profit Margin} = \frac{\text{Net income}}{\text{Revenue}}$$

- **Gross profit margin:** Gross income should be more than 20% of revenue:

$$\text{Gross Profit Margin} = \frac{\text{Gross income}}{\text{Revenue}}$$

- **Debt–equity ratio:** Total liabilities should be less than shareholder equity, so a ratio of less than 1:

$$\text{Debt/Equity Ratio} = \frac{\text{Total Interest-Bearing liabilities}}{\text{Shareholder equity}}$$

- **Dividend yield:** An annual dividend payout of more than 5% of the share price would be ideal, though usually it's about 3%:

$$\text{Dividend Yield} = \frac{\text{Annual payout}}{\text{Share price}}$$

Judgment Calls

- **Management transparency:** Look for full disclosure, openness to discussion.
- **Related party transactions:** Scrutinize any contracts with companies owned by executives or their relatives for arms-length pricing.
- **Parent company fees:** Watch out for foreign companies charging fees for use of a brand name or logo as a way of creaming profit.
- **Tag along rights:** Check minority shareholders are entitled to the same price, terms and conditions as majority owners in the event of a buyout.
- **Majority control:** Caution is needed on any company mostly owned by one person or family with unchecked control, look for written protection.
- **Corporate governance:** Avoid companies with different share classes that give one group fewer votes or that block independent directors getting on the board.

Macro Factors

- **Economic outlook/risk of instability:** One key measure is the misery index, adding together the rate of inflation and unemployment, the two biggest causes of public dissatisfaction.
- **Executives linked to government:** Assess the risk of this becoming a negative for the company should the executive fall out of political favor.

- **Infrastructure improvement benefits:** Look for companies set to benefit from boosts such as improved transport links or more reliable electricity.
- **Construction contracts:** Identify companies that could benefit more directly through selection for major projects.

Portfolio Structuring: Andy Ho's Investing Criteria

The most important consideration is **strong management.**
Some questions to ask:

1. Does money **leak** from the business?
2. Is there a corporate **governance** system in place that creates a culture of good practice?
3. Is the company involved in activities that are socially or environmentally **unfriendly**, e.g. polluting or engaging in child labor?

> "Most businesses we look at in the beginning are probably breaching some kind of social and environmental practices. It's natural. They're entrepreneurs. They don't think about this stuff, they think about buying and selling and creating. Over time, as they build into a larger organization, we need to convince them that it's good for them, good for society, and makes sense for the business, because if one day they get caught polluting the river then the whole value just drops."

Endnotes

1. Amnesty International (2011) Available at: http://www.amnesty.org/en/news-and-updates/rwandan-opposition-politician-jailed-exercising-rights-2011-02-14.
2. The World Factbook (2014) Central Intelligence Agency. Available at: https://www.cia.gov/library/publications/the-world-factbook/geos/vm.html.
3. Anonymous (2014) Gold demand in Vietnam seen plunging as inflation slows, Bloomberg News. Available at: http://www.stoxplus.com/News/144576/1/191/gold-demand-in-vietnam-seen-plunging-as-inflation-slows.stox.
4. ASEAN Exchanges. Available at: http://www.aseanexchanges.org/exchange/HOSE.

III - Panacea

Drugmaker Imexpharm is suffering the side effects of government remedies.

To clamp down on corrupt hospital managers overpaying for medicine in return for kickbacks, the Ministry of Health has instructed that only the cheapest medicines are to be purchased.

For Imexpharm, which imports higher quality ingredients from Europe and charges among the top prices as a result, sales to hospitals have plummeted.

The decline has deterred investors, causing its shares to trail returns on Vietnam's benchmark equity index. While Vietnam's stocks have typically been priced at twice the value of their assets, Imexpharm has languished at 1.5 times its book value.[1,2]

The stock has been performing worse still by Franklin Templeton's own metrics. The amount in the company accounts used to calculate book value understates the true worth of assets. Along with machinery, Imexpharm's core physical assets are acres of factory, warehousing and office space in the Mekong Delta region – real estate that's been rapidly appreciating in price. Yet accounting standards require the company to depreciate the value each year.

Rather than relying on the stated book value, Mark's colleagues run their own estimates of net asset value. Their higher valuation shows Imexpharm's stock price equivalent to just half of its assets, with a price-to-NAV ratio of 0.5.

As the largest shareholder after the government, with a stake of over 15%, Mark has taken a hit from the underperformance. The stock has lost 36% in five years while his holding in rival DHG Pharmaceuticals has made him a 131% gain (Table 5.1).

TABLE 5.1 Franklin Templeton's top five holdings in Vietnam vs. Imexpharm.

Company	Percentage Stake in Company	Total Market Value ($m)	Annual Return %
1. DHG Pharmaceuticals	12.3	384	25.3
2. Vinamilk	0.5	4641	34.4
3. PetroVietnam Drilling	2.9	1072	7.0
4. PetroVietnam Technical	3.4	687	−7.1
5. Binh Minh Plastics	10.0	142	49.1
Vs: Imexpharm	**16.4**	**50**	**3.1**

Source: Data compiled by Bloomberg as of December 2014. Annual return is the average for 2007–2013. Petro-Vietnam Technical is from first full-year data in 2008. Holdings data from Franklin Templeton as of end 2013

Inspecting the factory and meeting with the company's CEO and her deputy will be key to deciding whether to take the hit and sell, or take advantage of the cheap price to buy more.

It's lunchtime as we enter the site, so we're whisked off to a private room at a restaurant a two-minute drive away. The five of us and two Imexpharm executives squeeze around a table that would seat four in any Western diner.

Mark orders an orange juice but quickly changes to a local beer to follow the lead of our lunch host, Vice General Director Nguyen Quoc Dinh. He pours a can of Saigon 333 for Dinh into a glass filled with a large slab of ice, the custom for keeping beer cool in the tropical heat. We follow suit by serving one another with drinks and from platters of Mekong river fish, fried beef and seaweed-wrapped shrimps, appreciative now of the close proximity of our plates.

Conversation moves quickly to Imexpharm's biggest challenge. The company can't compete with the cheaper drugs being sold to hospitals, says Dinh. Nor would it want to. These drugs are not only less effective in treating symptoms but could expose patients to dangerous side effects, he claims.

"There are a lot of unwanted ingredients and with low technology they can't extract those harmful ingredients," says Dinh.

Many of the drugs bought by the hospitals are supplied by Indian and Chinese companies, taking advantage of a zero-tax rate on certain medical imports.

Imexpharm ships all of the ingredients for its antibiotics, fever and pain-relief tablets, vitamins and specialist drugs from Spain. Importing from the European Union ensures the raw materials meet the highest international safety standards, says Dinh, but they don't come cheap.

We cross back through town to the CEO's office in a shiny low-rise building overlooking the factory and research labs. Tran Thi Dao, a lifelong pharmacist, has been with the company 30 years. Health policies will swing back to the company's favor before long, she says, citing a proposed legal amendment to give priority to locally produced drugs.

"The prospects seem brighter because they will protect the local companies," says Dao. "But then I worry that there will be fierce competition among local companies themselves to become low-cost producers."

The solution, says Dao, is to reduce Imexpharm's reliance on the cost-conscious hospital managers altogether. The company is shifting its focus to drug stores. Pharmacies play a bigger role in dispensing medicine in Vietnam than in other countries because they can sell antibiotics without a doctor's prescription. Imexpharm earned 60% of its revenue from hospitals and 40% from pharmacies in 2012. Now that's been reversed and the company is driving toward 70% from over-the-counter sales.

It's exactly what Mark wanted to hear. "I like OTC better," he says. "It has more profit margin." He nods keenly as Dao sets out her strategy of "slow but stable growth," paying dividends to shareholders and staying No. 1 for quality among Vietnam's drugmakers.

Even her stated reluctance to entertain offers from foreign companies for fear of compromising quality control wins Mark's endorsement.

We leave the CEO's office for a tour of the factory but first we need to be dressed for the occasion. The investor controlling over $40 billion is handed plastic flip flops and a pajama-style blue shirt and trousers to minimize the risk of contamination. The matching night cap seems overkill on Mark's bald head.

We inspect bags of white-powdered antibiotics – doxycycline, produced in Spain – and a sugar-like coating used for the casings – maltodextrin. Giant machines dry and granulate the raw materials before shooting the deposits through a funnel for compression into tablets – 20,000 of them every hour. A processor, made in India, counts 2.5 million pills. The machines run day and night with operators taking 8-hour shifts.

In another room, thousands more tablets are being color coated in a giant tumble dryer that sprays a pink paint every few seconds. The process takes 12 hours.

Though Mark has clearly done this kind of tour a hundred times, he has the enthusiasm of Charlie in the chocolate factory. "You see," he points, "you need to get every single one with the same coating."

We stop to watch a worker – dressed exactly as we are – scooping up a few hundred pills and inspecting them for 30 seconds, before giving her sieve a shake and repeating the process again and again.

"I've been through a number of factories and you can see this company has very good quality control," says Mark. "And they're running 24 hours, so they're utilizing the equipment very effectively."

We climb into the van for the long drive back to Saigon.

"The CEO reminded me of my mother," says Mark. "Kind but firm. The fact that she's not willing to succumb to a takeover by foreign investors is probably a good thing for us if they can improve the licensing, get more products and promote OTC."

To Mark's mind now, the problem of government cost controls for hospitals has turned into a big opportunity. "It's actually a blessing in disguise because it's forcing them to promote OTC and to promote the brands."

While Mark is impressed by Dao's restraint on expenditure and zero debt, the company is going to need to spend more on marketing its products to ramp up OTC sales.

"I'm sure many investors are skeptical of them being able to make the change, but most people are not aware of what we saw. This is one of the advantages of getting out to see the company. If they can keep the standard high and the image of top quality, the market will move up to them with incomes going higher."

"Dao openly admitted this is going to be a tough year, but that's the time to buy, when things are looking bad."

Q&A Highlights: Mark Mobius Interviews Imexpharm Executives
(Shortened excerpts)

Q: What are the major illnesses causing death in Vietnam?

A: Cardiovascular or heart attacks and strokes, then hepatitis, pneumonia and cancer, diabetes as well.

Q: What are your biggest selling drugs?

A: Antibiotics. Vietnamese people take a lot of antibiotics. You can just have flu and they give you three days of antibiotics over the counter without a doctor's prescription. They're very easy to get.

Q: Is there any chance you can make the raw material here in the future?

A: It's unlikely that local companies can produce the ingredients for three reasons. The first is the technology, second is the investment and third is the scale – it must be produced on a big scale to make it competitive and a local company cannot compete with a large producer.

Q: Any contact with Indian firms about cooperation?

A: We do have discussions but with the Indian companies everything must be cheap, from production to selling, so we haven't achieved anything yet.

Q: If you lower the price, what would the profit margin be? Can you still make money?

A: There are two risks from a lower price: first, if the raw material price fluctuates, we can easily run into a loss because the margin is so low; and second, if you want high volumes from the hospitals, the receivable days are very high.

Q: How many days for receivables?

A: It's 60–90 days on the contract but in reality it takes six months to a year to be paid because it depends on the medical insurance payment.

Q: And for the OTC market, what sort of period for receivables?

A: If you sell direct to the pharmacy 40 days, but if you sell to a distributor it will be 60–90 days.

Q: How much of your spending goes on research and development?

A: Only about 5%, not much because it's generic so we only modify the compilations to fit the facilities. These aren't brand new drugs.

Q: Can you export?

A: We export to Moldova and to France, and then France will sell to African countries.

Q: Any new products or plans?

A: About five new products are registered and waiting for approval – mostly antibiotics and cardiovascular/digestive drugs to reduce cholesterol.

Q: What's the turnaround time for approval?

A: It's about two years to get approval for new products. The manufacturing process has to be approved and the drug itself has to be approved, and if you want a price increase, that also has to be approved.

Q: Is it like China here where you have to give a lot of money and payments under the table for the doctors to prescribe it?

A: A few companies adopt that practice but not this one.

Q: How do you encourage the doctors to prescribe?

A: We hold conferences at hospitals so the doctors will attend, we introduce our products and their advantages.

Q: Are you going to be entering into joint ventures?

A: We don't want to compromise quality or profits by going into joint ventures or cooperating with a foreign company. For foreign companies, their strategy is to localize their products for wholesale so our company must be very careful in any association with foreign companies, because it might not bring much profit to us.

Q: And how do you plan to get the new drugs that are created overseas, how can you get the technology?

A: For new drugs it's very hard to approach the technology because of financing and patents. We try to evaluate which patent is going to expire and register with the Ministry of Health in order to get the producing license.

Q: How much do you spend on advertising?

A: There are restrictions on advertising prescription drugs. We don't do much advertising. Instead we go to the pharmacies and do promotions and discounts. We have conferences.

Stocks Box: Imexpharm Vs. Vietnamese Drugmakers

Company & Trading Platform	Average Annual Return	Price-Book Ratio	Return on Equity	Gross Dividend Yield	Market Value ($m)	Top Holders %
Imexpharm	3.1% since listing 2006	1.4	8.4%	3.9%	50	Vinapharm 27.4% Franklin Resources 16.4% Free float 53.8%
DHG Pharmaceutical	25.3% since listing 2006	3.8	27.5%	1.6%	384	Franklin Resources 13.0% Vina Capital 7.2% Free float 91.5%
Ben Tre Pharmaceutical	-0.5% since listing 2009	1.6	11.8%	5.6%	6.7	Lien Thanh Seafood 15.0% Tin Duc Pharma 2.7% Free float 79.0%
OPC Pharmaceutical	38.1% since listing 2008	1.9	14.1%	5.1%	36.2	VinaPharma 18.5% SSI Asset Management 10.2 % Free float 56.8%
Hatay Pharmaceutical	5.4% since listing 2008	1.5	26.7%	5.7%	10.2	Trong Nguyen Hoang 10.0% Van Lo Le 8.4% Free float 42.1%
Pharmedic	34.3% since listing 2009	2.7	39.3%	2.0%	21.6	Sai Gon Pharm 43.4% Be Mai Thi 0.3% Free float 54.7%
Cuu Long Pharmaceutical	18.5% since 2008	1.7	14.6%	1.2%	24.2	State Capital 36.3% Red River 3.8% Free float 57.3%

Source: Data compiled by Bloomberg as of December 2014

Investor Analysis: Templeton's Mark Mobius on Imexpharm

<u>Bottom Line</u>

- If you look at it in a global context this company is very **cheap**.
- This factory you can see has been here since 1997 and it looks brand new. It's beautifully maintained, and yet it's probably written off because of **depreciation** requirements. This is the reason we do NAV rather than book value.
- If you look at the structure of the industry, this isn't an area you can start up in overnight, there are **barriers to entry**.
- We **probably will go up** to a level where we're owning maybe 20% of the company, depending on availability of shares, because, like most of these Vietnamese stocks, it's relatively illiquid.
- It will be a really good stake to own over the next **2–3 years** and then you'll probably see this thing shoot up.

<u>Buy/Sell Triggers</u>

- The only doubt I have is the company's ability to get new products, new drugs, and to **promote**, because they've got to shift gear now. In the past, you would just tender and you'd get the job. Now they have to become much more aware of company image, product differentiation, etc.
- The CEO says the government has a restriction on **advertising**, which is true, but that's on product advertising, not on brand advertising. They can promote the company brand itself, that's very important.

Endnotes

1. Imexpharm shares climbed 5.67% in 2013, compared with 22% gain for the Vietnam Ho Chi Minh Stock Index/VN-Index. The following year the stock had jumped 85% by August, compared with a 19% advance for the index.
2. Imexpharm vs. VN-Index price-to-book ratios based on data compiled by Bloomberg as of Aug. 15, 2014.

IV – Equitization

The Communist Party of Vietnam introduced a new word to the lexicon of capitalism: equitization.

The *Collins English Dictionary* defines it as the privatization of state businesses in Vietnam, though in reality the government mostly retains its control.

To encourage companies to equitize – raising cash for the state – they're offered 50% tax exemption. If they go on to list on the stock exchange, more incentives accrue.

Binh Minh Plastics, the pipes producer we're on our way to visit, equitized in 2004, transforming from a state-owned enterprise into a joint stock company. Then, in July 2006, it listed on Vietnam's stock exchange. Claiming both tax breaks, it skipped payments in 2004 and 2005 and cut the bill in half from 2006 to 2010. In retrospect, the Ho Chi Minh City Department of Taxation ruled, the company should only have been entitled to one concession at a time. It demanded payment of arrears plus a fine for administrative violations.

As we drive for an hour northeast from Saigon, we're briefed by Mark's head of research in Vietnam, Nguyen Thu Lam. "The tax department is changing the rules and the company is trying to appeal to various authorities," she says. "It's not their fault. The tax department can't wait five years and then go back and say there's something wrong."

Franklin Templeton owns 10% of Binh Minh, having increased its stake from 7% and reaped a doubling of the share price in 2013.

"The fact that Vietnam has this tax break is very encouraging," says Mark. "It means the government would like to see these companies listed. There are a few other countries that have these incentives but not that many."

"We've recommended to a number of countries that if they really want to get companies listing, they've got to give a tax break, especially in areas where there's a lot of tax evasion. It doesn't pay for a company that's been evading taxes to go listed and become transparent, so you've got to give them a carrot."

We sweep through Binh Minh's main gate into a yard with wide crates stacked with pipes of every size and color. Blue pipes or black ones with a blue line are for water supply, while yellow is for gas and orange for electricity and telecoms. That's the coding in Vietnam at least.

"There's unfortunately no united international standard for pipes," says CEO Nguyen Hoang Ngan, leading us past the workers' canteen to a private dining area next to the board room.

Over noodles, Ngan recounts how the company's appeal against the tax decision is still dragging on. "Because it's a very complicated problem, they have to get the opinion of the prime minister."

A decision against the company could cut annual profit by about a quarter, he says.

Binh Minh's pre-tax earnings are around 500 billion dong ($24 million) a year. It makes about $24 for every $100 of sales for a gross profit margin of 24%. By Mark's criteria, anything above 10% looks positive. The high margin here is especially impressive given that plastic piping is normally a low-margin high-volume kind of business.

Binh Minh's margin is higher, says Ngan, because its prices are higher than competitors. "It's better quality, a better brand."

It's also about size. The wider the pipe, the higher the profit margin and Ngan scours the world for the technology to grow ever-bigger. There are only five or six companies in Vietnam making large-diameter pipes, he says, which enables Binh Minh to charge top prices.

"Smaller companies can't compete," he says. "We supply for some public projects, but some years the government projects will just stop."

When the government does place an order, it can take over two years to pay. "Sometimes the government tells me the time I have to wait for payment depends on the Asian Development Bank or the World Bank," says Ngan. "Small players can't do the projects, they can't wait that long."

Ninety-five percent of Binh Minh's pipes are used for water and construction. Larger pipes are for longer distances before the line gets dispersed regionally.

"Last month," says Ngan, "I was in Dusseldorf at the biggest plastics fair, where there are plastic pipes displayed from all over the world. They can produce a plastic pipe with a diameter of four meters."

"Wow!" enthuses Mark. "If they can do that, that's tremendous because they can do long distance."

In all the excitement and stretching of arms to gauge the size, Mark's water bottle topples over, narrowly missing our host. Then his investment analyst does exactly the same.

"In Vietnam," says Ngan, "spilling water is considered an omen of prosperity."

Q&A Highlights: Mobius Interviews Binh Minh Plastics Executives
(Shortened excerpts)

Q: Where do you see this company in five or ten years?

A: In the future there will be a lot of opportunities for plastic pipes – in irrigation, water supply, electricity production, telecommunications and medical care. There are some very small plastic hoses for medical use and for wire in the automotive industry.

Q: Any plans to export?

A: We export to Cambodia and Laos but not that much because the transportation fee is a lot – 500 kilometers, that's OK, but when you want to export the pipes 600, 700, 800 kilometers, the transport cost is very high.

Q: Even though it's small now, would you think about exporting to Myanmar?

A: Everybody says that's the last golden land in southeast Asia, but I don't think it's for us because in Myanmar right now there are three very big players – China, Japan and Thailand. In the south of Myanmar, it borders with Thailand, in the north with China, and Japan is looking at the market very carefully, giving a lot of money. We are studying the market very carefully but it's still a small market.

Q: And you can't sell to China?

A: No. It's not so difficult, but the price – how can we compete?

Q: How did you get into the plastic piping business?

A: I worked for the People's Committee of Ho Chi Minh City. After two years I went to the army, I was a soldier. Then in 1988, I started working in a plastics firm.

Q: Has your army experience helped you?

A: It taught me: "Don't fear. Remember that you are a soldier so go ahead!"

Stocks Box: Binh Minh Plastics

Company & Trading Platform	Description	Average Annual Return	Price–Earnings Ratio	Price–Book Ratio/ NAV	Return on Equity	Gross Dividend Yield	Market Value ($m)	Top Holders %
Binh Minh Plastics Ho Chi Minh Stock Exchange	Pipes producer	49.1% since listing 2006	8.4	1.8	23.2%	3.0%	142	State Capital & Invest 29.5% Free float 31.0%
Tien Phong Plastic Ho Chi Minh Stock Exchange	Pipes producer	29.1% since listing 2007	9.1	2.0	23.5%	4.7%	129	State Capital 37.1% Nawaplastic 23.8% Free float 19.6%

Source: Data compiled by Bloomberg as of December 2014

Investor Analysis: Mark Mobius on Binh Minh Plastics

Bottom Line

- One of the key factors for this company is it's able to make these very **large diameter pipes**. There's not a big market but the margins are good, and not very many people make those pipes so they have a leg up.
- Mention of **medical piping** shows they're keeping an open mind as to what they might want to go into. Medical or hospital piping is very specialized. It would be a new area, but it's the same idea, extrusion technology is what we're talking about, and they clearly have expertise in that.
- It's not a very positive situation for **exports**. They might be able to export to Myanmar but it's a long shot. He was very leery of establishing a plant until he knew what the market would be, which I think is positive. You don't want to be too daring in a market like that where you really don't know what's going on and the Japanese are all over the place.
- The **Japanese** are spending like crazy in these countries because Japan isn't that welcome in China, and therefore they're putting more and more money into southeast Asia.

- Probably the **tax bill** is written into the share price; the market knows about it. If it goes against them, it's a one-off payment they'd have to make and he said the maximum would be about a quarter of earnings. If they win then that would be very good.
- On **dividends** he said they'll probably have a 30% payout, which is good. I've got a feeling they might maintain this dividend payout in the future.
- We might increase because it's **not expensive**, the markets are very good; they meet our criteria for profit margins and other ratios.

<u>**Buy/Sell Triggers**</u>

- Usually this kind of plastics manufacturing is not a high-margin business; it's production at a high rate, utilizing the machinery 24 hours a day, so this is unusual. One of the reasons may be the lack of tough **competition** but that could come because you see a company like this that's been in business for a while, and the money attracts competitors like flies to honey, so we have to watch this.
- They have to be careful because the **Japanese** could come in with a lot of money and manufacturing expertise. My guess is that the Japanese would go for the upstream – supply of raw materials – rather than the downstream business of pipes, because pipe manufacturing is somewhat localized and specialized. We saw that the number of SKUs (stock keeping units) is over 500 – different types of pipes and connectors. That means you've really got to get a sense of demand because you can't stop the machines, you've got to keep producing. You've got to have a feel for what demand is going to be in the next five or ten months, and the only way you're going to do that is by getting close to your customers.

V – Automata

Fifty kilometers north from the chaotic streets of Saigon is an oasis of calm driving, courtesy and order. Vehicles give way to one another in plenty of time. There's no congestion or drivers tooting their horns. In fact – there are no drivers.

Welcome to Vinamilk. In an area the size of 20 football pitches, laser-guided vehicles go about delivering pallets stacked with cartons of milk. They offload to machines in a temperature-controlled warehouse. The machines then lift the crates 17 stories high onto shelves. On the way back down they pick up the milk first in to stack in trucks.

At a cost of $110 million, this ranks among the world's most advanced factories. The German-made automata churn out more than a million liters of milk a day nonstop, overseen by a few humans in white hats and lab coats.

Vinamilk is the stock market's star performer, soaring 50%-plus every year from 2011. Its popularity has lifted the portion held by foreign investors to the government-set limit, and that means anyone wanting to buy must pay a premium of somewhere between 5 and 10% to convince another foreigner to sell.

Franklin Templeton owns less than 1% of the stock. While the price at 17.4 times annual earnings is more than the average of 14 for Vietnam, it's below the price–earnings ratio of 24 for Nestlé, the second biggest milk producer in Vietnam, after Vinamilk. Across the border in China, equivalent dairy companies have been trading at p/e multiples above 30. Meanwhile, Vinamilk's profit margin is twice the average in Vietnam at 26% while Nestlé's is 15%.[1]

The new factory – with enough spare capacity to double production – will enable earnings to grow in the order of 20% a year, estimates Mark's colleague Lam. Even after the building cost, Vinamilk has a lot of cash and no debt, so dividend payouts could go higher, she says.

Outside the factory in the Binh Duong province, giant milk vats tower over manicured lawns and sculpted hedges interspersed with fountains and concrete cows.

A real-life herd is the next big investment. Most of Vinamilk's produce comes from milk powder shipped in from New Zealand, Australia, the USA and Europe. The company plans to cut its reliance on imports by expanding its dairy herd of 8200 to 30,000 or 40,000.

"When we import from overseas or from third parties, there's some risk about the price and the quality," explains plant director Trinh Quoc Dung. "So Vinamilk would like to increase local supply in order to better control our chain."

Stocks Box: Vinamilk Vs. Dairy Producers

Company & Trading Platform	Description	Average Annual Return	Price–Earnings Ratio	Price–Book Ratio/ NAV	Return on Equity	Gross Dividend Yield	Market Value ($m)	Top Holders %
Vinamilk Ho Chi Minh Stock Exchange	Vietnam's biggest milk producer	34.4% since listing 2006	17.4	5.5	33.2%	2.0%	4641	State Capital & Invest 37.6% Fraser & Neave 11.0% Free float 57.5%
Nestlé SIX Swiss Exchange	World's biggest food producer	6.9% since 2006	24.3	4.0	15.8%	3.0%	242,143	Blackrock 3.7% Norges Bank 2.7% Free float 99.8%
Bright Dairy & Food Shanghai	Milk & dairy producer in China	41.4% since 2006	38.6	4.5	11.8%	1.3%	3170	Shanghai Milk 29.9% Bright Food 24.7% Free float 43.5%

Source: Data compiled by Bloomberg as of December 2014

Q&A Highlights: Mobius Interviews Vinamilk Executives
(Shortened excerpts)

Q: What's driving sales of your health drinks or "liquid meals"?

A: In the past, when the economy was still difficult, people just thought about how to get their stomach full. Now people are getting richer and they're looking for quality of life.

Q: I've been reading about TH Milk. How does their strategy complement or compete with yours?

A: They focus on fresh milk, and fresh milk is only a portion of the total.

Q: Do you see demand growing for fresh milk as people become richer?

A: The problem is refrigeration. We have pasteurized milk but we only sell it in the supermarkets where we are confident about the quality. Pasteurized can't sell in an open market. The trend is for fresh milk but it will grow gradually.

Q: What about condensed milk, is that rising or falling?

A: It's declining. Our other three categories – powdered milk, liquid milk and yogurt – are going up.

Investor Analysis: Mark Mobius on Vinamilk

Bottom Line

- Vinamilk is a very **impressive** factory, particularly the UHT unit, which was operated by only four people in the control room, everything else was automated.
- They're **ready** for any wage hikes and increases in demand. First, they foresee the day when labor rates will go up, and second, it's to make sure that the quality is top notch.
- They're now expanding their **dairy farms**. They're going to be producing more fresh milk in Vietnam so they want to have assured supply as a kind of insurance policy, and they can also have better quality control.
- A lot of people still can't afford milk of any form, so you're going to see the **market expanding**. They'll still be going for UHT, processed milk, that sort of thing, milk with a long shelf life. But it's also true that more people will be drinking fresh milk.
- We'd love to get more of the stock. Foreigners who hold it aren't selling and if they are, the chances are they'll only sell at a **premium**.

Buy/Sell Triggers

- The important thing with milk is the **trust** in the brand, the safety. So far they have not had any scandals or anything like that.
- My guess from the numbers we have seen previously is that this market is really **not penetrated yet**. Their being in a dominant position means lots of potential. If they continue promoting and growing, they should do very well.

Endnote

1. Data compiled by Bloomberg as of August 2014.

VI – From Noodles

A future Vietnam lies 5 kilometers south of the capital city Hanoi.
The shiny new Royal City Mega Mall, set over six floors and sprawling 230,000 square meters, is the country's biggest indoor retail space. It groups over 170 restaurants, Vietnam's only ice-skating rink and southeast Asia's largest indoor water park.

Teenagers and families wander mesmerized by glossy displays – posing for pictures next to perfumes, handbags and impossible snow scenes.

Few can afford to do much more than look on incomes averaging little over $2000 a year. Still, that's twice the level of five years ago. If the trend continues, young minds fantasizing of luxuries as unreal to their present lives as the Lapland snow will start having disposable income before too long. Capture the imagination of the aspiring consumer and you have a dedicated follower when they achieve spending power.

Royal City is the creation of Vietnam's first billionaire, Pham Nhat Vuong. After scooping a fortune from an instant-noodle and mashed potato business in Ukraine, he sold to Nestlé and returned home to pour his money into property development.

Vietnam, says Vuong at the Hanoi HQ of his company Vingroup, is just reaching a "golden age" when its young population is starting to enter the workforce and spend money. Half of the population is under 30.

Along with this demographic trend is a shorter-term boost. The government is expected to pump up the economy in time for the 2016 National Assembly meeting to elect a new leader.

"Everyone wants the economy to be good by then," says Vuong. "You'll see the stimulus policies coming out."

One proposal already in the works is permitting foreigners to buy property for the first time under communism. The plan was approved by the National Assembly in late 2014 to become law.

Confidence building measures have steadied the currency, the dong, after it depreciated more than 30% from 2008 through 2011.

"Just a few years ago, if you were buying a car, a motorbike or a house, people used to pay in gold," says Vuong. "That doesn't exist anymore, but the move has been so smooth that people could hardly notice."

Stocks Box: Vingroup Vs. Developers

Company & Trading Platform	Description	Average Annual Return	Price–Earnings Ratio	Price–Book Ratio/ NAV	Return on Equity	Gross Dividend Yield	Market Value ($m)	Top Holders %
Vingroup Ho Chi Minh Stock Exchange	Vietnam's largest property developer & mall operator	27.4% since listing 2007	16.7	3.7	20.9%	3.0%	3293	Nhat Vuong Pham 29.1% Vietnam Inv 12.4% Free float 49.6%
New Europe Property Investments Johannesburg Stock Exchange	Developer of mostly Romanian shopping malls & office blocks	35.2% since shares issued 2009	N/A	-2 (based on co. data)	N/A	4.35%	1,840	Resilient Property 9.6% Fortress Income 7.6%
Yoma Strategic Singapore Exchange	Biggest listed Myanmar business. Spans property, transport, autos, agriculture.	166% from 2011, when reforms paved way for sanctions easing	37.0	2.2	4.5%	N/A	703	SergePun 37.3% Aberdeen 7.1% Free float 62.1%

Source: Data compiled by Bloomberg as of December 2014

CHAPTER 6

Nigeria

I – Eko Beach

My faithful four-wheel, hundred-liter suitcase has followed me through five countries but I leave it behind as I head to Nigeria. It's too big to pass as hand luggage and I've heard enough stories of hours of delays and worse to know to avoid baggage reclaim in Lagos. Everyone on board had the same idea. The overhead lockers are jammed with cases and Harrods bags.

I last visited Nigeria a decade ago for a gathering of Commonwealth heads of state. The airport arrivals process hasn't got any quicker – 1½ hours waiting for one immigration officer to check through all foreigners. But it does seem more orderly. People didn't used to queue. I remember having to push my way through a crowd and then watching and praying as someone wearing a uniform snatched my passport and disappeared for a few minutes.

When the Commonwealth conference was over, my arduous reporting task was to find out why Guinness sales were going through the roof in Africa to the point where they overtook the core market in the UK and Ireland. It turned out the stout was gaining a reputation in Nigeria as some kind of aphrodisiac. My favorite quote came from a Lagos taxi driver. "It makes me feel powerful," Rasheed Adegbite had said. "If I have three stouts, my wife knows she had better watch out. I have energy in my body."

Now back again in Lagos, I'm excited to find it's Rasheed's cab firm picking me up from the airport. I'd brought the newspaper cuttings with the story just in case. It turns out to be a different driver, named Billy, so I ask him to pass my regards to Rasheed. The next morning I ask again after Rasheed. Billy gets a leaflet from the glove pocket he hadn't wanted to show me when I arrived. Rasheed was picking up a client from Lagos airport when a car flipped from the opposite carriageway and landed on his windscreen. The other driver was killed instantly and Rasheed died 20 minutes later. The leaflet was for his funeral just a month earlier.

"Driving is very dangerous here," says Billy, blinking a tear.

Nigeria's roads are the fifth most deadly of 175 countries and regions tracked by the World Health Organization, with 34 deaths for every 100,000 people.[1] Life expectancy at 52 ranks 11th worst.[2]

Reckless drivers aren't the only hazard on the road. Dodging rogue policemen and extortionists is part of the daily routine.

One morning I'm at the five-star Radisson Blu hotel overlooking the Lagos Lagoon with Aberdeen Asset Management's emerging markets fund manager, Kevin Daly, along with a client of his and a colleague of mine. We need a car in a hurry as the taxi we'd booked went to the wrong address. I walk to where I've seen a few cabs and haggle a price with a driver. But before we can climb into his car a large woman blocks our path.

"You cannot take this car," she screams, slamming the passenger door and almost taking off my fingers. "You must take an approved car."

The driver leans across to the passenger side shouting: "Why you take my customers? Get away from them."

Marching round to the driver, the woman tells him he shouldn't be here. With the passenger side clear, and only a few minutes to make our meeting, the four of us jump in the car but before we can pull away the woman lands a punch through the open window at our driver. I have to pull him back from retaliating by threatening to leave.

"Did you see?" he says as we speed off, "she was pregnant, so it's lucky I didn't hit her." According to our driver, she's part of a mafia that dominates taxi ranks across the city, intimidating drivers from encroaching on their patch.

The next morning I'm across the lagoon on Lagos Island at the sprawling Balogun market. Women balance on their heads 6-liter pans loaded with porridge; others tap-tap two-prong forks on square glass food containers. I'm with another cab driver, Gbenga. As we're leaving, we see a teenager waving his arms and shouting with incredible rage at a bewildered-looking man parked in the street. "This is his area," explains Gbenga. "He wants money for allowing him to park." There are few official parking restrictions, just gangs of youths – area boys. They want 2000 naira – over $12. The driver has no choice but to pay up.

We pass a squat dark-blue police car built like a tank with grills across the windows for riot control, and then turn left next to a set of traffic lights.

As soon as we're round the corner a gray-shirted policeman flaps his arms and shouts at us to stop.

Gbenga slows down but carries on driving, so the cop pulls open the door behind me and climbs in the back seat.

"You're a terrible driver," the beefy officer says, catching his breath.

"Why, what have I done?"

"You skipped the red light, it's very bad driving. Pull over now!"

Gbenga is indignant. He's actually accelerating. "There was no red light for turning left," he says calmly. "I went left!"

The policeman thrusts forward, crashing his bulk against Gbenga's skinny right arm and makes a grab for the ignition key. Gbenga is quick and uses his back and elbow to shove him away. But now the cop's hands have slipped from the key to the automatic gear stick and he's trying to push it into Park.

Gbenga wrenches the sausage fingers off the gear only to get a punch across his face.

"Tell your driver to stop now!" the cop shouts at me.

Blood is dripping from Gbenga's nose onto the steering wheel. He tries to reason with the cop that he'll drive with him to the police station to resolve the issue.

It's a smart move. Going to the station is the last thing this officer wants as he would need to explain why he pulled Gbenga over and risks being admonished by his superiors. He'd also lose the chance to pocket the on-the-spot fine he wants to slap on Gbenga.

"No, no. You stop here, now!" He lunges for the ignition key, again blocked by Gbenga, and then the gear stick but Gbenga hammers his hand off.

I unbuckle my seat belt to avoid getting pinned down if the cop pushes to the front. "That's right, you get out, leave, it's OK." I tell him I'm not leaving my driver.

And at that point, with the car still moving, the cop jumps out, shouting, "we'll come after you, we'll be following you."

The policeman is trying to save face. He has no car to chase us.

Still, Gbenga's not taking any chances. He stamps the accelerator to the floor, speeding south across Lagos Island toward Victoria Island. We keep going for a few minutes before stopping at a red light.

Gbenga's whole body is trembling. The pristine white shirt and tie he wore to take me around the market in the 40 degree heat is stained with blood. He fumbles for his wristwatch under his feet. The strap is broken, the spindle bent. "My Swiss watch!" he fumes, with tears welling.

The next day I'm back with Billy. We're heading north from Lagos Island to the Mainland on Africa's longest bridge. A third of the way over, we turn off and circle underneath. Stretching as far as the eye can see is row upon row of tin-roof wooden huts built on stilts in the lagoon. This is Makoko, one of the biggest slum areas of Africa's largest city.

We drive along a pot-holed dirt track and pay some area boys to park. They introduce us to Samuel Pelumi. His name means "God is with us."

He helps me and Billy onto a dug-out canoe and we paddle through this swamp version of Venice. Babies and infants are everywhere – some swimming in the dark, shallow water, others as young as three at the oars of their own canoes. Families in Sunday best row to church. I'm a curiosity. They giggle and call "oyibo, oyibo" – "white man." At every corner, music spills out from church services, makeshift drums banging out a rhythm.

Watering hole in Tsavo West, Kenya.
Photography by Gabriel Rotich, A24 Media

Burmese days: Fishing in the Irrawady River in Mandalay

Net revenue: Paddling a haul of fish to market

Balloonrise in Bagan, Burma

Icon: The lady & the "fighting peacock." Against the golden bust is a photo of Barack Obama seated between Suu Kyi and her right-hand man Tin Oo

Cashpile: Few accept plastic in Myanmar

For richer, for poorer: Family on the street in Buenos Aires, their washing hangs on park railings. The children wait while their parents pilfer bread for lunch

What they think of Buenos Aires Mayor Mauricio Macri: garbage, oppressor

Good morning, Vietnam! Rush hour in Saigon

Boom or bust? Mobius stands by Ho Chi Minh

River bank: Cyclist in conical *non la* hat in Hoi An, Vietnam

Bullish call: Search for greener pastures in Hoi An

Rowing up in Makoko

"Land of aquatic splendor": Makoko's shanty sprawl

Pointing to the future: David Frame shows the new Lagos rising from the ocean at Eko Atlantic

Firing questions: Aberdeen's Daly quizzes Lamido Sanusi

Monetary stimulus: Central Bank of Nigeria

One for the album: Sunset by world's tallest fountain, in Riyadh

His & hers: Toeing the line at Al Faisaliah mall, where religious police patrol for Romeos

Beach boys in Jeddah

On the road to Kilinochchi in northern Sri Lanka, land mines lie undetonated years after civil war ended

Displaced: Family home destroyed in the Tamil north

Making its headlines: Editor Prem with a report of the day he returned to the newsroom to find two colleagues dead and another wounded

Mr. S. Suhirtharajan
Journalist
Killed on 24.01.2006

One of the Rising Sun journalists killed in Jaffna, Sri Lanka

Fish dry in the sun in Jamestown square, Ghana

Door of no return: From the women's slave dungeon in Cape Coast Castle, they filed to the waiting boats

Taking the rise in Accra

Questions for the road home

We stop at random at a hut painted bright blue with a sign saying Makoko Independent Baptist Church, and clamber onto loose wooden planks. Pastor Abandy Bedolph, in a white shirt and blue tie, is about to start his service. The building has seats for 30 but only four children and his wife are inside. They sing "Onward Christian Soldiers" and chant "praise ye Lord, hallelujah" before the pastor's sermon on the origins of sin and its penalty, to which his young congregation replies in unison: "Death!"

Years ago Pastor Abandy studied classical music at the English seaside village of Deal, a 30-minute drive from my own home. Nowadays he travels 3½ hours each way by bus twice a week to reach his tiny congregation.

"These people mostly make their living from fishing, and sometimes they don't catch anything," he says. "Their income is very low, you can tell by their faces what is going on here. We feed them with the word of God."

A woman floats by, her children at the paddles. She has a bowl of small fish in her lap collected from her husband's net. She guts the haul on the way to a smoking hut, leaning over the side to rinse off. The bacteria from the polluted lagoon will remain in the fish as it's smoked, says Samuel.

In the stagnant, shallow water, murky with oil and debris from the city and feces from the shanty latrines, some fish swept in with the tide float dead. Even the drinking water collected from boreholes dug deep below ground is often infected by seepage from the lagoon. Many of the children splashing about in it get diarrhea. Others pick up typhoid and malaria. With limited access to medicine, each can be fatal.

Samuel has lived here since his family fled tribal fighting 200 kilometers east in Ondo State. His father was killed aged 38. His mother, now 48, travels 7 hours to earn an income as a hospital nurse, leaving at 1 a.m. on Mondays and sleeping over. It's down to 24-year-old Samuel to keep things going through the week with his three younger brothers.

There are no hospitals, police or any other state services in Makoko because the government deems this century-old settlement illegal. That makes it a magnet for violent criminals, says Samuel. "In the ghetto life, murderers can just hide away."

In 2012, the state deployed armed squads to destroy the huts as part of an official campaign to clear the city slums.[3] Up to 30,000 people were forced out by police firing live bullets as their shacks burned in the water. Families were left to sleep in their canoes.[4]

Amid the international media outcry came a literal beacon of hope. Two Dutch architects with the help of the United Nations Development Program built a three-story, triangular-shaped floating school.[5] Bobbing atop 256 blue plastic barrels it's visible from the Third Mainland Bridge towering overhead.

Samuel lives a 5-minute paddle from the school, opposite "Chelsea Football Club," as the painted blue sign says. His is the only hut around with glass windows and a satellite dish. Electricity from a generator powers a Phillips flat-screen TV in front of a cracked leather armchair. By local standards, they've made it big.

With the limited aid of a broken laptop, Samuel is studying for a degree, traveling to Lagos University for lectures. Rather than follow his mother into medicine, he's studying zoology with a focus on pollution control. Instead of treating symptoms, he says, "I need to find solutions."

Ten kilometers south from Makoko, another group of people are building on the water. There are no stilts or bobbing barrels here but drawings of skyscrapers, designer shopping malls and a marina complex. Where the Atlantic waves lap will be a vast area of reclaimed land as big as Manhattan – but more modern.

"It looks a bit like Monaco," says developer David Frame, showing me artists' impressions of Lagos Atlantic – or Eko Atlantic in the region's Yoruba language.

It reminds me of Dubai. Either way, the concept is mind boggling. Monaco and Dubai – the playgrounds of billionaires – have all the money in the world to push back the ocean for super-yacht marinas and islands in the shape of the world.

But this is Nigeria, where over 60% of the population live on less than $1.25 a day, the world's highest rate of poverty after Madagascar, Zambia and Malawi.[6] We're in a country where land rights are so compromised owners daub "This House is Not for Sale" on their walls to prevent their home being sold when they're out.

In the country where Frame has had his own camera smashed in the belief photographs steal the soul, tourists will flock to seven-star hotels and white-sand beaches, according to the Eko Atlantic managing director.

The project was sparked by a crisis. In 2005, an Atlantic surge swept across the main highway on the city's southern coast, flooding properties lining Victoria Island, one of the more desirable residential and business zones.

Former Lagos Governor Bola Ahmed Tinubu reached out for ideas for a permanent sea defense. Rather than a monster wall along the beach, the billionaire Lebanese–Nigerian Chagoury brothers proposed building it 2½ kilometers out to sea along the original pre-erosion coastline. That way the area in between could be reclaimed for lucrative real estate. The Chagoury brothers would obtain a title deed for the reclaimed land in compensation for their investment in the project. It wouldn't cost the government a kobo.

The "great wall of Lagos" is now well under way. One hundred thousand interlocking concrete Accropodes, each weighing 5 tons, form the backbone of the vast sea defense. A constant stream of trucks trundle boulders to place on top while a dredger volleys rainbow arches of sand collected from the ocean 25 kilometers offshore.

Five and a half square kilometers has been reclaimed so far. What are now 4-meter craters in the sand will be underground car parks for office blocks lining the eight-lane Eko Boulevard at the heart of the business district.

Banks have already started buying along with energy companies buoyed by recent oil and gas discoveries 60 kilometers off the coast of Lagos. Plots are selling from $1250 per square meter, while those along the new coastline are going for twice that amount. That's still cheaper than elsewhere on Victoria Island or Ikoyi where, according to Frame, the cost runs to $3000 – close to prices in Buenos Aires or Bucharest. In Nairobi, property is a third of the price.[7]

Housing costs are sky-rocketing as the city's 18 million population increases by 6% a year. Growth at the same pace for the next decade could make Lagos the world's third largest city after Mumbai and Tokyo at over 25 million.[8] Nigeria overtook South Africa as the continent's largest economy in 2014.

It's the increase in the 15s to 50s population that excites investors because of the potential for a wider pool of workers consuming and buying goods. It's also the biggest source of tension, as the nation's energy and transport infrastructure already can't cope. Plans for a light rail network and ring road around the city are aimed at relieving Lagos's notorious traffic "go-slows." While most Nigerians might get less than 5 hours of uninterrupted electricity and 18% get none at all, power generation is inching higher with the sale of some of the country's power stations to the likes of Transnational Corp.[9]

"All the elements are starting to fall into place," says Frame as we stand on the new Eko Beach imagining the future for the city that calls itself with a sense of irony the "land of aquatic splendor". "You look at what's happening in China where BMW and Daimler have their assembly factories – they can do that here. We've got 180 million people in Nigeria, it's just a huge market."

Top Down Data

Country	Population	GDP on PPP Basis ($)	GDP/ Capita on PPP ($)	Inflation (% pa)	Unemployment (%)
Nigeria	177,155,754	478,500,000,000	2800	8.7	23.9
Vietnam	93,421,835	358,900,000,000	4000	6.8	1.3
Argentina	43,024,374	771,000,000,000	18,600	20.8	7.5
Romania	21,729,871	288,500,000,000	14,400	3.2	7.3
Myanmar	55,746,253	111,100,000,000	1700	5.7	5.2
Kenya	45,010,056	79,900,000,000	1800	5.8	40.0

Source: CIA World Factbook, December 2014
[1] Population data from July 2014 estimates.
[2] GDP at purchasing power parity (PPP) exchange rates is the sum value of all goods and services produced in the country valued at prices prevailing in the USA, based on 2013 estimates.
[3] GDP per capita (PPP) divided by population, based on 2013 estimates.
[4] Inflation rate shows the annual percentage change in consumer prices in 2013.
[5] Unemployment rate shows the percentage of the labor force without jobs in 2013, except for Nigeria (2011) and Kenya (2008).

Fund Factbox

Company & Assets in Emerging Markets	Emerging Market Fund	Performance & Peer Ranking	Portfolio Manager: Kevin Daly
Aberdeen Asset Management $13 billion	Aberdeen Global Select Emerging Markets Bond Fund	35th highest total return among 3033 offshore emerging market funds over 5 years at 85% (annualized 13.1%)	Kevin manages $13 billion in emerging market debt including $1 billion in frontier markets for Aberdeen Asset Management in London. His Aberdeen Global Frontier Markets Bond Fund had 7% of assets in Nigeria. Kevin spent a decade at the credit ratings company Standard & Poor's, transferring in 1998 from Singapore to London, where he joined Aberdeen in 2002. Aged 54, he lives in London with his wife and three children

Source: Data compiled by Bloomberg as of June 2014

Endnotes

1. World Health Organization (2013) Report on Road Safety 2013, WHO. Note: Pacific Island of Niue is excluded from reference as population of <2000 skews data. Report available at: file:///C:/Users/Traveler/Downloads/9789241564564_eng.pdf.
2. Life Expectancy at Birth, Total (Years), The World Bank. Available at: http://data.worldbank.org/indicator/SP.DYN.LE00.IN?order=wbapi_data_value_2011+wbapi_data_value&sort=asc.
3. (2012) Destroying Makoko, *The Economist*. Available at: http://www.economist.com/node/21560615.
4. Morka, F. (2012) Violent Forced Evictions Of 30,000 People As Homes In Nigeria's Makoko Community Are Demolished, Social and Economic Rights Action Center. Available at: http://accproject.live.radicaldesigns.org/article.php?id=711.
5. Glancey, J. (2014) Learning from Lagos: floating school, Makoko, *Architectural Review*. Available at: http://www.architectural-review.com/buildings/learning-from-lagos-floating-school-makoko-nigeria-kunl-adeyemi-nl/8652311.article.
6. Poverty Headcount Ratio at $1.25 a Day (PPP) (% of population), The World Bank. Available at: http://data.worldbank.org/indicator/SI.POV.DDAY?order=wbapi_data_value_2010+wbapi_data_value&sort=desc.
7. Global Property Guide (2014) The World's Most Expensive Cities. Available at: http://www.globalpropertyguide.com/most-expensive-cities#most-expensive-cities.
8. Awofeso, P. (2011) One out of every two Nigerians now lives in a city: There are many problems but just one solution, *World Policy Journal*. Available at: http://muse.jhu.edu/journals/world_policy_journal/summary/v027/27.4.awofeso.html.
9. Thompson, C. (2014) Privatisation shines a light on Nigeria's route out of the Dark Age, *Financial Times*. Available at: http://www.ft.com/cms/s/0/fcd5b44a-bb15-11e3-948c-00144feabdc0.html#axzz30ku9I3yA.

II – Crude Politics

The old system works too well for some people who are entrenched, and until we understand that – understand how well entrenched they are, understand how they need to be dislodged, how their thinking can be affected – then you're not going to succeed

Sanusi Lamido Sanusi, Emir of Kano
Ex-central bank Governor

Abuja has got a bit rougher around the edges since my last visit. It needed to.

World leaders converging on Nigeria's newly built capital for the Commonwealth meeting in 2003 saw neatly manicured hedges and irrigated lawns with floral displays and fountains, and not a soul around. In the once-empty three-lane highways, hawkers now trawl between cars and yellow *danfo* minibuses offering sachets of water from bowls of ice on their heads while street stalls grill kebabs in fiery peanut-tomato *suya*.

What hasn't changed here is the sense that every aspect of life revolves around the government. We're sitting in a go-slow for two hours between the airport and the city center because security has closed a main artery for a government meeting. We pass the Abuja National Stadium where fanatically revered Arsenal was billed to play the Nigerian Eagles but canceled citing unspecified "complexities" after the sports minister said he wouldn't rush re-grassing the pitch for the match.[1,2] The work was finally completed over a year later at a cost of $600,000, and to complaints of water logging in the sparse Savanna rain.[3]

Sweltering in the heat, the driver next to us forgets to put his brake on and rolls back into the car behind. The two men lean out shouting at each other but neither bothers getting out. Both cars are so bashed up it would be hard to tell if this latest knock added any more damage.

Guards with AK-47s stand chatting as we edge toward the government district. The city has been a repeat target for Boko Haram, the Islamist terror group translating to "Western education is a sin." In a single day in 2014 the group killed 75 people commuting into Abuja by exploding a car bomb next to a bus station and abducted 276 school girls, forcing them into marriage with militiamen. Targeting the capital marks a ratcheting up of the terror campaign that's claimed at least 13,000 lives in attacks predominantly in the northeast since 2009.

Nigeria's center of power runs in an arch from the golden dome of the Abuja National Mosque up Constitution Avenue to the green-domed presidential State House with the dark monolith of Aso Rock for its backdrop and the National Assembly beside it. Next are the ministries and then the domineering cross-shaped glass tower of the Central Bank down Independence Avenue. Just how much independence the central bank has was tested to the limit in early 2014 before President Goodluck Jonathan fired its Governor.

Sanusi Lamido Sanusi was born into northern Nigerian royalty as the grandson of the Emir of Kano and son of the highest ranking official in the Ministry of Foreign Affairs.[4] He studied Sharia law in Sudan and lectured in economics there before switching career to banking, becoming the chief risk officer for United Bank of Africa and First Bank of Nigeria. In 2009, he was made the CEO of First Bank and six months later appointed central bank Governor by President Umaru Yar'Adua, a fellow northern Muslim aristocrat.

It was the height of the global financial crisis hitting emerging markets. Nigeria's stock market had plunged 70% and banks were on the brink of collapse from loans sliding into arrears. While the same picture was being repeated in countless countries, the difference in Nigeria was the scale of systemic corruption. Sanusi accused bankers of raiding depositors' funds to lend themselves money to buy properties, private jets and their banks' own shares to inflate the stock price.

According to Sanusi, they got away with it because their controller was asleep. The body bringing together financial supervisors, the Financial Services Regulation Coordinating Committee, hadn't met for two years, he said.

With the global credit crisis sending bank shares into freefall, people's savings for their retirement, school fees and medical bills were being wiped out, he reflected in a 2010 university lecture. "How many honest businessmen have been rendered bankrupt? How many people have committed suicide? How many have died because they were unable to pay medical bills as their money was trapped in these institutions?"

Sanusi concluded he was up against a conspiracy of bankers and politicians. "Here is the reality," he told the students at Kano's Bayero University, named after his great grandfather. "The owners and managers of banks, the rich borrowers and their clients in the political establishment are one and the same class of people protecting their interest, and trampling underneath their feet the interest of the poor with impunity. So this time we turned the tables and said enough is enough."

Within four months of being appointed he fired the heads of eight banks. Five CEOs were jailed. Wealthy debtors to the banks were warned to pay up or face prosecution. Then he injected 620 billion naira ($3.8 billion) to prevent the institutions collapsing.[5-7]

"What we have done," he told the students six months later, "is to fire the opening salvo in what could potentially be a revolutionary battle against the nexus of money and influence that has held this country to ransom for decades."[8]

Genteel almost to the point of meekness, Sanusi doesn't strike as a revolutionary. Bespectacled with graying hair in a mandarin collar pinstriped suit, he jokes affably about how his father took all the diplomatic blood, leaving him a more controversial character. It's not a convincing argument. One of Sanusi's less heralded initiatives in 2009 was to organize retreats for the central bank's policymakers and those chief executives who survived his cull to build a consensus on the objectives of monetary policy and the banking industry.

The entire central bank board flew off to Malaysia to study the policy response to Asia's financial crisis that had most impressed Sanusi – recapitalizing banks, purchasing their non-performing loans and restructuring the debt. "I used that to fix the crisis in Nigeria," he tells us. The next year the board studied mobile banking in Brazil and then inflation targeting in South Africa.

When it came to the monthly policy meetings, the retreats paid off, with broader alignment on whether to raise, cut or freeze interest rates.

After the bank rescues, the biggest problem was that executives were now too worried about running up further losses to lend to anyone except the safest of borrowers. While agriculture represented over 40% of the economy, farmers had little prospect of getting a bank loan because they couldn't prove they had the stable earnings to repay the debt. Most had to take whatever price was offered for their produce at the time of harvest because of a lack of storage facilities and processors.

As a starting point, Sanusi commissioned a study on the tomato industry in 2011. He found that most tomatoes were left to rot in the fields even though four-fifths of the 80 million rural population lived in poverty and the country was importing $360 million of tomato paste for suya and other dishes, much of it from China.[9] Sanusi teamed up with Africa's richest man, Aliko Dangote, a fellow native of Kano, to build a tomato paste factory that would buy at a fixed price from 8000 farmers in the northern Kadawa Valley region. With their contracts proving stable income, farmers were able to borrow to buy their seeds.

"Now we're getting to a point where 4 to 5% of the loan book of banks is in agriculture," says Sanusi. The output from Dangote's factory will allow Nigeria to cut tomato paste imports by a third. It's a model that could be used to create finished products in other sectors of the economy. "It's the same process moving from cassava to starch and from hides of skin to leather goods."

In northern Nigeria – once known for its pyramids of groundnuts and exports of rice, cotton and cowpeas – it's one answer to the poverty that's made this fertile ground for Boko Haram's recruiters.

"Boko Haram isn't really a Muslim–Christian thing because they've killed many more Muslims than Christians," says Sanusi. "When you have a system in which 90% lives in poverty, 70% in absolute poverty, you're likely to have one problem or another. A few years ago it was in the Niger Delta; now we're seeing it in the religious tensions in the north."

In Nigeria's main crude-producing Delta region, kidnappings of foreign workers and theft from pipelines cut oil output by 29% in the three years to 2009. The violence eased that year as thousands of fighters accepted a government amnesty offer and disarmed. But the following year, as President Yar'Adua's death led to succession by Goodluck Jonathan, a Christian from the Delta, Boko Haram started its terror campaign. In 2013, theft from the Delta's pipelines was flaring up again, reducing output to a four-year low.[10]

It was the nation's disappearing oil revenue that Sanusi took up in his final act as central bank governor. Like Norway and Abu Dhabi, Nigeria has kept a rainy day fund for the past decade to set aside revenue during good years of oil exports. But while Norway's fund has quintupled in eight years to $850 billion[11] and Abu Dhabi has stashed away $800,000 for every man, woman and child,[12] Nigeria's assets have shrunk. The kitty of $20 billion in 2008 dwindled to $3.45 billion in March 2014 – or $20 per person.[13]

The Excess Crude Account, established under President Olusegun Obasanjo, was seen early on by Sanusi as a key tool for economic stability. In his speech to the students in 2010 he envisaged the fund providing a boost when the economy needed it, while in a good year it would soak up oil revenue before it created inflationary pressure in the economy.

While theft from oil pipelines in the Delta contributed to a drop in production to 2.2 million barrels a day from the projected 2.5 million in 2013, Sanusi calculated that higher oil prices should have resulted in a top-up for the Excess Crude Account. Oil prices had ranged between $87 a barrel and $111, while the government had based its budget on a lower price of $79,

Sanusi reasoned. But instead of receiving new money, the ECA had been drawn down, hitting a low of $2.11 billion.

"Arithmetic doesn't explain it and also it's not explained by a huge increase in government spending because there wasn't," he says in our meeting. "Obviously there is a leakage."

A private letter was sent to President Jonathan in late 2013 suggesting that the Nigerian National Petroleum Corp. be made to account for nearly $50 billion that should have come to the government. "This was not meant to be a public issue," says Sanusi. "An invitation to investigate somehow became read as the conclusion of an investigation, and that wasn't it. This was an initial report that, for me, raised sufficient concern to have an investigation so we can know exactly where that money is."

Finance Minister Ngozi Okonjo-Iweala told reporters in December that a review showed unaccounted oil receipts stood at $10.8 billion. Sanusi told a Senate finance committee two months later that $20 billion was outstanding.

"There are a number of numbers that I'm looking at," Sanusi told us. "The principle remains: no one has the right to retain money that should come to the federation account. Constitutionally it should come, and then, if expenses are legitimate, they should be presented transparently and properly approved. To even admit that you haven't brought back $10 billion or $12 billion and say this is what I did with it is, frankly speaking, not even the beginning of an argument."

The wider issue for Sanusi was that if the government is drawing down the Excess Crude Account when oil prices are around $100 a barrel and production is more or less stable, then what would happen in the event of a serious drop in oil revenue? The central bank has a legitimate interest, argued Sanusi, because it needs to show the country has enough reserves to withstand pressure on the currency or financial system.

In February 2014 – four months before his term was due to end – Sanusi was suspended from office by Jonathan for "financial recklessness and misconduct." Security officials seized his passport at the airport.[14]

International investors who had lauded Sanusi for his rescue of the banking industry and steady monetary policy were horrified. Shares tumbled as the naira hit an all-time low and the country's main international bonds sank by a record amount.

Jim O'Neill, the ex-Goldman Sachs analyst who coined the BRICs acronym for the go-go economies of Brazil, Russia, India and China and identified the MINT nations of Mexico, Indonesia, Nigeria and Turkey as the next in line, had reserved for Sanusi what for him as a Manchester United fan was the highest recognition of merit: "The Alex Ferguson of central bankers". "If I were a leader in this country, I'd pay attention to the fact that the markets didn't like how that was done," O'Neill said on Bloomberg TV. "Clearly a lot of oil revenue has gone missing and the issue needs to be placed on the table and brought into more public focus. He's certainly done that."

The Lagos federal high court two months later ordered the State Security Service to return Sanusi's passport and issued a perpetual injunction preventing any government law enforcement agency from arresting or harassing him without following the "due process of law."

Then, in mid-June, the 83-year-old Emir of Kano, Nigeria's most powerful Islamic figure after the Sultan of Sokoto, died, after reigning for more than half a century. Sanusi, at 52, was appointed heir, becoming Muhammad Sanusi II after his grandfather. In place of his pinstriped suits, Sanusi now wears an embroidered white cloak with an elaborate turban wound around his head and tied at the top like rabbits' ears. The royal dress code includes a mouth veil, conveying a tradition that the Emir speaks only through his aides. Convention is to rise above the political fray, to speak in the language of diplomacy.

Sanusi has already made a break with his predecessor by leading the Friday sermon at the main mosque in Kano.

"This whole process for me," Sanusi said in our meeting before his appointment, "is one in which we need to force greater transparency over oil revenues."

"The old system works too well for some people who are entrenched, and until we understand that – understand how well entrenched they are, understand how they need to be dislodged, how their thinking can be affected – then you're not going to succeed."

* * *

Someone who knows that old system inside and out is Ken Saro-Wiwa Jr, the son of the activist executed in 1995 as the Ogoni people campaigned against pollution in the Niger Delta.[15]

Ken continued his father's struggle, leading a landmark court case in 2009 against Royal Dutch Shell for complicity in the abuse, torture and death of Saro-Wiwa and eight others. Shell settled with a $15.5 million payment to compensate the families of the victims and establish a trust for the Ogoni people.[16]

More recently, Ken has been the senior special assistant to President Jonathan. Meeting us for breakfast at the Hilton in Abuja, he reflects on what his father would make of politics today.

"Nigeria has changed so much, he would barely recognize the country. He'd be surprised that there's a president from the Niger Delta." Then he pauses to consider his legacy – "I am more dangerous dead!" his father had said defiantly – "But then, maybe not so surprised."

Saro-Wiwa's "judicial murder," as Britain's then Prime Minister John Major put it, led to Nigeria's suspension from the Commonwealth and tougher sanctions against the regime of Sani Abacha. After the dictator's death in 1998, his successor, Abdusalam Abubakar, began transitioning the country toward an elected civilian government in 1999.

For the next 15 years, only one party governed – the People's Democratic Party. The main reason for that is – just like in Kenya – the rules are stacked against newcomers. A president needs to win not only the most support in total but also at least a quarter of votes in two-thirds of the country's 36 states.

"If you don't have the ability to reach all those polling stations, you're not even getting started," says Ken.

Before the 2015 election, when Jonathan was challenged by former military dictator Muhammadu Buhari of the All Progressives Congress - an alliance of the three main opposition parties - the biggest political battle was within the PDP itself.

The leadership is decided by the party's 2000-strong electoral college. Nigeria's media reports the salaries and extra allowances make their senators among the world's highest paid lawmakers.[17]

A series of defections in 2013 caused the PDP to lose its majority in the House of Representatives. Yet, by early 2014 it had won its majority back. There were no by-elections. Instead, five members of the opposing All Progressives Congress party crossed over to the PDP.[18]

"The consensus of Nigeria has always been negotiated," says Ken. "Here, you don't get by through gentle persuasion."

Yet the power base is starting to shift, he says. While Abuja is dominated by politics, Lagos is increasingly the domain of entrepreneurs who aren't waiting on the government.

"There has been a democratization of information. You're starting to get people making money that the politicians have no control over."

Country Factbox: Corruption

Nigeria ranks among the 35 worst countries for graft of 177 surveyed by Transparency International.[19]

My Nigeria: Sanusi Lamido Sanusi

"We need to separate the economic argument from the moral. As a moral issue everybody condemns corruption, but corruption hasn't stopped growth in China or in India or in Brazil or in Russia, so one must accept that it's too simplistic to blame corruption."

An official pocketing 5% for the construction of a power-processing plant would be an example of corruption, but if the plant adds electricity and creates jobs, the benefit might outweigh the money stolen. If, on the other hand, the same amount was spent buying transformers that didn't work, then you've the cost of corruption on top of wasted expenditure.

"I like focusing on the economic policies: Where is the money going? Are we investing in human beings? Are we building capacity? Do we have the right trade and tariff regimes? If you have that, the scope for corruption begins to close off. If you don't, then there's this pot of money and everyone's seeking a part of it."

Q&A Highlights: Kevin Daly Interviews First Bank Nigeria's Treasurer Ini Ebong (*Shortened excerpts*)

Q: Beyond oil, what are the biggest opportunities in the economy?

A: It's clearly retail. The retail opportunity here is just huge, with Shoprite leading the way and others coming in. We are slowly beginning to monetize the population. We've always had a large informal economy and we're beginning to capture that.

Q: What's your perspective on the violence in the north?

A: When the Brits came here, the north was a feudal society. It had an Emir and he had his Sheikhs. Everyone had their income and paid homage to the Emperor. The Brits left the feudal structure in place. The south didn't have that structure, so we're more entrepreneurial, but the food basket of the nation is up there. The north needs to find its own identity. Boko Haram is really people revolting that they're poor. The northern leaders are now beginning to have those discussions about empowerment.

Investor Analysis: Aberdeen's Kevin Daly on Politics & Policy

<u>Bottom Line</u>

- The security **situation in the north** remains tenuous. The government's response to the Boko Haram threat has been seen as ineffectual. From a purely financial perspective, if the terrorist threat dampens the economic interests of the north and also spills into the south, this could weigh on investor sentiment.
- The **president's control** of the purse strings is key to retaining support. The state-owned oil company, Nigerian National Petroleum Corp. (NNPC), is seen as an important source for the PDP to influence voters, as it's an opaque organization that doesn't open its books to the public.
- The allegations against Sanusi were a joke. The episode should remind investors that Nigeria's **country risk is high**. One should be wary when you have a weak leadership and a strong-willed central bank governor who is taking on the establishment.
- Looking ahead, Godwin **Emefiele** is clearly a different central bank governor to Sanusi, I just hope he's able to do his job without government interference.

<u>Buy/Sell Triggers</u>

- Softer oil prices and increased political noise will continue to **test the resolve** of the central bank's Monetary Policy Committee.

Ethical Investor Analysis: Axel Röhm, Head of Emerging Market Debt at PGGM

Axel Röhm, a client of Kevin's, invests 6 billion euros of assets on behalf of seven Dutch pension funds in emerging-market and frontier government bonds. Along with seeking to maximize financial returns, Axel also focuses on the social impact of investments. Here are some of his observations from our meetings:

- The economic growth story was broadly confirmed. A lot of **construction** is going on – visible especially in Abuja (roads, railroads and buildings). There is a need for much more infrastructure investment as witnessed by the heavy traffic and electricity blackouts.

- With regard to **corruption**, I was surprised how openly everybody spoke about it (even naming specific amounts – how much it cost to buy votes from the 2000 delegates of the PDP) and accepting that this was the way things work. Views on the elections come down to power, "entrenched interests" and "money changing hands." Corruption can take many forms: whereas corruption in Russia hinders growth, especially for smaller companies, it seems to be in Nigeria mainly a problem in the government and state-owned enterprises such as the NNPC.
- More people need to profit from the oil-driven economic growth, i.e. lifted above the **poverty line**. The oil sector is creating revenue but very few jobs, so the challenge is to build employment in other parts of the economy. Hopefully, the local companies expected to buy some of the onshore oil fields will manage the relations with the local population better and improve the situation around sabotage, oil theft and pollution.
- The hope for the **north** is that farming and other sectors develop from the current situation of producing only raw crops to processing food.
- Nigeria has many of the ingredients needed for continued strong economic growth. However, the quality of **governance** will decide whether a large part of the population participates in this growth and if there's a corresponding increase in welfare (creating an inclusive society). School fees make a good education unaffordable for the majority of people living below the poverty line. Paying doctors is also not within the financial possibilities for a large part of the population, so many people are excluded from healthcare. This, in turn, is important for political stability and a prerequisite for the future continuation of economic and social growth.

Portfolio Structuring: Picking Bonds

- Aberdeen's main emerging-market **hard-currency funds** had 0.45% of assets in Nigerian Eurobonds, equal to the weighting for the country in the benchmark JPMorgan EMBI Global Diversified Index, along with an additional 0.23% allocation to Zenith Bank Eurobonds.
- **Government Eurobonds in dollars due in 2018** are among the most widely traded of Nigeria's debt securities. The yield has been relatively low because Nigeria has one of the smallest debt burdens relative to GDP in emerging markets at about 20%, reducing the risk of default.

- Federal Government of Nigeria (**FGN**) Eurobonds denominated in naira are more sensitive to local politics than the bonds in dollars. Aberdeen owned FGNs due in 2017, opting for the shorter maturity than the securities due in 2022 to reduce the risk of price swings.
- **Treasury bills** have a shorter maturity than the FGNs. They're useful as a way to take a position on the naira without adding to the credit risk by buying bonds. Aberdeen cut its holdings of local-currency government bonds to zero in the run-up to the 2015 presidential election amid violence and plunging oil prices.
- Nigerian **bank bonds** offer attractive yields. Banks are very well capitalized after Sanusi's reforms. Guaranty Trust Bank (GTB), First Bank Nigeria (FBN) and Zenith Bank have the highest capital adequacy ratios in the region at 20–25%, while Access Bank, Diamond Bank and Fidelity Bank are around 15–18%.
- **GTB** is the best known Nigerian bank to foreign investors, as it has been in the market since 2007 and hence benefits from this familiarity. Aberdeen owns GTB 2016s and GTB 2018s. We also own **FBNs** due in 2016 and 2018. **Zenith** Bank bonds trade at about the same yield as GTB, which reflects the similar credit quality.
- Aberdeen's **total holdings** of Nigerian corporate bonds amounted to 2% of overall emerging-market corporate bond fund assets - double the weighting in the benchmark JPMorgan CEMBI Broad Diversified corporate bond index.

Bond Box: Nigeria

Security & Trading Platform	Asset Description	Maturity/Amount Outstanding	Average Annual Price Change	Coupon/ Interest	Yield
Republic of Nigeria Euroclear/ Clearstream	Sovereign Local currency	2017 35b naira ($190m)	−4.8% since issued in 2012	15.1%	14.0%
Guaranty Trust Bank Euroclear/ Clearstream	Corporate Dollars	2018 $400m	N/A Issued late 2013	6%	6.7%
FBN Finance Euroclear/ Clearstream	Corporate Dollars	2020 $300m	N/A Issued mid 2013	8.25%	9.1%

Source: Data compiled by Bloomberg as of December 2014

Stocks Box: Nigerian Equities

Company & Trading Platform	Description	Average Annual Return	Price–Earnings Ratio	Price–Book Ratio/NAV	Return on Equity	Gross Dividend Yield	Market Value ($m)	Top Holders %
Dangote Cement Nigerian Stock Exchange	Nigeria's biggest company; Africa's No.1 cement producer	30.2% since listing 2010	16.5	5.4	34.3%	3.9%	17,160	Dangote Industries 92.8% Aliko Dangote 0.2% Free float 7.0%
Dangote Sugar Nigerian Stock Exchange	Nigeria's biggest sugar producer	0.5% since listing 2007	8.2	N/A	N/A	8.6%	468	Dangote Industries 67.7% Dangote Aliko 5.4% Free float 26.8%
Guaranty Trust Bank Nigerian Stock Exchange	Nigeria's biggest bank by market value	50.2% since data starts 2002	8.4	2.29	27.7%	6.27%	4913	Oppenheimer funds 1.69% FIL Ltd 0.78% Free float 99.81%
FBN Holdings Nigerian Stock Exchange	Nigerian lender	24.8% since data starts 2002	4.9	0.7	14.4%	11.1%	1817	Franklin Resources 2.8% Fidelity 1.5% Free float 98.4%

Source: Data compiled by Bloomberg as of December 2014

Stocks Box: ETFs

Security/ Trading Platform	Issuer Description	Average Annual Return Since Inception	Top 10 Index Holdings	
Global X Nigeria Index ETF	ETF incorporated in the USA seeking to provide investment results that correspond generally to the price and yield performance, before fees and expenses, of the Solactive Nigeria Index	N/A	Nigerian Breweries plc	18.6%
		Inception mid 2013	Guaranty Trust Bank plc	11.0%
			Zenith Bank plc	9.9%
New York Stock Exchange			Nestlé Nigeria plc	8.2%
			Ecobank Transnational	4.7%
			Guinness Nigeria plc	4.0%
			Dangote Cement plc	4.0%
			FBN Holdings plc	3.6%
			Forte Oil plc	3.5%
			Transnational Corp.	3.5%

Source: Data compiled by Bloomberg as of December 2014

Country Factbox: Nigeria

Nigeria's economy barely grew from 1950 and was poorer in 2000 than in 1974 when high oil prices briefly bumped up its per capita income.
Tyler Cowen & Alex Tabarrok Modern Principles: Macroeconomics Worth Publishers (2010).

Endnotes

1. Anonymous (2012) Arsenal cancel pre-season trip to Nigeria, BBC Sport. Available at: http://www.bbc.co.uk/sport/0/football/18732474.
2. Anonymous (2012) Soccer: Arsenal cancels match with Nigerian Eagles; "complexities" in Abuja, USAfricaOnline. Available at: http://usafricaonline.com/2012/06/27/soccer-cancelled-arsenal-clash-with-nigerian-eagles-on-august-5-in-abuja/.
3. Adebowale, S. (2013) House doubts N97m re-grassing cost for Abuja stadium. Available at: http://theeagleonline.com.ng/house-doubts-n97m-re-grassing-cost-for-abuja-stadium/.

4. Central Bank of Nigeria (2011) Available at: http://www.cenbank.org/aboutcbn/TheBoard.asp?Name=Mr.+Sanusi+Lamido+Sanusi+(CON)&Biodata=lamido.

5. Ajayi, Y., Abiodun, E. (2014) Sanusi: reformer with an irrepressible streak, This Day. Available at: http://www.thisdaylive.com/articles/sanusi-reformer-with-an-irrepressible-streak/172077/.

6. Yedder, O. B. (2013) Interview with Sanusi Lamido Sanusi, Governor of the Central Bank of Nigeria, African Business. Available at: http://africanbusinessmagazine.com/features/finance/sanusi-lamido-sanusi-too-much-wealth-in-too-few-hands.

7. Anonymous (2009) Arrest threat for Nigeria debtors, BBC News. Available at: http://news.bbc.co.uk/1/hi/8208932.stm.

8. Sanusi, L. (2010) "The Nigerian Banking Industry: What Went Wrong And The Way Forward," Convocation Lecture delivered at the Convocation Square, Bayero University, Kano. Available at: http://www.cenbank.org/OUT/SPEECHES/2010/THE%20NIGERIAN%20BANKING%20INDUSTRY%20WHAT%20WENT%20WRONG%20AND%20THE%20WAY%20FORWARD_FINAL_260210.PDF

9. Mbachu, D., Olofu, E. (2013) Nigeria's Dangote vies with China over tomato market, Bloomberg News. Available at: http://www.bloomberg.com/news/2013-06-30/africa-s-richest-man-vies-with-china-in-nigeria-tomatoes.html.

10. Kay, C. (2014) Africa's richest man Dangote mulls buying Nigeria oil fields, Bloomberg News. Available at: http://www.businessweek.com/news/2014-01-20/africa-s-richest-man-dangote-considers-buying-nigeria-oil-fields.

11. Milne, R. (2014) Norway scraps oil fund ethics committee, *Financial Times*. Available at http://www.ft.com/cms/s/0/92cef506-bbe3-11e3-84f1-00144feabdc0.html#axzz2zdhz6VbO.

12. SWF Institute (2014) Available at: http://www.swfinstitute.org/swfs/abu-dhabi-investment-authority/.

13. Emejo, J. (2014) Nigeria's excess crude account now $3.45 billion, says Okonjo-Iweala, This Day. Available at: http://www.thisdaylive.com/articles/inflation-drops-to-7-7-in-february/173926/.

14. Kay, C. (2014) Nigeria Central Bank independence at risk with Sanusi ousted, Bloomberg News.

15. The Death of Ken Saro-Wiwa, Remember Saro-Wiwa. Available at: http://remembersarowiwa.com/background/the-death-of-ken-saro-wiwa/.

16. Press release (2009) Settlement Reached in Human Rights Cases Against Royal Dutch/Shell. Available at: http://wiwavshell.org/documents/Wiwa_v_Shell_Settlement_release.pdf.

17. Babalola, L., Ugbodaga, K. (2010) Nigeria's Federal Legislator Earns More Than Obama-Prof. Itse Sagay. Available at: http://saharareporters.com/news-page/nigeria%E2%80%99s-federal-legislator-earns-more-obama-prof-itse-sagay.

18. Kay, C. (2014) Nigerian ruling PDP regains lead in Parliament's lower house, Bloomberg News.

19. Transparency International (2013) Available at: http://www.transparency.org/country#NGA.

III – Sugar King

Like the suya kebab stalls using Chinese puree while tomatoes rot in the fields, drivers in Africa's biggest oil-producing nation load up with imported fuel.

Most of the two million-plus barrels of crude extracted every day from the Niger Delta and offshore in the Gulf of Guinea take a voyage for processing as petrol or plastics before re-entering Nigeria. While the country has four refineries – three in the Niger Delta and one in the north in Kaduna – the theft of funds, fires and neglect have cut output to a fifth of capacity.[1]

Having invested $25 million in home-grown tomato paste, the oil industry is the next port of call for Africa's richest man. It fits Aliko Dangote's pattern since the 90s of replicating imports with local production.

"We were known as the sugar kings," recalls Devakumar Edwin, who moved from India to Nigeria in 1992 after being approached by Aliko to run his textile mills. He's now Dangote's chief executive officer for the cement business. "We were importing all the sugar requirement for Nigeria before expanding into rice and other businesses."

Then, in 1998, Dangote decided to stop importing and start producing. One industry led to another as the company sought to own its production line. "Most of the products need bags so we had to produce them," says Edwin, describing a strategy labeled backward integration. "Otherwise we could be held to ransom by a supplier."

Dangote's headquarters in the middle of Lagos Island is a hectic fusion of its businesses dotted around the continent and beyond. Suited executives talk with engineers as workers run around with cardboard boxes of noodles. The empire spans telecoms to salt plants to flour and steel.

The biggest business is cement, taking a billion dollars of investment in 2014 alone and paying out more in profit. The oil venture will dwarf even that business.

The refinery and petrochemical plant will cost around $9 billion. The group took a $3.3 billion loan and plans to borrow a further $2.2 billion.

Based near Lagos, it should be up and running in 2017, refining 400,000 barrels of crude a day to begin and rising to 500,000, says Edwin. That's around the level of Exxon Mobil's Baton Rouge in the USA or Saudi Aramco's Ras Tanura among the top dozen refineries. Eventually, production will ramp up to a million barrels a day, ranking it the second biggest worldwide, says Edwin.[2] There's been no scaling back of the project amid the slump in oil prices.

Dangote's super-refinery could change lives. The problem of low production at existing refineries is compounded by a frequent shortage of foreign fuel. Many of the importers ran out of credit after defaulting on loans in 2012.[3,4] More recently, they're alleged to have pocketed billions of dollars in energy subsidies without ever supplying the discounted fuel.[5] For Nigerians it all adds up to wasted hours spent queuing at gas stations and inevitable fights in the struggle to fill up. The shortages hit commuters to freight operators to families cooking on kerosene stoves to businesses needing diesel for their electricity generators, the essential backup in the face of constant power outages.

To economists, Nigeria's reliance on oil magnifies the impact of gyrations in global crude prices on the naira and the nation's finances.

Beyond fuel, Dangote's refinery will produce urea for fertilizers and petrochemicals for plastics.

Even before the refinery has been built, Dangote is working out the backward integration from refining to supplying the oil. With the violence and thefts reducing their crude output, the likes of Shell and Chevron are switching to offshore fields they can more easily control, and Dangote is moving in.

Given the history from Ken Saro-Wiwa to the present day, it's conceivable a Nigerian company would have a better chance of resolving the issues plaguing the Niger Delta.

"Because we are on the ground, we know the terrain much better, we know the risks and we believe that the risks can be managed," says Edwin. Where Dangote extracts limestone, for example, the company has agreements in place with each of the communities.

While oil is the ultimate expansion for Dangote within Nigeria, it's also pushing to replicate its African operations across other continents. Dangote's limestone miner is branching out to Indonesia and Nepal and reviewing three South American countries, says Edwin. Part of the rationale is to increase the company's overall value by diversifying its risk from a single country. Dangote expects to generate 60% of its business from outside of Nigeria before a planned listing on the London Stock Exchange.

All of this activity increased Dangote's wealth to over $20 billion, ranking him among the world's 35 wealthiest people, before the plunge in Nigerian assets triggered by sliding oil prices and pre-election violence cut his ranking to No. 53 by early 2015. He remained Africa's wealthiest person.

"Whoever would have thought," reflects Lamido Sanusi, "that Nigeria and not South Africa would have the continent's richest man. We've seen with Dangote proof of what can be done with structural reform."

Dangote is inspiring plenty of wannabes. A husband-and-wife company making roof nails found the metal for the caps cost $160 a ton in Nigeria but only 30 cents in China. Using the same model of backward integration, Alhaji Kamoru Yusuf and his wife Bolanle built Nigeria's first cold roll steel mill.

Like tomato paste and petrol, steel is a natural industry in Nigeria where an estimated five billion tons of iron ore lies untapped. Governments have tried and failed to build an industry since General Yakubu Gowon's regime created the National Steel Development Authority soon after the Biafran War in 1971.[6]

Finance Minister Ngozi Okonjo-Iweala has been studying the Yusufs as an example of what's right and wrong in the economy.

"They've been married 25 years, they've invested in the manufacturing of nails, and now they have the cold roll steel mill, and they go borrow $200 million," says Okonjo-Iweala, raising her index finger, "at 18% – and do this for three years."

That's not right, she says.

"You can't expect people to borrow short term, for three years, to invest in a 15-year endeavor. There's a missing institution – a missing link – so we're creating this institution."

A future Mr and Mrs Yusuf will be able to tap a new lender being created with the help of the World Bank and advice from development banks in Germany and Brazil. Like the German KFW and Brazilian BNDS, Nigeria's development bank will take advantage of state backing to obtain cheaper financing. It will borrow from foreign investors, particularly targeting those like Axel Röhm at PGGM who have a mission to make a positive "social impact." That way, says Okonjo-Iweala, it will have to be fully transparent, ensuring it doesn't become another corrupted institution. The bank will channel money to existing state and commercial lenders to provide credit to businesses.

The same kind of idea is being applied to the housing market in an attempt to kick-start home ownership. Africa's largest nation needs 17 million additional homes by official estimates, and this so-called housing deficit is growing by two million every year.

The home shortage – whether manifested in people living on the streets or in unsanitary and overcrowded slums like Makoko – feeds into the wider social problems of crime and corruption.

"Everybody wants a home, no matter which country, what color their skin, it's a primary human need to have a roof over the heads of your family at some point," says Okonjo-Iweala. "If you don't have any means of accessing it then you start looking for ways and means to gather that money."

The government plans to spur cheap lending by creating the Nigeria Mortgage Refinance Co. to run in a similar way to America's Fannie Mae. It will obtain a $250 million line of credit as a starting point from the World Bank at zero interest for 40 years. This guaranteed funding will enable the company to sell long-maturity bonds at low rates and pass the money along for home loans. Right now, from Nigeria's population of 170 million, there are probably only about 50,000 mortgage accounts, says Okonjo-Iweala.

One component of the housing program is a "lease to own" initiative where a tenant becomes the owner of the property after 20 years. The legal entitlement would be portable for people moving house.

"If we can create this institution so a young couple just starting out knows that within 20 years they can buy their home, it helps curb any temptations to do the wrong thing," says Okonjo-Iweala. "I see it as a form of social inclusion. It's also a form of tackling corruption."

According to United Nations estimates, by 2050 Nigeria's population will overtake America to rank third after India and China.[7] "For the demographics to work, people must have a certain amount of purchasing power, we cannot just have large numbers of people who can't really buy anything."

While oil is the biggest money earner for Nigeria, it's other sectors that have kept the economy growing by 7% a year and created jobs and wages – led by telecoms, manufacturing and construction.

Okonjo-Iweala sees future growth coming from non-oil minerals yet to be exploited – zinc, copper, bitumen, tantalite and gemstones – and from its best-loved industry: Nollywood.

Going by the number of movies made – as opposed to box office earnings – Nigeria's film industry ranks second only to Bollywood, with Hollywood a distant third. Monetizing that output is the next step, says Okonjo-Iweala.

"It's amazing to me," she says, "when I'm in the Caribbean, people say are you Nigerian? We've been watching your movies. The potential to service the black diaspora and beyond is amazing, we've only just begun to plumb that."

"Nigeria has the potential to be another California."[8]

Stocks Box: The Dangotes

Company & Trading Platform	Description	Average Annual Return	Price–Earnings Ratio	Price–Book Ratio/ NAV	Return on Equity	Gross Dividend Yield	Market Value ($m)	Top Holders %
Dangote Cement Nigerian Stock Exchange	Nigeria's biggest company; Africa's No.1 cement producer	30.2% since listing 2010	16.5	5.4	34.3%	3.9%	17,160	Dangote Industries 92.8% Aliko Dangote 0.2% Free float 7.0%
Dangote Sugar Nigerian Stock Exchange	Nigeria's biggest sugar producer	0.5% since listing 2007	8.2	N/A	N/A	8.6%	468	Dangote Industries 67.7% Dangote Aliko 5.4% Free float 26.8%

Source: Data compiled by Bloomberg as of December 2014

Investor Analysis: Aberdeen's Kevin Daly on Nigeria

Bottom Line

- International oil companies are continuing to sell their **onshore oil** operations to indigenous companies as they shift their focus to offshore exploration. While offshore has higher lifting costs at $20–25 a barrel versus $6–10 for onshore, there's less risk of pipeline theft.
- **Oil theft** remains a big concern, with the estimate of lost annual revenues ranging from $6–12 billion.
- Prospective **oil industry investment** through Dangote and other companies could reach $100 billion. The long-awaited Petroleum Industry Bill is to set the ground rules.

Buy/Sell Triggers

* Nigeria is the one country in Africa you could see having its international credit rating increased to **investment grade** over the next ten years. Improvement in its debt relative to GDP along with a current account surplus and already pretty strong foreign-currency reserves could boost the rating and spur a rally for the bonds.
* Plans to increase **electricity output** are moving ahead. This will be a positive driver for growth over the medium to long term.
* A further sustained collapse in the price of **oil** is by far the biggest risk.

Endnotes

1. Bala-Gbogbo, E. (2012) Nigeria faces prolonged fuel shortages on import disruptions, Bloomberg News.
2. Rachovich, A., Rachovich, D. (2011) World's top 21 largest oil refineries, Petroleum Insights. Available at: http://petroleuminsights.blogspot.co.uk/2011/02/worlds-top-21-largest-oil-refineries.html#.U2dH3_ldUuc.
3. Associated Press (2014) Nigeria, Africa's biggest oil producer, dogged by fuel shortages blamed on corruption. Available at: http://www.foxnews.com/world/2014/04/05/nigeria-africa-biggest-oil-producer-dogged-by-fuel-shortages-blamed-on/.
4. Bala-Gbogbo, E. (2012) Nigeria faces prolonged fuel shortages on importers' poor credit, Bloomberg News. Available at: http://www.bloomberg.com/news/2012-11-14/nigeria-faces-prolonged-fuel-shortages-on-importers-poor-credit.html.
5. Omisore, B. (2014) Nigerians face fuel shortages in the shadow of plenty, *National Geographic*. Available at: http://news.nationalgeographic.com/news/energy/2014/04/140411-nigeria-fuel-shortage-oil/.
6. Adegoke, O. (2014) Meet the couple behind Nigeria's largest steel sheet factory, Ventures. Available at: http://www.ventures-africa.com/2014/02/bonds-of-steel-kam-industries-a-new-mega-factory-for-nigeria/.
7. UN News Center (2013) World population projected to reach 9.6 billion by 2050 – UN Report. Available at: http://www.un.org/apps/news/story.asp?NewsID=45165#.U2e1Y_ldUuc.
8. Anonymous (2009) Nigeria surpasses Hollywood as World's second largest film producer, UN News Centre. Available at: http://www.un.org/apps/news/story.asp?NewsID=30707#.U1lWKvldUud.

CHAPTER 7

Egypt

I – Revolution II

*The biggest enemy of the regime is if life goes back to normal and people
start asking why they wasted three years of their life on a revolution when
nothing very much has changed.*

Wael Ziada
Head of Research
EFG Hermes

I land in Cairo on the anniversary of Egypt's uprising against three decades
of military dictatorship – the revolution that inspired rebellions from Bahrain
to Libya and Syria.

The mood is tense. Four bombs have exploded here in the past 48 hours.[1]

In Tahrir – or Liberation – Square, the central thoroughfare for the Arab
world's biggest city, barbed wire blocks every entry and exit point.

Soldiers watch nervously.

In front of them, a carnival plays out into the evening.

Patriotic music blasts from cars draped with flags and pictures of Abdel
Fattah el-Sisi, the army general turned president. Men dance and clap, women
sit on plastic chairs with picnics.

"I am so happy with the new Egypt," says Mohamed, standing with his
two infant daughters, their faces daubed in red, white and black. They pose
for my camera making victory signs, the girls struggling to hold up an el-Sisi
poster bigger than them.

"We came here to celebrate with the people," he says. "This is the most
beautiful country in the whole world. Our hopes are with el-Sisi."

Those less enamored with the new Egypt have been kept well away – over
a thousand of them arrested and 49 killed in clashes with security forces.

After the 2011 uprising came the "Second Revolution" when el-Sisi's army
deposed Egypt's first democratically elected civilian government in July 2013.[2]
President Mohamed Morsi was jailed on charges ranging from inciting murder
by breaking up demonstrations against his Muslim Brotherhood government, to
conspiring with Hamas and Hezbollah to commit terrorism, and killing guards
in a jailbreak during the overthrow of ex-President Hosni Mubarak.[3]

In the polarized political climate, those questioning the second revolution are terrorist conspirators. Twenty journalists from Al-Jazeera TV including an Australian and Canadian were imprisoned days before the anniversary
on allegations they were making up stories to harm national security.[4,5]
A Facebook page "CNN Supports Terrorism" and Twitter hashtag

#CNN_STOP_Lying_About_Egypt reflected official indignation at head-
lines describing the 2013 overthrow as a "coup" – a loaded term as it would
have meant the USA automatically halting aid.[6]

Heading from the el-Sisi fiesta I meet Hasan, a 22-year-old walking
home from his shift as a mobile phone services operator for Etisalat. Proudly
he shows me the spot where in 2011 protestors stood before water cannons
to block army trucks, their images beamed around the world.

"What I can't understand now," he says, "is why the international media
has turned against Egypt." My taxi driver from the airport made the same
remark.

The concern outsiders have, I tell him, is that the democracy you stood
here and fought for is being swept away under the cloak of a crackdown on
terrorism.

"But that's not true," says Hasan. "The army will never have so much
power again, and if they do, the people will just rise up again."

Before 2011, Egypt's most significant uprising was the "bread riots" of
1977, triggered by the rising cost of flour, cooking oil and other staples. The
demands of the people forced President Anwar Sadat to reinstate subsidies.
Then the army cracked down on the demonstrators, killing 80, injuring 800
and imprisoning over a thousand.[7]

But that was 15 years before Hasan was born. Abdu, a father of three
scratching a living as a multilingual guide for the dwindling number of tourists to Cairo, has a longer memory.

"For the first time in my life, I could say what I wanted, I was free," he
says. "Where is our democracy now?"

The Muslim Brotherhood used to provide donations to his children's
school, he says. "They were good people."

It's not a commonly heard view. To Hasan, the army rescued Egypt from
an inept and dangerous administration that had perverted democracy. The
Brotherhood came to power telling Muslims if they didn't vote for them
they might not go to heaven. Morsi appointed inexperienced rank and file
Brothers to key government positions, ignoring calls for a more inclusive
government, while widespread union strikes shut down entire industries.
Economic growth slumped to the slowest in 20 years, barely keeping pace
with population increases, as the stock market sank to half its 2008 peak.[8–11]

After his ousting, the financial markets rallied as monarchies in the Per-
sian Gulf region poured in $15 billion of aid, relieved to see the back of a
party regarded as a threat for bringing in political Islam via the ballot box.[12]
The only Gulf country to support the Muslim Brotherhood government was
Qatar – the owner of Al-Jazeera.

Even with the Gulf aid, Egypt's real economy remains weak. A quarter of youths are unemployed.[13] Government subsidies on bread and fuel pushed the budget deficit to an unsustainable 14% of gross domestic product. Yet el-Sisi has enjoyed rock God status – his face emblazoned on cookies, chocolates and women's pajamas.[14] Officials at the May 2014 election claimed el-Sisi won more than 96% of votes, and his sole opponent, Hamdeen Sabahy, 3.9%.[15] Meanwhile, hundreds of Muslim Brotherhood supporters have been sentenced to life imprisonment or death on charges relating to violence around Morsi's ousting.[16]

"As long as the Muslim Brotherhood are seen as terrorists, people will support the military," says Wael Ziada, the head of research at EFG Hermes, Egypt's biggest investment bank. "The biggest enemy of the regime is if life goes back to normal and people start asking why they wasted three years of their life on a revolution when nothing very much has changed."

Top Down Data

Country	Population	GDP on PPP Basis ($)	GDP/Capita on PPP ($)	Inflation (% pa)	Unemployment (%)
Egypt	86,895,099	551,400,000,000	6600	9.0	13.4
Nigeria	177,155,754	478,500,000,000	2800	8.7	23.9
Vietnam	93,421,835	358,900,000,000	4000	6.8	1.3
Argentina	43,024,374	771,000,000,000	18,600	20.8	7.5
Romania	21,729,871	288,500,000,000	14,400	3.2	7.3
Myanmar	55,746,253	111,100,000,000	1700	5.7	5.2
Kenya	45,010,056	79,900,000,000	1800	5.8	40.0

Source: CIA World Factbook, December 2014

[1] Population data from July 2014 estimates.
[2] GDP at purchasing power parity (PPP) exchange rates is the sum value of all goods and services produced in the country valued at prices prevailing in the USA, based on 2013 estimates.
[3] GDP per capita (PPP) divided by population, based on 2013 estimates.
[4] Inflation rate shows the annual percentage change in consumer prices in 2013.
[5] Unemployment rate shows the percentage of the labor force without jobs. Data from 2013 estimates, except for Nigeria (2011) and Kenya (2008).

Endnotes

1. Kirkpatrick, D.D. (2014) Clashes kill 49 Egyptians on uprising's anniversary, *New York Times*. Available at: http://www.nytimes.com/2014/01/26/world/middleeast/egypt.html.

2. Cofman, T. (2005) The 2005 Egyptian elections: How free? How important? Saban Center for Middle East Policy at the Brookings Institution. Available at: http://www.brookings.edu/research/papers/2005/08/24middleeast-wittes

3. Anonymous (2014) Lawyers for Egypt's Morsi walk out of latest trial, BBC News Middle East. Available at: http://www.bbc.co.uk/news/world-middle-east-26214732.

4. Anonymous (2014) Canadian Mohamed Fahmy among Al-Jazeera staff charged in Cairo, CBC News. Available at: http://www.cbc.ca/news/world/canadian-mohamed-fahmy-among-al-jazeera-staff-charged-in-cairo-1.2515275.

5. Loveluck, L. (2014) Why Al Jazeera's journalists are being targeted in Egypt, Global Post. Available at: http://www.globalpost.com/dispatch/news/regions/middle-east/140202/al-jazeera-journalists-targeted-egypt.

6. El Sharnoubi, O. (2013) 'Revolution not coup': Anti-Morsi Egyptians tell CNN, AhramOnline. Available at: http://english.ahram.org.eg/NewsContent/1/64/75881/Egypt/Politics-/Revolution-not-coup-AntiMorsi-Egyptians-tell-CNN.aspx.

7. Egyptians riot in the streets in 1977, CBSNews.com. Available at: http://www.cbsnews.com/news/egyptians-riot-in-the-streets-in-1977/.

8. Anonymous (2012) Muslim Brotherhood bribing voters as Egypt chooses new leader. Available at: http://rt.com/news/egypt-president-elections-fraud-026/.

9. Anonymous (2013) Who's who: Egypt's new ministers, AhramOnline. Available at: http://english.ahram.org.eg/News/70884.aspx.

10. El-Tablawy, T., Shahine, A. (2013) Egypt replaces finance minister as cabinet shuffle announced, Bloomberg News. Available at: http://www.businessweek.com/news/2013-05-07/egypt-replaces-finance-minister-as-cabinet-shuffle-announced.

11. Lynch, D., Marroushi, N. (2013) Workers adding to Egyptian chaos as strike wave disrupts economy, Bloomberg News. Available at: http://www.bloomberg.com/news/2013-02-27/workers-adding-to-egyptian-chaos-as-strike-wave-disrupts-economy.html.

12. Shahine, A., Carey, G. (2014) Saudi King sees Egypt too big to fail under friendly general, Bloomberg News. Available at: http://www.bloomberg.com/news/2014-01-15/saudi-king-sees-egypt-too-big-to-fail-under-sympathetic-generals.html.

13. Anonymous (2014) Youth unemployment rises to 29% in 2014: CAPMAS, Cairo Post. Available at: http://thecairopost.com/news/121714/news/youth-unemployment-rises-to-29-in-2014-capmas.

14. Anonymous (2013) Women's 'Sisi pajamas' hit the Egyptian market, Al Arabiya News. Available at: http://english.alarabiya.net/en/variety/2013/11/30/Women-s-Sisi-pajamas-hit-the-Egyptian-market.html.

15. Anonymous (2014) Egypt declares El-Sisi winner of presidential election, CNN. Available at: http://edition.cnn.com/2014/06/03/world/africa/egypt-presidential-election/.

16. Anonymous (2014) Egypt court sentences two Mohamed Morsi supporters to death, *Economic Times*. Available at: http://economictimes.indiatimes.com/news/international/world-news/egypt-court-sentences-two-mohamed-morsi-supporters-to-death/articleshow/41169582.cms.

II – Cleopatra

The political temperature started rising on the streets of Cairo in 2010, influenced by a record heat wave in Russia and Ukraine.

Egyptians, with their love of pitta, are the world's biggest importers of wheat. As scorched fields caused grain prices to double and Russia to halt exports, the Mubarak administration struggled to keep state-owned bakeries stocked with enough subsidized flour for the 220 million loaves demanded every day.[1] Bread queues formed and protests followed.

While Egypt does grow its own wheat, the higher gluten content of Russia and Ukraine's makes it better suited to soft, unleavened pittas.[2] Wheat farmers are deterred by lower prices for their disfavored local crop.

The other main staple of Egyptian life – tobacco – is almost 100% imported. Back in the 1800s, Egyptian tobacco accounted for 9% of the Treasury's earnings.[3] It was so fashionable it spawned foreign imitations like Camel and even got a mention in the tales of the legendary pipe smoker Sherlock Holmes. Egypt was persuaded to stop farming tobacco in 1890 as part of an imperialist trade deal.

These days, religious authorities have taken over from the British colonialists in maintaining the ban. Even though 38% of men are regular cigarette or shisha smokers, the tobacco plant is viewed as either makruh (to be avoided) or haram (forbidden). The former Grand Mufti of Egypt went a step further and issued a fatwa in the 90s against smoking, though few paid any attention – smoking more than doubled between 1990 and 2007. While in America and Europe restrictions on smoking in public places have helped marginalize the habit, the number of Egyptian smokers is rising by 4–5% a year. The poorest families spend more than a tenth of their income on tobacco. Egypt has gone from a leading exporter to the world's ninth largest importer.[4–9]

Most of the tobacco is turned into cigarettes and shisha molasses by the government-controlled Eastern Tobacco Co., accounting for around 80% market share. I arrive in the midday heat at the company's headquarters near the pyramids of Giza with Andrew Stobart, who's been managing emerging market equities for Baillie Gifford in Edinburgh for the past decade.

It turns out Egypt's second revolution has been good for business at the Middle East's biggest tobacco manufacturer. "The main thing has been the security situation," says Abdelrahman Eissa, the deputy head in the financial division. "The knock-on effect from increased security against terrorism is better checks against counterfeit cigarettes."

While contraband had jumped to 30% of the market, it's now come down to around 5%, according to Eissa. Authentic branded packets are stamped with an official watermark to help customs officers spot imitations.

The political and economic turmoil has been no bad thing either for Eastern. "In stressful times people don't consider cigarettes to be a choice. A simple man would buy his cigarette and not his food if that was a choice he had to make."

The tobacco is imported from China, India, America and Brazil to factories dotted around Cairo and Alexandria that churn out 82 billion cigarettes a year. The company wants to reach an optimal production level of 100 billion by 2020, says Eissa.

Although shisha is the traditional pastime here, the molasses that sit atop burning charcoal produce less than 5% of sales revenue. The biggest profit comes from retailing the likes of Marlboro and Rothmans under license from Philip Morris International and British American Tobacco, which supply the raw materials for Eastern to manufacture locally.

Among the domestic brands, Eastern's Cleopatra is the most popular by far, at least among older Egyptians. The company is working on a new brand for younger smokers. "Adolescents like to show off and it's still the prevalent mentality that smoking is cool," says Eissa. "But they don't want to be seen with these old Cleopatra cigarettes."

Women are Eastern's biggest challenge. Only 0.2% of women smoke manufactured cigarettes and 0.3% do shisha.[10] "Women in Egypt tend to find shisha has a little less stigma, so we're trying to attract more women through that."

A less ethically challenging consumer stock is Juhayna, the country's biggest dairy and fruit juice producer. In contrast to bread and tobacco, consumption of milk, yogurt and fruit juice is among the lowest worldwide. The average Egyptian eats two kilograms of yogurt a year; Moroccans eat six times that amount and Turks 15 times more.[11]

"The food habits are very bad in Egypt," says Seif Thabet, the son of Juhayna's founder, Safwan Thabet. "We eat a lot of fatty food, we smoke a lot, we use ghee in our cooking."

The World Health Organization estimates two-thirds of Egyptians are overweight, the eighth highest rate worldwide after the USA and Saudi Arabia.[12] Whereas in Vietnam, where obesity is only 5%, ordering more food than you can eat would be culturally obtuse, Egyptian hospitality is geared around loading the table with more food than can possibly be consumed. Women in Egypt are the heaviest in the world.[13] Professor Osman Galal of the International Health Program at the University of California

Los Angeles cites a "cultural preference for female plumpness."[14] Egyptians spend 40% of their wages on food.

"For a country where people love eating, dairy and fruit juice consumption is too low," says Seif, the deputy CEO to his father.

A study of Egyptian teenagers showed most were drinking three times more soda than milk.[15]

"It's all about good eye-level placing on shelves," says Seif. "We want to compete with Coke, so we keep the juices in the chilled section."

Unlike Eastern Tobacco, Juhayna uses locally grown produce for its mango, orange and other juices and has 80 dairy farms supplying milk. The company, named after a local tribe, is increasing production by 20–25% a year. A new factory will boost yogurt output from 600 kilos a day to at least 800. Juice sales jumped 76% in the year to September 2013.

Growth in Egypt's population of 85 million plays a big part in the rising demand for dairy, with 2.4 million babies born every year. Higher incomes and food awareness could push Egyptian sales to the level of Turkey or Brazil in the next few years, says Seif. "Our main strategy isn't to take share from our competitors. Our main strategy is to increase the pie."

Fund Factbox

Company & Assets in Emerging Markets	Emerging Market Fund	Performance & Peer Ranking	Portfolio Manager: Andrew Stobart
Baillie Gifford $12 billion	Baillie Gifford Emerging Markets Growth Fund	14th highest total return among 636 UK-registered global emerging market funds over 10 years at 301% (annualized 14.9%)	Andrew joined Baillie Gifford in 1991. He specialized in smaller companies in Japan and the UK before switching to emerging markets in 2007. He has specific responsibility for Latin America and the Europe, Mideast and Africa region. Andrew, 50, has an MA in Economics from Cambridge University. He lives in Edinburgh with his wife and son

Source: Data compiled by Bloomberg as of June 2014

Stocks Box: Fast-Moving Consumer Goods (FMCG) Companies

Company & Trading Platform	Description	Average Annual Return	Price–Earnings Ratio	Price–Book Ratio/ NAV	Return on Equity	Gross Dividend Yield	Market Value ($m)	Top Holders %
Eastern Tobacco Cairo Stock Exchange	Mideast's biggest tobacco manufacturer	18.4% from 2005, year of share offering	8.1	1.9	25.1%	4.9%	1225	Chemical Industries 55.0% Investec Africa 5.0% Free float 44.1%
Juhayna Food Industries Cairo Stock Exchange	Egypt's biggest dairy and fruit juice producer	55.1% since IPO in 2010	54.6	3.6	7.1%	N/A	1122	Pharoah Investment 51.0% Aberdeen 1.9 Free float 47.9%
Vinamilk Ho Chi Minh Stock Exchange	Vietnam's biggest milk producer	34.4% since listing 2006	17.4	5.5	33.2%	2.0%	4641	State Capital & Invest 37.57% Fraser & Neave 11.0% Free float 57.5%

Source: Data compiled by Bloomberg as of December 2014

Investor Analysis: Baillie Gifford's Andrew Stobart on Consumer Stocks

<u>Bottom Line</u>

- Eastern Tobacco is 55% owned by the Egyptian **government**, which needs both the tax revenues from tobacco and the dividend from the company to boost public finances.
- Its production of **foreign brands** is becoming a larger part of the total and this carries higher profit margins.
- Overall **revenue growth** is likely to be slow rather than spectacular.
- Juhayna has many of the attributes common to successful companies. Controlled by the founding Thabet family, it has **created a market** (traditionally people would buy milk in churns off the back of a cart) and now has the leading market share.
- It has built **strong brands** and continually invests in organic growth by developing production facilities and diversifying into related areas (from milk to dairy to juice and so on).
- It has established a leading national **distribution** network, where it rents refrigerators to its retail customers and, over time, can sell more products through its many sales channels.

<u>Buy/Sell Triggers</u>

- Eastern Tobacco's cash flow should increase at a faster pace than sales and allow healthy growth in the **dividend** payment.
- In the short term, Juhayna has suffered from raw material cost pressures, but in the **long run** this is likely to be a leading consumer goods company in Egypt.

Portfolio Structuring: Consumer Comes First

Whether it's Kenya, Myanmar, Vietnam or Egypt, for frontier investors the consumer *is* king.

That's because in poorer countries, an increase in income has a greater proportional effect in boosting consumer demand.

People earning less than $1000 a year can typically only afford basic, unbranded commodities. Go above this level and purchases of branded food, beverages and clothing become possible. By $5000 or $6000, most of the consumption is in branded goods. At the point when earnings start to reach developed economy levels at around $25,000, the proportionate increase in consumption from any further boost to income starts to slow.

FIGURE 7.1   S curve for passenger cars

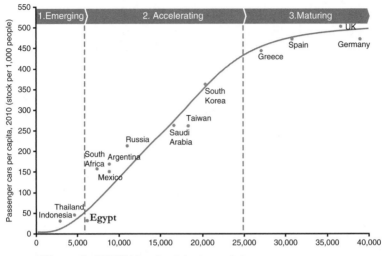

GDP per capita, 2010 (US dollars at market exchange rates)

1. Emerging	2. Accelerating	3. Maturing
Demand is still in its infancy because most consumers can't afford to buy a car – e.g. Thailand and Indonesia.	At a certain threshold (around US\$6,000), greater affordability sees demand growth outstrip increases in GDP per capita – e.g. Argentina and Mexico.	Beyond this point, increases in GDP per capita don't translate into significant demand growth – e.g. Germany and Spain.

Sources: All non-Egypt data from Egan, H., Ovanessoff, A. (2011) Gearing Up for Growth: Five Impera-tives for Success in Emerging Markets, Accenture. Available at: http://www.accenture.com/SiteCollection-Documents/Local_France/Accenture_Gearing_Up_for_Growth.pdf.

Egypt data on passenger cars per capita from GB Auto Investor Presentation, First Quarter 2014, p.10. Available at: http://ir.ghabbourauto.com/testbed/gbauto-email/earning-release/1q2014/downloads/GB%20IRP%20Investor%20Presention%201Q14.pdf. Egypt GDP data is on PPP basis, from 2013 estimates in CIA World Factbook.

The S Curve shows this pattern (Figure 7.1). Frontier markets are typically right in the high-growth portion of the S curve. Egyptian average incomes have stayed around \$6600 since 2010 while Vietnam's are about \$4000, Kenya's are \$1800 and Burmese earn \$1700.[16] Any increase can be expected to drive a spurt of consumption, whether for Juhayna's juices, Vinamilk's milk, Athi River Mining's cement or City Mart's tissues.[17,18]

Endnotes

1. Anonymous (2010) Egypt's wheat subsidy system under strain, Middle East Online. Available at: http://www.middle-east-online.com/english/?id=41084.
2. Hardy, R. (2013) Egypt, wheat and revolutions, The Globalist. Available at: http://www.theglobalist.com/egypt-wheat-and-revolutions/.
3. Hakim, T. A. (1995) International Centre for Advanced Mediterranean Agro-nomic Studies, A brief history of Egyptian agriculture, 1813–1992. Available at: http://om.ciheam.org/om/pdf/b09/CI950942.pdf.

4. Global Adult Tobacco Survey (GATS), Egypt Country Report, 2009, World Health Organization. Available at: http://www.who.int/tobacco/surveillance/ gats_rep_egypt.pdf.

5. Tobacco control laws: Explore tobacco control legislation and litigation from around the world, Campaign for Tobacco-Free Kids. Available at: http://www. tobaccocontrollaws.org/legislation/country/egypt/summary.

6. The economics of tobacco and tobacco taxation in Egypt (2010) International Union Against Tuberculosis and Lung Disease. Available at: http://global.tobac-cofreekids.org/files/pdfs/en/Egypt_Tobacco_Economics_en.pdf.

7. Tobacco education in Cairo: Is there an effect on adolescent smoking, Tobacco Control (2012). Available at: http://www.ncbi.nlm.nih.gov/pmc/articles/ PMC1759751/pdf/v008p00440a.pdf.

8. How much do you know about tobacco and the millennium development goals? Facts and figures on tobacco use in low and middle income countries, Smokefree Partnership. Available at: http://www.smokefreepartnership.eu/IMG/ pdf/Tobacco_and_the_MDGs.pdf.

9. See (3).

10. Global Adult Tobacco Survey, Egypt Country Report, 2009, World Health Organization. Available at: http://www.who.int/tobacco/surveillance/gats_rep_ egypt.pdf.

11. Consumption per capita in kg, Chart from Juhayna, citing AC Nielson data; based on Egyptian consumption at 2 kg, Moroccan at 12, Turkish at 30.

12. Country Global Obesity and Overweight Chart, Procon.org, citing World Health Organization (WHO), "Global Database on Body Mass Index: Tables," apps.who.int/bmi/index.jsp (accessed July 22, 2011). Available at: http://obesity. procon.org/view.resource.php?resourceID=004371.

13. Bloomberg Visual Data (2013) Heaviest Women: Countries. Available at: http:// www.bloomberg.com/visual-data/best-and-worst/heaviest-women-countries.

14. Galal, O. M. (2002) The nutrition transition in Egypt: Obesity, undernutrition, and the food consumption context. Available at: http://journals.cambridge.org/ download.php?file=%2FPHN%2FPHN5_1a%2FS1368980002000204a.pdf& code=0df2575139a8e3b73a840b894cced959.

15. Anonymous (2014) What we eat, Al Ahram. Available at: http://weekly.ahram. org.eg/2004/704/li1.htm.

16. The World Factbook, Central Intelligence Agency. Available at: https://www.cia. gov/library/publications/the-world-factbook/geos/eg.html.

17. The statistical pattern was developed by Roger Babson in the 1920s and Michael Howell adapted it to emerging economies in 1992.

18. Sinha, A., The S Curve, Amit Sinha, Indicus Analytics. Available at: http://www. indicus.net/blog/index.php/indian_economy/amit/the-s-curve/.

III – Sahl Hasheesh

A t the entrance to the Great Pyramid of Giza, a dozen harnessed horses and camels idle in the 35 degree heat.

Ahmed used to lead two or three treks a day around the best-known of the Seven Wonders of the World. He hasn't had a customer in a fortnight.

"Who would come to Cairo for a holiday with all the bombings and warnings of terrorism?"

He points to the Three Lions emblem on his red England football shirt. "I'm seeing so few Londoners now, I'm starting to forget my cockney." He flashes a toothless grin. "Lovely jubbly!"

Hotels reported a third fewer guests since the 2011 revolution, at 9.5 million in 2013. Tourism earnings halved to $6 billion as lower occupancies drove hoteliers to slash room rates. In Luxor, vacancies reached 99% while Red Sea resorts had 80–90% of rooms available.[1]

As in Kenya, tourism is critical to the economy, accounting for 12% of GDP and around a tenth of employment.[2]

Across the Red Sea from Sharm el-Sheikh's famous beaches is the bay of Sahl Hasheesh. In an area two-thirds the size of Manhattan, developers are busy building a new town of hotels and holiday homes. A marina, golf courses, sports clubs, shopping mall, a hospital and even a university are planned within a few years. Egyptian Resorts Company has struggled to sell the development plots and attract tenants. Its share price has tumbled from a peak of 8 Egyptian pounds in 2007 to below 2.

History, says ERC's Finance Director Wael Abou Alam, shows tourism will pick up.

"For people going to the Cairo Museum and the pyramids, definitely the numbers are affected right now," he says. "But the tourist sector has always been resilient."

It's true that even the reduced tourist numbers now are still over 50% up from the six million a decade ago. While some governments including the UK have applied travel restrictions to parts of Egypt from time to time since 2011, the Red Sea destinations like Sharm el-Sheikh and Sahl Hasheesh have been excluded from the bans because of enhanced security in these areas.[3,4]

"Security is the most crucial thing," says Abou Alam. "The economy and political stability are important to us but if you have security you can attract tourists."

Stocks Box: Egyptian Resorts vs. Frontier Developers

Company & Trading Platform	Description	Average Annual Return	Price–Earnings Ratio	Price–Book Ratio/ NAV	Return on Equity	Gross Dividend Yield	Market Value ($m)	Top Holders %
Egyptian Resorts Co. Cairo Stock Exchange	Developer building a new town in Red Sea resort of Sahl Hasheesh	93.2% since data starts 2003	N/A	1.7	-7%	N/A	180	Kato Investment 11.9% Rowad Touristic 10.0% Free float 52.0%
Vingroup Ho Chi Minh Stock Exchange	Vietnam's largest property developer & mall operator	27.4% since listing 2007	16.7	3.7	20.9%	3.0%	3293	Nhat Vuong Pham 29.1% Vietnam Inv 12.4% Free float 49.6%
New Europe Property Investments Johannesburg Stock Exchange	Developer of mostly Romanian shopping malls & office blocks	35.2% since shares issued 2009	N/A	~2 (based on co. data)	N/A	4.35%	1840	Resilient Property 9.6% Fortress Income 7.6%
Yoma Strategic Singapore Exchange	Biggest listed Myanmar business. Spans property, transport, autos, agriculture.	166% from 2011, when reforms paved way for sanctions easing	37.0	2.2	4.5%	N/A	703	Serge Pun 37.3% Aberdeen 7.1% Free float 62.1%

Source: Data compiled by Bloomberg as of December 2014

Investor Analysis: Baillie Gifford's Andrew Stobart on Egyptian Resorts Co.

Bottom Line

- Egyptian Resorts Company describes itself as the country's "leading developer of **mega communities**." It's trying to attract Egyptians by creating more than just a honeymoon destination.
- After first acquiring land in 1995, hotels and apartments started going up in 2007. While progress has slowed recently because of the political uncertainty, it has benefited from close **relations** with the government.

Buy/Sell Triggers

- This is a **volatile** business with significant uncertainty and where land sales account for half of the revenue base.
- Even if Sahl Hasheesh succeeds in becoming the thriving community ERC hopes for, it's not clear how equity investors make good **returns**.

Endnotes

1. Kingsley, P. (2014) Tourist desert – Egypt desperate to woo back visitors after years of unrest, Feb. 11, 2014, *The Guardian*. Available at: http://www.theguardian.com/world/2014/feb/10/egypts-tourist-resorts-ghost-towns.
2. World Tourism Organization, Tourism Key to the Economic Recovery of Egypt. Available at: http://media.unwto.org/en/press-release/2011-05-31/tourism-key-economic-recovery-egypt.
3. Resilience, Returning Tourists and Continued Investment, Investor Presentation 3Q 2013, p. 40, ERC citing Beltone Financial.
4. Foreign Travel Advice: Egypt, Foreign & Commonwealth Office, Feb. 23, 2014. Available at: https://www.gov.uk/foreign-travel-advice/Egypt.

IV – Audacity of Hope

In Egypt's moribund economy, two things have been selling like hot cakes: flags and tuk tuks.

Demand for the black and yellow motorized rickshaws is partly the result of a micro-financing initiative from the largest automaker on North African stock markets. In a country where less than 10% of people have a bank account and even fewer have any kind of formal loan,[1] Egypt's Ghabbour Auto has started extending millions of pounds in credit and in the poorest slums.

Banks have had little incentive to lend money to people for cars or homes – let alone those in slums with no collateral to guarantee payment – because they were earning interest rates above 10% from the government on Treasury bills with less risk and work involved.

"That's the opportunity we saw," says Menatalla Sadek, GB Auto's corporate finance and investment director. "With T-bill rates so high, why should they bother testing out cars to see if they should finance them? All the banks have grown lazy."

GB Auto paid 12% interest for its capital and charged its customers around 40% for one-year hire purchase agreements. After a flat 2010, its tuk tuk sales jumped more than 50% in 2011, the year of the revolution. By 2012, the company was shifting twice the amount of four years earlier.[2]

"There are almost no defaults because this is the main source of income for the borrower," says Sadek. There's also a sense of family responsibility integral to the contract as it requires two guarantors including a female relative, she says.

"We're not a bank and that helps – it's not like you're getting a loan. You sign checks for the installments, so to the customer this is just the price you're going to pay over a year."

GB Auto assembles the tuk tuks from parts under license by Bajaj of India. The vehicles sell for 20,000 Egyptian pounds, or just under $3000, which is about a quarter of the starting cost for a new Hyundai car, for example. Each tuk tuk creates three jobs on average, or three shifts of 8 hours in a 24-hour period.

At least 16 million Egyptians live in slum areas, mostly on the outskirts of Cairo[3] where there's little or no public transport. "They can't go home without a tuk tuk," says Sadek. "This is the only product Mubarak had in his campaign. Everyone realizes that this is not only a source of transport, it's a means of existence."

The company, founded by Raouf Ghabbour and 60% owned by his family, has broadened its financing to also fund tractors, microbuses and cars. The company sells about 28% of all new cars in Egypt.[4]

Even with the introduction of credit to help buyers, auto sales at 144,000 a year are only a third of the amount in Algeria despite Egypt's population being three times larger. Egyptians have about 30 cars for every thousand people, compared with 76 in Libya, 77 in Iraq, 119 in Algeria and 165 in Jordan.[5]

"Algeria has seen its market grow in the past three years, while we have seen ours shrink," says Sadek. "We had two revolutions in three years. If we have three years of stability this is where we should get to."

Among 85 million Egyptians, probably only two million have bank accounts, an executive at Egypt's largest lender, Commercial International Bank, told us. CIB has just over half a million deposit holders but it lends to less than a third of them. Even before the revolution and the global financial crisis, a World Bank study found 87% of small- and medium-sized companies in Egypt had no access to formal finance.[6]

"The government has been borrowing at very nice rates for us, so we have been making a lot of money but it isn't by doing a lot of business," says the executive.

CIB is opening about 20 new branches a year to expand its customer base but lending won't pick up until lower government borrowing costs reduce the rate for everyone else.

"We have very few mortgages," says the executive. "If we can charge 10% or less then the door would open."

One-year Treasury bills were paying as much as 16% in 2012 as the political turmoil drove investors to increase the premium for lending to Egypt. Ratings firm Moody's cut the country's international credit score six times between 2011 and 2013 to the fifth lowest of its 21 categories (Figure 7.2).

"We had the Olympic record for downgrades," says the CIB executive. "No one wanted to put their money in Egypt."

The starting point for el-Sisi to rehabilitate Egypt's image in the market was to wean the nation off decades of energy subsidies that cost the government around $20 billion a year.[7] Within two months of the election, he hiked the price Egyptians pay for a liter of fuel by 41% and lifted the cost for taxi drivers using compressed natural gas by 175%. The president refused to approve the government's budget until the finance minister trimmed the planned fiscal deficit to 10% of GDP from 12%.[8] His administration then announced plans to double revenue from the Suez Canal through its first expansion in a century and a half. Investors were cheered. In those two months, the country's main equity index rallied 19%.[9]

Egypt will come under pressure to improve its finances from its Gulf nation creditors along with the International Monetary Fund and some of the government's own members, according to Ahmed Heikal, who oversees billions of dollars invested in Egypt, the Middle East and Africa as the

FIGURE 7.2   "Nice Rates": Egyptian Treasury Bills Yields

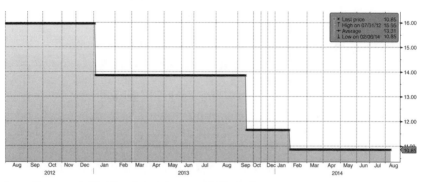

Source: Data compiled by Bloomberg. *(Function: EGPT1Y Index GP GO).*

chairman of Citadel Capital. Before the election, Citadel committed to a $3.7 billion oil refinery to halve Egypt's diesel imports.[10] Cuts to fuel subsidies were key to its profitability.

Within days of the election, the UAE minister overseeing assistance to Egypt called on el-Sisi to shore up the nation's public finances and invest in infrastructure to revive the economy.[11]

"Egypt is going into a new regime, it will create humungous opportunities," Heikal told us.

On the wall of his office, with a serene view across the Nile, is a framed letter from the former US Treasury Secretary, Larry Summers. He expresses admiration for Heikal's "audacity of hope."

Investor Analysis: Baillie Gifford's Andrew Stobart on GB Auto

Bottom Line

- GB Auto has the **leading** market share in cars in Egypt, at 30%, and a strong position in Iraq. It's expanded into selling buses and two- and three-wheelers, as well as related products such as tires, lubricants and batteries.
- It now covers the full automotive **value chain** including manufacturing, servicing and financing.
- It has a diverse range of **partners** including leading global brands – Hyundai, Mazda, Geely, Bajaj, Volvo and Goodyear.

Buy/Sell Triggers

- Given the low level of **penetration** in the country (30 cars per 1000 people), the market should grow for many years to come. It is also well placed to take advantage of opportunities in other countries in the region.
- In addition, it is strengthening its **competitive** position by improving its level of service and offering financing on attractive terms.
- A resurgent Egyptian economy is likely to have a positive impact on **demand** for passenger vehicles.

Stocks Box: Money & Cars

Company & Trading Platform	Description	Average Annual Return	Price–Earnings Ratio	Price–Book Ratio/ NAV	Return on Equity	Gross Dividend Yield	Market Value ($m)	Top Holders %
Ghabbour Auto Cairo Stock Exchange	North Africa's largest listed automaker	10.7% since IPO in 2007	22.1	2.0	9.0%	N/A	584	Ghabbour Raouf Kamal 20.6% Ghabbour Nader Raouf 12.9% Free float 37.9%
Commercial Int'l Bank (CIB) Cairo Stock Exchange	Egypt's biggest private sector bank	26.6% since IPO in 1996	13.0	3.3	27.5%	2.0%	6302	Oppenheimer Funds 4.5% Wentworth Insurance 4.4%
EFG Hermes Cairo Stock Exchange	Leading Egyptian investment bank	4.2% from 2009, year of share offering	N/A	1.2	–1.7%	N/A	1531	DF EFG 1 11.7% Rahman Abdel 7.7% Free float 72.9%

Source: Data compiled by Bloomberg as of December 2014

Investor's Notebook: EFG Hermes Co-CEO
Karim Awad

- Egypt's biggest publicly traded investment bank is focusing on increasing its presence outside of the country. The proportion of fees and commissions EFG Hermes earned from the Middle East and North Africa region **beyond Egypt** doubled to 40% in the first nine months of 2013 from a year earlier.[12] By 2018, probably 60% of the investment bank's revenue will come from outside of Egypt through brokerage, advisory, private equity and asset management services.
- As for Egypt, the fundamentals are there for **recovery**. "There is a depth of industry here that's probably as large as anywhere else in the Arab world. It's not an economy that's built just on, let's say, the real estate sector but there is also a large contracting sector, a very large industrial sector, services and so on. People are looking closely, seeing when the best entry point is."

Investor Analysis: Baillie Gifford's Andrew Stobart
on Financial Stocks

Bottom Line

- **Banking penetration** in Egypt is low, with household debt equivalent to 8% of GDP. The mortgage market is nascent.
- CIB is a **well-run** bank, with a good record on credit quality and a focus on cost control. It has an impressive list of corporate clients and a growing base of SME and individual customers.
- Citadel Capital is an investment **holding company** with interests across the region but a strong bias to Egypt. The thesis behind many of the holdings is to have dollar revenues and mainly Egyptian pound costs and borrowings. CEO Ahmed Heikal and other employees own 27% of the equity and so are aligned with other shareholders. Dividend pay-out ratios will be high.
- Despite being a listed entity, EFG Hermes has a **partnership-like** culture, with strong loyalty among its employees, reflected in its success.

New management is focused on reducing the cost base to protect profits in a weak environment. They now use only half the space in the new HQ they moved into in 2010 and are looking to rent out the other half, for example. The bank is returning cash to shareholders in the form of a share buy-back, and aims to improve return on equity (ROE).

Buy/Sell Triggers

- Banks often represent an attractive way of getting **exposure** to an economy. CIB is a good example of this. With stability and a growing economy, confidence should improve, generating greater demand for credit and boosting CIB's profits. Falling interest rates would accelerate this process.
- Citadel is a fascinating company with some potentially very exciting invest-ments. **Hope** will reap rewards one day, but a lot of things outside Citadel's control need to happen before it does.
- EFG has **survived** all that regional markets and economies could throw at it. It remains a highly operationally geared play on ongoing expansion in financial activity in the MENA region. As well as restructuring, EFG will look to play to its strengths and grow the business.

Bond Box: Egyptian Government Debt

Security & Trading Platform	Asset Description	Maturity / Amount Outstanding	Average Annual Price Change	Coupon/ Interest	Yield
Arab Republic of Egypt	Sovereign Dollars	2016–2040	–2.25% since issued in 2010	5.75%	4.1%
Euroclear/ Clearstream		Among the larger bonds is a $1 billion issue due in 2020			

Source: Data compiled by Bloomberg as of December 2014

Stocks Box: ETFs

Security / Trading Platform	Issuer Description	Average Annual Return	Top 10 Index Holdings	
Market Vectors Egypt Index ETF New York Stock Exchange	ETF incorporated in the U.S. with objective to replicate as closely as possible, before fees and expenses, the price and yield performance of the Market Vectors Egypt Index	−4.4% since inception in 2010	Commercial Int'l Bank	8.9%
			Global Telecom Holding	7.2%
			EFG-Hermes	7.1%
			Talaat Moustafa Group	6.9%
			Telecom Egypt	6.2%
			Six of October Dev't	5.4%
			Juhayna Food	5.1%
			ElSwedy Electric Co.	5.0%
			Egypt Kuwait Holding Co SAE	4.9%
			Orascom Telecom Media An	4.7%

Source: Data compiled by Bloomberg as of December 2014

Investor Analysis: Baillie Gifford's Andrew Stobart on Egypt

Bottom Line

- Egypt's economic **problems** aren't new: significant and distorting subsidies, particularly for fuel; a large fiscal deficit and a current account deficit made worse by the collapse in tourism; inflation at 10% plus; a crawling currency peg regime which inflates the value of the Egyptian pound; low foreign reserves; and under-investment because of the political turmoil.
- There are many **positives** too. The population is sizeable and young; wages are low by regional standards (minimum wage EGP700/month or $100/month); and the starting position is low, with expectations for Egypt subdued and investment in particular very depressed in light of the political situation.
- For too long Egyptian governments have shied away from confronting the long-term problems. The two main contributors to the fiscal **deficit** are interest payments and subsidies.

- The UAE, Saudi Arabia and Kuwait will continue to fund the country. It's unclear what conditions, if any, have been attached to their grants. Such a situation is **unsustainable** in the long run.

Buy/Sell Triggers

- The **fiscal deficit** looms over the economy and will break Egypt unless the authorities begin to address it. The government is beginning to focus on the fuel subsidy problem, which is an encouraging start. Additional reforms would drive a virtuous circle of improved confidence towards Egypt, a more favorable investment climate, increasing tourism, more job creation, a better fiscal position and sustainable GDP growth approaching 5%.
- There are arguably parallels between Egypt now and Turkey in the 1970s, with similar levels of GDP per capita and secular military leaderships encountering Islamic-leaning governments. Stronger GDP and particularly increasing income levels will help the potential for a shift to **inclusive democracy**.
- El-Sisi's war on terror will continue to foment the **radical terrorism** it resolves to destroy. Egypt has a weak institutional framework, such that the risk is a return to the crony capitalism of the Mubarak era.
- Egypt will continue to be a **white knuckle ride** but seems likely to enjoy a better macro-economic outcome than the doomsayers predict.

Endnotes

1. Number of bank accounts estimated at 8 million, number of unique account holders estimated at 2 million, estimate from executive at CIB.
2. Investor Presentation, Third Quarter 2013, p.14, GB Auto; sales increased from 36,615 FY08 to 61,722 FY11 and 68,527 FY12.
3. Khalifa, D. (2013) Egypt's slum crisis persists amid housing abundance, Ahram Online. Available at: http://english.ahram.org.eg/NewsContent/3/12/62321/Business/Economy/Egypts-slum-crisis-persists-amid-housing-abundance.aspx.
4. Investor Presentation, Third Quarter 2013, p.13, GB Auto.
5. GB Auto Investor Presentation, First Quarter 2014, p.10. Available at: http://ir.ghabbourauto.com/testbed/gbauto-email/earning-release/1q2014/downloads/GB%20IRP%20Investor%20Presention%201Q14.pdf.
6. Nasr, S. (2006) Access to finance and economic growth in Egypt, World Bank. Available at: http://siteresources.worldbank.org/INTEGYPT/Resources/Access_to_Finance.pdf .
7. Figure from Wael Ziada at EFG-Hermes.

8. Anonymous (2014) Pharaonic frailties, *The Economist*. Available at: http://www. economist.com/news/finance-and-economics/21607850-new-regime-attempts-foster-growth-pharaonic-frailties.

9. Said, S., Parasie, N. (2014) Egypt's Suez Canal expansion plan raises some questions, *Wall Street Journal*. Available at: http://blogs.wsj.com/middleeast/2014/08/10/ egypts-suez-canal-expansion-plan-raises-some-questions/.

10. Namatalla, A. (2012) Citadel capital closes $3.7 billion financing for refinery, Bloomberg News. Available at: http://www.bloomberg.com/news/2012-06-14/ citadel-capital-closes-3-7-billion-financing-for-refinery-1-.html.

11. Habboush, M., Fam, M. (2014) U.A.E. urges Egypt to trim budget as Gulf aid pours in, Bloomberg News. Available at: http://www.bloomberg.com/ news/2014-06-05/u-a-e-urges-egypt-fiscal-consolidation-to-help-revive-economy.html.

12. Investor Presentation, Third Quarter 2013, p. 16, EFG Hermes.

V – Zahma!

On my last day in Cairo, I leave Andrew at the hotel and take a walk to the Egyptian Museum close by Tahrir Square.

I cross the 15th of May Bridge (Egypt's maps are a compendium of Arab–Israeli War dates) to a bustling clothes market stocked with "I Love New York" sweaters and thick overcoats.[1] Then I hook back toward the Nile along a narrow alley with dark shisha cafes and a crumbling butcher's shop attracting only flies to the hunks of camel meat hung outside.

Approaching the white bulk of the Maspero state TV tower, a barbed-wire mesh road block is now partially pulled aside to let pedestrians pass.[2] On my right is the lush green lawn of a security compound. Beyond the perimeter railing next to me, a soldier with a rifle slung around his shoulder rustles in the bushes. I walk a few paces further and stop cold.

Ten meters from the barbed-wire barricade, next to the security compound, a man lies curled on the ground, his arms shielding his face.

I'd seen people sleeping rough in the streets in Cairo – one man the night before on the side of a road surrounded by onions ready to sell when he woke up – but this is midday, by a military road block.

Four people walk by, stepping around him.

Checking if he's alright or calling for medical help doesn't seem a safe option, so my instinct is to go for the next best alternative: I look to document it.

I don't see any soldiers or police watching so I quickly unzip my backpack and grab my auto-focus camera, take a snap behind my knee without looking, and stow it back in my bag.

Immediately a man marches toward me, holding up his palm, beckoning for my camera.

"What are you taking a photo of?" he demands.

We're about 15 meters from the man on the ground.

Edging to a point where he's out of view, I point vaguely. "I was just taking a photo of the road block."

The man, dressed in jeans and a dark sweater, presses the play button on my camera with one hand while ushering me to a group of soldiers and police seated on plastic chairs by the roadside.

The camera passes between them. The man on the ground is a pin prick on the tiny screen of my camera. "Why are you taking photos?" one of the men asks. "Are you a journalist? What are you doing here?"

My time in Cairo had mostly been spent meeting company executives and financial analysts, though I'd also spent a day with a TV crew recording interviews for a news broadcast.

"I was just on my way to the Egyptian Museum and was taking some pictures along the way," I reply. "I've been in business meetings all this week and doing the tourist thing now."

"Where are you from?" he asks, now scrolling through my pictures of the crowds and soldiers on Tahrir Square a week earlier.

"I'm from England."

"Would you take photos of soldiers in England?"

"Well, actually, yes."

"Are you a Muslim or Christian?"

Given the limited choice available I opt for Christian.

"Show me your passport."

I deliberately left my passport in the hotel safe for security, so I offer my driver's license.

"Unzip your bag."

He pulls out my reporter's notepad and leafs through the pages. "What's this?"

"It's just notes from my meetings with companies, for my research."

His finger hovers over words like "Mubarak," "jailed" and "bombings."

"Why would you write about these things?"

I explain that the notes relate to a company I'd met. It had a change of management to remove executives connected with Hosni Mubarak, though in the end only Mubarak and his sons were tried in court and jailed. Then we discussed how the terrorist bombings are causing road blocks around the city, disrupting business, I tell him.

"What language is this?"

"It's shorthand."

They confer briefly until one in a green woolen jumper and dark glasses stands up. "Come this way."

We walk a few yards to a café. The policeman sits down at a table, takes a puff of shisha and then offers it to me. We smoke for ten minutes in silence. Then a black car with blacked out windows pulls up. I'm hustled into the back seat. We weave eastward from the Nile for five minutes and arrive at a black metal gate. A guard salutes and we pass into a sandy courtyard. I'm led up a steel external staircase and along a dusty corridor. At the end is a jail with a rusty grill and shiny padlock. An old man in a traditional white tunic paces about inside.

We stop at a room halfway along. The policeman sits in a leather executive chair and beckons me to sit opposite, offering a Marlboro red.

A guy in his 20s wearing a royal blue jersey with shoulder pads in the style of 80s ladieswear sits next to me. He speaks a little more English than my silent host.

He takes rudimentary details – name, age, nationality, occupation. Mindful I'm in the country ranked the most dangerous for reporters after Syria and Iraq by the Committee to Protect Journalists, I err on the side of caution: Financial research.[3]

We wait. Several men come and go with reports for the older cop. Then he pops out through a frosted glass door behind his desk and kneels facedown on a prayer mat. Like many observant Egyptian men he has a carpet burn on his forehead known as a zabeeba, or raisin. The Samsung mobile he's left on his desk plays Koranic verse for a ringtone.

He returns and the two officers chat as cartoons play on a TV. "What's happening?" I ask.

"We get someone speak English more good."

A man in a bell boy's beige uniform with a bronze badge saying Mohamed appears. He asks me the same questions and then pores through my notebook.

Finally he asks, "so why aren't you staying my hotel?" It's welcome humor.

I'm led to another room while the bell boy conveys his findings. I've been detained three hours now and I'm thinking my wife will start worrying soon if I'm not back at our hotel. This was the one trip in the entire project Jules came along for. She was last here in 1976 when tensions were high in the run-up to the bread riots. Her memories are of cockroaches on the walls, mass street protests and nightclubs being bombed.

Egypt is also the only place other than Myanmar where my mobile refuses to work, leaving me reliant on email via my Blackberry.

I needn't have fretted about reaching Jules. I'm called back to the chief's office. I'm to leave my backpack at the police station and collect my passport from the hotel. Along with my room key, I quickly snatch my wallet and press ID card.

My escort is a beefy guy in a gray track suit with a likeness to Popeye's Bluto. He leads me out of the police compound and hails an equally burly bloke on a scooter. Bluto motions for me to hop on and then to move closer to the driver. He then swings on behind me.

Crushed between two beefcakes with legs at right angles and my heels clinging to the foot rest, we heave out of the compound. We're saluted as we go along the wrong side of the road, through the market, my knees under my shorts brushing the winter coats.

We arrive at the grandeur of the Marriott but the hotel security guards aren't convinced by these plain-clothed cops and demand ID. Bluto huffs and eventually pulls out a crumpled business card from his trackies with no photo. Linking my arm, he leads me inside.

By now it's 4 pm so I explain that I need to let my wife know where I am. He agrees. We trek to the pool, arm-in-arm, trailed by the bike driver and two Marriott staff. Somehow hotel security manage to talk the police out of actually walking up to the poolside, but Jules knows immediately by my face something's wrong. I show her my phone with security numbers to call if they decide to arrest me.

Back at the station I wait. Two teenagers are sent to keep an eye on me. One in skinny jeans and flip flops offers me a cigarette. I decline but he seems so insulted I quickly say "shukran," figuring it's best to keep everyone on side. He tries to tell me something important. He makes a noise like a machine gun and then points two fingers at his head and jolts it back.

What, here? I ask, pointing my index finger down. He nods.

Then he seems to mime putting on a back pack. "Money!" he says, rubbing his fingertips, before waving his hand snake-like toward the door.

If it's a plan to get me out I'm not convinced, given the chief has my passport and I'm meant be going through security checks at the airport tomorrow morning for Saudi Arabia. But I also don't want to get on the wrong side of him and need to be open to the idea that his boss may be in on the plan, so I nod agreeably.

Then he pulls out a tiny silver revolver. It has an infrared beam. He points it to make a dot on his friend's forehead and pulls the trigger. He laughs hysterically. It's a cigarette lighter.

Six prisoners walk by in the corridor straight into the 2-meter-square cell. They crouch on their feet, talking urgently.

Having just snuffed out my laugh-a-minute guard's cigarette and trying to remoisten my dried out tongue, his mate comes over with another. By now I know not to refuse.

I catch the green sweater of the police chief flash by, so I move to the door. He flaps a hand to say they're working on it. In his office across the corridor I can hear the TV flipping through news channels. Now I'm on edge partly because my recording from the week is scheduled to play around 6 o'clock and the last thing I need is to pop up on their TV screen. But mostly because they've had my passport for two hours, they've had a chance to look more closely at the photo on my camera and I'm guessing the police will clock off soon, which means releasing me or keeping me in overnight.

I've been careful to keep my Blackberry out of sight to avoid the police snooping through my emails, but while the boys are goofing about in the corridor I quickly check. Jules – aware they could be combing through my emails by now – just sends a kiss, "u ok?" My company's security asks innocuously for my itinerary for the rest of the week. I fill both in on the latest situation.

By 7 o'clock I'm pacing by the door. "Five minutes, five minutes," says a guy in a white cotton shirt and jeans who I haven't seen before. Ten minutes later he escorts me down the staircase and across the dusty yard to the main part of the police station.

It's dark. I don't know whether I'm being led to the gate or the prison.

He talks with a group of seven officers in black uniform and hands them my passport.

"Where you from?" asks one, thumbing through the pages. "Ah, England. I like Chelsea!"

We swap football names for a few minutes until the white-shirt guy returns. He takes my passport back from the policeman, hands it to me and makes a horizontal clap to show the matter is finished.

I try to look nonplussed and ask for my backpack. "No, nothing else," he says. "That's it."

I insist I need my back pack, doing the same mime of putting it on my shoulder as my teenage warden, so he leads me back up the stairs toward the cell. My camera and notepad are safely inside.

I walk out as fast as I can without breaking into a run. I'm disorientated and use tall buildings as my compass to get to a main road. I hail taxis, tuk tuks, any passing car to get me away.

A white cab stops. I'm in an emotional state. I tell the driver, who doesn't speak a word of English, what happened – "man down," I say, and then motion taking a photo and point at the police building.

He shakes his head and hands me a cigarette. "Zahma!" He points his finger in a circle. "Gaysh, gaysh, gaysh, gaysh!" These are two words of Arabic I've picked up by now: Madness! Army, army, army, army! As soon as my cigarette's out the window he hands me another, and writes his name and mobile number for me should I need him.

Back in my room, Jules and Eddie, the cameraman I was with earlier in the week, have been running a military operation of their own, coordinating with the UK Foreign Office and the local embassy, and security and legal agents in New York, London and Dubai.

After a hug, Jules scolds me for stinking of tobacco and being stupid enough to take a photo. I show her the picture, zooming in on the man on the ground. She cries. I choke back tears and order double brandies from room service.

"Nothing's changed, it's just the same as '76," she says.

"No," says Eddie, shaking his head at the floor. "It's worse."

Endnotes

1. First Arab–Israel War: 15 May 1948, PalestineHistory.com. Available at: http://www
.palestinehistory.com/history/war/war1948.htm.
2. Maspero: A Massacre of Christians in Egypt, Dec. 15, 2013, 60 Minutes Overtime, CBS News. Available at: http://www.cbsnews.com/news/maspero-a-massacre-
of-christians-in-egypt/.
3. Abou Bakr, S. (2014) Journalism in Egypt, a dangerous business, *Daily News Egypt*.
Available at: http://www.dailynewsegypt.com/2014/01/26/journalism-in-egypt-
a-dangerous-business/.

CHAPTER 8

Saudi Arabia

I – Virtue and Vice

Attempting to bring standup comedy to Saudi Arabia, Yaser Bakr sketches the scene at his country's first aquarium. The dolphins are the star attraction but after a few days in Saudi Arabia, they're swimming up to shows 15 minutes late, growing too fat for their hoops and their smiley faces turn serious.

It's a recognizable stereotype. In place of in-flight entertainment between Cairo and Riyadh, an imam intones to images of a mosque and Koranic script. The call to prayer echoes around the immigration hall as we line up at passport control. Women, dressed head to toe in black, are in a separate queue. When we've stood for over an hour the officer in front of us shuts his booth for a break. We're left waiting until he decides to return half an hour later. The men huff but no one dares speak out loud.

This is the border crossing I've been dreading the most since filling out my visa application: name, religion, sect, mother's maiden name. As an agnostic Ashkenazi Jew I seek advice from an agency in Riyadh. "They shouldn't discriminate, but if you want it processed quickly . . ." So I write: "Christian, Church of England, Lieberman." Oy vey!

I'm silently rehearsing my lines as I finally reach the officer. I hand over my British passport and the man jabbers at me in Arabic. I tell him I don't understand. "Why come if no speak Arabic?" he sneers while stamping my passport.

At baggage reclaim the conveyer belt has long since spat out my suitcase, so I grab it from a pile and head for the customs gate. The warning that anyone found with drugs faces death is a tad disconcerting given my case has been left unattended for over an hour.

Outside a London black cab awaits with all the leg room to park your luggage at your feet. But the familiarity ends there as we career off, jerking between traffic lanes, my suitcase swinging around on its wheels.

A white train on a mono rail glides serenely by in the desert, its two carriages empty. I wonder aloud why I didn't get the train from the airport to town. I'd have had a long wait, says the cabbie. The mono rail is for a women-only university.[1] The government is just starting work now on a train line to connect its cities.[2]

Infrastructure in the world's largest oil-exporting nation is surprisingly lacking. There's less rail track here than in Syria, a country a tenth of the size. Internet connectivity lags the likes of Bulgaria and Belarus. From time to time raw sewage seeps onto Jeddah's streets.[3-6] The wait I experienced at Riyadh airport is nothing unusual.

The government is responding, spending at least $7 billion on a Riyadh to Jeddah railway, $22 billion on the country's first metro system for Riyadh and $70 billion on four "economic cities" or smart zones with fast internet connections.[7–9] Tens of billions of dollars more are going on projects to boost the capacity of airports and improve water and waste sanitation. The money being shelled out is itself a draw for investors scouring for the winners of contracts and the potential unlocked when an oil-enriched population becomes better connected.

When it comes to health infrastructure, however, Saudi Arabia is already streets ahead. The World Health Organization ranks it above the USA, Canada and Australia for access to medical services. Hospitals are signposted on every road in the center of Riyadh and Jeddah.[10,11]

Saudis need all of their 500 hospitals and more. Nearly a quarter of Saudi adults are diabetic, the biggest proportion globally. For every 1000 Saudi babies, 81 have birth defects. Only Sudan ranks higher.[12,13]

While the incidence of diabetes is put down to sedentary lifestyles and unhealthy food, medics attribute birth abnormalities to marriages between cousins. A third of Saudi weddings are between first cousins and more than half are between blood relatives, according to the *Reproductive Health Journal*.[14]

Adding to the hospitals' workload is some of the craziest driving. Giant SUVs weave and clunk over metal studs inset in the roads in the vain hope of triggering awareness as drivers switch lanes. Saudis pull in front of hapless taxis without a signal. The cabbies – mostly immigrants from south Asia and north Africa – don't dare honk. A Saudi taking umbrage could seriously complicate their life. At one point I'm in a taxi stuck in traffic when a Saudi in a jeep rolls back and hits us. My Indian driver curses under his breath and drives on.

Immigrant workers typically pay a few hundred dollars a month to a Saudi who acts as their official sponsor and in theory as their employer. Many sponsors simply collect multiple fees while keeping the immigrant's passport as a guarantee they won't abscond. Domestic maids work to a similar arrangement.

Labor laws give both the employer and worker the right to end a contract at a month's notice, but in practice the odds are stacked in favor of the sponsor. A story in the *Saudi Gazette* tells of 31 mostly Sri Lankan maids held in detention after quitting their jobs and requesting deportation. The maids won't be allowed home until they compensate their sponsors for the cost of their recruitment. The Riyadh Shariah court set the payment at 43,000 riyals ($11,500) each for three of the maids. It would take them five and a half years to earn that much. The article didn't say why the women had quit.[15–18]

According to Human Rights Watch, maids are extremely vulnerable to abuse and exploitation. If they run away, they may face spurious accusations of theft, witchcraft, adultery or fornication, offences punishable by imprisonment or death. They struggle to access lawyers and translators and may be prevented from contacting their embassies.[19]

Life for immigrants became more precarious when the government tightened the visa rules to prevent workers moving between sponsors. The authorities deported a million foreigners in 2013, chartering up to a dozen planes a day for Ethiopians alone.[20]

The regulation is part of a wider campaign to get more Saudis earning their own living. Economists estimate between 60 and 70% of working age Saudis don't have a job and those who do are mostly employed by the state.[21] The spoils of oil have made many reluctant to work, cosseted by wealthy relatives and government benefits paying up to 2000 riyals ($533) a month, more than triple the average maid's wage.[22]

For women, jobs have been limited by religious decrees restricting their interaction with men.

At the Al Faisaliah mall in Riyadh's iconic tower topped with a golden glass ball, ladies and family zones enable women to shop without the risk of encountering an unmarried man. Yet, for Saudis who actually want to meet a member of the opposite sex who isn't a cousin, the malls are as good a hunting ground as any. With shops staying open late into the evening, the amorous take their chances.

Forty-five minutes before midnight a 20-something Saudi man in a white shirt and casual gray blazer presents a dozen red roses to a woman dressed in full abaya and niqab. The woman looks ecstatic as she reads the card with a girlfriend. Romeo turns on his heel and scurries down the nearest escalator. A security guard witnessing the scene radios for help. Two bearded men wearing the traditional full-length thawb and carrying prayer beads appear. The guard points in the direction Romeo headed and the religious police scuttle after him, trying to maintain a dignified pace without running. Having lost him they quick-march to the taxi rank to wait there on the chance he'll need a cab to get home.

The next morning I head away from the shiny shopping malls to the historic clay and mud-brick Masmak Fort, whose capture in 1902 by Ibn Saud began the rule of the House of Saud.

I'm stopped by a guard at the giant palm-trunk gate. "Sorry, it's families only today, come back tomorrow."

I tell the guard I'll be in Jeddah tomorrow and anyway it clearly said on the website that this was a men's day. He tells me to come back at 9:30 am to give the women an hour to take their leave. It's an interesting area and a clear blue-sky morning so I'm happy to wander around.

Outside, a small crowd is gathering. Facing the group of men are guards in beige uniforms with revolvers and batons. Next minute, three police cars and a white van arrive, sirens flashing. A dozen Saudis with red and white ghutrah on their heads stand in the middle of a square. One has a meter-long curved sword like a samurai. A prisoner in a brown thawb is led out. He kneels. The sword comes down on the back of his neck. His decapitated body is covered in a blanket and taken away on a stretcher to the white van. The guards brush their hands to show the crowd there's nothing more to see.

I talk with a young Saudi as the crowd scatters. I'd seen him discussing what was happening with the guards. The prisoner was Mohammed Ramadan, aged about 26, from Pakistan. "He was found with alcohol," he tells me.

As the white van and police envoy whisk by, the Saudi introduces himself as Salman, flashing a smile with teeth clasped in a silver brace. Salman works for his father's money-lending firm and was on his way to drop off a check. The business conforms to Shariah rules barring the payment or receipt of interest by providing the refrigerator, mobile phone or car the borrower wants to purchase rather than the money. The client pays Salman and his dad a price 20% higher after ten months.

Trying my best to affect only a passing interest, I express mild surprise that we've just witnessed a man being executed simply for possessing alcohol. "He was found drunk," says Salman. "He was not good man to have here."

In a souq across the street, every fifth stall sells ceremonial versions of the swords used in the beheading along with tunics and incense. At the end of the road a soldier stands guard on the back of a pick-up truck, thumbing his gun on a pivot. Nearby is a police station. Opposite, a line of old men sit at typewriters, slowly punching with an index finger letters for anyone in need of official paperwork.

I walk back toward the fort. The execution area, marked by removable tiles underfoot and a large drain, has been hosed down. A plaque above reads General Presidency of the Promotion of Virtue and Protection from Vice.

When I get back to my taxi, the driver is excited. "In 15 years, I've never seen a head cut," he says. "You were very lucky."

The killing is reported the next day in the *Arab News* as a snippet at the bottom of page 3: "A Pakistani was executed for smuggling drugs into the Kingdom. Mohammed Asharaf Ramadan was caught attempting to smuggle into the Kingdom an amount of heroin that he swallowed, the ministry said in a statement carried by the Saudi Press Agency. The Kingdom executed 78 people last year."

As we drive away from the place I now know from locals as "chop-chop square," young boys in T-shirts and girls in abayas run along the road with fish loose in their hands they've just stolen from the back of a truck stuck in traffic. We turn left into a neighborhood of crumbling mud-clay houses with missing roofs and floors.

Begging in a wheelchair by the side of the road, wearing a white thawb and red-checkered ghutra, is Mohamed Abdullah Sheri. He's over 80 and paralyzed. With a miswak chewing stick, he points to the ruined house he says he lived in for decades with his mother and father since the era of King Faisal – three reigns before King Abdullah took the throne in 2005. The family used to come and go between here and their native Yemen to trade. Recently the government evicted him because the building isn't safe, so he moved to another tumbledown nearby with his three sons and five daughters. None can find work, he says. "Still, Allah will give."

A few kilometers west in Diriya, the capital city under the first Saudi monarchy in the 1700s, the same mud-brick buildings are being ripped down for palaces. They're homes for some of the country's thousands of princes including the most senior, Crown Prince Salman Bin Abdulaziz Al Saud – who succeeded his half-brother as King in 2015 – flanked by a wall stretching hundreds of meters and topped with barbed wire and CCTV cameras.

Close by in the heavily guarded diplomatic quarter, Patrick and his partner Robert entertain with sparkling wine and a fine 12-year-old single malt whisky. From here, Riyadh doesn't seem like a hardship posting though it's classified as just that. Patrick is soon to move on to his next assignment. I ask what he'll miss most about Riyadh. There's a long pause. "I'll tell you what I'll miss least – having to be so careful when we go out together, having no intimacy." Homosexuality is punishable by death under Shariah law.[23]

The next day in Jeddah I'm at the swanky Al Nakheel restaurant. Men chug on giant hookahs with maroon pipes the size of bicycle tire tubes. Women smoke smaller pipes flavored with water melon. Their hair and faces are uncovered. Abayas are worn loosely over jeans. They sit chatting with single male friends.

I think of the religious police, the mutaween, in Riyadh monitoring the shopping mall. "They wouldn't dare come in here," explains Zeinab, a marketing manager for an international conglomerate.

For the more liberal Saudis in Jeddah, the breakthrough came with the advent of smart phones and social media. If the mutaween came here, videos of them would be posted all over the internet, says Zeinab. They'd end up looking foolish.

Zeinab believes in Islam, she just doesn't think the religion obliges her to hide her face. After all, she argues, female pilgrims entering the holy city of

Mecca are required to have their faces showing before Allah. "Covering the face is covering my identity and I don't believe Islam wants me to live my life faceless."

Women came closest to burning their niqabs on Saturday, 26th October, 2013. Saudi Arabia is the only country in the world to ban female drivers. In protest, a social media campaign called on women to get in cars and drive, wherever they happened to be, and to post their pictures on Facebook and Twitter.[24]

Like most Saudi women, Lamis doesn't have a driver's license, so she hopped in a car with a girlfriend who had a foreign permit and they drove around their neighborhood in Jeddah. They saw a policeman at one point and sped up. Luckily he didn't chase them.

"You just don't know what would happen if they stopped you," says Lamis. "Fifty lashes? No one wants to be the example."[25]

The single biggest humiliation to both Zeinab and Lamis is the guarantor system, which requires a husband or father to give written permission for a woman to leave the country. If there's no father or husband, a mother must ask her son for permission. Twenty-four-old Lamis has permission from her father automated on her passport. Even so, when she booked a holiday in Turkey last year, officers refused to let her travel without written consent. She had to wake up her father who drove to the airport to say she could go.

Zeinab and Lamis are among 20 women in an office of 120. They sit at desks alongside the men. Down a corridor is a separate room with 20 desks and computers lying dormant. If the mutaween come knocking, the women will scurry to their office and fire up their computers.

Their company is further ahead than most. Along with Saudization of the workforce, the government is trying to tackle unemployment by removing the stigma of women working. The *Saudi Gazette*, which, like all domestic media, is monitored by the Ministry of Information and Culture, complains of female hospital receptionists having to contend with daily abuse from men hostile to being served by a woman, and all for a wage of 2000 riyals, equal to unemployment benefit. The same month the paper appointed its first female editor-in-chief.

Ten kilometers from Jeddah at the private Dream Beach, where the Red Sea, alive with rainbow coral, laps white sand, Naziya sits in a wetsuit with a girlfriend smoking from a hookah.

Naziya quit her job as a hospital receptionist three years ago and has been trying to find work ever since. Of Yemeni descent, she was married in her teens to her father's friend. They argued every day because she refused to wear her niqab. When they divorced, Naziya, 29, moved back with her family.

She gets to see her two children once a week after school when her ex-husband allows her to visit.

For comfort, she bought a puppy Rottweiler, but her mother says the dog is haram and so they argue every day about whether she can keep it. When she walks to the supermarket she gets scolded by the mutaween and called a bitch by local boys for not covering her head.

"I hate Saudi Arabia," she says. "I would live anywhere else, I don't care."

Top Down Data

Country	Population	GDP on PPP Basis ($)	GDP/ Capita on PPP ($)	Inflation (% pa)	Unemployment (%)
Saudi Arabia	27,345,986	927,800,000,000	31,300	3.7	10.5
Egypt	86,895,099	551,400,000,000	6600	9.0	13.4
Nigeria	177,155,754	478,500,000,000	2800	8.7	23.9
Vietnam	93,421,835	358,900,000,000	4000	6.8	1.3
Argentina	43,024,374	771,000,000,000	18,600	20.8	7.5
Romania	21,729,871	288,500,000,000	14,400	3.2	7.3
Myanmar	55,746,253	111,100,000,000	1700	5.7	5.2
Kenya	45,010,056	79,900,000,000	1800	5.8	40.0

Source: CIA World Factbook, December 2014

[1] Population data from July 2014 estimates.
[2] GDP at purchasing power parity (PPP) exchange rates is the sum value of all goods and services produced in the country valued at prices prevailing in the USA, based on 2013 estimates.
[3] GDP per capita (PPP) divided by population, based on 2013 estimates.
[4] Inflation rate shows the annual percentage change in consumer prices in 2013.
[5] Unemployment rate shows the percentage of the labor force without jobs. Data from 2013 estimates, except for Nigeria (2011) and Kenya (2008).

Endnotes

1. Schwatz, A. (2013) This gorgeous campus is the world's largest women's university – and it's in Saudi Arabia, Co.Exist. Available at: http://www.fastcoexist.com/3020619/this-gorgeous-campus-is-the-worlds-largest-womens-university-and-its-in-saudi-arabia.

2. Anonymous (2014) New railway projects to link eastern and western regions, *Arab News*. Available at: http://www.arabnews.com/news/450962.

3. CIA, The World Factbook, Country comparison: Railways, total length of railway network. Available at: https://www.cia.gov/library/publications/the-world-factbook/rankorder/2121rank.html?countryname=Saudi Arabia&countrycode=sa&regionCode=mde&rank=81#sa).

4. WorldAtlas.Com, Countries of the World (by largest land area, including indigenous water). Available at: http://www.worldatlas.com/aatlas/populations/ctyareal.htm.

5. The 50 most wired countries in the world: ranking, Bloomberg. Available at: http://www.bloomberg.com/visual-data/best-and-worst/most-wired-in-the-world-countries.

6. Anonymous (2014) Saudi Arabia: dengue fears from leaking sewage in Jeddah, *Arab News*. Available at: http://crofsblogs.typepad.com/h5n1/2014/02/saudi-arabia-dengue-fears-from-leaking-sewage-in-jeddah.html.

7. Anonymous (2013) US Firm Fluor to Manage $7 Billion Riyadh–Jeddah Railway Project, Royal Embassy of Saudi Arabia, Washington DC. Available at: http://www.saudiembassy.net/latest_news/news01021302.aspx.

8. Gayathri, A. (2013) Saudi Arabia unveils Riyadh metro project worth $22.5 billion; Bechtel, AECOM among foreign companies part of the project, *International Business Times*. Available at: http://www.ibtimes.com/saudi-arabia-unveils-riyadh-metro-project-worth-225-billion-bechtel-aecom-among-foreign-companies.

9. Saudi Arabia invests US$70 billion in economic cities project, Cisco. Available at: http://www.cisco.com/web/about/ac79/docs/success/Saudi_Arabian_General_Investment_Authority_SAGIA_Engagement_Snapshot.pdf.

10. World Health Organization ranking of health systems. Available at: http://en.wikipedia.org/wiki/World_Health_Organization_ranking_of_health_systems_in_2000.

11. List of hospitals in Saudi Arabia. Available at: http://en.wikipedia.org/wiki/List_of_hospitals_in_Saudi_Arabia.

12. Diabetes prevalence (% of population ages 20 to 79 who have type 1 or type 2 diabetes), International Diabetes Federation, Diabetes Atlas. Available at: http://www.indexmundi.com/facts/indicators/SH.STA.DIAB.ZS/rankings.

13. The Hidden Toll of Dying and Disabled Children, March Of Dimes Foundation, White Plains, New York. Available at: http://www.neonatology.org/pdf/MODBDExecutiveSummary.pdf.

14. Consanguinity rates in Arab populations, *Reproductive Health Journal*, 2009. Available at: http://www.reproductive-health-journal.com/content/6/1/17/table/T1.

15. Labor and Workmen Law 1969, The Labor Contract, Article 73, Royal Embassy of Saudi Arabia, Washington DC. Available at: http://www.saudiembassy.net/about/country-information/laws/Labor_and_Workmen_Law-2of4.aspx.

16. Anonymous (2014) Maids asked to compensate sponsors for quitting jobs, *Saudi Gazette*. Available at: http://www.saudigazette.com.sa/index.cfm?method=home.regcon&contentid=20140203194581.

17. Anonymous (2013) Number of Lankan runaway maids swells, *Arab News*. Available at: http://www.arabnews.com/news/447411.
18. Chamberlain, G. (2013) Saudi Arabia's treatment of foreign workers under fire after beheading of Sri Lankan maid, *The Guardian*. Available at: http://www.theguardian.com/world/2013/jan/13/saudi-arabia-treatment-foreign-workers.
19. Anonymous (2013) Saudi government fired 7,500 foreign workers, deported 1 million illegals in 2013, *World Tribune*. Available at: http://www.worldtribune.com/2013/12/22/saudi-government-fired-7500-foreign-workers-deported-1-million-illegals-in-2013/.
20. Sambira, J. (2013) Saudi Arabia deports illegal migrants from Yemen and Ethiopia, United Nations Radio. Available at: http://www.unmultimedia.org/radio/english/2013/11/saudi-arabia-deports-illegal-migrants-from-yemen-and-ethiopia/.
21. McDowall, A. (2014) Saudi Arabia introduces employment insurance, Reuters. Available at: http://www.reuters.com/article/2014/01/06/saudi-unemployment-idUSL6N0KG1VX20140106.
22. McDowall, A. (2012) More than 1 million Saudis on unemployment benefit, Reuters. Available at: http://www.reuters.com/article/2012/03/28/us-saudi-unemployment-subsidy-idUSBRE82R0L320120328.
23. Saudi Arabia: Treatment of homosexuals by authorities and by society in general; recourse available to those who have been targeted because of their sexual orientation (2004–2007), United Nations High Commissioner for Refugees, Refworld. Available at: http://www.refworld.org/docid/469cd6ab3.html.
24. McDowall, A. (2013) Saudi authorities warn of punishment for women drivers, Reuters. Available at: http://www.reuters.com/article/2013/10/24/us-saudi-womendriving-idUSBRE99N0SA20131024.
25. Abu-Nasr, D. (2011) Saudi woman driver sentenced to 10 lashes after king grants women the vote, Bloomberg News. Available at: http://www.bloomberg.com/news/2011-09-27/saudi-woman-driver-sentenced-to-10-lashes.html.

II – Socialist Monarchy

Topping the bestsellers list at the Jarir book store in Riyadh is the story of a jinni who falls in love with a girl as they communicate through a Ouija board.

H W J N – pronounced as "Hawjan," the imaginary name of the spirit – was banned for several months pending investigation by the witchcraft division of the Commission of the Promotion of Virtue and Prevention from Vice.

Author Ibraheem Abbas successfully argued that jinnis are mentioned in the Koran and the books were returned for sale.

For business development manager Safi Al-Safi, it's another chapter in the constant evolution of what's acceptable. He avoids playing music in the shop for fear this would be frowned upon. Only recently it wasn't lawful to allow a woman to serve male customers; now he's hiring his first female cashier.

"Society is changing very, very fast," says Safi. Women can have face-to-face interaction with customers as long as it's in an open area.

Bringing the female half of Saudi Arabia's 30 million people into the formal economy represents a massive opportunity to fund manager Sean Taylor. Women earning their own money means increased spending on consumer items from food and fashion to laptops and mobile phones. Jarir – which, along with selling books, is Saudi Arabia's biggest retailer of smart phones, tablets and laptops – employs only four women among its 200 managers. All are in roles where they don't interact on the shop floor.

Sean, 47, brings a deeper understanding than most foreign investors of the changes happening in Saudi society. The son of a mining industry executive, he lived here for eight years as a child.

"Saudi Arabia went from being liberal when we first arrived to very strict," says Sean. "I don't feel now there's a tension on the streets or in the malls like there was then."

After serving in the British army, Sean returned to the Middle East in 1997 to create the first fund for foreign investors focused on Arab countries – the SG Arab Fund. He went on to run emerging and frontier market hedge funds for GAM before joining Deutsche Asset & Wealth Management in 2013, taking over a 7.5 billion-euro portfolio as the head of emerging market equities.

Walking around the store, he stops to pick up a book entitled *Behavioral Attitude – The Cause for High Unemployment in Saudi Arabia*.

"This shows you the degree of openness in discussing the challenges," says Sean. "You wouldn't think it, but the Saudis are in many ways much more open than other countries in the region."

The book argues for a transition from the traditional notions of virtue that contribute to unemployment. "Saudi tribal societies regard being a barber, a butcher or a painter as contemptible," writes Abdullah M. Anazi. "A Bedouin who digs a well to provide clean water for his family will reject doing something similar for money."

Saudi aversion to the trades and paid labor is reinforced by family wealth and state handouts. The government subsidizes everything from health to bread and petrol in a system described as a "socialist monarchy" by one banker we met. Healthcare is free, even to the extent of air lifting patients to Germany if necessary for specialist treatment.

The subsidized fuel prices are the lowest in the world at 0.45 riyals a liter, or 12 US cents. That compares with 90 cents in America and $2.20 in Germany and Britain.[1] Water is more than twice the price at 1 riyal for a 600 milliliter bottle.

Cheap fuel encourages Saudis to drive GMC 4x4 monster trucks, air-condition their grocery stores to wintry levels and leave the air con running at home for weeks while on vacation abroad. Energy consumption will only rise further as the population – two thirds of which is under the age of 29 – expands by 2% a year (Figure 8.1).[2] A report by Citigroup warned the country risks having to import oil by 2030 as Saudis might consume their entire output.[3]

"There is a new lifestyle of ease," writes Anazi in his book. "Real economic growth and development can occur only when the people, society and the government succeed in changing Saudi youths' work attitudes."

Jarir's chairman is doing his bit. Having taken over the business from his father who built Jarir from a book stall, Muhammad Alagil refuses to employ his own children or family members until they have worked "successfully"

FIGURE 8.1 Population in millions

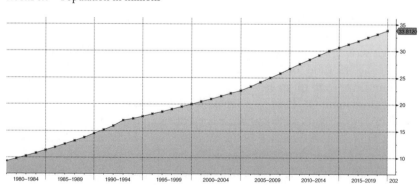

Source: IMF data compiled by Bloomberg. *(Function: IPOPSAU GP).*

for at least three years outside the company to encourage their financial independence. They can take up any other vocation, he says.

To break down class barriers and align the interests of staff with the company and its shareholders, all managers work on the shop floor for at least six months. Their bonuses are directly determined by takings in the stores. If revenue grows above 10%, the 40 or so top managers earn a 50% increase in their bonus.

"As a family we have made enough money not to work, so it's all about reputation and ethics for us," says Alagil. "Part of it we learnt from the US."

Under the government's program to encourage more Saudis into the workforce known as Saudization or nitaqat, companies are graded on a scale of red, yellow, green or excellent depending on the proportion of their workforce that are nationals. Red companies – those with a low proportion of Saudis – won't be allowed to renew work visas for their foreign employees while yellow companies can renew for up to six years. "Excellent" companies can expect strong state support.

Exactly what percentage needs to be Saudi depends on the sector and number of employees. A company with 10 to 50 security guards, for example, should have 75–84% Saudis to score green. A company with the same number of delivery drivers – a job deemed less desirable – will go green at 10–19% Saudization.[4] Companies with more foreigners than Saudis are liable for a levy of 2400 riyals per foreign worker. Studies show the overall cost to the private sector will run into billions of dollars.[5]

Sean is skeptical. "The analysts are all wrong on this."

"Absolutely!" says Alagil. "We have an expat salesman who's paid 3500 riyals a month but on the top of that we pay him tickets home, housing and other perks, taking his pay to 4500. When we hire a Saudi we pay him the same amount but as cash. Maybe we have a difference of 500. But people get it wrong. They just look at the payslips and see 3000 for an expat and 4500 for a Saudi."

Far from being stung by higher labor costs, Jarir's earnings have soared. The company translates a book every 30 hours to produce a range of new titles for its stores. But its biggest income is from selling Apple iPads and Huawei tablets, along with Samsung mobiles and iPhones. Jarir has increased net profit by at least 15% and dividends by 17% every year since 2008, helping the company lure mutual funds targeting high income to its shares, says Alagil.

For Sean, that all translates to a positive score on a key investment metric: return on equity. Jarir has earned the equivalent of at least half the value of its equity each year. A figure above 20% is a positive indicator under Mark Mobius' guidelines.

One reason for the high number is the company doesn't need to spend much of its earnings paying interest on debt, says Alagil. Jarir's borrowing was equivalent to 22% of its equity as of September 2013.[6] Anything below 100% gets a tick under the Mobius criteria.

Demand for Jarir drove the share price up 55% in 2013 and 28% in the first eight months of 2014. The rally increased the valuation to 27 times expected annual earnings.

"Retail companies seem a really good bet and Jarir seems like a core holding," says Sean. "The whole Saudization process and employing women can only help boost consumer spending."

Fund Factbox

Company & Assets in Emerging Markets	Emerging Market Fund	Performance & Peer Ranking	Portfolio Manager: Sean Taylor
Deutsche Asset & Wealth Management $10 billion	DWS Top Asien Fund	27th highest total return among 986 Asia Pacific equity funds over 10 years at 118.64% (annualized 8.13%)	Joined in 2013 from hedge fund manager GAM to head emerging market & Asia equity funds. Awarded while at GAM "Best Frontier Hedge Fund" of 2010 & "Emerging Fund of the Year" in 2007 by Hedge Fund World

Source: Data compiled by Bloomberg as of June 2014

Stocks Box: Jarir

Company & Trading Platform	Description	Average Annual Return	Price–Earnings Ratio	Price–Book Ratio/ NAV	Return on Equity	Gross Dividend Yield	Market Value ($m)	Top Holders %
Jarir Saudi Arabian Stock Exchange	Biggest Saudi retailer of books, smart phones, tablets, laptops	29.1% since data starts in 2003	23.9	12.7	56.4%	3.9%	4455	Al Aqeel Nasser 9.0% Al-Aqeel Abdulsalama 9.0% Free float 54.2%

Source: Data compiled by Bloomberg as of December 2014

Endnotes

1. Fuel-Prices Europe.Info, world prices as of Feb. 17, 2014. Available at: http://www.fuel-prices-europe.info/index.php?sort=4.
2. Murphy, C. (2012) Saudi Arabia's youth and the Kingdom's future, New Security Beat. Available at: http://www.newsecuritybeat.org/2012/02/saudi-arabias-youth-and-the-kingdoms-future/.
3. Daya, A., El-Baltaji, D. (2012) Saudi Arabia may become oil importer by 2030, Citigroup says, Bloomberg News. Available at: http://www.bloomberg.com/news/2012-09-04/saudi-arabia-may-become-oil-importer-by-2030-citigroup-says-1-.html.
4. Nitaqat: Percentage of new Saudization program in different sectors – Saudi Labor Law, Expat Corner GCC. Available at: http://expatcornergcc.com/?p=739.
5. Saudisation to cost nearly $4bn in 2013 – study, Arabianbusiness.com, May 1, 2013. Available at: http://www.arabianbusiness.com/saudisation-cost-nearly-4bn-in-2013-study-500254.html.
6. Jarir Marketing Co., Investor Presentation, Balance Sheet Highlights.

III – Desert Farming

Eighty kilometers southeast of Riyadh on the edge of the world's largest sand desert is a natural oasis.

Irrigated by fossil water formed deep underground by ancient forests, Al-Kharj has, for centuries, been a place of date palm trees and small farms. More recently, farming here has gone supersize.

The idea of breeding cows in the 50 degree desert heat of the Rub' al-Khali, or Empty Quarter, was conceived out of fear. After halting oil exports in protest at American military aid to Israel in the 70s, it occurred to the Saudis they'd be vulnerable in the event of a retaliatory boycott on food imports. The government set out on a mission for the country to become self-sufficient.[1] The task went to Prince Sultan bin Mohammed bin Saud Al Kabeer, and in 1976, he founded Almarai, meaning pasture.[2]

Today, Almarai is the world's largest integrated dairy foods company and among the biggest Arab consumer brands,[3] making 60-year-old Al Kabeer a multi-billionaire.

Its seven farms are spread over a vast tract of desert, punctuated with green crop circles producing alfalfa for feed. Trucks deliver the fodder in neat rows to Almarai's 145,000 black and white Holstein cows in air-conditioned barns. Outside they're sprayed with water to keep them cool and clean before lining up at automated milking stations. Artificial insemination is used to produce 200 calves every day.

The meticulous routine has made Almarai's cows more productive than their field-grazing cousins abroad, producing an average 13,325 liters of milk a year compared to 7000 in Europe and 5000 in New Zealand (Figure 8.2). The water to hose the cows and electric for the air conditioning are paid for by government subsidies.

The quid pro quo of the state's aid is the government dictates how much Almarai can charge per liter of milk. Prices last rose in 2008 from 3 riyals to 4 riyals, or $1.07. That increase was the first since 2000.

Almarai attempted to raise its price for two-liter bottles of milk by 1 riyal to 8 riyals in 2011. Fired up by the power of social media in bringing a revolution to Egypt, Saudi consumers campaigned on Twitter and Facebook for a boycott against Almarai. The commerce minister revoked the increase a week later.

"We're much more prudent now," says an executive at Almarai's headquarters in Riyadh. "We're not the first one to push for price increases any more. But we feel the pinch because there is tremendous inflation pressure in the Kingdom, and if we can't change our price, that would be a threat to our business."

FIGURE 8.2 Competitive cows.

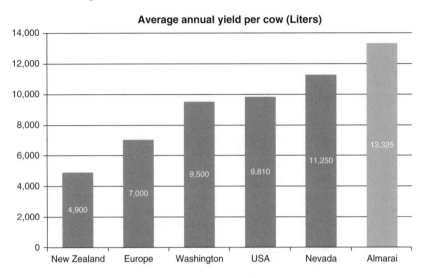

Source: Almarai's data. Almarai Investor Presentation, p.40, Average Yield Per Cow (Liters), Q1 2014.

Almarai tries to limit the effect of some cost pressure by buying contracts that produce a profit when commodity prices rise. But these derivatives can't shield the company from increases in its single biggest expense: wages. Paying its 34,000 employees accounts for about half of Almarai's costs.

The Saudization rules will have an impact on labor costs, but it's unlikely to amount to more than 1% of the total wage bill.

"Where it has affected us more is on the consumer side," says the executive. "Some of the smaller shops we distribute through have closed because they didn't have the required paperwork."

By one estimate, up to 40% of private companies looked set to shut because of the Saudization program.[4]

From cows, Almarai has diversified into poultry.

It's a logical move. Saudis love chicken – whether wrapped in flatbread with tahini as a shawarma or fried and boxed at the hugely popular Al Baik fast-food chain. Saudis eat about as much chicken as Brits – a nation twice its size – providing two thirds of their protein intake.[5,6]

Almarai's poultry business expanded rapidly until a nationwide disease outbreak sent chicken mortality rates soaring to over 50% at some medium-sized farms. While the rate for Almarai was between 10 and 20%, it was losing heavily as its facilities for 60 million birds a year worked below capacity. The company developed its own vaccines from Jordan to combat the airborne disease, bringing the mortality rate down.

The Saudi ban on alcohol makes soft drinks another lucrative area. Almarai supplies 41% of the fruit juice in Saudi Arabia and the rest of the Gulf Cooperation Council countries. Egypt and Jordan have generated the biggest growth in sales overall, with a PepsiCo. joint venture supplying Almarai and Tropicana brands. The company is also stepping up competition with the Egyptian dairy producer Juhayna.

Water, ice cream and confectionery are next on its menu.

Stocks Box: Food and Dairy

Company & Trading Platform	Description	Average Annual Return	Price–Earnings Ratio	Price–Book Ratio/ NAV	Return on Equity	Gross Dividend Yield	Market Value ($m)	Top Holders %
Almarai Saudi Arabian Stock Exchange	World's largest integrated dairy foods company	12.3% since data starts in 2005	27.8	4.1	15.8%	1.4%	11,740	Savola Group 36.5% Al-Saud Sultan Moham 28.6% Amraan & Partners 5.70% Free float 26.4%
Juhayna Food Industries Cairo Stock Exchange	Egypt's biggest dairy and fruit juice producer	55.1% since IPO in 2010	54.6	3.6	7.1%	N/A	1122	Pharaoh Investment 51.0% Aberdeen 1.9% Free float 47.9%
Vinamilk Ho Chi Minh Stock Exchange	Vietnam's biggest milk producer	34.4% since listing 2006	17.4	5.5	33.2%	2.0%	4641	State Capital & Invest 37.6% Fraser & Neave 11.0% Free float 57.5%

Source: Data compiled by Bloomberg as of December 2014

Investor Analysis: Deutsche Asset & Wealth Management's Sean Taylor on Almarai

Bottom Line

• Almarai **reduced its debt** load to 76% of equity from over 100% by refinancing in 2013 with a perpetual Sukuk (equivalent to a combination of debt and equity). The cost of borrowing on the perpetual is about 90 basis points higher than on its regular debt. The borrowing shouldn't present a problem.

Buy/Sell Triggers

• Almarai could **surprise on upside** as the poultry problems are resolved.
• The investment process isn't just about identifying whether the company will continue to make a loss on poultry, but **what is being anticipated** by the mass of individual investors who make up 90% of trading on the Saudi exchange.

Endnotes

1. Pendleton, D. (2013) Hidden billionaire milking Saudi dairy fortune in desert, Bloomberg News. Available at: http://www.bloomberg.com/news/2013-01-14/hidden-billionaire-milking-saudi-dairy-fortune-in-desert.html.
2. Sabri, S. (2001) The House of Saud in Commerce: A Study of Royal Entrepreneurship in Saudi Arabia, I.S. Publications.
3. Anonymous (2006) Forbes Top 40 Arab brands. Available at: http://www.forbes.com/2006/10/17/top-arab-brands-biz_cz_fas_1018toparabbrands.html.
4. Nitaqat: Percentage of new Saudization program in different sectors – Saudi Labor law, Expat Corner GCC. Available at: http://expatcornergcc.com/?p=739.
5. KSA Poultry Market, Q1 2014 Almarai Investor Presentation.
6. USDA Foreign Agricultural Service, Global Agricultural Information Network, Aug. 29, 2013. Available at: http://gain.fas.usda.gov/Recent%20GAIN%20Publications/Poultry%20and%20Products%20Annual_Riyadh_Saudi%20Arabia_8-26-2013.pdf.

IV - Opening Bell

S audi Arabia is the odd ball in a book about frontier markets. The typical
Saudi earns more than the average Spaniard, Italian or New Zealander.
The country's stock exchange at over half a trillion dollars tops most emerging
and developed nations (Table 8.1).

It's excluded from the emerging markets universe for one reason: foreigners
haven't been allowed to buy shares.

At least, not directly.

To invest in companies, fund managers like Sean have had to go through
a local brokerage, which buys the securities and then issues so-called partici-
patory notes. The buyer of these p-notes will collect dividends and capital
gains just like they owned the underlying stock.

But while p-notes are held by some big investors like Franklin Templeton,
most steer clear of them largely because of the extra risk of having to entrust
millions of dollars of assets with a local broker.

The other problem is that p-note holders have zero say in the company's affairs. Unlike shareholders who have a vote on everything from board

TABLE 8.1 Richer than Italians: GDP per capita on purchasing power parity basis

Rank	Country	$
1	Qatar	102,100
2	Liechtenstein	89,400
3	Macau	88,700
14	United States	52,800
36	Japan	37,100
41	European Union	34,500
44	**Saudi Arabia**	**31,300**
46	New Zealand	30,400
47	Spain	30,100
48	United Arab Emirates	29,900
51	Italy	29,600

Source: The World Factbook, CIA. Available at: https://www.cia.gov/library/publications/the-world-factbook/rankorder/2004rank.html

appointments to mergers and remuneration, p-note owners don't even have the right to attend the annual meeting.

The alternative to p-notes is to enter a contract in which the counterparty agrees to pay an amount equivalent to any gain in the shares and the investor stands to lose should the stock go down. But these swap agreements would have the same problems for fund managers wary of p-notes, as it would mean taking on board the risk of the counterparty failing to pay up and zero voting rights.

Saudi Arabia is gradually opening its door. The government introduced p-notes in 2008 as a first step – bringing in foreign capital without the risk of ceding control over the economy. Then, in 2013, it shifted its weekend from Thursday and Friday to the Middle East standard of Friday and Saturday.[1] This meant only one day rather than two when trading activity isn't aligned with the rest of the world.

Now we're entering the third phase. The Capital Market Authority announced plans in mid-2014 to open the Saudi bourse to qualified foreign financial institutions.

The market still won't look like the US or western Europe. Like Vietnam, the kingdom may impose restrictions preventing foreign investors buying a big enough stake to control a company. Voting rights might also be limited. Buyers could be required to pay immediately for their shares rather than having a couple of days to settle as is the norm in markets operating under *T+2* rules.

Even so, the announcement triggered a surge in the Saudi Tadawul All-Share Index to a six-year high on anticipation of foreign demand once the market opens up. Overseas investors owned just 1.6% of the capital listed on the stock exchange in 2014. The proportion could easily triple to 6%, according to Habib Oueijan, who manages one of the largest private portfolios in Saudi Arabia as the head of public equities at Olayan Saudi Investment Co. in Riyadh.

Oueijan is in a good position to know. Back in the 90s he was working for the World Bank's private-sector financing arm, the IFC, setting up the equivalent of the FTSE 100 Index or Dow Jones Industrial Average for emerging markets including Egypt and Saudi Arabia.

Indexes have become a critical part of the investment decision process. Some fund managers follow rules preventing them from deviating too much from the securities included in a benchmark index. The MSCI Emerging Markets Index is the gauge tracked the most by investors in developing countries along with the smaller and newer MSCI Frontier Markets Index.

Saudi Arabia has been excluded from both because of its ban on direct investment. When it opens up, the country is likely to go straight into the larger MSCI Emerging Markets Index, says Oueijan. It should make up at least 3% of the index, equivalent to Turkey and Poland combined, based on the current market size and the amount of trading, he says. MSCI says Saudi Arabia could become eligible for the index in 2017 and account for about 4% of the measure (Table 8.2).[2]

With the market opening up, investors will rush for the biggest companies first, says Oueijan. "They'll go for the blue chip companies that are well researched." (Table 8.3).

TABLE 8.2   Big as Poland and Turkey combined: MSCI Emerging Markets Index weightings

Name	% Index Weight
China (99 members)	15.5
South Korea (106 members)	14.4
Taiwan (101 members)	12.3
Brazil (70 members)	9.6
South Africa (50 members)	7.8
India (64 members)	7.2
Mexico (30 members)	5.1
Hong Kong (40 members)	4.9
Russia (22 members)	3.9
Malaysia (42 members)	3.7
Indonesia (30 members)	2.7
Thailand (32 members)	2.5
Turkey (25 members)	1.8
Poland (24 members)	1.7

Source: Data compiled by Bloomberg as of December 2014

TABLE 8.3 Blue Chips: Biggest Saudi listed companies.

Company	Weighting (%)
Al Rajhi Bank	8.3
Saudi Basic Industries	6.7
National Commercial Bank	3.6
Savola	3.6
Jabal Omar Dev't	3.4
Riyad Bank	3.2
Samba Financial Group	3.1
Etihad Etisalat	2.7
Banque Saudi Fransi	2.7
Alinma Bank	2.7

Source: Tadawul All Share Index, data compiled by Bloomberg as of December 2014

Stocks Box: Saudi ETFs

Country	Security / Trading Platform	Issuer Description	Average Annual Return	Top 10 Index Holdings
Saudi Arabia	HSBC Amanah Saudi 20 ETF	Incorporated in Saudi Arabia, the Fund seeks to track the performance of the HSBC Amanah Saudi 20 Index, before excluding fees and expenses	20.7% since inception in 2011	No holdings reported

Source: Data compiled by Bloomberg as of December 2014

Endnotes

1. Anonymous (2013) It's a Friday-Saturday weekend, *Arab News*, June 23. Available at: http://www.arabnews.com/news/455923.
2. Hankir, Z., Khan, S. (2014) Saudi stock opening shut to some as hot money unwanted, Bloomberg News. Available at: http://www.bloomberg.com/news/2014-07-22/saudi-stock-opening-will-be-closed-to-some-as-hot-money-unwanted.html.

V – White Balloons

It's like a pressure cooker: If you just release it,
it might explode in your face.

Yaser Bakr, Saudi Comedian

Like the dolphins losing their smiles in his joke, Yaser Bakr found his humor fading as he went from class clown to devout Muslim adult with a management job and family responsibilities.

Then social media exploded.

"It became my outlet," says Yaser.

With few competitors for Saudi gags, Yaser quickly amassed a big following on Twitter.

In Saudi Arabia especially, being big in social media is far more powerful than appearing on TV. Saudis download more YouTube videos than any other nationality.[1] Fifty-one percent of Saudis with internet access are active on Twitter, the highest rate worldwide.[2]

Yaser went from joking online to standup and finally quit his job as a vice president for Group 4 Securicor in late 2012 to set up the nation's first comedy club.

His shows have two big differences from the routines in other countries. The first is alcohol.

"That's something we struggle with," says Yaser. "It's much harder to get laughs here simply because people are sober."

The second is that improvised comedy just doesn't work. "We didn't go through the open mic structure of anyone coming up and giving his bit because of all of the sensitivity," says Yaser. "We have auditions first and then if we think the act is solid from a comedy point of view, we can make it safe to be presented to the audience."

The comics, so far, are all men.

Yaser, bearded with a shaved head and wearing a traditional thawb, does a routine as the hen-pecked husband. "I think my marriage is great until noon when she wakes up …"

While Saudi men have all the rights and there are countless instances of domestic abuse, it's the woman who has the real power, according to Yaser.

"The running joke is always of the wife as the boss – we call our wives the Ministry of Interior – so if someone isn't in the kind of marriage that's more of a partnership, where the woman has as much say as the husband, he might look at his marriage differently after the sketch."

Keeping the religious and political authorities on board requires treading a fine line. "What we do is self-censorship. We try something new and quietly we're freaking out, just hoping no one gets angry, and if no one does, then you know that that's OK. If you get a very negative reaction from everyone then you know that this is a red line."

I tell Yaser my personal comedy moment: seeing a man photographing his wife whose face was completely covered. "We wouldn't joke about it," he says, "because it's everyday life."

"But we would definitely be the people laughing hardest at an expat seeing this because we'd remember how weird this would look."

We drive in Yaser's massive GMC Sierra truck as the sun sets on Jeddah's Al Corniche beach. We're about to witness the city's first mass-participation expressive arts event. The idea is everyone draws or writes their dream or feelings on a piece of paper which is then stuck to a balloon.

Some artists have been helping illiterate migrant workers write their name for the first time in their lives. They draw childlike match-stick men with a strip of blue sky and yellow circle sun. Young girls draw hearts, hoping it will fall to the right guy. A thousand white balloons float to the sky.

From there we head to an exhibition for Jeddah Art Week. In one corner, a collection of mirrors gives the effect of seeing yourself from every angle. Felt-tip pens are strewn about the floor, inviting the visitor to draw or write their own thoughts and ideas. Like the balloons, this could be politically provocative. Yet the writing on the wall is a bunch of names and kisses – no complaints about human rights or demands for change.

"Society here was very conservative," says Yaser. "They put a lot of rules in place that we got stuck with for now. Everyone wants to change them. But it's like a pressure cooker: if you just release it, it might explode in your face."

Endnotes

1. Young Saudis getting creative on YouTube, Reuters, Nov. 18, 2013. Available at http://www.reuters.com/article/2013/11/18/us-saudi-youtube-idUSBRE9AH0 GY20131118.
2. Anonymous (2013) In the Middle East, Twitter rules: majority of internet users in Saudi Arabia are active Twitter users, e-Marketer. Available at: http://www. emarketer.com/Article/Middle-East-Twitter-Rules/1009737#sthash.Qmmmy-KAS.dpuf.

CHAPTER 9

Sri Lanka

I – Family Economy

*Let us overcome jungle law with justice, barbarism with courtesy,
foolish family nepotism with noble wisdom.*

Maithripala Sirisena
President
Democratic Socialist Republic of Sri Lanka

A giant yellow Buddha beams down on arrivals at Colombo's main air-port, making a first photo opportunity for tourists ignoring the bright red sign with a cross through a camera.

Airport security isn't minded to enforce rules. The crowd masses its way toward the immigration booths, uncertain of who lines up where. Passports are stamped without questions.

It's a relief. Sri Lanka had the longest visa process of all ten countries, keeping my passport for 12 days.

We pass through a long corridor to baggage reclaim. Fridges, washing machines and TVs line both sides. I'm wondering who would buy a fridge from the airport, but plenty of money is changing hands. It's all tax-free. Many will end up being sold on for a profit.

Minutes later I'm gliding along an open road to the city center. It's Mon-day morning, the busiest time to arrive in Colombo, but there are no traffic jams. The new Airport Expressway has cut the journey to a third of the hour-and-a-half it would have been only a few months earlier. A 300 rupee ($2.30) toll limits vehicles to the time conscious.

The radio plays "YMCA" and "Pretty Woman" – "music for cruising around the emerald isle" – as we cross a glimmering lagoon with the blue Indian Ocean beyond.

Friendly, curvy Sinhalese symbols with English beneath – the adopted second language – announce the city's approach. Next to the swanky white-stucco Kingsbury Hotel is the beginning of a land fill project called Port City.[1]

Turning left along the coast road is the old parliament. It was abandoned by politicians for a new building 20 kilometers out of town. No need to take up prime real estate.

Beside it, a construction site stretching several hundred meters will be a $400-million, 500-room Shangri-La tourist complex. Then there's an

ITC hotel going up, and on the opposite side, right on the beach front, is the gray concrete shell of a 43-story tower block soon to become a Hyatt Regency.[2] It was being built by the Ceylinco Group until the company ran out of money. The Economy Ministry – then headed by former President Mahinda Rajapaksa's brother, Basil – seized the building and handed it to Sinolanka Hotels & Spa, a developer run by then presidential aide Gamini Senerath.

The government could do these things because it owns the land. It falls under the Urban Development Authority, which is part of the Defense Ministry. That was run by another brother, Gotabaya Rajapaksa.[3] A third brother, Chamal, oversaw Parliament as the Speaker.

Between them, the three brothers controlled at least 45% of Sri Lanka's budget and the most important ministries, with the president doubling up as the minister of finance and planning, defense and urban development, ports and highways and law and order.[4–6]

In the Democratic Socialist Republic of Sri Lanka, that equated to control of the economy. Over 300 government-owned enterprises dominate insurance to ports to aviation and banking.[7]

Many have been running up big losses. Budget transfers to help state-owned enterprises more than doubled since Rajapaksa came to power in 2005.[8]

In contrast to many of the other frontier markets, like Romania or Vietnam, there's little talk yet of inefficient state companies being sold. "This is not the era to sell government entities but to regain those privatized ones," Rajapaksa said in 2013.[9] President Maithripala Sirisena's 2015 election manifesto lacked any detailed commitment to privatization.

We sweep into the five-star Cinnamon Grand Colombo, owned by the biggest of Sri Lanka's conglomerates, John Keells. I find myself trailing a procession of whirling men in red and white costumes banging drums as a bride and groom and hundreds of guests flood through the lobby to one of several designated wedding areas.

In a country where the average wage is under $3000 a year, Sri Lankans outspend everyone on weddings – one making the Guinness Book of World Records for having 126 bridesmaids.[10] In Colombo's main shopping area, an entire street is devoted just to wedding stationery. Another caters to wedding saris. Credit plans are available: HSBC offers a "Lifestyle Wedding Loan" of up to 3.5 million rupees ($27,000) for customers earning 20,000 rupees a month.[11]

Amid the marital hubbub I meet Tim Drinkall, Morgan Stanley's frontier markets fund manager. This is his fifth trip to Sri Lanka. The last was a little under a year ago. After flying overnight from New York, the island has already made a positive impression. The quicker route from the airport gave him an extra hour's rest in his room before our first meeting.

Top Down Data

Country	Population	GDP on PPP Basis ($)	GDP/ Capita on PPP ($)	Inflation (% pa)	Unemployment (%)
Sri Lanka	21,866,445	134,500,000,000	6500	4.7	5.1
Saudi Arabia	27,345,986	927,800,000,000	31,300	3.7	10.5
Egypt	86,895,099	551,400,000,000	6600	9.0	13.4
Nigeria	177,155,754	478,500,000,000	2800	8.7	23.9
Vietnam	93,421,835	358,900,000,000	4000	6.8	1.3
Argentina	43,024,374	771,000,000,000	18,600	20.8	7.5
Romania	21,729,871	288,500,000,000	14,400	3.2	7.3
Myanmar	55,746,253	111,100,000,000	1700	5.7	5.2
Kenya	45,010,056	79,900,000,000	1800	5.8	40.0

Source: CIA World Factbook, December 2014
[1] Population data from July 2014 estimates.
[2] GDP at purchasing power parity (PPP) exchange rates is the sum value of all goods and services produced in the country valued at prices prevailing in the USA, based on 2013 estimates.
[3] GDP per capita (PPP) divided by population, based on 2013 estimates.
[4] Inflation rate shows the annual percentage change in consumer prices in 2013.
[5] Unemployment rate shows the percentage of the labor force without jobs. Data from 2013 estimates, except for Nigeria (2011) and Kenya (2008).

Fund Factbox

Company & Assets in Emerging Markets	Emerging Market Fund	Performance & Peer Ranking	Portfolio Manager: Timothy Drinkall
Morgan Stanley $25 billion	Morgan Stanley Galaxy Frontier Emerging Markets Fund	21st highest total return among 2571 offshore-domiciled global emerging market funds over 5 years at 118% (annualized 16.9%)	Tim joined Morgan Stanley in New York in 2007 from Gustavia Capital in Stockholm. He commutes in from Connecticut where he lives with his wife and three sons. He takes to the road about once a month to visit frontier markets and meet investors. With the 49-year-old at all times is his Nike fuel watch to clock his exercise

Source: Data compiled by Bloomberg as of June 2014

Portfolio Structuring: Tim Drinkall's Investing Criteria

Tim Drinkall's Frontier Emerging Markets Equity Fund invests over $1 billion in those countries **excluded from the main indexes** for emerging and developed markets, including Saudi Arabia. Nigerian Breweries and Argentina's YPF were among his top 10 holdings in 2014. In Sri Lanka, the fund owns shares in John Keells and Commercial Bank of Ceylon, the island's biggest non-state lender.

His investment style is "**top down**," looking from a broad macro perspective to identify the country first. There are parallels here with TCW's approach in Kenya of assessing potential negative shocks or positive surprises to calculate a risk-adjusted return. It's the reason Tim's fund wasn't invested in Ukraine before Russia's annexation of Crimea in 2014 despite the country being a key part of the MSCI Frontier Markets Index. The economy was a mess and the currency was over-valued, says Tim.

The Morgan Stanley way is to keep fund managers for the most part as independent operators – creating a "**house of boutiques**." One portfolio manager might be more tolerant on the level of corporate indebtedness than another, for example. While compliance will pre-screen stocks for money laundering, fraud and legal issues, there's no investment committee that needs to approve purchases.

Like Andy Ho in Vietnam, Tim looks primarily for **strong management** with a proven ability to execute strategy, along with regular earnings growth and strong market share.

Other criteria accord with Mark Mobius's selection process, though there are distinctions in the way these metrics are assessed:

Debt

Drinkall: Total borrowing should be less than 0.5 times earnings before interest, taxes, depreciation and amortization (Ebitda) – or the company should have a credible plan to bring it down to that level.

Mobius: Liabilities should be less than shareholder equity, so a ratio of less than 1.

Cashflow

Drinkall: Companies should be generating cash from operations – i.e. their operating free cashflow should be positive.

Mobius: The stock price should be less than 10 times the revenue stream, preferably less than 5 times.

Return on Equity

Drinkall: The proportion of net income generated from equity capital should be higher than the cost to obtain capital. For a company whose weighted average cost of capital is 12–13%, for example, ROE should be at least 15%.

Mobius: Annual net income should be at least 20% of equity.

Additional Criteria

• **Working capital** should be well managed. Any increase in the time taken for payment, or days receivables, would raise a flag.
• Industries or economies in **structural decline** are best avoided.
• **Socially responsible** investment (SRI) considerations make tobacco companies off limits, though alcoholic beverages and casinos are fair game.

Endnotes

1. SLPA confirms commencement of US$ 15bn Port City Project (2014) Sri Lanka Ports Authority. Available at: http://www.slpa.lk/news_events_12046.asp.
2. Anonymous (2013) Colombo hotels to add 700 rooms, *Daily News*. Available at: http://www.dailynews.lk/?q=business/Colombo-hotels-add-700-rooms.
3. Daniel, F.J. (2012) Sri Lanka's "People's Dynasty": Help or harm for growth? Reuters. Available at: http://www.ft.lk/2012/11/20/sri-lankas-peoples-dynasty-help-or-harm-for-growth/.
4. Anonymous (2013) Who are the Rajapaksas? Channel 4 News. Available at: http://www.channel4.com/news/sri-lanka-mahinda-rajapaksa-commonwealth-meeting-2013.
5. Ministry of Defence & Urban Development. Available at: http://www.defence.lk/main_abt.asp?fname=contacts.
6. Policy Research & Information Unit of the Presidential Secretariat of Sri Lanka Government ministers. Available at: http://www.priu.gov.lk/Govt_Ministers/Indexministers.html.
7. Central Bank of Sri Lanka, Annual Report 2013.
8. Guruge, P. (2013) Lankan public enterprises need an urgent solution, *Sunday Times Sri Lanka*. Available at: http://www.sundaytimes.lk/131103/business-times/lankan-public-enterprises-need-an-urgent-solution-67608.html
9. Anonymous (2014) Sri Lanka credit to SOEs surge in December, Lanka Business Online. Available at: http://www.lankabusinessonline.com/news/sri-lanka-credit-to-soes-surge-in-december/2032037434.

10. Anonymous (2013) No, no and no to privatization, *Daily News*. Available at: http://www.dailynews.lk/local/no-no-and-no-privatization.

11. Anonymous (2013) Sri Lankan couple break Guinness record for a wedding with the most bridesmaids for a bride, Times Online. Available at: http://www.sundaytimes.lk/top-story/39694.html.

12. Wedding Loan, HSBC. Available at: http://www.hsbc.lk/1/2/personal/lifestyle-loans/wedding-loan.

II – China City

From Colombo's World Trade Center, Lakshman Jayaweera oversees foreign investment with a bird's eye view of the biggest: Port City.

On his board table is Sri Lanka's flag with its golden lion. Next to it, the golden stars of China.

Having overtaken Japan and India as Sri Lanka's biggest investor, China is about to build a 2-square-kilometer extension of Colombo where the ocean stretches to India and Africa.[1,2] Like the Eko Atlantic land reclamation in Lagos, the $1.4 billion Port City plan involves swanky hotels, shopping malls and leisure areas. There's talk of a marina and even a Formula 1 race track to boost tourism.

"For a country's development you really need a vision," says Jayaweera, chairman of the Board of Investment. "Just being an island doesn't make economic sense. We need to say 'we are here, we have the airports and the ports.'"

Along with grand infrastructure projects, Chinese investment is also arriving in smaller buckets. The flags on the table are the remnants from a meeting a day earlier with officials from the southern Guangdong province.

"They've had very active manufacturing operations as one of China's booming provinces," says Jayaweera. "But what they're finding now is per capita income is rising to $14,000, and so they're looking for places to relocate."

Wages here are a third less than in China and while adult literacy is similar at over 90%, Sri Lanka scores higher in UN data for secondary school enrollment and education quality.[3,4]

"If you look at the number of scientists, mathematicians, doctors – we're not making proper use of them. We're looking at whether we can get contract research like nanotechnology here."

Among the companies moving onto the island is an Australian solar panels maker, Energy Puzzle, which is investing $190 million in a production plant. Another Australian manufacturer that produces Hyflex industrial gloves called Ansell has opened a research center.

Sri Lanka's traditional strength is in textiles. GAP, Marks & Spencer and Victoria's Secret are all supplied by local companies Brandix Group and MAS Holdings, making garments the country's biggest export (Figure 9.1).[5]

"It's a mature industry," says Jayaweera. "Now we're speaking with some of our existing investors about really investing. We want to find a way of expanding just like Singapore or Hong Kong. We want to bring the materials in and create an environment to be a hub operation."

FIGURE 9.1   Export growth

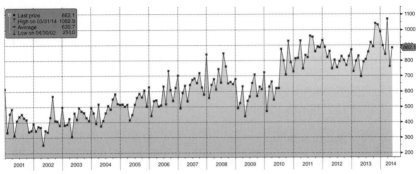

Source: Monthly export revenue in millions of dollars, data compiled by Bloomberg. (*Function: SNEX-TOT$ Index GP GO*).

With this in mind, Sri Lanka's tax policy nets out the cost of importing materials by providing rebates on export. Energy Puzzle gets a further tax break by locating its operation at the Board of Investment's new Export Processing Zone near the southern port city of Hambantota.

Along with creating a Hong Kong or Singapore type hub, investments in technology could mark the start of the "next Silicon Valley," Jayaweera says. "We would like to see Sri Lanka being the next Malaysia, maybe in ten years' time," he says in another breath.

Malaysia grew its economy by almost 8% annually between the early 80s and the mid-90s by creating a manufacturing base for technology such as semiconductor components and solar panels. Investment was helped along by the discovery of oil and gas, contributing about 40% of the federal budget.

The Sri Lankan economy grew by more than 8% in 2010 and 2011 after the end to a quarter of a century of civil war. Growth slowed to a little over 6% in 2012 and then recovered toward 8% in 2013 and 2014.[6]

Meanwhile, Cairn India is exploring for oil in the north and west of the island. "There are some hopes," says Jayaweera. "It's not an area that has been explored very well in the past. This could be a belt that has oil and gas."[7]

* * *

Seven kilometers southeast from the twin towers of the World Trade Center is a small anonymous house serving as the constituency office for the the United National Party's economy spokesman. The only marker from the street is a tiny arrow under a green elephant, the party's emblem.

Up a creaky narrow staircase in his office, Harsha de Silva is poring over official data that show the near 8% growth figures. The numbers are rigged, he says. Take 2011. Cement imports dropped, yet the figures showed construction booming with 25% growth. "How do you corroborate these numbers?"

Transparency International, the anti-corruption watchdog, has been asking the same question. In early 2014, it wrote to the parliamentary speaker and party leaders demanding an investigation on concern "concocted data" risk encouraging "disastrous" policies.

"There appears to be a significant gap between the figures in some areas like inflation, the cost of living, etc., and the actual situation of the country," wrote Executive Director S. Ranugge. "There is enough evidence before us to believe that the Department of Census and Statistics has been manipulating national socio-economic data."

Rajapaksa's government had to show there's been a "peace dividend" for the economy, reasons De Silva. But in reality the state's increased dominance smothered growth, he says.

"The state is like an octopus – whether it's hotels, golf courses, airlines, retail, banks, insurance or lucrative infrastructure contracts."

The contract for Port City, Sri Lanka's biggest-ever infrastructure project, was awarded without any transparent bidding process, alleges De Silva. The terms handed a part of the development on a 99-year lease to China Communications Construction Co.[8] Two months later, in September 2013, a further concession to expand the Mattala airport in Hambantota was also awarded to CCCC. It's the same Chinese government-linked group that Kenya contracted for its record infrastructure project – the Nairobi to Mombasa railway – despite protests that the company has been debarred from projects by the World Bank citing accusations of fraud the company disputes.[9,10] Port City - fully financed by CCCC with no government funding - will position Colombo as the International Business Centre of South Asia, boosting employment and tourism, the company said in a 2014 statement in the Sri Lankan Daily Mirror.

Nevertheless, the project and associated loans would be investigated by a UNP-led government, De Silva said before the 2015 election. Now, the UNP is part of the Sirisena coalition, elected on pledges to challenge the nation's increasing economic dependence on China.

"The land that White Man took over by means of military strength is now being obtained by foreigners paying ransom to a handful of persons," Sirisena wrote in his manifesto. "If this trend continues for another six years, our country would become a colony and we would become slaves."

Bond Box: Sri Lanka's Dollar Debt

Security & Trading Platform	Asset Description	Maturity / Amount Outstanding	Average Annual Price Change	Coupon/ Interest	Yield
Republic of Sri Lanka	Sovereign Dollars	2015 – 2022 Longest dated matures 2022 with $1bn outstanding	–12.4% in 2013 after issue in 2012	5.875%	5.2%

Source: Data compiled by Bloomberg as of December 2014

Investor Analysis: Morgan Stanley's Tim Drinkall on Policy

Bottom Line

- They're definitely **delivering on development**. The highway coming in was very quick and smooth. It's a much nicer, cleaner city than it was, and you can really see how it's going to be very different again in a few years.
- Jayaweera at the Board of Investment is right, they need the **infrastructure** in place first, and the rest can follow.
- In terms of the economy's **competitiveness**, while wages may be lower than China, the cost for a company finding that it suddenly needs to scale back its operations may be higher in Sri Lanka because of tougher labor laws.

Buy/Sell Triggers

- Post-conflict countries should be able to achieve economic **growth** above 8% a year, assuming they have slack in their labor markets and the economy isn't running at close to full capacity. The Sri Lankan economy doesn't have that slack, so growth rates at 7%-plus tend to fuel inflation, leading to higher interest rates and a slowdown in growth.

Endnotes

1. Anonymous (2013) China, Sri Lanka's biggest lender, *Ceylon FT*. Available at: http://www.ceylontoday.lk/22-48493-news-detail-china-sri-lankas-biggest-lender.html.
2. Media Center for National Development of Sri Lanka. Available at: http://www. development.lk/news_details-7-757.html.
3. Central Intelligence Agency (2013) The World Factbook, Country Comparison: GDP Per Capita (PPP). Available at: https://www.cia.gov/library/publications/ the-world-factbook/rankorder/2004rank.html.
4. United Nations Development Program (2010) Education. Available at: https:// data.undp.org/dataset/Table-8-Education/mvtz-nsye.
5. Economic and Social Statistics of Sri Lanka 2013: Key Socio-economic Indicators, Central Bank of Sri Lanka. Available at: http://www.cbsl.gov.lk/ pics_n_docs/10_pub/_docs/statistics/other/econ_&_ss_2013_e.p
6. Sri Lanka misses 2012 growth, deficit targets, *Daily Mirror*, April 10, 2013. Available at: http://www.dailymirror.lk/business/economy/27958-sri-lanka-misses-2012-growth-deficit-targets-.html.
7. Anonymous (2013) Cairn India bids for one block in Sri Lanka, *The Economic Times*. Available at: http://articles.economictimes.indiatimes.com/2013-12-06/ news/44864529_1_mannar-basin-cauvery-basin-cairn-india-ltd.
8. Anonymous (2013) Chinese firm to build $1.4 billion Sri Lanka 'Port City', AFP. Available at: http://foxnews.com/world/2013/07/24/chinese-firm-to-build -14-bn-sri-lanka-port-city/.
9. World Bank (2011) World Bank Applies 2009 Debarment to China Communications Construction Company Limited for Fraud in Philippines Roads Project. Available at: http://www.worldbank.org/en/news/press-release/2011/07/29/ world-bank-applies-2009-debarment-to-china-communications-construction-company-limited-for-fraud-in-philippines-roads-project.
10. Anonymous (2014) Sri Lanka opposition slams deal with blacklisted China firm, Lanka Business Online. Available at: http://www.lankabusinessonline.com/ news/sri-lanka-opposition-slams-deal-with-blacklisted-china-firm/915963676.

III – Pawn

One Saturday a month, a Colombo branch of Sampath Bank becomes an emporium. Watches, rings, necklaces, bracelets and brooches go under the auctioneer's hammer.

All are heirlooms put up as collateral for loans that have fallen into arrears.

With the end of Sri Lanka's long civil war feeding optimism of more prosperous times ahead, banks were falling over themselves to provide so-called pawning loans. Along with taking jewelry as security, the lenders would charge interest at twice the rate they paid for deposits.[1,2]

One of the biggest of the pawning loan providers among non-state banks was Sampath.

"These are people who have no other collateral to offer to get loans," says Ranjith Samaranayake, the chief financial officer at Sampath, sitting at his desk piled with paperwork. "They come with whatever jewelry they have in their house for working capital for their shop or fisheries."

Banks were lending close to the full value of the jewels as gold prices soared and the economy expanded through 2011.

Then growth slowed in 2012. More and more borrowers couldn't make their loan payments. When gold started dropping in price, bankers realized the collateral they owned was worth less than the money they were owed.

Non-performing loans at banks increased from 3.7% in 2012 to 5.6% by the end of 2013, with three-quarters of the increase driven by pawning loan defaults.[3]

As the bad debt crept up, Sampath increased its jewelry auctions from once every three months to one a month. It also slowed its growth in pawning loans from 80% in 2010 to 20% in 2013, partly by cutting the amount it would provide from 80% of the value of jewelry to 65%, Samaranayake tells us. Sampath reduced the number of loss-making branches from 37 to nine during 2013 and had the highest net interest income growth among its peers, according to Samaranayake.

At Colombo's central bank, deputy governor Ananda Silva draws parallels with America's mortgage meltdown. In the same way US lenders provided home loans close to the full property value, Sri Lanka's regulator hadn't set any loan-to-value limits for pawning loans.

"It was like the subprime issue," says Silva. "We didn't have rules on LTVs – that was the problem – so they lent up to 85%."

As the defaults mounted, banks made pawning loans less attractive to borrowers. At a time when commercial loan rates were falling, banks increased the interest on pawning loans to almost 19% by the end of 2013.[4]

But just like the credit squeeze triggered by the US mortgage meltdown, policy makers then fretted that the drop-off in lending, particularly to farmers and small businesses, was damping economic growth – cutting the "peace dividend." In 2014, the central bank switched tack – creating a loan guarantee scheme to spur banks to boost loan-to-value rates back to 80%. In return for taking on the risk of defaults, the central bank required lenders to cut their interest rates on pawning loans to 16% or less to spur more borrowing.[5,6]

While the guarantees covered licensed banks, the most enthusiastic providers of pawning loans – and the worst hit by the crisis – weren't actually banks at all but leasing companies offering finance on retail purchases. Defaults had driven some of the non-banking financial institutions, or NBFIs, close to collapse.

The central bank's solution was to ask banks to take on one or two of the NBFIs each to reduce the number of lenders.[7]

The idea of banks being coerced to bail out the NBFIs doesn't sit well with Tim Drinkall as a shareholder in Sri Lanka's biggest non-state lender, Commercial Bank of Ceylon. Tim would rather the central bank dealt with the problem by creating an asset management company to take over the NBFIs' bad debt, even if it meant charging a fee to the industry to cover some of the cost. He tells Silva as much.

"For me as an investor in a bank, if you're going to charge me 0.5% of assets to deal with the problems, I can model that out, that's OK, but when you're asking banks to buy NBFIs, I don't know what that cost looks like."

Rather than causing losses for the banks, responds Silva, the consolidation will be an opportunity to expand in a sector that accounts for 7% of all lending. "It's only two or three companies that have a problem."

Bank of Ceylon and Peoples Bank – the two main state-owned lenders – are among the banks most exposed to pawning loans, while the largest of the NBFIs to fail was an unregulated credit card company called Golden Key.[8–10]

"In order to strengthen the industry and ensure there are no further failures amongst these companies that could cause stress to the financial system, the central bank is determined to push for consolidation," says Ruwan Manatunga, chief strategy officer at Hatton Bank in Colombo.

At Commercial Bank, Managing Director and CEO Ravi Dias says they have always gone slow on pawning loans, focusing instead on personal loans, home loans and leasing as well as small- and medium-sized enterprise and corporate loans.

"We would look at pawning as a product to support the agricultural and micro-finance sector for the villages and may gradually reduce the existing pawning book in the main cities," says Dias.

Meanwhile, Commercial Bank has been expanding overseas, with 18 outlets in Bangladesh. That operation is bringing in around 12 to 15% of overall profits for the bank.

Investor's Notebook: Central Bank
Deputy Governor Ananda Silva ▬▬▬▬▬▬▬▬▬▬▬

- Spending on roads, ports and railways should keep **GDP growth** above 7% in the next few years while inflation will stay below 5%.
- After using $2 billion of reserves in 2011 in an effort to stem the rupee's weakening, the central bank switched its policy to let the currency depreciate. The rupee slid 12% against the dollar in 2012, helping exporters. It's likely to **go on depreciating** by 2 or 3% a year.

Stocks Box: International Bank Comparison

Company & Trading Platform	Description	Average Annual Return	Price– Earnings Ratio	Price– Book Ratio/ NAV	Return on Equity	Gross Dividend Yield	Market Value ($m)	Top Holders %
Commercial Bank of Ceylon Colombo Stock Exchange	Sri Lanka's biggest non-state bank	58.2% from 2009, year civil war ended	12.2	2.2	17.8%	2.8%	1029	DFCC Bank 14.8% Franklin Resources 13.6% Free float 75.7%
Hatton National Bank Colombo Stock Exchange	Sri Lankan non-state bank	46.9% from 2009	9.4	1.3	14.0%	4.5%	549	Sri Lanka Insurance 14.8% Employee Provident 9.9% Free float 31.7%
EFG Hermes Cairo Stock Exchange	Leading Egyptian investment bank	4.2% from 2009, year of share offering	N/A	1.2	–1.7%	N/A	1531	DF EFG 1 11.7% Rahman Abdel 7.7% Free float 72.9%
Guaranty Trust Bank London Stock Exchange	Nigeria's biggest bank by market value	23.3% since listing 2007	N/A	N/A	N/A	2.2%	4120	FMR 1.5% Fidelity 1.2% BankInvest 0.4%

Company & Trading Platform	Description	Average Annual Return	Price–Earnings Ratio	Price–Book Ratio/ NAV	Return on Equity	Gross Dividend Yield	Market Value ($m)	Top Holders %
FBN Holdings Nigerian Stock Exchange	Nigerian lender	24.8% since data starts 2002	4.9	0.7	14.4%	11.1%	1817	Franklin Resources 2.8% Fidelity 1.5% Free float 98.4%
BRD-Groupe Bucharest Stock Exchange	Romania's second-largest bank	34.5% since listed 2001	N/A	1.1	–7.0%	N/A	1595	Société Générale 60.2% SIF3 4.6% Free float 38.8%

Source: Data compiled by Bloomberg as of December 2014

Investor Analysis: Morgan Stanley's Tim Drinkall on Banking

Bottom Line

- We take a long-term view, so a reasonable **devaluation** of the currency is a good thing. You don't want an over-valued currency eroding competitiveness.
- It is concerning that the central bank allowed the **NBFIs** to happen and then asked the banks to fix its mess. I'm surprised the central bank doesn't regulate the pawning loans industry. Capital adequacy ratios could come under threat, yet they don't force banks to make sure they're properly provisioned. It's a little Pollyanna-ish.
- It's more the **principle** that annoys me than the actual cost. I don't like it when a company I hold is told it has to buy something. I'm put in a position where I have to decide whether I want to play a part in the clear-up as an innocent bystander.
- I've never been a fan of **pawning loans**. The whole "know your customer" consideration goes out the window. It's a much riskier business than normal bank lending. It's better to bring in the unbanked population through deposit services, rather than rushing to lend. There's also no cross-selling opportunity.
- The pawning loans aren't a problem in a **systemic risk** sense as indebtedness is very low.

- Within the banking sector, Commercial remains the **standout**. It offers the highest return on equity at around 18% and gold pawning loans are a very low percentage of the business.
- **Hatton** said it wants to dethrone Commercial Bank as the most profitable bank – but that's why I like Commercial Bank, because it's already the most profitable.

Buy/Sell Triggers

- Commercial Bank has a **return-on-equity target** of 20%, though that's going to be tough. If it can keep around the level of 18% seen in 2013 that would be fine.

Stocks Box: Comparing Industries

Company & Trading Platform	Description	Average Annual Return	Price– Earnings Ratio	Price– Book Ratio/ NAV	Return on Equity	Gross Dividend Yield	Market Value ($m)	Top Holders %
Ceylon Tobacco Colombo Stock Exchange	Manufactures and markets cigarettes and smoking products	84.5% from 2009	22.3	42.2	194%	4.0%	1558	British American Tobacco 84.1% FTR Holding 8.3% Free float 5.7%
Tokyo Cement Company Lanka Colombo Stock Exchange	Sri Lanka's largest cement manufacturer	22.9% from 2009	8.8	1.5	26.2%	2.5%	140	St. Anthonys 27.5% Nippon Coke & 23.7% Free float 16.3%
Chevron Lubricants Lanka Colombo Stock Exchange	Manufactures and sells petroleum-based lubricants	55.7% from 2009	14.8	6.9	49.2%	5.6%	313	Chevron Ceylon 51.0% Aberdeen 24.6% Free float 40.3%

Source: Data compiled by Bloomberg as of December 2014

Investor's Notebook: Ceylon Tobacco Co. ▬▬▬▬▬

- **Second biggest** stock on Colombo exchange by market capitalization.[11]
- **Exports** to Afghanistan and Maldives with consent from majority owner British American Tobacco. Pricing in Sri Lanka is government controlled.
- **Innovative** products: A click in the cigarette butt switches the flavor to menthol on Dunhill Switch and Dunhill Ice.
- Overall market direction is **declining;** income levels are insufficient for electronic cigarettes.

My Sri Lanka: Securities and Exchange Commission Chairman Nalaka Godahewa
Ten-Point Plan for the Colombo Stock Exchange

1. **Demutualization:** Open up the ownership of the exchange beyond the 15 main brokerages; prepare for listing as soon as 2016.
2. **Bonds:** Initiatives to encourage companies to list bonds include removing a 10% withholding tax. This spurred 400% growth of the market in 2013.
3. **Back office:** Harmonization among the brokering houses and modernization with the latest technology.
4. **Education:** Improve financial literacy and understanding of the capital markets.
5. Central **counterparty** system: Reduce the risk of failed transactions by trading through a single clearing system; completion targeted for end of 2015.
6. **Regulation:** Fine-tune the regulatory framework to provide civil and administrative enforcement powers in addition to the current criminal sanctions.
7. **Unit trusts:** The fund industry is a major focus to attract more retail investors.
8. **Portfolio expansion:** Products in the pipeline include derivatives, exchange-traded funds and real estate investment trusts.
9. Company **listings:** We have 293 listed companies and about 45 that are discussing a listing by 2017.
10. **New investors:** Roadshows in the USA, UK, Dubai, Hong Kong, Singapore and India are part of the process of attracting a wider group of foreign investors along with locals.

Endnotes

1. Commercial Bank Lending and Deposit Rates, Central Bank of Sri Lanka. Available at: http://www.cbsl.gov.lk/htm/english/_cei/ir/i_4.asp?date=&Mode=2&Page=11.
2. Anonymous (2011) Sri Lanka Sampath Bank's pawning business up 80 pct in 2010, Lanka Business Report. Available at: http://lbr.lk/fullstory.php?nid=201102142040022048.
3. Anonymous (2014) Guarantee on pawning loans credit positive for banks: Moody's, *Daily Mirror*. Available at: http://www.dailymirror.lk/business/features/47556-guarantee-on-pawning-loans-credit-positive-for-banks-moodys-.html.
4. Anonymous (2014) CB introduces credit guarantee on pawning loans, The Nation. Available at: http://www.nation.lk/edition/breaking-news/item/29355-cb-introduces-credit-guarantee-on-pawning-loans.html.
5. Anonymous (2014) New credit guarantee scheme for pawning advances, *Daily News*. Available at: http://www.dailynews.lk/?q=business/new-credit-guarantee-scheme-pawning-advances.
6. Anonymous (2014) Sri Lanka's Bank of Ceylon profits down 1.9-pct, cushioned by loss reversals, Lanka Business Online. Available at: http://www.lankabusinessonline.com/news/sri-lankas-bank-of-ceylon-profits-down-1.9-pct,-cushioned-by-loss-reversals/82760471.
7. Anonymous (2014) NBFI Sector consolidation on course with more mergers, *Daily News*. Available at: http://www.dailynews.lk/?q=business/nbfi-sector-consolidation-course-more-mergers#sthash.F1KVhXg8.dpuf.
8. Sirimanna, B. (2012) State banks reduce gold pawning business, *Sunday Times*. Available at: http://www.sundaytimes.lk/120722/business-times/state-banks-reduce-gold-pawning-business-6472.html.
9. World Finance Banking Awards (2012) Banking in Sri Lanka. Available at: http://www.banking-awards-2012.worldfinance.com/development-in-sri-lanka.
10. Bloomberg data as of June 2014.
11. Data based on internal estimates from Ceylon Tobacco Co., 2013.

IV - Kilinochchi

The last train to the Tamil north left Colombo two decades ago, so I buy a ticket for the Sri Lanka Air Force service.

Cadets are on a pre-dawn jog around the airport perimeter as I arrive. Officers in light blue and navy uniforms check my handwritten receipt against their paper records and guide me to a scale to be weighed with my luggage. In the lounge, painted the same uniform blues, an officer sits with his wife and two children, while a couple of Chinese tourists plan their stay in Trincomalee, a resort in the northeast that's our first stop. Two Airtel salesmen in matching red polo shirts play with the phones they sell. I'm seated with one of them on board. Sri Lanka's fourth largest mobile provider after the leader Dialog has an outsized presence in the north after entering the market as soon as the region opened up in 2010, he tells me.

The plane is almost full as we fly for 40 minutes over thick, hilly jungle before touching down in "Trinco." The town is lined with mile upon mile of unspoiled white beaches. Most of the passengers on our 50-seater plane disembark, heading for the few hotels near the town.

From Trincomalee we hug the coastline across a landscape of shallow green lagoons. We're heading northwest to the very top of the teardrop of India – as Sri Lanka was known through its long civil war. Every acre is farmed, even tiny islands.

Baggage reclaim at Jaffna airport consists of a man with a half dozen suitcases. We take a beige airforce minibus to an army checkpoint nearby in Kankesanthuray. KKS, as it's known to locals with the Indian habit of turning everything into initials, is 100 square kilometers of pristine shoreline, fertile grasslands and palmyra forests. A rusting white light-house marks the spot where a customs office once monitored ships ply-ing the 30-kilometer Palk Strait to India. Close by is the Aitken Spence Harbor View Hotel. Like everything else here, it has been taken over by the army.

The pride of KKS is the Thalsevana Holiday Resort. On a bandstand with wicker chairs on a polished red floor I meet Ghanan. In "the good old days" before the war, his parents used to bring him and his five siblings here for tea at the small rest house. The army has turned it into a 30-room hotel.[1] In place of bell boys and porters are green-fatigued soldiers.[2] The old harbor wrecked by the Tsunami in 2004 has been moved down the coast by the military.[3]

Ghanan's family moved to KKS in 1967. Dad was a civil servant and his mother a teacher. They took the train to Colombo for a family wedding one day in 1984. Clashes broke out between Tamil Tiger and government forces that week, closing down the railway, so they stayed in the south.

We drive by the track where the train station stood. Across a sandy road are the disused council offices where Ghanan's father worked, alongside shut-down government stores and a glass maker's workshop. A parched field beyond is where Ghanan used to play football with his friends, just next to the old school bus stop. Nadeswara College is 2 kilometers up the road. The remains of its yellowy-cream walls and red skirting are just as Ghanan remembers.[4]

We drive on. To our right, grassy plains sink down to a huge lime-stone quarry, and towering above is the idled hulk of the KKS cement factory.

A soldier patrols, an automatic rifle by his side. "Look to your right," says Ghanan, "and remember what you see." There's nothing but a pile of old bricks. When the soldier is out of sight, Ghanan stops the car and pulls a photo from the glove box.

"That pile of rubble was our home." The picture shows a grand Italianate house with a red-tiled roof supported by two Roman pillars. Wide stone steps lead to a porch with a dining table for eight. Above are brown shuttered windows topped by a rose-colored arch and framed figurine. Apart from a few missing tiles, the house seems beautifully intact.

Ghanan shows me another photo. It's him and his sister holding hands outside the house. The photo was taken less than four months earlier, when his mother and sister came to visit. A week later, newspapers reported that the military had demolished some houses in KKS and the chief minister for the northern region, CV Wigneswaran of the Tamil National Alliance, was refused permission to visit.

"I assumed our house was still standing because I'd only just seen it," says Ghanan. "It was only last week when I came here with a friend that I realized. In fact, it was my 8-year-old son who saw it first. I said don't be silly, that's not our house – but he was right."

We drive past dozens more rubble piles and then rows of empty yards. Each has a gray stone circle around a deep hole. "You can tell where the houses were because there was no running water here. Everyone had to dig their own well."

Around 40,000 people lived in KKS before the war. "Even if they come here now, there are no houses," says Ghanan. "It's heart-breaking. They're systematically blocking the prospect for families to resettle."

Ghanan is no Tamil Tiger rebel. He condemns the Liberation Tigers of Tamil Eelam and the governments of the time for the wartime atrocities and failing to reconcile differences when they were in positions of strength. The Indian Peace Keeping Force that forgot its mission with its massacres around here is equally to blame.

"I'm tough on everyone letting down this region," says Ghanan.

"There are too many people playing politics. Once people get power they become deaf and dumb."

Among the Tamils who fled, 100,000 went to Britain and twice as many headed for Canada.[5,6] The Rajapaksa government said it had resettled all internally displaced people.[7]

"Instead of resettling they've actively aided displacement," says Ghanan. "Thank God for the Jaffna people, they have relatives abroad to send money. Otherwise we'd have been another Sudan."

Three kilometers from the center of Jaffna is the region's main shrine, the Nallur Kandaswamy Kovil. Tuk tuk drivers slow down, nod their heads to the temple and touch their hearts. Across the road, a widow sets up a makeshift altar for prayers and money. Cows drift by and stray dogs bark it out and mark their territory.

In the next street is the blue and white steel gate of the United Nations. The UN was given a mandate in March 2014 to investigate alleged war crimes by Sri Lankan government forces and Tamil Tiger rebels in the final throes of the war.[8] The UN says at least 40,000 Tamil civilians were killed in the last few months of the conflict, mostly by government artillery. Its resolution – opposed by Rajapaksa as a conspiracy for regime change that will damage reconciliation efforts – also calls on the UN to probe human rights abuses up to the present day.[9] The inquiry was "triggered by the failure of the Sri Lankan government to stand by its promises to credibly and independently investigate alleged violations," said British Prime Minister David Cameron. It represents a victory for Sri Lankans who need to know what happened, he said.[10] Prime Minister Ranil Wickremesinghe said the new government will engage with the UN Human Rights Commission in a positive manner, though all matters should be determined by domestic jurisdiction.

A couple of doors from the UN building is the Heritage Hotel where I drop my bags. Outside my bedroom window, a man on a motorbike delivers a garland of flowers to decorate the hotel's shrine to the elephant god

Ganesha, the remover of obstacles. I head down to watch the ceremony, wary of intruding. I'm welcomed with thumbed dabs of red and yellow powder to my "third eye." A white substance in a small pot heated over a flame – the traditional dried cow dung – is smeared across my forehead.

The hotel owner's sister-in-law is an MP in Jaffna. His brother was too. Famous for removing his shirt in parliament in protest at the humiliating treatment of Tamils, Thiyagarajah Maheswaran said on TV he would be presenting parliament with details of the terror campaign being waged from Colombo. The interview in late 2007 was his last. While visiting a temple on New Year's Day 2008, he was shot dead.

In the center of Jaffna, the red and yellow of Hindu ceremonies color the temples and walls, before giving way to the branded maroon of Cargills. Sri Lanka's biggest retailer has just opened a shopping mall on the wreckage of the Jaffna Cooperative Stores, closed since a blast in the early 80s.

The new building's star attraction is the Tamil north's first-ever escalator. "People really didn't know how to get on it," says Samuel Neshakumar, who views the mall from every angle on a security monitor in his office as Cargills' manager in Jaffna.

Like the Page family that built the Cargills business, Nesha – as he's known to just about everyone here – is a Tamil Christian born in Jaffna. When the Indian Peace Keeping Force invaded the town of Urumparai in 1986, they shot dead seven of his relatives. The family moved south and Nesha married a Sinhalese colleague. When the war ended, he became the first manager of a major company to relocate to the north. He arrived in November 2009 after driving for 12 hours from Colombo with a military convoy for the last leg.

Across from his glass-walled office is the northern region's only KFC, offering spiced-up chicken and vegetable biryani. Next door is a three-screen, 600-seater cinema, returning the Page family business to its roots as a movie theater operator. In its heyday – when it was supported by a cement factory, a chemicals plant and a salt mine – the Jaffna region had more than 15 cinemas. The movies showing now are mostly light-hearted Hindi imports from Bollywood that inexplicably have the audience in hysterics.

At the foot of the escalator is Cargills' Food City, a bright, modern supermarket with seven types of rice lined up in sacks and large, unblemished fruit and vegetables.

The produce comes from a collection center a 20-minute drive north from Jaffna in Allaveddy. Smallholders drop off here while Cargills makes the rounds to collect from bigger vendors. Crates of green chillies are being sorted as we arrive.

The soil, reddened by heavy limestone and ferric content, makes the region suited to growing a wider range of produce than the rest of the island, including vegetables better known to damp European climes like beetroot, carrots and cabbage.

One of Allaveddy's biggest suppliers is a 5-minute drive from the sorting depot. Long-necked chickens with sturdy legs coveted for cock fighting stride about the yard as fluffy yellow chicks peck at some cabbage. Tiny red garlic-like onions used in curries are piled ready for pick up.

Running the place is Mutthiah, a lean, unshirted Hindu who looks about 50 but is 71. Mutthiah moved to the farm with his father and his brother in the 80s. In 1987, the Indian Peace Keeping Force invaded his home. They tortured his brother, accusing him of supporting the Tamil Tigers. After a series of interrogations, Mutthiah's brother poisoned himself. His gravestone looks out over the farm.

While taking up arms is a "source of shame," Mutthiah supports the Tigers "100 percent." For all their mistakes, the LTTE maintained peace and fought crime when they controlled the territory. Mutthiah points to where thieves cut the electricity wires connected to a neighbor's house to sell as copper a few weeks earlier. "When there are so many army check points, how can this happen?" he says.

Mutthiah feels sad for the people who "sweated to build their house" only for it be expropriated by the army. "It's hugely wrong," he says.

As for himself, Mutthiah is making good money. He's quadrupled the land he farms since 2010, earning a million rupees ($7650) a year.

Cargills turns some of Mutthiah's fruit and vegetables into chutneys, jams, juices and sauces 90 kilometers south from here at the processing plant in Kilinochchi.

The road to Kilinochchi is littered with remnants of the war. Some of the palmyra trees are bare trunks, their tops blown off by shelling. Grassy plains are dotted with red and yellow sticks denoting unexploded landmines.

Kantharuban walks by the side of the road to a waiting bus after a day sweeping with the Halo Trust, the world's largest humanitarian mine clearance organization. Each person covers around 8 square meters a day. It's dangerous work. Neither side left maps of the mines they planted. Inter-connections were rigged to trigger multiple explosions. The team finds mines every day, says Kantharuban, and detonates them.

By the roadside near the Elephant Pass salt mine is the wreckage of a bulldozer. The LTTE painted it in camouflage green and tried to drive it through an army camp. A billboard above shows a photo of Lance Corporal Hassalaka Gamini Kularatne. He was posthumously awarded the highest military honors for climbing on to the bulldozer and blowing it up, along with himself.

To the left is a giant water tank toppled on its side. A plaque reads: "Kilinochchi Water Tank, destroyed by LTTE terrorists in December 2008, is declared open as a public attraction." Next to it, the "Souvenirs Galore" store sells postcards.

According to the pro-Tamil website TamilNet, most of the buildings around here were destroyed by continuous shelling from the Sri Lankan military.[11] A few hundred one-bedroom houses make up India's resettlement project at Palai. There had been talk of 50,000.

Nearby is the industrial area of Kilinochchi. A sprawling factory makes sportswear and lingerie for MAS Holdings to supply fashion outlets like Victoria's Secret and GAP.

Opposite, at the Cargills processing plant, the fruit and vegetables from Mutthiah and other farmers are washed, skinned, chopped and fed into a blender for pulp. Most of the 55 women on the production line are the wives of men disabled or killed in the conflict, or divorcees. The LTTE's policy of compulsory conscription for unmarried men created a scramble to get hitched. Many of the marriages of survival didn't last after the war.

Serving tea and lunch for the women here is 62-year-old Sarojinidevi. Thirty years ago she was fleeing from fighting across the jungle when her husband got crushed by an elephant, leaving him severely disabled. They resettled until the army approached again in early 2009. Again they escaped, taking their three children and nine grandchildren to a camp in Puthumathalan. When the army came to Puthumathalan, there was nowhere left to go. Bombardment of the camp killed Sarojinidevi's 39-year-old son and grandsons aged 15 and 8. Sarojinidevi lifts her blouse to show shrapnel in her left rib. She's still taking painkillers. At home in her Indian-built displacement house she suffers severe post-trauma depression. "Having a job with people around is good," she says. "It helps me cope."

Stocks Box: Conglomerates

Company & Trading Platform	Description	Average Annual Return	Price–Earnings Ratio	Price–Book Ratio/ NAV	Return on Equity	Gross Dividend Yield	Market Value ($m)	Top Holders %
Cargills Colombo Stock Exchange	Sri Lanka's biggest retailer; businesses span beer to broking	73.2% from 2009	N/A	2.9	2.4%	1.3%	264	CT Holdings 70.0% Page Valentine 6.4% Free float 11.7%
John Keells Colombo Stock Exchange	Largest Sri Lankan listed company; businesses include Cinnamon hotel group, Keells Super groceries, ports, bunkering	65.7% from 2009	18.5	1.88	11.7%	1.5%	1824	Capital SE 13.9% Broga Hill 10.5% Free float 59.4%
Aitken Spence Colombo Stock Exchange	Largest inbound travel operator through 50:50 joint venture with TUI Travel	74.8% from 2009	10.8	1.26	12.4%	2.0%	309	Melstacorp 39.8% Aberdeen 16.9% Free float 32.1%

Source: Data compiled by Bloomberg as of December 2014

Investor's Notebook: Colombo Conglomerates ▬▬▬

1. Cargills: Ranjit Page, Deputy Chairman

- **Origins** in a general warehouse, import and wholesale business established in 1844 by William Miller and David Sime Cargill. Bought in 1982 by Albert Page, expanding his business from a chain of cinemas.
- **Flagship products:** Oldest retailer in Sri Lanka, with Cargills Food City supermarkets. Produces Magic ice cream, Kotmale fresh milk, yogurt and cheese, Kist fruit jams, juices, sauces, biscuits, and Goldi & Sams processed meats. Holds KFC & TGI Fridays franchises. The parent company, CT Holdings, spans broking to property development.
- **Next big push:** Building a banking network to use technology and the group's regional presence to bring financial services to a wider socio-economic group; seeking international partner with same vision that can unlock liquidity.
- **Perspective:** "Sri Lankans have suffered from many decades of terrorism and frankly I never thought I would see the bloodshed end in my lifetime. The government was bold enough to make this happen. Now it's up to us as corporates to contribute towards transforming the absence of war to sustainable peace. The process of reconciliation is never easy, but engaging the communities, empowering them towards employment and income generation is certainly a pivotal part of this process. We are trying to empower people to move forward and not become victims of their past."

2. John Keells: Ajit D. Gunewardene, Deputy Chairman

- **Origins** in the brokering business of English brothers Edwin and George John in the early 1870s that helped build tea production and exports, and the acquisition of another Colombo broker, Keell & Waldock Ltd, in 1960. The purchase of Walkers Tours & Travels and the Mackinnons' Group began diversification toward today's 70-member conglomerate.[12]
- **Largest** company on the Colombo Stock Exchange.
- **Flagship products:** Cinnamon hotel group, Keells Super supermarkets, Elephant House soft drinks and ice cream, ports, bunkering.
- **Next big push:** "Waterfront"- a 4 million square foot integrated resort complex in Colombo including an 800-room hotel, 450+ apartments in two towers, commercial office tower, conference space, shopping mall and a 160,000-square-foot area to be leased out to a foreign casinos operator.

- **Growth** in supermarket footfall has been very encouraging – we plan to add about 10 stores a year to the current total of 46. Soft drinks and ice cream sales continue to increase with the rise in disposable incomes. Colombo's port should grow in volume as the Indian economy expands. The fastest tourist growth is from China: 25,000 in 2012 rising to 50,000 in 2013 and a likely 100,000 in 2014. Sri Lankan Airways will fly direct to Shanghai and some other cities, cutting the route time to 5½ hours. We're tweaking our business model – Chinese menus, Chinese-speaking staff, guides etc.
- **Challenges:** We saw ourselves slightly outpriced and so we adjusted our hotel room prices downwards by 8–10% in 2013, which has resulted in a sharp jump in occupancy and the overall performance of our resorts. The first quarter of 2014 was the best we've had, with 100% occupancy. The bunkering business suffered a narrowing of margins because of competition.
- **Macro:** Local currency devaluation benefits us because 70% of our profit is from businesses that earn foreign currency.
- **Perspective:** The property market here isn't speculative, with most purchases being for accommodation rather than investment. The yield on property is around 6% in dollar terms. Payment is 10% upfront, followed soon after by an advance of 15% and then tranches of 25%, with the final settlement on handover. Commercial real estate has to be the next big development push.

3. Aitken Spence: Nilanthi Sivapragasam, Chief Financial Officer

- **Origins** with British entrepreneurs focusing on trading and maritime services in 1868.
- **Largest** inbound travel operator through a 50:50 joint venture with TUI Travel Plc, representing over 200 of the leading tour operators and handling around 12% of total genuine tourist arrivals.
- **Flagship products:** A leading player in hotels, travel, maritime services, logistic solutions and power generation. Significant interests in plantations, insurance, financial services, IT, printing and garments. Operations in six countries in south Asia, the South Pacific, the Middle East and Africa.
- **Growth:** More tourists are coming in from southeast Asia and the Middle East. Western Europeans remain the largest group at 33%, but the growth has come down. Southeast Asia is a close second at around 26%.

- **Challenges:** When the war was over we increased our rates; we never reduced the rates, even in mid-2013. It was a challenge – occupancies were not so good. There are a large number of travel agents/tour operators in the country, so we do have competition. The power purchase agreements for two 20-megawatt power plants run by Aitken Spence weren't extended because the government switched its focus to coal.

4. Hemas: Husein Esufally, Non-Executive Chairman

- **Origins** in business established in 1948 by Sheikh Hasannally Esufally and listed in 2003.
- **Largest** baby care producer with Baby Cheramay.
- **Flagship products:** Colgard toothpaste and Velvet beauty soap contribute to over 20% share of the personal care market. Hemas also operates three private hospitals and five hydropower plants with a combined capacity of 11.4 megawatts. Hemas Transportation is the general sales agent for Emirates and Malaysian Airlines. The leisure business comprises four hotels and destination management.
- **Next big push:** Operations in Bangladesh are growing rapidly; Bangladesh is easier to bite than getting into India. We tried to get our baby care creams to India, but it takes a lot of money.
- **Growth:** Owns four hotels with a total of 400 rooms and building three more hotels on the southern coast for another 350 rooms. Revenue is about equally split in three. The first area is fast-moving consumer goods (FMCGs), mainly personal care products. The next is healthcare – pharmaceuticals and private hospitals. The last third is the leisure, transportation and power sectors.
- **Challenges:** Hemas entered the power generation business 10 years ago with a 100-megawatt thermal power plant. That's coming to an end. The government isn't likely to extend the license as it's cheaper to use coal. Hemas appointed Steven Enderby as the group's first non-family chief executive officer in 2014. Husein Esufally, the former group CEO, becomes non-executive chairman.
- **Macro:** 2012 and 2013 were tough because of currency depreciation; a lot of the ingredients are imported from India, China and Europe.
- **Perspective:** It's all about trying to get scale so you can attract talent and access capital more efficiently. We're at a point where we're trying to narrow down to focus on wellness and hospitality. Our strategy is not to get into high-end hospitals but deliver affordable family healthcare.

Colombo Stock Exchange

Company Name	% Index Weight
John Keells Holdings PLC	8.4
Ceylon Tobacco Co PLC	7.2
Commercial Bank of Ceylon PLC	4.5
Nestlé Lanka PLC	4.0
Dialog Axiata PLC	3.7
Carson Cumberbatch PLC	3.0
Sri Lanka Telecom PLC	3.0
Bukit Darah PLC/The	2.6
Distilleries Co of Sri Lanka PLC	2.1
Hatton National Bank	2.1
DFCC Bank	2.0
Lion Brewery Ceylon PLC	1.8
Lanka Orix Leasing Co PLC	1.5
Chevron Lubricants Lanka PLC	1.4
Aitken Spence PLC	1.4
National Development Bank PLC	1.4
Sampath Bank PLC	1.4
Access Engineering PLC	1.3
People's Leasing & Finance PLC	1.3
Hemas Holdings PLC	1.2
Cargills Ceylon PLC	1.2
Lanka IOC PLC	1.1
Asian Hotels & Properties PLC	1.1

Source: Data compiled by Bloomberg as of December 2014

Investor Analysis: Morgan Stanley's Tim Drinkall on Conglomerates

Bottom Line

- John Keells remains a **core holding** because of the exposure to a lot of the good growth areas in the economy. Around 1.8% of the frontier fund is in John Keells.
- The company is still very positive about property and tourism. I'm pleased they cut room rates aggressively when they realized they'd priced themselves out of the market. That flexibility clearly had an impact and put **occupancy** ahead of Aitken Spence, who are sticking to the higher-end clients.
- John Keells is also developing its land bank to **diversify** across residential, port businesses and bunkering, whereas Aitken Spence is almost purely tourism now.
- The **retailing** businesses hadn't been profitable, so it's very good to see John Keells finally reached profit on the supermarket business.
- The **Waterfront Project** with its mixed use of malls, office and residential space and a casino will also be very positive. The rules aren't clear on casinos but it's good they're moving in anyway. Others risk missing the boat by waiting.
- Normally I'm averse to companies **over-diversifying** but this is an exception. They have a very strong management team.
- **Outside of the conglomerates** the textile companies – MAS and Brandix – are very big. Ceylon Tobacco has the monopoly here. Dilmah is the big tea exporter but that's privately held.

Buy/Sell Triggers

- There are a lot of moving parts – the **risk of property** prices falling being the main one. The John Keells model is to pre-sell, which helps to fund the next property. If the market dries up and they aren't able to pre-sell, that will be problematic.
- While buying of the shares has been international, selling has been local. The **price** has been looking high. It traded at 19 times earnings per share compared with an average of 14 times for companies in the Sri Lanka Stock Market Colombo All-Share Index.
- On the positive side, the **tourist numbers** are really nothing yet – 1.2 million a year. They haven't reached critical mass. There's a lot of potential.

Endnotes

1. Ministry of Defence & Urban Development (2010) Commander of the Army declares open 'Thalsevana', the luxurious holiday resort in Jaffna. Available at: http://www.defence.lk/new.asp?fname=20101003_02.

2. Sri Lanka Army (2014) Defence Seminar. Available at: http://www.defseminar.lk/about-us/Theslarmy.php.

3. India–Sri Lanka Friendship, Rehabilitation of Kankesanthurai (KKS) Harbour. Available at: http://www.hcicolombo.org/images/cover_pdfs/Rehabilitation_of_KKS.pdf.

4. Palakidnar, A. (2014) KP's Alma Mater demolished, *Ceylon Today*. Available at: http://www.ceylontoday.lk/16-48860-news-detail-kps-alma-mater-demolished.html.

5. Sri Lanka Demographics Profile (2013) Index Mundi. Available at: http://www.indexmundi.com/sri_lanka/demographics_profile.html.

6. Diversity Watch, Ryerson University School of Journalism. Available at: http://www.diversitywatch.ryerson.ca/backgrounds/tamils.htm.

7. Ministry of Defence & Urban Development (2013) Resettlement completed – A milestone reached by the Government of Sri Lanka. Available at: http://www.defence.lk/new.asp?fname=RESETTLEMENT_COMPLETED_20121022_03.

8. Cumming-Bruce, N. (2014) U.N. approves investigation of civil war in Sri Lanka, *New York Times*. Available at: http://www.nytimes.com/2014/03/28/world/asia/un-rights-council-sri-lanka.html?_r=0.

9. Anonymous (2014) Sri Lanka rejects the UN resolution approving an International probe, Colombo Page. Available at: http://www.colombopage.com/archive_14A/Mar27_1395933963CH.php

10. Anonymous (2014) 'Victory for Sri Lankan people': UN to probe 'War Crimes,' Channel 4 News. Available at: http://www.channel4.com/news/sri-lanka-united-nations-vote-resolution-war-crimes-video.

11. Anonymous (2009) Sri Lankan troops seize rebel HQ, BBC News. Available at: http://news.bbc.co.uk/1/hi/world/south_asia/7807908.stm.

12. John Keells plc Annual Report 2007/08. Available at: http://www.cse.lk/cmt/upload_report_file/731_1215148010.pdf.

V – Rising Sun

Outside the headquarters of Jaffna's main newspaper, seven Compaq computers are stacked on shelves. The monitors are smashed, the hard drives ripped out.

Inside, white walls are pocked with five holes. Bullets are lodged in two. Framed photos show the bloodied faces of three journalists, a marketing manager, a nightshift worker and a driver killed in raids here between 2001 and 2007. Another shows a journalist still missing.

After the civil war, the killing stopped and a campaign of violence began. Snaps from 2013 show a motorbike loaded with newspapers set ablaze by thugs who attacked the driver with iron bars wrapped in barbed wire. The paper's printing press is riddled with bullets and burnt; a video camera is mangled.

The photos end with a visit by British Prime Minister David Cameron in November 2013, the first by a foreign head of state to the Tamil north. Cameron told the newspaper's staff he wouldn't forget what he'd seen.[1] The next day he warned Sri Lanka that unless it took credible action to tackle human rights issues, Britain would push for the UN Human Rights Council to investigate allegations of war crimes.[2]

With the international focus, violence was downgraded to threats. In January 2014, an army officer seeing a journalist taking photos of homes being demolished in KKS threatened to kill him if the pictures were published, says the editor. The paper was facing nine defamation lawsuits from officials, each demanding between half a billion and a billion rupees, or up to $7.7 million. Any one of the cases could have shut down *Uthayan* – the Rising Sun.

"Their tactics have changed," Editor Thevanayagam Premananth said before the 2015 election, "but their intention hasn't. They think we are fueling the aspirations of the Tamils, that's the reason they want to suppress us."

Prem, as he's known, was 8 years old when the Indian Peace Keeping Force burnt down his family's home. Seven years later, he was among half a million displaced when Sri Lankan troops drove the Tamil Tigers out of Jaffna in 1995.

Prem's family moved in with relations 150 kilometers southeast in Mullaittivu. Without a university in reach, Prem got his journalism degree through a distance learning course and joined *Uthayan* in 1998. He returned to the newsroom from an assignment one day in 2006 to find two colleagues dead and another being rushed to hospital.

With gallows humor he says the situation helped his promotion. At the age of 30, he's about the oldest here. "Once a journalist gets married there's no way his wife will let him work here."

After the main printing press was torched and sprayed with bullets in the 2013 raid, *Uthayan* had to cut its print run to 25,000 from 40,000. Advertising dwindled to a few statements from the temples, says Prem. "A company would have faced huge pressure from government if it was advertising with us."

Not that there would be much money among local businesses to spend on advertising anyway. While the local fishing industry provided 43% of the national supply before the war, its contribution has dwindled to just 7%.[3]

"If we upgrade techniques and have multi-day trawlers then we can boost the fishing industry again," says Prem. "We still have the small boats and motors that need to return in the evenings."

Wealthy entrepreneurs among the Tamil diaspora are keen to invest if they can be assured the government won't take over their assets, says Prem. Discussions on reviving the salt, chemical and cement factories have been ongoing since 2009 without a result.

The Cargills mall and factories, built with help from USAID, are positive but it's a drop in the ocean. "We can see this one example in five years," says Prem. "Four hundred job opportunities aren't enough. Without a solution in the Tamil–Sinhalese issue, we can't have any serious development."

President Sirisena campaigned on a promise to ease religious and ethnic tensions, winning him backing from the Tamil National Alliance. Six years earlier, during the closing weeks of the civil war, Sirisena was acting defense minister. He remained part of the Rajapaksa government until two months before his election as president.

"Everyone's expecting peace and harmony, and we don't want war – the people have already suffered a lot," Prem said before the election. "But the government should be treating the Tamils with equal rights and dignity. If they don't, it's my belief there will be an armed struggle again."

Endnotes

1. Anonymous (2013) British premier's historic Jaffna visit raises Tamil hopes, *Tamil Guardian*. Available at: http://www.tamilguardian.com/article.asp?articleid=9227.
2. Anonymous (2013) Sri Lanka refuses to give timeline on human rights issues, *New Indian Express*. Available at: http://www.newindianexpress.com/world/Sri-Lanka-refuses-to-give-timeline-on-human-rights-issues/2013/11/17/article1896050.ece#. Uzkye2fjhy0/.
3. Krishnaswamy, P. (2014) Northern fishers heave a sigh of relief, *Sunday Observer*. Available at: http://www.sundayobserver.lk/2014/01/19/fea05.asp.

CHAPTER 10

Ghana

1 – Goatanomics

Because goats don't cross the road in America.

Kwesi Essel Blankson
Barack Obama's Tour Guide
Cape Coast Castle

Accra from the air is a patchwork gray-brown sprawl of tin-roof and timber shacks stretching endlessly from the deep blue of the Atlantic. Dotted between are bright flecks of yellow, red, green and blue. These are more upscale dwellings: converted shipping crates.

Cutting a vertical path upwards from the coast is Oxford Street. The focal point is Frankie's, one of the first concrete high-rises here at four stories. It serves burgers and fast food (in relative terms – nothing in Accra happens fast). Hanging outside are teenagers from New York University. Unlike in Nigeria or Kenya, foreigners can be in the street without much risk of hassle beyond a constant tooting of taxis vying for a fare. As a result, Accra has become a mecca for student programs and NGOs.

Politically this is as harmonious as it gets in Africa. Since Jerry Rawlings ended military rule by standing for election in 1992, Ghana has alternated peacefully between his National Democratic Congress and the New Patriotic Party. While NPP leader Nana Akufo-Addo challenged the 2012 election count, he then accepted the Supreme Court verdict ratifying the result and congratulated President John Dramani Mahama.[1]

Down a side street past Shoprite – the South African supermarket spreading across the sub-Sahara – youth volunteers with the Peace Corp. and USAID down Friday night beers in the neighborhood of Osu. Most of the stallholders here are from Cote D'Ivoire, part of an exodus in the past decade from the civil war that raged across Ghana's western border. They cook *poulet braise* on charcoal spread over halved oil barrels. The chicken is flown 4000 kilometers from Brazil. Local meat is expensive and tasteless, says the cook in French.

The penchant for foreign produce from tomatoes to toothpicks is throwing the economy off kilter, with Ghanaians spending $5 billion more on imports than exports.[2,3]

On Saturday morning at the Accra Arts Center – a large market shaded under a canopy from the burning sun – business is slow. A hundred stallholders compete for a dozen tourists. A woman selling bracelets playfully bates the man she says has made her like this, pointing to her belly. She needs 50 cedis ($19) to go to a maternity hospital for a checkup. Ghana's "free healthcare" model switched to a paying system known as "cash and carry" under Rawlings and then to the National Health Insurance Scheme.[4] The woman makes a grab for the man's pocket but it contains nothing but his mobile. "I'll sell your phone to pay the hospital," she jokes. I buy a leather strap bracelet for 50 cedis that would be half the price in London.

Everything is expensive here. My Movenpick hotel room costs $340 a night, compared with $140 for an equivalent room in Colombo. Prices, climbing 14% a year, have been pumped by imports growing ever-more expensive as the cedi depreciates, continuing its two-decade, straight-line 91% drop.[5] The currency ranked among the three worst in the world since the start of 2008.[6] Feeding the inflationary cycle, public sector wages have been soaring – sucking up 70% of tax revenue and driving the government's budget deeper into deficit (Table 10.1).

At the edge of the craft market, two guys crouch over a newspaper circling lottery numbers going back three years. They've concluded the number most likely to win is 14. Their odds of making money look better than the stallholders'.

I head back toward the airport to the wealthy district of Villaggio. Overlooking the Accra Polo Club are two new tower blocks, one clad in red, another in green. A third, under construction, will be yellow to make a skyline in the colors of the flag.

TABLE 10.1   Worse than Iran, Syria and Venezuela in currency rankings.

Country Spot	Value
Ukrainian Hryvnia	−58.3
Argentine Peso	−61.5
Iranian Rial	−63.3
New Sudanese Pound	−64.4
Malawian Kwacha	−64.5
Syrian Pound	−65.4
Venezuelan Bolivar	−65.8
Ghanaian Cedi	−71.9
Belarusian Ruble	−79.1
Myanmar Kyat	−99.3

Note: Ghana's Cedi ranks among the 3 worst currencies worldwide since the start of 2008.
Source: Data compiled by Bloomberg as of August 2014. *(Function: WCRS GO)*

The property market is tough right now, says Jan Du Preez, an executive for Trasacco Group, which sells and maintains the apartments. From the swimming pool roof terrace of the red building, Du Preez points to a dozen cranes on the coast. "All these buildings are popping up but not many are getting sold," he says. "We're OK here because we've got revenue and a good customer base from years ago, but a lot of new developers who expected a flood of expats because of the oil boom have been disappointed. It seems to be less of a boom and more of a slow, tedious process."

While Ghana began producing oil 60 kilometers from the shore at the Jubilee field in 2010, production starts in earnest from 2016 to 2021.[7]

Meantime, the country lacks the energy to meet its electricity needs. Power outages can last for days at a time. To conserve supplies, the Electricity Company of Ghana switches off regions by rota. A three-page spread in the *Daily Graphic* newspaper shows the schedule for each place. On the front page the headline warns the "dumsor dumsor" – or on-off on-off – could trigger a rise in crime.

There's no follow-up story. Ghana's crime rate is lower than America's or Japan's. Interpol puts robberies at 2.15 per hundred thousand people compared with 4.08 in Japan and 144 in the USA. Burglaries were 1.3 in Ghana to 233 in Japan and 728 for the States.[8] Ghanaians point to the influence of the local community and the church.

Churches and church billboards are everywhere. Early on Sunday morning I head back to the Osu neighborhood and follow signs to the Lighthouse Chapel. It's like a multiplex cinema for Christianity. Circled around a gravel yard packed with a thousand cars are six chapels offering a choice of reverend, language and prayer mode.

My ears guide me to the smallest but noisiest. It's a whitewashed building with a wooden spire. The Reverend Enok is lead vocals accompanied by backing singers, an organ, drums and bongos. There are no hymn sheets – everyone knows the words, sung in the local Twi with hands waving in the air or banging on tambourines. People are either grooving in the isles or prostrate on the floor in devotion. After 20 minutes, the Reverend Enok tells us all to shake hands with one another before belting out the next hit hymn.

The biggest gathering here is a service in English, Ghana's official language since colonial days. On an arena-style stage with a giant video screen and bright neon cross, a hundred-strong choir is led by a young female singer. The glitzy show goes out live on the web, the church's FM radio station and in its private hospital.

Next door, the chapel has no pews. Dozens of men and women pace frenetically in every direction – muttering, exclaiming, shouting and waving their fists. Their zombie trance continues for 15 minutes. Then the pastor says "shush!" In unison they smile and break into a soothing Twi hymn. Then it's back to the shouting and fist waving.

"People are getting laid off," explains Psalmist, the rector for the "Charismatic" denomination. "They don't have enough food to eat. You walk around this area and some people are homeless, sleeping in the street. We do this to get rid of the frustration of the people in the English church. We want to help them, otherwise they'll hang themselves. We give hope."

Accra, with a population of over four million, draws people from all of Ghana's ten regions, making it crowded and pushing up housing costs, says Psalmist. He pays 500 cedis ($188) a month for a room. Landlords can demand three or four years' rent in advance, he complains. "Then you find out the toilets and sanitation are bad, but it's too late, you've already paid."

In the neighborhoods with access to piped water, the taps often run dry. Raw sewage festers in canals dug by the side of streets in lieu of underground sewers.

"You wake up and the electricity isn't working and there's no water and it's frustrating," says the Reverend Ben Johnson. "That frustration needs to be controlled, otherwise it turns into violence. Our help comes from God. Yes, you're frustrated with the system and the economy, but you have hope."

With the Lighthouse Chapel's Sweet Melodies on the taxi's radio, I head west to Jamestown, a fishing community on the edge of one of Accra's biggest and poorest slums.[9] Men on brightly painted wooden rowing boats sing prayers for God's protection in the sea as they unravel nets on the beach ready for their next trip. Much of their catch – sardines or sprats – is spread on the ground until fish covers every inch of the main square. It's left there to dry until Tuesday when it's collected for use in pastes. Cleared of fish, the area then becomes a football ground for the day before the cycle starts over again.

Beyond the rainbow line of fishing boats along the shore, an infant wheels an old tire outside a shelter for orphans and the children of homeless parents. It's funded by a drumming band that tours European folk festivals like Womad.[10]

Towering above is the landmark red and white lighthouse by the James Fort slave prison. It's where Ghana's founding father Kwame Nkrumah was jailed before leading the country to independence in 1957.

The larger slave forts are a couple of hours' drive west of Accra. Cape Coast Castle, a white fortress used by European colonialists as a trading post for ivory and gold, became the grim holding pen for slaves, many of them destined for America.

Kwesi Essel Blankson leads me through the dungeon where the men and women sold by rival tribe leaders rotted in pitch black, fumbling through feces for food thrown in by soldiers. Those who survived would file through the "door of no return" onto waiting boats. Two centuries later, a sign on the beach side reads "door of return," welcoming back the descendants of survivors.

It was Kwesi who led Barack Obama and his family around the castle in 2009, his first visit to Africa as US president.

"They were very emotional," says Kwesi. "It has that effect. My friend who's a journalist said it's the first time he'd seen that side of Obama as he's normally very cool." Obama told his children how history can take cruel turns and it was an obligation to fight oppression, recalls Kwesi.

Sixty percent of visitors to the castle are Ghanaian. The rest are mostly European with a few Americans, says Kwesi. But the biggest increase is in Chinese, visiting on Sundays after business meetings during the week. Few are tourists.

Along the coast between the coconut trees and a turquoise sea are some of the most captivating beaches where Atlantic lobsters are reeled in and barbequed wherever you choose to sit, watching bare-back horse riding as ambient reggae wafts from beach bars.

"Tourism is suffering because of the costs in this country," says Kwesi, who has a degree in tourism and is studying for his masters. It's hard for a hotel to make a profit after paying for the building, electricity and water. At the same time, he says, more are being built, further crimping the potential for profits.

Most are styled on an American or European format. At the Movenpick, there's a St Patrick's Day theme running through my entire stay, with Irish music pumping across the pool and the dining area serving Irish stew and chicken nuggets.

"We have to recognize and build on our own identity to really attract tourists," says Kwesi. "We should be giving people a different experience from anything they're used to in America or Europe, because goats don't cross the road in America."

On the drive back from Cape Coast we slow several times for goats ambling between grazing before finally stopping at a police road block. A cop dressed in black inspects the red, yellow and green circle stickers on the cab's windscreen to check for road tax and insurance and then flicks over the driver's license. Everything's in order yet the policeman requests Emi step out. He leads him behind the car where I can't see.

Three minutes later Emi comes back fuming. "Everything OK?" I ask as we drive away.

"Yes, but I had to pay."

The policeman had shown Emi a speed monitor displaying 160 kilometers an hour. There's no way we were even doing half that. The cop demanded 50 cedis. Emi offered 10. They met at 20.

I'm shocked. We'd had a whole conversation on the drive out about how the police aren't corrupt here. He says it's the first time in his life he's had to pay a bribe to police. The cops in Accra are good, he says, and in the city he'd report an abuse like this straight away at the station, but here he doesn't know where to go.

By the amount of people we stop to ask directions, it's clear Emi doesn't often travel beyond the city limits.

Just before the outskirts of Accra, we slow down at another road block. A policewoman named Joyce says something to me in Twi. She's smiling, so I assume it's a pleasantry and wave amicably. As we pull away I ask Emi what she said.

"She asked if you got something for her family."

Top Down Data

Country	Population	GDP on PPP Basis ($)	GDP/Capita on PPP ($)	Inflation (% pa)	Unemployment (%)
Ghana	25,758,108	90,410,000,000	3500	11.0	11.0
Sri Lanka	21,866,445	134,500,000,000	6500	4.7	5.1
Saudi Arabia	27,345,986	927,800,000,000	31,300	3.7	10.5
Egypt	86,895,099	551,400,000,000	6600	9.0	13.4
Nigeria	177,155,754	478,500,000,000	2800	8.7	23.9
Vietnam	93,421,835	358,900,000,000	4000	6.8	1.3
Argentina	43,024,374	771,000,000,000	18,600	20.8	7.5
Romania	21,729,871	288,500,000,000	14,400	3.2	7.3
Myanmar	55,746,253	111,100,000,000	1700	5.7	5.2
Kenya	45,010,056	79,900,000,000	1800	5.8	40.0

Source: CIA World Factbook, December 2014

[1] Population data from July 2014 estimates.

[2] GDP at purchasing power parity (PPP) exchange rates is the sum value of all goods and services produced in the country valued at prices prevailing in the USA, based on 2013 estimates.

[3] GDP per capita (PPP) divided by population, based on 2013 estimates.

[4] Inflation rate shows the annual percentage change in consumer prices in 2013.

[5] Unemployment rate shows the percentage of the labor force without jobs. Data from 2013 estimates, except for Ghana (2000), Nigeria (2011) and Kenya (2008).

Endnotes

1. Anonymous (2013) Nana Addo congratulates President Mahama, Ghana Broadcasting Corp. Available at: http://www.gbcghana.com/1.1506501.
2. Hinshaw, D. (2014) Ghana tries to cut dependency on imports, *Wall Street Journal*. Available at: http://online.wsj.com/news/articles/SB10001424052702304558804579377373278889450.
3. Sulaiman, T., Kpodo, K. (2013) Ghana pays a premium as it sells $750 Mln 10-year Eurobond, GhanaWeb. Available at: http://www.ghanaweb.com/GhanaHomePage/economy/artikel.php?ID=280745.
4. Durairaj, V., D'Almedia, S., Kirigia, J. (2010) Obstacles in the process of establishing a sustainable National health insurance scheme: Insights from Ghana, World Health Organization. Available at WHO: http://www.who.int/health_financing/pb_e_10_01-ghana-nhis.pdf.
5. Bax, P. (2014) Ghanaians cut savings to keep babies fed as prices soar: economy, Bloomberg News. Available at: http://www.bloomberg.com/news/2014-02-27/ghana-mothers-slash-savings-to-ensure-babies-fed-as-prices-soar.html.
6. Bloomberg data, World Currency Rankings, WCRS GO 12/31/07-current, Cedi ranks among three worst currencies worldwide.
7. Bax, P. (2013) Technip to double Ghana office as offshore crude output, Bloomberg News. Available at: http://www.bloomberg.com/news/2013-11-22/technip-to-double-ghana-office-as-offshore-crude-output-t.html.
8. Winslow, R., Crime and society: A comparative criminology tour of the world, San Diego State University. Available at: http://www-rohan.sdsu.edu/faculty/rwinslow/africa/ghana.html.
9. Anonymous (2010) Four communities in accra have been identified as poverty endemic according to a Co-Operative Housing Foundation International (CHF) Report. Available at: http://ama.ghanadistricts.gov.gh/?arrow=nws&read=34941.
10. Jaynii Foundation website. Available at: http://www.jaynii.com/about-the-foundation/.

II – Highlife and Death

Q sits drumming his hand to a jazz beat while nursing a Polish vodka. It's an experiment to kick the gout he blames on Russia's vodka.

"They're good," he says of the five-piece Frank Kissi & the Electric Band. "I might record them."

Q has served Accrans over the years with some of the greats – Shabba Ranks, Jermaine Jackson, Isaac Hayes – along with the local jazz fusion known as highlife. Ghana's foremost concert promoter and album producer, he counts Bono among industry associates. When he turned 44 a dozen or so years ago, Stevie Wonder called to sing "Happy Birthday." To younger Ghanaians, he's known for appearing on the reality TV show *Icons: Divas Edition* as a local Simon Cowell.

Quantos Ackah-Yensu, to use his full name, uses the nightclub named +233 after Ghana's dialing code as a sounding board. Tonight, as every other night this week, he's with his oldest friends from Christ the King School in Accra. It's time for the boys to kick back as their wives are on a trip overseas.

While many of their set left Ghana in the 80s when the economy was shrinking and food shortages drove hyperinflation and mass unemployment, these guys stayed on, growing their network of business interests.

Sat around Q's table outside, watching the band through a glass wall, is +233 owner Dr Adrian Nii Oddoye. By day, he runs a private medical clinic.

Then there's Francis Baffour, an investment consultant. He's playing host this week to a Chinese delegation thinking of spending millions of dollars on a power plant. Next to him is David Addo-Ashong, a banker who led eight of the initial 15 listings on the Ghana Stock Exchange at its inception in 1992.

Our introduction comes through David's business partner, Adam Greenberger. The New Yorker worked back in the day with Q's dad and he's godfather to Adrian's son. "Greenie" also just happens to be an old school chum of the investor I'm trailing around Ghana: Derrick Irwin from Wells Fargo Asset Management.

Business is one third social mixed with vodka, whisky, Ghanaian Club lager, football and complaints of gout between +233 and "the house" (David's place where Greenie crashes when he's over from the States).

At Dr Oddoye's private hospital, the same Louis Ghost transparent chairs from +233 are in the waiting room. Highlife plays on a stereo. A modern abstract painting of a traditional woman in hazed reds, blues and gold hangs above his desk.

Oddoye quit the state health sector in frustration at requirements to see 120 patients a day. "I've always pushed preventative medicine," he says, "and for that you really have to sit down with people and talk. I work in 30-minute slots, that's the time you need."

To build his practice, Oddoye borrowed $1.2 million in 2009 at an interest rate of 36% to buy the latest-spec MRI scanner. The rate has since dropped to 24%.

"Ultimately we've built a small facility that can do all the stuff people used to have to go to South Africa to do," he says."All of this will raise the bar for local healthcare."

Unlike in Europe and America, most Ghanaians pay their own hospital bill in cash. Private health insurance is mainly limited to big companies. Consultants' fees start at 100 cedis ($40).

"Right now, we're each out here on our own as private hospitals but one or two will eventually emerge as leaders," says Oddoye. "If wages go up and the economy is doing well, private health insurance has got to take off."

For now, the insurers are focused more on death.

Funerals are the biggest expense for Ghanaians after housing, topping healthcare, education and weddings.

Families come under pressure to go all out for the final farewell as an expression of respect and status.

Coffins – some elaborately carved as fish, football boots or beer bottles, depending on the deceased's passions – processions of bands and dancers, transport for hundreds of relatives of relatives and keeping the body in a morgue for weeks while the funeral is being planned all add to bills running to thousands of dollars.[1,2]

Daniel Larbi-Tieku and his family spent over $10,000 on the funeral for his sister. Conveying the body from Accra to their home in the eastern region after 27 days in the mortuary cost $2000. Then there was the seventh day "celebration" that serves as a type of funeral planning meeting, preparation of the body for viewing, the casket, the buffet lunch, drinks and transport for 550 guests. "It was a fairly standard funeral."

He should know. Larbi-Tieku is the finance manager for Enterprise Life. The company started offering funeral cover in 2001. Selling the product meant breaking through layers of superstition that prevented people discussing death, let alone planning financial arrangements.

"It was really difficult," says his colleague CC Bruce Jr, executive director. "People would say, what happens if my father dies next week? You'll have caused it."

Five years later, Enterprise had grown its funeral cover business to a point where it contributed nearly half of the life company's revenue. Its parent, Enterprise Group, has soared sixfold in the stock market since the start of 2012. It had the second best performance among the 35 companies included in Ghana's benchmark GSE Composite Index, rising 292% in 2013, before flatlining in 2014.[3]

Policies to meet school fees contribute around a third of revenue. "The middle class in Ghana has been growing, especially in the last five years or so, and they want to educate their children in top class schools," says CC Bruce.

Around a fifth comes from illness and income protection cover, known as lifetime needs. This was the starting point for the company under a venture with the World Bank's International Finance Corp. To drum up more business, Enterprise has teamed up with the mobile phone provider Airtel, offering up to 250 cedis of free cover to its mobile phone subscribers. The campaign brought in 21,000 customers in the first month. The next phase is to offer those customers a top-up for a monthly premium.

Fund Factbox

Company & Assets in Emerging Markets	Emerging Market Fund	Performance & Peer Ranking	Portfolio Manager: Derrick Irwin
Wells Fargo Asset Management $12.4 billion	Wells Fargo Advantage Emerging Markets Equity Fund	17th highest total return among 638 US-registered emerging market stock funds over 10 years at 253% (annualized 13.4%)	Derrick, 44, co-manages the emerging markets fund, focusing on Europe, the Mideast, Africa and India Joined Wells Fargo in 2005 bringing experience from Goldman Sachs and Merrill Lynch

Source: Data compiled by Bloomberg as of June 2014

Stocks Box: Enterprise Life

Company & Trading Platform	Description	Average Annual Return	Price– Earnings Ratio	Price– Book Ratio/ NAV	Return on Equity	Gross Dividend Yield	Market Value ($m)	Top Holders %
Enterprise Group Ghana Stock Exchange	Ghana's second biggest listed insurer	70.1% since data starts 1995	6.0	2.8	36.9%	13.0%	65.0	Ventures & Acquisition 41.1% ELAC 8.0% Free float 38.5%
Sanlam Ltd. Johannesburg Stock Exchange	Financial services inc. life insurance, retirement annuities, unit trusts, health insurance	18.1% from 1999, when data starts	15.9	3.7	23.5%	2.7%	14,319	Ubuntu-Botho 13.5% Government Employee Pension 12.1% Free float 63.4%
Standard Bank Group Johannesburg Stock Exchange	Africa's largest lender	15.1% from 1999	12.6	1.6	13.0%	4.1%	19,904	Industrial & Commercial Bank 20.1% Government Employee Pension 11.3% Free float 56.9%

Source: Data compiled by Bloomberg as of December 2014

Investor Analysis: Wells Fargo's Derrick Irwin on Finance Industry

Bottom Line

- Don't die in Ghana, it's too expensive. But it makes **funeral insurance** a great business to be in.

- I'd take a long, hard look at Enterprise Group. It seems self-sufficient on capital and looks like a good opportunity to get exposure to the economy as **demand** for insurance will increase as incomes grow.
- The company's market **capitalization** at $85 million makes it too small realistically for Wells Fargo, but it bolsters the case for part-owner Sanlam, the South African financial services group.

Buy/Sell Trigger

- The key will be for Enterprise to keep its solid **market position** and increase insurance penetration and customer sophistication.

Local Investor Analysis: Afina Capital's David Addo-Ashong on Finance Industry

- Healthcare, insurance and financial services are some of the **best positioned** sectors. The influx of expats and returning Ghanaians adds to the demand. There is still an open first-mover advantage for the group that can build Ghana's first private world-class hospital.
- At the top end, the banking industry is quite **crowded**. International banks jostle with Nigerian and South African regional powerhouses to compete with the entrenched local Ghanaian players. The real opportunity is in the rapidly expanding world of micro-finance. There is a virtually endless demand for capital to help grow these institutions.

Endnotes

1. Gross National Income (2012) World Bank. Available at: http://data.worldbank.org/country/Ghana.
2. Bax, P. (2013) Ghana's dancing pallbearers, insurers lead funeral boom, Bloomberg News. Available at: http://www.bloomberg.com/news/2013-08-01/ghana-s-dancing-pallbearers-insurers-lead-funeral-boom.html.
3. Data compiled by Bloomberg. Function: GGSECI Index MRR GO.

III – Gold Diggers

Two hundred kilometers southwest from Accra, just before Ghana dips to its southernmost point in the Atlantic, is the town of Takoradi.

At a tiny military airport, men wearing Tullow Oil, Schlumberger and Halliburton corporate polo shirts collect colleagues in SUVs with blacked-out windows. The pot-holed mud roads of Accra and Cape Coast give way to smooth tarmac. Shops offer new bicycles, three-piece sofa suites, designer kitchens and manicures.

This is Ghana's most happening city. Takoradi has it all – beautiful beaches, gold mines and oil.

Tullow has been pumping 100,000 barrels a day offshore from here. Output from the Jubilee field will more than double to 250,000 by 2021 as companies partner the government by investing $20 billion – nearly 40% of Ghana's entire economy.[1]

And there's more to come. West of Jubilee is an area collectively known as the TEN project after the regions of Tweneboa, Enyenra and Ntomme. This zone is expected to generate a further 80,000 barrels a day from late 2016.[2]

The British oil producer Tullow has stakes in both Jubilee and TEN, along with the US-listed Kosmos Energy and Anadarko Petroleum, and has remained committed to the project while scaling back elsewhere amid falling crude prices. Schlumberger and Halliburton are among the companies servicing the industry with technology, project management and construction.

While an exploration rig towers over the shoreline, most people's lives are untouched by the development going on around them – except for the one change everybody here understands: inflation. At Schlumberger's office in Takoradi, 30 striking oil workers in blue overalls and red bandanas wave placards declaring EXPATS ARE ENJOYING AT THE EXPENSE OF GHANAIANS and WE CANNOT WORK LIKE ELEPHANTS AND FEED LIKE ANTS. Trombones, trumpets, whistles and drums play highlife.[3,4]

From Takoradi we drive north for an hour to Tarkwa where Ghana's biggest gold producer has its Iduapriem mine. Women walk by with tree trunks balanced on their heads – fuel for stoves in their bamboo-frame mud huts. An array of pastel-painted coffins is stacked in the street for sale. Our driver, from AngloGold Ashanti, toots his horn at meandering goats. He relocated to Tarkwa ten years ago from the company's main Ghanaian mine at Obuasi, some 150 kilometers further north. His wife refuses to join him here because the living costs are too high.

For NGOs, it's the cost to the environment here that's a bigger concern. Under a yellow and green bridge advertising De-Luxy paint, nine boys clamber down a steep rocky incline from the rainforest to bathe in the Bonsa River. The water is dirt brown. Studies have shown traces of mercury in the fish along with other mining waste – lead, cadmium, manganese and arsenic.[5,6] One township built on waste deposits left from a mine here decades ago is known simply as Cyanide.[7] Communities in the Tarkwa mining area run an "excess risk" of cancer from the pollution, according to the *Science Alert* journal.[8]

Showing us around the Iduapriem Mine is South African Tebogo Mushi. He was working in a liquor store in his native Soweto when he heard a company was looking for young miners and willing to give bursaries for university degrees. Mushi started in a coal mine in South Africa, then a gold mine in Guinea before arriving in Ghana in 2012 as the senior manager for mining.

Folding long dreadlocked hair under a hard hat, he drives us to the highest point, tests the brakes with an emergency stop and dips down into the canyon. I'm expecting men chiseling for nuggets but instead we see lots of bulldozers and trucks. "In South Africa, you can actually see the gold in the rocks," says Mushi. "Here you don't see it."

That's because South African mines contain up to 14 grams of gold per ton of rock. The gold content starts to increase the further north we head in the 4½-kilometer Iduapriem pit, but it doesn't go much above a gram per ton.

The lower content is a blessing in some ways for AngloGold. While it means shifting 80,000 tons of blasted rock – 900 fully loaded 777F dumper trucks – to make a single 18-kilo gold bar, it makes theft less of an issue.

At AngloGold's much larger Obuasi mine, the gold content is four times higher. The mine's location right in the heart of the town makes it easy prey for men known locally as galamsey – a vernacular distortion of "gather 'n' sell." Any attempt to move the galamsey, employees on the ground warned their chairman, could "start a war."[9]

"You have to appreciate Obuasi is a community that has completely overwhelmed the mine," says Alex O-Bediako, the business improvement manager at Iduapriem. He moved here from Obuasi with his wife and children. "Everything depends on the mine. If the mine isn't doing well, you have to face the community."

The illegal plundering along with a drop in the price of gold and production inefficiencies lifted the cost of mining an ounce of gold at Obuasi to $1530 – 18% more than the price the bullion was fetching. The world's third-biggest gold producer responded by closing the mine to restructure as a smaller, more efficient operation.[10]

According to Mushi, it's the illegal or "artisan" miners – increasingly operating with heavy machinery – that cause the biggest environmental problems by dumping the chemical waste. "When it's people and shovels, that's okay," says Mushi. "But when it's mechanized it causes damage and pollution."

From the mine face we cross to what looks like the surface of Jupiter – a silver-brown marble swirl forming an enormous lake. This is liquefied waste

from the blasted ore mixed with cyanide. It's encircled by a 45 degree slop-
ing wall built successively higher to encase the sludge coming in at a rate of
660 tons an hour. Twenty-five meters deep right now, it will go to twice that
amount before being sealed off and left to harden. It's an earlier version of
this so-called tailing storage facility that the township of Cyanide is built on.

Pollution risks from cyanide prompted Romania's parliament to reject
Canadian plans to build Europe's biggest gold mine in 2013. Memories are
scarred by the continent's worst environmental disaster after Chernobyl,
when a burst dam caused cyanide to contaminate rivers in 2000.[11,12]

Through the bog in front of us, two tree roots protrude with bright green
leaves. A lonely bird drifts above.

"It's not toxic," says Mushi. "You get more birds flying around on the
weekend when there's less activity."

From here we head to the main production plant. It's surrounded by a
high fence topped with circles of barbed wire and warning signs: No usage of
mobile phones, random searches taking place and "use condom wisely." We
file through, blowing into a machine to test for alcohol.

On a giant conveyer belt, boulders of rock are broken down into stones
and then crushed in machines by steel balls. Cyanide is then used to separate
the gold particles. The mixture is heated and poured into a series of slab
molds. As the heaviest element, the gold deposits collect at the first casting
as red hot slag slops to the next. The first mold is then plunged into water
to cool and solidify before being polished with a giant electric toothbrush.
Finally, the gold bar is weighed, stamped with a serial number and stacked for
helicopter dispatch to Johannesburg.

Three gold bars are produced in the half hour we're there. We're frisked
and made to empty our boots twice on the way out.

Doing bicep curls with a fresh gold bar, Derrick is in seventh heaven.
He studied geology at university and two decades on is quizzing the mine's
geologists as a shareholder. There's also a family connection as his father was
a long-time investor in AngloGold through a fund he listed on the New York
Stock Exchange.

The shares have been a drag on Derrick's portfolio as gold prices dropped.
"I should have sold down the gold stakes," says Derrick, "but we felt cost control would mitigate any weakness in the gold price. It turned out the price of
gold fell more than we thought and cost control was slow in coming."

Now the discounted valuation could be an opportunity. The potential
is there for a positive surprise from a jump in the gold price, discovery of
new deposits or an improvement in Obuasi's fortunes. On the other hand,

a worsening situation at Obuasi could put its Ghanaian operation out of business.

Ghana accounts for about a third of AngloGold's output from the continent outside of its base in South Africa.

While AngloGold cut production at Iduapriem to less than a third of its target in 2014 to use up stockpiles as gold prices were low, the company has become more reliant on its smaller and lower-yielding pit with Obuasi in disarray. AngloGold aims to move 36 million tons of rock a year on average at Iduapriem, amounting to about 16 gold bars a week.

"Obuasi at the moment is struggling," says Sicelo Ntuli, the managing director responsible for the Iduapriem mine. "But we believe it can catch up."

The company will initially reduce production from the mine at Obuasi to focus on gold nearer the surface while it reviews the next step. "Our intention," says Ntuli, "is to breathe new life into a massive gold deposit that needs to be mined with more modern, productive techniques to make it viable for the long term."

Stocks Box: AngloGold Ashanti vs. Newmont

Company & Trading Platform	Description	Average Annual Return	Price–Earnings Ratio	Price–Book Ratio/ NAV	Return on Equity	Gross Dividend Yield	Market Value ($m)	Top Holders %
AngloGold Ashanti	Ghana's mines contribute a third of the non-South African gold	-3.6% from 2004, year of AngloGold merger with Ashanti	N/A	1.2	-5.8%	N/A	3617	Government emp pension 7.6% Free float 87.3%
Newmont Mining Corp.	Africa is 15-20% of production	-4.2% from 2004	15.9	0.9	-6.1%	0.5%	9177	Blackrock 7.2% State Street 5.7% Free float 99.8%

Source: Data compiled by Bloomberg as of December 2014

Investor's Notebook: Newmont Mining Corp. Executives ▬▬▬▬

- Africa represents 15–20% of production for Newmont.
- The cost at $600 an ounce, and $815 all in, is one of our lowest globally.
- We get petty theft but nothing significant.
- The biggest issue in Ghana is power. If you're not getting steady and reliable power it certainly adds to problems.
- Newmont looked at its global position with the price of gold falling. We had to scale back certain projects such as the mill at Ahafo, one of the company's flagship Ghanaian mines.
- The government understands the problems of the gold industry, they know there aren't windfall profits to tax.

Investor Analysis: Wells Capital's Irwin on Gold ▬▬▬▬

Bottom Line

- While many of the large gold mines in Ghana are operating profitably at current prices, AngloGold's **Obuasi mine** is a serious problem. It is unlikely to ever approach historical levels of output and probably will shrink dramatically. This will be a drag on growth and employment.
- **Illegal mining** is a continuing problem in Ghana (as it is in the rest of Africa). Environmental and safety standards are very poor, creating real pollution issues and tarnishing the entire industry's reputation.
- I am encouraged by the intense focus from Newmont and AngloGold on **cost control** and capital management. This has been missing in recent years. If this continues, we may see returns and cash flow improving for the more efficient gold producers.

Buy/Sell Triggers

- AngloGold has announced it will **restructure** its Obuasi mine. This is in keeping with its improving capital discipline, and should add value to the company. However, if the process takes longer than expected, or is more expensive, it would be negative for the share price.
- While aggressive cost cutting was required, once those efforts bear fruit, future earnings growth will increasingly depend on the **price of gold**.
- Gold is a major source of foreign currency and a key **economic driver** for Ghana. The increase in the price of gold until 2011 was an important tailwind. Barring another jump in the gold price, this growth driver will need to be replaced.

Endnotes

1. Interview with Augustus Obuadum Tanoh, chairman of HML Marine Power & Energy Ltd.
2. Dontoh, E. (2013) Ghana oil output to more than double by 2021 with new fields, Bloomberg News. Available at: http://www.bloomberg.com/news/2013-04-24/ghana-oil-output-to-more-than-double-by-2021-with-new-fields.html.
3. Opoku, E. (2014) Oil service workers go wild, *Daily Guide*. Available at: http://www.dailyguideghana.com/oil-service-workers-go-wild/
4. Ghana Broadcasting Corp. (2014) Schlumberger workers embark on strike. Available at: https://www.youtube.com/watch?v=DgMrQvvjfKk.
5. Balfors, B., Jacks, G. (2007) Contamination of water resources in Tarkwa mining area of Ghana: Linking technical, social-economic and gender dimensions, Department of Land and Water Resources Engineering, Royal Institute of Technology (KTH). Available at: http://www.diva-portal.org/smash/record.jsf?pid=diva2:477471.
6. Ato, A., Samuel, O. (2010) Mining and heavy metal pollution: assessment of aquatic environments in Tarkwa (Ghana) using multivariate statistical analysis, *Journal of Environmental Statistics*. Available at: http://www.jenvstat.org/v01/i04/paper.
7. Anonymous (2013) Cyanide Retains Tarkwa Tigo Community Soccer Title, Global Newsreel. Available at: http://globalnewsreel.com/index.php?option=com_content&view=article&id=2484:cyanide-retains-tarkwa-tigo-community-soccer-title&catid=26:sports&Itemid=160.
8. Armah, A., Kuitunen, M. (2012) Non occupational health risk assessment from exposure to chemical contaminants in the gold mining environment of Tarkwa, Ghana, *Science Alert*. Available at: http://scialert.net/fulltext/?doi=tasr.2012.181.195.
9. Crowley, K., Dontoh, E. (2014) AngloGold faces 'enormous' challenges in Ghana, Mboweni says, Bloomberg News. Available at: http://origin-www.bloomberg.com/apps/news?pid=conewsstory&tkr=ANG:SJ&sid=aspFh0Lu2i1E.
10. Seccombe, A. (2014) AngloGold Ashanti to retrench hundreds in Ghana, Business Day Live. Available at: http://www.bdlive.co.za/business/mining/2014/08/12/anglogold-ashanti-to-retrench-hundreds-in-ghana.
11. Savu, I. (2013) Europe's biggest planned gold mine may face Romanian Referendum, Bloomberg News. Available at: http://www.bloomberg.com/news/2013-09-02/europe-s-biggest-planned-gold-mine-may-face-romanian-referendum.html.
12. Ilie, L. (2013) Romania rejects massive Canadian gold mining project, *The Star*. Available at: http://www.thestar.com/news/world/2013/11/11/huge_canadian_mining_project_to_be_rejected_by_romania.html.

IV – Cassava King

Before running for president, Augustus Obuadum Tanoh tried a more humble route to developing Ghana.

Goosie, as he's better known, sold cassava to Europeans to make tapioca puddings, flour and animal feed. He ended up shipping 80,000 metric tons, pioneering West Africa's export of the brown root vegetable before winding down the business to lead the National Reform Party in the 2000 election.

A decade and a half on, he's back in the cassava trade but now, instead of Europe, he's focusing on China. And rather than puddings, he's offering fuel.

Across Africa, cassava is a staple as a hardier alternative to rice and maize that thrives in the driest soil. It's also the most efficient crop for ethanol production, giving a better yield than wheat, corn or sugar cane.[1]

China triggered a surge in demand for cassava when the government started pushing for ethanol fuel as a substitute for petroleum. The world's biggest nation probably has enough appetite to import $3 billion worth of the carrot-shaped vegetables every year, a gap Ghana could plug on its own, says Goosie.

Many of the frustrations of exporting 20 years ago still remain. Poor infrastructure means it's more expensive to transport from Ghana than other producing countries, making it tough to compete.

"In the 90s," says Goosie, spooning instant coffee and pouring hot water from a teapot before passing it along to Derrick, "I had to literally build roads myself from the farm to the processing factory and the ports."

Nowadays it's the storage depots, automatic loading bays and conveyer systems commonplace in modern ports that are missing in Ghana. While 1000 tons of cassava chips could be loaded in a day at Accra's state-owned port, 40,000 could be stacked in the same time in Thailand, he says.

It's only because cassava commands a higher price as a biofuel that exports could still be profitable from Ghana. Goosie tried to export red sorghum, the key ingredient for Chinese alcoholic drinks like maotai and kaoliana. "We realized that Australians could do it cheaper," he says. "We also tried exporting ground nuts but we found that when the Chinese came on the market, we weren't competitive."

Exporting cassava won't be easy either, with low-cost exports coming from Vietnam, the country that crashed the coffee market in 2001 by cutting prices.[2]

But to Goosie – who received little over 1% of the vote in 2000 for his manifesto pushing for local governance and public accountability – it's worth a shot. He estimates Ghana has a ten-million-ton surplus of cassava and plans to start exporting a million tons in the next five years. His demand for more efficient port facilities will drive improvements, he hopes.

"In this part of the world, sometimes you need to drag the state along. Show that something works and the state will follow and invest."

Developing agriculture is every bit as important as oil to improving Ghana's economy, says Goosie. He has experience of both. A former Attorney General in the Rawlings government and delegate to the UN, Goosie also ran the finance and administration for Ghana National Petroleum Corp. until 1992.

"The oil will come and most of it will go abroad," he says. "Being able to generate surplus agriculture is the substantial change needed as that frees up labor. Right now, cassava rots in the ground."

Investor Analysis: Wells Fargo's Derrick Irwin on Commodities

Bottom Line

- Goosie's point is spot on. Revenue from oil and gas projects is great for Ghana, but unless that revenue translates into more investment and increased efficiency, it won't generate long-term sustainable growth. This is a **classic trap** for low-income, commodity-exporting countries.
- Ghana has a fairly responsible government, a smart and ambitious population and robust rule of law, so I think their **odds are better** than for many oil-producing peers.

Local Investor Analysis: Afina Capital's David Addo-Ashong on Commodities

- As basic **infrastructure** projects are completed, access to markets for the agricultural sector is poised to grow significantly.
- There are big **opportunities** with existing and newly formed cold storage management companies, port service providers and regional transportation companies.

Endnotes

1. Ethanol, Agro2. Available at: http://www.agro2.com/our-products/ethanol/.
2. Coffee, Fairtrade International. Available at: http://www.fairtrade.net/coffee.html.

V - Egg and Stone

If you keep the egg and the stone at the same temperature,
a chicken will come out of the egg but never from the stone.
Kwesi Botchwey, Finance Minister 1982–95
& Chairman of Ghana National Gas Co., quotes Mao Zedong

D r Kwesi Botchwey was a 30-something law professor when he was called
in by the military leader Jerry Rawlings to sort out the economy.

It was 1982. The country was imploding. A three-year drought was made
all the more devastating by a 10% jump in the population as Nigeria expelled
Ghana's economic migrants. Rawlings turned to academia for help.

"We were at the brink of total national disintegration," says Botchwey.
"And here we were – a bunch of left-leaning intellectuals – who were suddenly
answering to the lieutenant. Our saving grace is we were honest intellectuals."

Taking over as finance minister, Botchwey organized forums with farmers,
workers and manufacturers in an attempt to win a consensus for policy
change. Farmers were angry because the propped-up exchange rate was
making imported wheat and maize much cheaper, pricing them out of the
market. They wanted the cedi to depreciate.

But Botchwey had to balance the goal to improve their competitiveness
against the risk of pushing up the cost of imports to a level where inflation
would surge. His compromise was a gradual process of exchange rate reform,
starting with quarterly adjustments through an auction system.

"It was a painful process because the exchange rate was so grossly
overvalued," says Botchwey, in his office in Accra. "The state gold-mining
corporation was collapsing and farmers were leaving cocoa to rot in the bush
rather than sell it to the Cocoa Board at a price that didn't cover their costs."

For Ghana's desperate farmers, the fix wasn't working fast enough.

"In the meetings, farmers would say, 'this exchange rate is killing us,
why don't you slap on high import taxes?'" recalls Botchwey. "And the
workers in the meetings showed solidarity with the farmers, so we started
with surcharges on imported wheat and maize to more or less equalize
the terrain."

The revenue from the import duties was used to help exporters cover
their cost of production. Botchwey then introduced a more structured framework to incentivize exporters using three different exchange rates.

As exports of gold and other commodities started recovering in the 90s,
the final step was to ease the currency controls. Botchwey approached illegal
money changers to set up as authorized foreign exchange bureaus.

"They thought initially that it was a trick to identify them and have them arrested," says Botchwey. "It was only when weeks went past and they realized no one was going to go after them that they agreed to register and the forex bureaus took hold."

Botchwey left office in 1995 as Ghana's longest serving finance minister, returning to academia.

Two decades on, the nation has found itself back in an economic tangle, with Ghana's high-cost producers unable to compete with imports and the budget and current account deficits soaring. "I began to ask myself whether we're going back to the same situation we saw in the 80s," says Botchwey.

While nervousness over the US Federal Reserve tapering its economic stimulus was impacting all emerging markets, Ghana was contributing to the problem.

"External factors by themselves never really wreak the havoc," says Botchwey. "It's a bit like an egg and a stone," he adds, quoting the Chinese Communist leader Mao Zedong. "If you keep the egg and the stone at the same temperature, a chicken will come out of the egg but never from the stone. External factors exercise their impact only through the agency of internal factors."

Labor costs soared from July 2010 as a result of a new system that placed all state employees under one salary structure, known as the "single spine."[1] The higher public wages drove increases in the fiscal deficit and inflation, and ultimately the currency's depreciation.

"We've been hampered by our internal situation – the budget deficit, the expenditure over-runs compounded by the growth in the wage bill."

The government now needs to focus on cutting costs. The extra expense from "single spine" could be more than covered by chasing down the pileup of payment arrears to state-owned enterprises and auditing who's on the government payroll that shouldn't be, says Botchwey. "It's not easy to weave out ghosts from the payroll."

The emphasis must be on efficiency gains, and not just increasing taxes to cover the budget shortfall. "You need greater efficiency in the collection of taxes before any new taxes are introduced."

But for the economy to really swing back to solid growth, the big challenge is delivering power. Gas and infrastructure projects will be critical, says Botchwey, who nowadays is the chairman of the Ghana National Gas Co. as well as leading Ghana's negotiations with the IMF.

The most ambitious is the Ghana 1000 Project – a plan to import liquefied natural gas to efficient GE turbines that will supply more than a thousand megawatts for the power grid. LNG is cheaper than the light crude used in most of Ghana's thermal plants. The first 360 megawatts are due in 2017 before completion in 2019.[2]

"It takes at least three years with the best effort to construct a full-blown gas infrastructure system," says Botchwey. "Gas supply will unleash the economy."

Bond Box: Republic of Ghana

Security & Trading Platform	Asset Description	Maturity / Amount Outstanding	Average Annual Price Change	Coupon/ Interest	Yield
Republic of Ghana	Sovereign Dollars	2017 – $750m 2023 – $1b 2026 – $1b	6.7% on 2017 bond since issued in 2007	2017: 8.5% 2023: 7.875%	2017: 6.3% 2023: 8.0%

Source: Data compiled by Bloomberg as of December 2014

Investor Analysis: Wells Fargo's Derrick Irwin on Ghana

Bottom Line

- Ghana undoubtedly benefited from the Federal Reserve creating ample **global liquidity** for investment in recent years. It will need to adjust to a more normalized liquidity environment, which may be a challenge.
- If **gas projects** come online as expected, and the country is able to deliver reliable power and drive efficiency improvements, it could set off a favorable growth cycle.
- The government of Ghana is well run and the democratic process is exemplary. However, the cycle of **over-spending** has to be replaced with more responsible, long-term planning.

Buy/Sell Triggers

- The progress of the **Jubilee and TEN** fields will be important to watch.
- Ghana has fairly shallow **capital markets**. However, banks are well run, the Ghana Stock Exchange is efficient and the country has access to global debt markets. If the capital markets in Ghana can become deeper and more liquid, it could usher in a new investment era. Increased domestic funding of the oil and gas projects could act as such a catalyst, although there is limited evidence of this occurring yet.

Local Investor Analysis: Afina Capital Partners' David Addo-Ashong on Ghana ▬▬▬▬▬▬▬▬

- There is no doubt that the challenges of local **currency swings** are a deterrent to mid- and long-term investment. Simple synthetic hedges to protect against losses from currency shifts really don't exist. One of the best hedges is real estate.
- Ghanaian law requires that any oil and gas development projects have a **local partner** with at least a 5% ownership stake. In addition, most of the services and infrastructure surrounding the petroleum industry must have 70–100% Ghanaian content by 2023 (most often measured in spend or man hours) which creates a huge amount of "baked-in" demand for local service providers.
- Access to inexpensive electricity coupled with Ghana's stability have the potential to make the country a regional **manufacturing hub** further down the road.

Endnotes

1. Single Spine Pay Structure in Ghana, Study Mode. Available at: http://www.studymode.com/essays/Single-Spine-Pay-Structure-In-Ghana-1556171.html.
2. Anonymous (2014) GE, Endeavor Energy and Finagestion team up on Ghana energy project, Renewable Energy Focus. Available at: http://www.renewableenergyfocus.com/view/38396/ge-endeavor-energy-and-finagestion-team-up-on-ghana-energy-project/.

Conclusion:
Journey's End

Journey's End

Our journey across frontier markets has taken us through poor, polluted slums, we've met people displaced and intimidated, we've encountered official corruption, police brutality and a beheading. In the Machiavellian world of developing-nation politics, one central bank chief we quizzed on the finer details of monetary policy was later hauled before a court to answer graft allegations; another was fired by the president for suggesting an inquiry into billions of missing dollars from oil exports. An opposition MP who warned us of mounting ethno-religious tensions was shot at by gunmen.

And yet, in the midst of turmoil, between the shanty towns and the glass towers of billionaires, we encountered courageous reformers and visionaries who are changing the landscape around them – people like Mwalimu Mati, the Kenyan lawyer building his database as a weapon against corruption, and Tin Oo, the 87-year-old comrade to Aung San Suu Kyi, driving democratic change after decades of confinement by the Burmese military he once served. Amid the latest financial crisis in Argentina, another octogenarian, Eduardo Eurnekian, works on drilling a tunnel through the Andes as a way to help provide the "competitive efficiency" he sees the next generation needing. In Romania, Fondul Pro-prietatea's analysts wage daily battles against malpractice at some of the biggest state enterprises.

Others are still fighting the fallout from conflicts a generation ago. On the road from Hanoi toward the Chinese border, mile upon mile of factories produce metals, cement, digital products and garments for global giants like Canon, Panasonic and Yamaha. I stopped off at one. Women are weaving beautiful wall tapestries with fine, colored threads. Leaning against some of the rows of tables are crutches, others have wheelchairs. These are the daughters of soldiers exposed to the chemical Agent Orange in the Vietnam War half a century ago.[1]

Having fled the ethnic clashes that killed his father, young Samuel Pelumi's determination to lift his community from a life of poverty, disease and violence spurs him to study pollution control on a broken laptop opposite "Chelsea Football Club" in the watery Lagos slum of Makoko.[2]

These are not the final frontiers. There are many – too many – more places with their potential drained by war, foreign isolation or poor governance, where even the more adventurous among investors don't dare tread for now – like Libya, with Africa's largest oil reserves, or Iraq, with the world's fifth-biggest. North Korea, rich in iron ore and largely untapped rare earth metals, and Cuba, with its sugar and nickel industries, are studied from a distance for signs of a thaw in relations with the West.[3,4]

Among these future frontier destinations – each with a legacy of external debt markets going back decades – the most compelling is Iran. While it's still too early for Western investors to wade in, here's an account of how the economy is shaping up from Charlie Robertson, the globe-trotting chief economist for the emerging-markets investment bank, Renaissance Capital.

Having visited roughly 65 countries, it's rare for me to land in a place with no idea of what to expect.

This is a country with 6000 years of civilization that was famously labeled "evil" by a president of a nation that didn't exist 300 years ago.

It's a place so isolated from global finance that your bank card won't work and you have to bring thousands of dollars to pay your hotel bill, meals and taxis. Blackberrys also don't work so you end up relying on phone calls costing $150 for a few minutes. There's no sign of the *Financial Times*, the *Economist* or the *Wall Street Journal*. Even Rwanda feels more connected than Iran. Twitter and Facebook are banned.

But Iran is full of surprises. Within a few hours, a friendly local has told me how to access social media and I'm reading the *FT*, checking Bloomberg screens and following President Hassan Rouhani and the Supreme Leader on Twitter and Facebook.

The roads in Tehran are smoother than New York's and the double-decker metro trains smarter than Amsterdam's. The ubiquitous yellow taxis seem to have been transplanted from Istanbul, and it's not long before the daytime traffic jams, the motorbikes and shops suddenly look familiar. This *is* just like Turkey – less Istanbul and more like conservative Ankara.

And yet, while some fear that Turkey is stepping back from modernity, in Iran the youth that attempted a "Green" Revolution in 2009 dress like LA teenagers. The women seem perhaps freer than in much of modern Turkey. Headscarves rest so far back on women's heads that they constantly slip to the shoulders. (The exception is in the central bank, where the chief economist had hers firmly covering her hair.) It took me three days to realize that women aren't allowed to shake hands with a man (in public) and to recognize the tell-tale plasters over noses that show how popular plastic surgery has become.

What's clear is that Iran's isolation is a temporary affair. The sense of freedom since the election of President Rouhani is evident. There's no way this highly educated nation of 78 million – like Turkey but with 9% of the world's oil reserves – will remain cut off for long. When sanctions on Iran are lifted, foreign investors will flock to a stock exchange formed almost half a century ago with a market capitalization of $150 billion.

Some Western companies are already here: Pepsi is beating Coke, locals tell us, and Danone is selling bottled mineral water at prices approved by authorities still struggling to understand why water should cost anything at all. While the formerly French-linked car manufacturers are in the doldrums today, the industry seems a first candidate for recovery.

Iran's companies pay wages below those in Vietnam and are as diversified in products as you'd find in any middle income country. Perhaps the most interesting was Butane Industrial Group. They believe their expertise in boiler heaters is ideal for the burgeoning economies of east Africa, just a few hours flight time to the south. They're keen to learn about my experiences in Kenya.

Iranians appear to have voted in favor of engagement and against the nuclear policy that was isolating the country. The energy companies want Western or Chinese investment to help them tap their share of natural gas and oil fields before they're sucked dry by neighboring Qatar and Iraq. Local bookshop owners stock Tintin in Farsi and English, and young lads on the street, wanting to practice their English, greet with a smile and conversation that makes Iran feel like a welcome throwback to the twentieth century – when tourists were still a novelty.

In short, Iran is ready to open up. We now have to see if the West can respond. That question was answered on my next flight to the USA – where my passport flagged me up as requiring extra security checks: not yet. Iran today is still beyond the frontier.

As Iran creeps slowly toward improved relations with the West, others have been at risk of sliding in the opposite direction. Kenya frustrated International Criminal Court prosecutors' attempts to bring its president to trial for crimes against humanity. Egypt provoked the ire of Western NGOs by detaining thousands suspected of links to the Muslim Brotherhood and jailing Australian, Canadian and Egyptian TV journalists the day after US Secretary of State John Kerry appealed for clemency.[5–9]

Unlike Iran, however, Egypt has strong allies to counterbalance the West's distaste. Saudi Arabia, the United Arab Emirates and Kuwait have provided billions of dollars to support el-Sisi's campaign to eradicate the Brotherhood, while China is bankrolling Kenya for its biggest-ever infrastructure project.[10]

Even without these powerful friends, it's hard to envisage the West taking a truly tough line against Egypt or Kenya so long as US foreign policy is defined by the war on Islamic terror. Kenya is a crucial front against the al-Qaeda linked al-Shabaab in Somalia while Egypt is key to American efforts to contain Israel's conflict with Hamas in Gaza.[11]

At the opposite end of the scale is Romania, cementing deeper ties in Europe by privatizing state companies in line with its IMF accord and bringing its budget deficit below the level of the EU's fiscal compact as it strives to adopt the euro as its currency in 2019.[12,13] In spite of Argentina's latest debt default and noisy protest against the New York court verdict favoring American "vulture funds," the country – even before its 2015 election – has been quietly mending bridges, compensating Spain's Repsol for its seizure of YPF and contracting with Chevron to explore Vaca Muerta.[14] Ghana received the biggest check to date from the Obama administration's Power Africa initiative, with an initial $498 million projected to spur at least a further $4 billion of private investment for the power sector.[15]

Though the ten frontier countries picked are as diverse as any in terms of foreign relations and most other criteria, there are also resounding common attributes.

The starting point is a need to reconcile long-term growth prospects against current political instability in a group that includes Egypt with its two revolutions, Nigeria and Kenya fending off continual terror attacks, Sri Lanka facing a UN war crimes investigation and Myanmar with its worsening ethno-religious violence. As bad as political tensions are on the ground, Egypt is tackling the country's widening budget deficit for the first time in years, Nigeria and Kenya are on a path of broadening access to credit in the same way Europe and America did half a century ago, Sri Lanka has peacefully thrown off creeping autocracy and Myanmar is emerging from decades of isolation. For Argentina, the repeat economic disarray has left the government in a position where it can't afford to remain a financial outcast.

Then there's the demographic makeup. Each of the ten countries has at least twenty million people, providing enough of a workforce to generate solid tax revenue for governments and a substantial consumer base for companies. More importantly, with the exception of Romania they all have many more youngsters ready to join the population of income earners than elderly retirees. Under-15s account for at least 24% of the population while over-60s are below 15%. In Nigeria and Kenya, the under-15s represent more than 40% and the over-60s less than 5% (Tables C1 and C2).

Finally, there's the sense of economic momentum. For Romania, the driving force is European integration, while in Myanmar and Vietnam it's about opening up trade relations. In Saudi Arabia, it's the effect of including work-shy men and work-deprived women in an expanded economy.

Momentum also comes from oil and gas exploration in the case of Argentina, Ghana, Kenya, Nigeria and Romania – even after the drop in crude prices. Yet oil's bounty also risks setting back economic development as politicians with inadequate accountability restraints line their pockets and ethnic groups wage war to control resources. In Nigeria, where oil has been synonymous with ethnic violence and official corruption for decades, the most inspiring perspective came from the finance minister. Wary of creating another corruptible institution, Ngozi Ikonjo-Iweala is targeting investors mandated to create a positive "social impact" to keep the new state development bank fully accountable.

While her vision of the Nollywood movie industry turning Nigeria into another California seems as far-fetched as Romania becoming the next Norway or Sri Lanka growing like Hong Kong or Singapore, who can say? Well, that was the point of this book. Though their investment styles and target markets are as diverse as the countries they picked, I asked each of the fund managers to stack the countries and securities reviewed on a scale of 1 to 10, with No. 1 being the best prospect for the decade ahead. Here are the results.

TABLE C1   Top down data.

Country	Population	GDP on PPP Basis ($)	GDP/ Capita on PPP ($)	Inflation (% pa)	Unemployment (%)
Kenya	45,010,056	79,900,000,000	1800	5.8	40.0
Myanmar	55,746,253	111,100,000,000	1700	5.7	5.2
Romania	21,729,871	288,500,000,000	14,400	3.2	7.3
Argentina	43,024,374	771,000,000,000	18,600	20.8	7.5
Vietnam	93,421,835	358,900,000,000	4000	6.8	1.3
Nigeria	177,155,754	478,500,000,000	2800	8.7	23.9
Egypt	86,895,099	551,400,000,000	6600	9.0	13.4
Saudi Arabia	27,345,986	927,800,000,000	31,300	3.7	10.5
Sri Lanka	21,866,445	134,500,000,000	6500	4.7	5.1
Ghana	25,758,108	90,410,000,000	3500	11.0	11.0

Source: CIA World Factbook, December 2014

[1] Population data from July 2014 estimates.
[2] GDP at purchasing power parity (PPP) exchange rates is the sum value of all goods and services produced in the country valued at prices prevailing in the USA, based on 2013 estimates.
[3] GDP per capita (PPP) divided by population, based on 2013 estimates.
[4] Inflation rate shows the annual percentage change in consumer prices in 2013.
[5] Unemployment rate shows the percentage of the labor force without jobs. Data from 2013 estimates, except for Ghana (2000), Nigeria (2011) and Kenya (2008).

TABLE C2   Young population: country ranking by % of population aged under 15 years.

Country	% of <15s	Ranking
Niger	49.8	1
Nigeria	43.2	16
Kenya	42.1	23
Ghana	38.6	42
Egypt	32.1	71
Saudi Arabia	27.6	94
Myanmar	26.4	103
Argentina	24.9	116
Sri Lanka	24.7	119
Vietnam	24.3	121
Romania	14.6	208
Monaco	11.7	227

Source: Thomas Brinkhoff: City Population, Citing CIA World Factbook. Available at: http://world.bymap.org/YoungPopulation.html

No. 10: Myanmar

Serge Pun's excitement for the tourist potential here is immediately understandable. To the visitor, the Burmese are the most hospitable people, with an undiluted and fascinating culture – from the thanaka painted faces and longyis to the monks, nuns and novices. And then there's the unique beauty of the country.

After our week of meetings I visited Bagan, a town nestled in a broad bend of Irrawaddy river toward the Bay of Bengal. From the overnight bus I went by horse and cart, the regular mode of taxi here, to a pagoda that indulges visitors to sit on its domed roof. A star shoots beside the full moon before cockerels, the clip clop of hooves and Buddhist chanting signal dawn. The sky turns a pale orange and a misty green landscape unfolds, dotted with a hundred sandstone-brick pagodas. As the chanting crescendos, light suddenly pierces a hole through the horizon and dozens of mauve hot-air balloons slowly rise with the sun. They drift to create perfect symmetry over the stupa domes. And then comes the epiphany. One by one, the balloons eclipse and release, eclipse and release the sunlight.

At a café by the bus stop heading back to Yangon, a couple of monks watch a Manchester United game. It's the 14th Waxing Day of Tazaungmone, a full moon festival, and the buses are jam packed with families coming together to pray at their local pagoda and party into the night. It's the only time I've seen Burmans drinking liquor – half bottles of whisky are on tables, knocked back with beer, fried vegetables and pop music. Police are standing by but there's no trouble. They have batons, no guns.

Beyond tourism, Myanmar's economy is almost a blank sheet. While opportunities from mining to banking to telecoms seem boundless, it's still years too soon for most foreign investors to buy meaningful stakes. The decades of self-imposed isolation followed by sanctions mean there's little experience of seeking outside capital and even less appetite for the sort of accountability investors would need to check for links to people on international embargo lists and that their money is properly spent.

Myanmar, as a result, offers the fewest real investment opportunities among the ten countries, with Pun's Yoma the only true Burmese business to issue shares. It's hard to envisage the leading indigenous companies like RedLink becoming investible any time soon. Eventually, the new stock exchange championed by the deputy finance minister Maung Maung Thein will become a reality. When it is, the untapped potential makes this one of the most exciting countries to watch. The Singaporean-family-owned City Mart and Silicon Valley whizz Daniel Michener's

Burst Networks point to the type of future opportunities. But before all of that can happen, everything rests on smooth transitions of power – first from the military to a democratic government and then devolution to the multitude of rivalrous ethnic groups.

No. 9: Ghana

Maybe it was because this was my last stop, maybe it was the company of Q, Greenie and the gang, or maybe it was the absolute absence of menace on the streets, but I had the most fun in Ghana. It's no wonder universities to NGOs to Bob Marley's widow have adopted Accra for their African home. With its reggae and homegrown highlife pumping from coconut-lined beaches, Ghana is possibly the most chilled out place on the planet.

For serious investment though, it's a little too laid back. It was harder to get company executives to commit to meetings in Ghana than in any of the other countries, and most government officials were a nonstarter. The lack of discipline in the economy in recent years has resulted in some of Africa's highest budget and trade deficits and fastest inflation rates. Holding stocks or bonds denominated in cedis has been anything but relaxing, with wild price swings making this among the most volatile of frontier markets.

While there are more investible securities here than Myanmar, it's hard to buy stakes in the leading contributors to the economy. The fortunes of AngloGold Ashanti rest more on the mines in its home country, South Africa, than in Ghana where it's downsizing the biggest after production dropped to a 30-year low at Obuasi.[16,17] While Ghana is the world's second biggest producer of cocoa, contributing 15% of the nation's economic output, most of the production is by smallholders and the main buyer is the state-run Cocoa Board. With farmers complaining of shrinking profits as the weakening cedi and inflation lift the cost of fertilizer, the industry shows no sign of scaling up.[18]

Just what is achievable here was demonstrated by Enterprise Group, with its rapid expansion of the insurance industry. The country's reputation for peace and low corruption is fairly unique in Africa and a contrast from the continent's biggest economy, almost on its doorstep: Nigeria. With more strategic direction, Ghana could leverage off this to become a hub for business, especially finance. For now, the country's finance industry is better known for flying a plane with $3 million in cash to Brazil to pay its World Cup footballers because most of them don't have bank accounts in Ghana.[19]

No. 8: Egypt

I have no way of knowing whether the man I saw curled up on the ground by the army checkpoint in Cairo was asleep, unconscious or dead. What is reported is that within a year of Mohamed Morsi's ousting on July 3, 2013, at least 16,000 people were arrested as support for the elected Muslim Brotherhood government was equated with support for terrorism. At least 80 died in custody and 1247 received death sentences in the first half of 2014. Trials were frequently without defense lawyers or even defendants and relied on statements extracted by torture, according to Amnesty International. Methods included suspension by handcuffs, electric shocks and rape.

On the day I arrived, 1491 people were arrested.[20] They included 18-year-old Mahmoud Mohamed Ahmed Hussein. His apparent crime was wearing a shirt with a logo of the 2011 revolution and a scarf with the slogan "Nation without Torture." He was blindfolded, beaten and given electric shocks to his testicles until "confessing" membership of the Muslim Brotherhood and possession of explosives. Around the time I was in detention, a 23-year-old student identified by the initials M.R.S. was dealt electric shocks, beaten with a stick on his penis, repeatedly raped by security guards and forced to sing a song in support of the Egyptian army. Amnesty International likened the abuses by state security forces to the darkest hours of the Mubarak era.[21] It's very important to understand, El-Sisi said in an interview with Bloomberg at the 2015 Davos World Economic Forum, that Egypt is "trying very hard after four years of turbulence to regain the rule of law."

Any notion that the new regime resembles the old hasn't been a negative for the stock market. During the year of democracy from the middle of 2012, Egypt's EGX30 Index fell 0.5%. In the year following the military overthrow, the benchmark jumped by 70%. Strong government – whether achieved by popularity or force – tells investors that the economic policies of today will continue tomorrow. And as long as the policies are working to improve the economy, that's a positive. Goaded by his financial backers in the Gulf, el-Sisi has taken important steps to cut the budget deficit and boost growth. It takes a strong government to lift fuel prices by up to 175% straight after an election. Expanding the Suez Canal shows strategic direction.

The money managers ranked Commercial International Bank, the biggest lender in Egypt not owned by the government, second best out of all 35 companies featured in this book. The buses-to-tuk tuk maker Ghabbour Auto also scores well.

Caution is needed. El-Sisi's popularity, said Wael Ziada at EFG Hermes, depends on maintaining the perception of the Muslim Brotherhood as terrorists lest "people start asking why they wasted three years of their life on a revolution." But the Brotherhood isn't the only entity Egyptians love to hate. When the US withdrew its supply of F-16 fighter jets, Apache helicopters and missiles from Egypt in protest at the crackdown in 2013, el-Sisi's popularity soared on the notion he was standing up to an America that backed the Brotherhood.[22] Anti-American sentiment is stronger in Egypt than any other country in the world, with 85% expressing an unfavorable view of Uncle Sam.[23] Putin's Russia ranks fourth. El-Sisi's first public engagement outside of the Arab world on seizing power and once again after winning the presidency was with Vladimir Putin.[24] On the agenda: supply of MiG-29 fighter jets, Kamov Ka-25 attack helicopters and Kornet anti-tank missiles.[25-27]

No. 7: Romania

Of all ten countries, Romania felt the most familiar, and not just because of my previous trips there. This is, after all, the EU country the British press obsesses over, and for all the wrong reasons – fear of immigrants, benefit scroungers and crime gangs.[28,29] Even Europe's more internationally minded media grew jittery of closer integration when Prime Minister Victor Ponta showed himself willing to compromise the rule of law and judicial independence in his battle to impeach the country's former president.[30,31]

With Ponta hurling legal missiles, I was expecting a government too distracted by its own political machinations to focus on the hard steps needed to revive the economy after the two-year recession, banking crisis and IMF bailout. I was wrong. For all Ponta's rhetoric against austerity, he hiked taxes, cut public spending and accelerated state share sales to produce one of the biggest budget deficit reductions in the EU. [32,33] By 2014, Romania was enjoying the fastest economic growth of the bloc and a rebound in the stock market to a six-year high.[12]

The pace of privatization is only accelerating. The government pulled off its biggest initial public offering to date by selling shares in the power distributor Electrica, while Fondul Proprietatea sold holdings in Transelectrica and Romgaz in 2014.[34-37] The privatizations are a further help in stabilizing the country's finances while the deepening market puts Romania on track for an upgrade to the more widely followed MSCI Emerging Markets Index. The fact that all of this is coming from a premier on the Socialist side of Romania's political spectrum makes more of the same the most likely outlook.

Romania still has its problems. Parts of the nation remain shockingly poor. One legacy of the communist era lives on beneath Bucharest's streets, where children infected with HIV through shared needles

in Ceausescu's neglected orphanages are now drug-addicted adults living in the sewers, some with their own addicted and infected children.[38]
Contributing to Romania's aging population relative to the other nine
frontier countries is the fact many young couples can't afford a place of
their own to raise a family.[39]

At the same time, Romania has the fastest internet connections after Hong
Kong and Japan and the cheapest after Ukraine and Mali.[40,41] World-class
infrastructure and the EU's second lowest wages is a combination that should
draw in more businesses, driving the economy's convergence with western Europe.
The potential from oil and gas exploration can only add to the momentum.

No. 6: Sri Lanka

"You can see for yourself," former President Rajapaksa told foreign visitors
a few months after the UN voted to investigate alleged war crimes, "how
the country and its people of all faiths and ethnic origins live in peace and
harmony today."[42]

I didn't have to look for long to see that the ex-president doesn't see as
those of other faiths and ethnic origins see – people like Prem, who saw his
newspaper's printing press unharmoniously riddled with bullets and burnt
and his delivery driver attacked with barbed-wire-wrapped bars; nor people
like Ghanan, who saw his family home turned to rubble five years after the
civil war ended. What I saw was a stunningly beautiful island divided by a
military occupation, intimidation and neglect of the economy of the north.

Yet it's likely Rajapaksa's audience in Colombo, driving on smooth, free-
flowing roads past grand tourist developments, would have seen just as he
sees. Here, the UN inquiry into the tens of thousands of deaths in the final
months of the war is widely derided as post-colonial meddling by countries
that no longer have a hold on Sri Lanka.[43]

China overtook the USA as Sri Lanka's biggest trading partner after India
in 2013. While Americans remain the largest holders of the government's
bonds, Chinese state lending has increased 50-fold over the past decade to
twice the amount from all Western countries and agencies combined. China,
voting against the UN resolution, said it has an "all-weather partnership"
with Sri Lanka and opposes interference in its domestic affairs under the "pre-
text" of human rights concerns. While the new government says it will work
positively with UN Human Rights Council members, all matters should be
resolved by domestic institutions.

The island's proximity to India 30 kilometers across the Palk Strait offers
perhaps the best potential for future foreign-exchange earnings. While in

2012 India backed America in urging Sri Lanka to investigate alleged abuses, it signaled a thaw in relations by abstaining from the UN vote in 2014.[44] India's importance will only grow as its population overtakes China's as the world's largest in the next decade or so.[45]

With President Sirisena's election pledge to challenge the growing dominance of China in Sri Lanka's economy, the island appears to be edging ever-closer to India.

No. 5: Kenya

When I told ordinary Kenyans the subject of my book, most were incredulous: Really? Kenya? A fast-growing economy? Are you sure? The world's most optimistic nation seems a generation past. Most I spoke with are cynical about every aspect of public life – politicians, healthcare, education, the economy, the police, the "injustice" system. During our stay, hundreds took to the streets in protest after three men alleged to have gang-raped a schoolgirl with violence that left her wheelchair-bound were simply ordered to cut the grass at the police station for a punishment.[46]

One of the few distinguishable policies in Uhuru Kenyatta's election campaign of 2013 was a pledge to provide a free solar-powered laptop for every child starting school. In a country entirely switched on to the transformational power of technology since the M-Pesa revolution, the idea of the nation's children having a head start was a vote winner. "It's never going to happen," said Gabriel Rotich, the photographer, on our way from Tsavo. His parents are both teachers. "The government is already struggling to pay teachers enough. Besides, most of these teachers won't know how to use the computers. How can they show pupils?" Kenya's children are still waiting for their laptops, the government blaming the delay on a legal dispute over the procurement contract.[47,48]

Opposition leader Mudavadi's faith in the checks and balances to keep governments in line isn't shared by his countrymen. The clubby nature of domestic politics allows corruption to breed while a partisan media lacks the credibility to harness real political action. Like the boy who cried wolf, the papers run so many sensationalist headlines on their adversaries it's hard for readers to spot genuine maleficence.

For all the admirable bravado of people like Brett Rowley refusing to yield to the terrorist threat, al-Shabaab's attacks are keeping those tourists with visions from "Out of Africa" out of Africa. Arrivals to Kenya fell by almost a fifth in 2013 amid the Westgate siege.[49]

And yet, there is the inescapable sense of an economy on the precipice of something big. M-Pesa is inspiring regional leadership in technology and finance[50] while helping Safaricom rank as the third favorite company among the investors in this book. The calm 2013 election nurtured foreign investor confidence. After discussing it for nearly two decades, the government's first issue of Eurobonds adds a layer of international scrutiny to government spending. And just in time: engagement with companies like Tullow Oil, BG Group and Randgold in oil, gas and gold contracts means big bucks are being passed around.

The same Kenyans incredulous that their country should be considered a strong candidate for future growth minutes later are listing reasons why actually it should. "The point is," said Mwalimu Mati, "that Kenyans have the capacity even in adversity to look on the bright side. But I don't want us to keep shattering their dreams. What would really keep me up at night is if, after all the oil exploration and discoveries, Kenya has nothing to show for it. That's happened in other countries. People are counting on this to bring development."

No. 4: Saudi Arabia

The shock of stepping out of a museum and seeing a man beheaded was topped only by the reaction of the random Saudi in the street: "He was found drunk, he was not good man to have here." Acceptance of systematic repression in the name of religion is the biggest imponderable. How can a protest movement demanding something as normal in every other country as the right to drive just fade away?[51] How is it possible at a mass-participation expressive arts event that none of the masses participating express any political expression? How is it that the international media reports cries for help from daughters of the late King Abdullah claiming they're being imprisoned and starved and then the story goes silent?[52]

The answer lies at least partly in the vast system of patronage where families are paid what in any other country would be a small fortune as an income whether they work or not – all funded by the world's biggest oil exports. The choice between this and risking jail, lashings or worse is no choice at all. There's also a sense of "better the devil you know," that the king and princes are the good guys relative to the religious zealots that might be in power without them. There's an understanding that the monarchy needs to carry the religious authorities with it on any steps toward liberalization or risk the fate of the Shah of Iran.

But it's another concern that compelled the king to liberalize more quickly shortly before his death than he ever had before. The oil revenue the monarchy uses to patronize the populace looks destined to dwindle. It's oil money, or rather the fear of less of it, that's pushing the leadership to diversify the economy. Forcing companies to start recruiting Saudis and particularly encouraging women to take up jobs, even in roles where they have direct contact with men, is a bold start. Spurring corporate competitiveness by opening the stock market to foreign investors is the next phase.

As Saudi Arabia starts to normalize, the opportunities for the first investors in are beyond compare. The country has better macro-economic fundamentals than any of the frontier markets in terms of GDP, credit quality and low indebtedness.[53]

Sean Taylor at Deutsche Asset & Wealth Management focused our trip on the companies set to benefit from consumers starting to spend their new earnings – especially women. Our starting point was the country's largest retailer of books, smart phones, tablets and laptops. Jarir was ranked 9th out of the 35 companies by our group of investors while Almarai, the world's largest integrated dairy foods company, was 20th. To Habib Oueijan's mind, it's the main stocks – the well-researched "blue chips" – that will receive the biggest influx of investors. These include Al Rajhi Bank, Saudi Arabia's top lender by market value, Saudi Basic Industries, the world's biggest petrochemicals maker, and Etihad Etisalat, the telecoms operator. Together they make up more than a fifth of the Tadawul All Share Index. Jarir is the 14th biggest and Almarai is 15th.

No. 3: Argentina

Argentina's ranking was the biggest surprise to me. Since its decline from the richest nations' league, it's resembled a fallen rock star still hooked on expensive habits and in need of rehab. Unaffordable borrowing triggered eight defaults in two centuries and won Argentina the dubious accolade as one the few countries to be downgraded from emerging market to frontier.[54]

Argentina's spending addiction is partly rooted in the early years of independence from Spain that gave way to fighting between the provinces and the richest of them all, the pampas and Buenos Aires. While states in the USA mostly have to balance their books to keep their combined deficit below 0.1% of total GDP, Argentina's powerful provinces run up far wider budget gaps. Governors are often the provincial party boss to whom members of Congress owe their allegiance. That also makes them the power brokers presidents depend on to pass legislation. As a consequence, the federal government has frequently bailed out the over-extended provinces.[55,56]

Unlike Kenya or Sri Lanka, Argentina isn't coming from a position of competitive advantage through lower production costs: the country's average income is higher than Russia's and ten times Kenya's or Myanmar's. And unlike Myanmar or Saudi Arabia – the only one of the ten countries with higher per capita income – Argentina is far from being a new market just opening up to the outside world.

While the politics of the moment are swinging toward free markets from the more populist Peronist era, those with long experience of Argentina's twists and turns, like Eduardo Eurnekian, see this as nothing more than a pendulum pre-destined to lurch back in a decade or so.

But a decade is a long enough horizon for most investors. One reason this time might just be different, perhaps even for the longer term, is the discovery of oil and gas. Vaca Muerta, the Dead Cow, sitting on the world's second largest shale gas and fourth biggest shale oil reserves, is just the tonic the economy needs. Much of the public overspend of the past has been on generous energy subsidies. Even with retreating fuel prices, Argentina's transformation to an energy exporter would go a long way to cutting public expenditure.

Vaca Muerta is the reason for YPF – the company swiped from Repsol's clutches by the government – being voted the best opportunity of all 35 securities included in this book. The shares of Argentina's largest company more than doubled in 2013 as it partnered with energy giants like Chevron to start drilling. George Soros's $28 billion family office more than doubled its stake in YPF, making this the investor's biggest US-traded stock holding in the second quarter of 2014.[57]

No. 2: Vietnam

No communist tour of Vietnam is complete without getting down and dusty in Cu Chi. This region of rubber tree plantations on the edge of Ho Chi Minh City is the entry point to a giant rabbit's warren of interconnecting tunnels that stretched across much of the country during the American War as it's known here. Termite mounds, some with sugar canes growing out of them, are interspersed with identical man-made replica earth piles where the canes form ventilation shafts to get air to tunnels below. Others are planted to look like ventilation shafts and tunnel entrances but below are bear traps to capture Americans.

Having normalized relations with the USA since the 90s, Vietnam is now preoccupied with an older adversary. The country has held back China since winning its independence in the tenth century. When China encroached on waters around the Paracel and Spratly Islands between Vietnam and the

Philippines in 2014, the government tolerated anti-China demonstrations before they morphed into riots causing over 20 deaths.[58]

The government is treading a fine line. China is the biggest foreign buyer of its goods while Vietnam's purchases represent less than 1% of Chinese exports.[59] The imbalance should compel Vietnam to diversify quickly.

One major front is closer integration with the ASEAN countries – Indonesia, Thailand, Malaysia, Singapore, the Philippines, Myanmar, Cambodia, Brunei and Laos. The bloc should give Vietnam a weightier political voice in talks with China, Europe or America, according to Dominic Scriven at Dragon Capital. It will also help boost the economy. In the same way as the free movement of people and goods within the EU multiplied flight connections, Dominic expects closer ties to shave hours from journey times across the South China Sea to the Philippines and beyond within a few years.

Besides the ASEAN, membership of the World Trade Organization since 2007 has opened the world stage to those companies efficient enough to compete. Vinamilk, with its factory of automata, sells its products in more than 23 countries including the USA, Australia, Canada, Russia, Turkey, Iraq and South Korea.[60] The investors ranked Vinamilk No. 5 of the 35 companies. Vingroup, the property developer owned by Vietnam's only billionaire, is No. 6.

The war helped shape the leadership profile of many of the companies here. Most notable is that women are running some of the most successful, including Vinamilk and Vingroup.[61] "A lot of people attribute that to the war," said Le Thi Thu Thuy, Vingroup's CEO until she recently handed over the reins to a female colleague to focus on building an internet business. "Pretty much all the men went south and the women had to take care of hard labors and everything else, so we never grew up thinking that because we're women we have to stay at home." Women, she says, are more careful, don't spend as much and really look at the numbers "instead of drinking and having fun."

No. 1: Nigeria

In more ways than one, Nigeria is Africa's Wild West. Like Saigon's never-ending markets, Lagos is alive with unbounded entrepreneurial drive. Everyone's trying to make a naira. Add to that a complete lack of law and order and you get a country as fiery as its chili suya.

The violence we witnessed during our time in Nigeria was, without exception, in the pursuit of money. That doesn't make it any more acceptable or easier to deal with, but in a country where over half the population lives below the poverty line, it at least gives some notion of resolution if incomes start to rise. Support for Boko Haram seems rooted more in the lack of opportunities for the young of the north than any sudden religious fervor.

The deadly northern insurgency amid the 2015 elections and the economic shock from collapsing oil prices sent Nigerian assets and the naira into free fall. It was Baron Rothschild who said "buy when there's blood in the streets." For all its turmoil, Nigeria's wildly discounted market seems impossible to ignore. This, after all, is the country that comes the closest to resembling the characteristics of the high-growth emerging economies of the past – Brazil, India and China. The UN projects Nigeria's population of 170 million will top America's by 2050 to become the largest after India and China, and exceed 900 million by the end of the century.[62,63]

Its economy has already overtaken South Africa as the continent's largest. The incongruous Dubai-style development springing from the Atlantic Ocean off Lagos shows how Africa's biggest city is literally on the rise.

Investors are focused on the nation's banks as a broad way to benefit from the growth in consumer activity. Nigeria's Guaranty Trust Bank ranks 4th best among the 35 stocks and FBN Holdings is 10th. The two lenders and Nigerian government securities in dollars and naira also make up the top four long-term picks from the bond market (Table C5). The risk of banks running out of cash has been vastly reduced since the global financial crisis by a strengthening of capital reserves.

While it's consumer spending that's luring investors, energy is at the root of the economy's prospects. More than 40% of daily business expenditure goes on power as companies run back-up generators to weather the continual electricity failures.[64] With the government's sale of power stations and Dangote's plan to create the world's second-largest oil refinery, Nigeria's shambolic energy sector might finally get fixed.

Amidst the optimism is the reality of a nation famed for its corruption. That demands extreme caution but it doesn't necessarily detract from the overall growth potential for the economy, according to the Nigerian who's done more to tackle graft than anyone in recent years. "As a moral issue everybody condemns corruption," says Lamido Sanusi. "But corruption hasn't stopped growth in China or in India."

Lagos seems a long way from Hollywood, but it just might start to resemble Bollywood (Tables C3–C5).

* * *

TABLE C3   Country rankings – money manager matrix

Country & Investor	Myanmar 10th	Ghana 9th	Egypt 8th	Romania 7th	Sri Lanka 6th	Kenya 5th	Saudi Arabia 4th	**Argentina 3rd**	**Vietnam 2nd**	**NIGERIA 1st**
Driehaus Capital Management Howie Schwab	6	9	4	10	2	5	7	8	3	1
Adelante Asset Management Julian Adams	10	8	5	2	9	7	6	1	3	4
Franklin Templeton Mark Mobius	9	9	5	4	8	7	1	6	3	2
Aberdeen Asset Management Kevin Daly	-	7	5	-	4	3	-	2	6	1
Deutsche Asset & Wealth Management Sean Taylor	10	9	5	7	8	6	2	4	1	3
Morgan Stanley Timothy Drinkall	3	10	9	5	8	7	2	1	4	6
Wells Fargo Asset Management Derrick Irwin	10	3	9	8	4	1	2	7	5	6
Anonymous	8	7	9	5	2	6	10	3	4	1
Anonymous	9	10	4	8	6	7	3	2	1	5
Ranking Average	7.22	7.20	5.50	5.44	5.10	4.90	3.67	3.40	3.00	2.90

Note: The investors ranked the 10 frontier markets from best long-term potential or most held at 1 to least favorite or least invested at 10. Fields are left blank where investors declined to disclose or have no view because the markets fall outside of their area of focus. The country ranking is based on the average of the scores submitted. The rankings were assigned between May & September 2014.

TABLE C4 Top of the stocks

Ranking	Company	Trading Platform
1	YPF Sociedad Anonima	New York Stock Exchange
2	Commercial Int'l Bank (CIB)	Cairo Stock Exchange
3	Safaricom	Nairobi Stock Exchange
4	Guaranty Trust Bank	Nigerian Stock Exchange
5	Vinamilk	Ho Chi Minh Stock Exchange
6	Vingroup	Ho Chi Minh Stock Exchange
7	Ghabbour Auto	Cairo Stock Exchange
8	John Keells	Colombo Stock Exchange
9	Jarir	Saudi Arabian Stock Exchange
10	FBN Holdings	Nigerian Stock Exchange
11	BRD-Groupe	Bucharest Stock Exchange
12	Dangote Cement	Nigerian Stock Exchange
13	OMV Petrom	Bucharest Stock Exchange
14	Romgaz	Bucharest Stock Exchange
15	Aitken Spence	Colombo Stock Exchange
16	EFG Hermes	Cairo Stock Exchange
17	Commercial Bank	Colombo Stock Exchange
18	Imexpharm	Ho Chi Minh Stock Exchange
19	ARM Cement	Nairobi Stock Exchange
20	Almarai	Saudi Arabian Stock Exchange
21	Yoma Strategic	Singapore Exchange
22	Juhayna Food Industries	Cairo Stock Exchange
23	Fondul Proprietatea	Bucharest Stock Exchange
24	Eastern Tobacco	Cairo Stock Exchange
25	Citadel Capital	Cairo Stock Exchange
26	Binh Minh Plastics	Ho Chi Minh Stock Exchange
27	Chevron Lubricants Lanka	Colombo Stock Exchange
28	Cargills	Colombo Stock Exchange
29	Dangote Sugar	Nigerian Stock Exchange
30	Transelectrica	Bucharest Stock Exchange

Note: The investors rated the frontier market stocks from best long-term potential or most held at 1 to least favorite or least invested at 10. The ranking is based on the average of the scores submitted. The rankings were assigned between May & September 2014.

TABLE C5 Best of the bonds

Ranking	Issuer	Country	Maturity	Currency	Trading Platform
1	Republic of Nigeria	Nigeria	2017	Naira	Euroclear/Clearstream
2	Guaranty Trust Bank	Nigeria	2018	Dollars	Euroclear/Clearstream
3	Republic of Nigeria	Nigeria	2018–2023	Dollars	Euroclear/Clearstream
4	FBN Finance	Nigeria	2020	Dollars	Euroclear/Clearstream
5	Sri Lanka	Sri Lanka	2015–2022	Dollars	Euroclear/Clearstream
6	Republic of Kenya	Kenya	2024	Dollars	Euroclear/Clearstream
7	Infrastructure Bonds	Kenya	2018–2025	Shilling	Nairobi Securities Exchange
8	Province of Buenos Aires	Argentina	2015–2035	Dollars/Euros	Euroclear/Clearstream
9	Aeropuertos Argentina 2000	Argentina	2022	Dollars	EuroMTF/Frankfurt/Luxemburg
10	Arab Republic of Egypt	Egypt	2016–2040	Dollars	Euroclear/Clearstream
11	Republic of Argentina	Argentina	2033	Euros	Euroclear/Clearstream
12	Republic of Ghana	Ghana	2017 & 2023	Dollars	Euroclear/Clearstream
13	Socialist Republic of Vietnam	Vietnam	2016–2028	Dollars	Singapore Exchange/Stuttgart

Source: Data compiled by Bloomberg
Note: The investors rated the frontier market bonds from best long-term potential or most held at 1 to least favorite or least invested at 10. The ranking is based on the average of the scores submitted. The rankings were assigned between May & September 2014.

Trading at the Frontier:
Practical Guidance Notes

With some ideas of what's out there to buy, how do you go about investing
in markets with an array of different rules, fees and restrictions? Below are
some guidance notes from the frontier-markets investment bank Exotix on
the likely transaction costs an investor might expect to be charged by a broker
on the stocks and bonds discussed (Tables C6 & C7), followed by a few last
tips from Mark Mobius.

TABLE C6   Fees, rules, restrictions – stocks

Country, Trading Platform & Chapter	Company	Costs Involved	
Kenya Chapter 1 Naironi Stock Exchange	Safaricom ARM Cement Infrastructure Bonds	CMA Transaction Levy	0.12%
		NSE Transaction Levy	0.12%
		CDS Transaction Levy	0.06%
		CMA Compensation Fund	0.01%
		CDS Guarantee Fund	0.01%
		Revenue Stamp	0.02%
		Broker Fees	0.90%
		Total fees	**1.24%**
Romania Chapter 3 Bucharest Stock Exchange	Fondul Proprietatea BRD-Groupe OMV Petrom Romgaz Trans-Electrica New Europe Property Investments	Margin fee: Buy 0.085% / 0.118% sell + Additional 0.04% for indirectly settled buy trades + Broker Fees 0.65% Total buy fees: **0.775%**	
Vietnam Chapter 5 Ho Chi Minh Stock Exchange	Imexpharm Binh Minh Plastics Vinamilk Vingroup	Sale consideration 0.10% Broker Fees 0.80% Total fees **0.90%**	

Country, Trading Platform & Chapter	Company	Costs Involved
Nigeria Chapter 6 Nigerian Stock Exchange	Dangote Cement Dangote Sugar Guaranty Trust Bank FBN Holdings	Buy trades: SEC Fee 0.30% Stamp Duties 0.075% Broker Fees 0.70% Total buy fees **1.075%** Sell trades: NSE Fee 0.30% (+5% VAT) CSCS 0.30% (+5% VAT) Stamp Duties 0.075% Broker Fees 0.70% Total sell fees **1.375%** (ex-VAT)
Egypt Chapter 7 Cairo Stock Exchange	Eastern Tobacco Juhayna Food Industries Ghabbour Auto Citadel Capital Commercial Int'l Bank (CIB) EFG Hermes	0.05% + 0.10% on buy trades + Broker Fees 0.40% Total buy fees: **0.55%**
Sri Lanka Chapter 9 Colombo Stock Exchange	Cargills John Keells Aitken Spence Chevron Lubricants Lanka Commercial Bank	Buy trades: CSE Fees 0.084% CDS Fees 0.024% SEC Fees 0.072% Share Transaction Fee 0.300% Broker Fees 0.64% Total buy fees **1.12%** Sell trades: CSE Fees 0.05% CDS Fees 0.02% SEC Fees 0.05% Share Transaction Fee 0.30% Broker Fees 0.64% Total sell fees **1.06%**

(Continued)

Country, Trading Platform & Chapter	Company	Costs Involved
Ghana Chapter 10 Ghana Stock Exchange	Enterprise Group AngloGold Ashanti	GSE Levy 0.35% SEC Levy 0.15% GSD Levy 0.15% Market Development Levy 0.05% Broker Fees 1.40% Total fees **2.10%**

Abbreviations:

CMA	*Capital Markets Authority*
NSE	*Nairobi Stock Exchange*
CDS	*Central Depository System*
SEC	*Securities & Exchange Commission*
CSCS	*Central Securities Clearing System*
CSE	*Colombo Stock Exchange*

Source: Data compiled by Exotix Partners LLP as of July 2014.

TABLE C7   Fees, rules, restrictions — bond listings

Trading Platform	Securities	Costs	Restrictions
Euroclear/ Clearstream	Romanian Sovereign Eurobonds Province of Buenos Aires Argentine Republic Socialist Republic of Vietnam Republic of Nigeria Guaranty Trust Bank FBN Finance Arab Republic of Egypt Republic of Sri Lanka Republic of Ghana	Basic charge for a Euroclear transaction starts ~30 euros per trade. Private-client brokers would then charge a percentage of the cash value of the trade, based on sliding scale from a maximum of around 1.5% downwards as the amount increases	The most prohibitive issue for retail investors is the minimum size of transactions. The standard minimum nominal amount is 200,000 units, which at face value would be 200,000 dollars or euros. In some exceptions, the minimum will be 50,000 or 100,000. Details of the minimum holding are included in the bond listing, e.g. on Bloomberg

Source: Data compiled by Exotix Partners LLP as of July 2014

Mark Mobius

One obvious way to start investing in frontier markets is to buy shares on the most easily accessible exchanges such as London, Toronto or Vancouver. The selection is limited since most are companies in the natural resource arena – digging for gold, drilling for oil and generally exploiting the rich mineral resources found in frontier markets, particularly in Africa.

The next step would be individual frontier market exchanges. This gets tougher because it involves establishing a custodial account in each of the countries, which can be an expensive and time-consuming process. It also requires dealing with illiquid securities, often with limited information.

A third route is to invest in frontier market mutual funds, of which there is a growing list (Table C8).

TABLE C8 Fund listings: The following funds have among the highest holdings of the companies featured above, based on data compiled by Bloomberg in June 2014
GLOBAL FRONTIER MARKET FUNDS

Fund Name, Description, Holdings & Assets Under Management	Fund Details	
First State Investments ICVC - Global Emerging Markets Fund is an open-end investment company incorporated in the UK. The aim of the Fund is to achieve long-term capital growth. The Fund invests in equities in emerging economies, including those companies listed on developed market exchanges whose activities predominantly take place in emerging market countries.	Top Ind. Group Allocation	
	Food	19.18%
	Banks	11.64%
	Beverages	8.54%
	Telecommunications	5.62%
	Insurance	3.80%
	Retail	3.29%
	Top Geo. Allocation	
	South Africa	12.92%
Holdings Include:	India	12.69%
Commercial International Bank, Egypt (London listing)	U.K.	9.37%
Tullow Oil plc	Chile	8.49%
Guaranty Trust Bank plc	Fund Info	
Juhayna Food Industries	Fund Type	OEIC
AngloGold Ashanti	Asset Class	Equity
	Economic Association	Emerging Markets
	Strategy	Blend

(Continued)

Fund Name, Description, Holdings & Assets Under Management	Fund Details	

Unilever Nigeria
Empresa Nacional de Electricid (Endesa)
Nigerian Breweries

Geo. Focus Region	International
Inception Date	12/30/92
Front Load	4.00%
Min Investment	GBP 1.00k
Min Subsequent	GBP 500.00
Current Mgmt Fee	1.75%

Assets   06/12/14   GBP 745.24M

Expense Ratio	1.61%

Goldman Sachs N-11s Equity Portfolio is an open-end fund incorporated in Luxembourg. The Fund's objective is long-term capital appreciation. The Fund invests in securities of companies in N11 Countries. N11 countries are Bangladesh, Egypt, Indonesia, Iran, Mexico, Nigeria, Pakistan, Philippines, South Korea, Turkey and Vietnam.

Top Ind. Group Allocation	
Banks	21.74%
Telecommunications	10.52%
Semiconductors	7.87%
Food	5.64%
Retail	5.43%
Oil &Gas	4.37%

Holdings Include:
Nigerian Breweries
Commercial International Bank, Egypt
Telecom Egypt
Vingroup
Zenith Bank
Guaranty Trust Bank
Nestle Nigeria
Dangote Cement
PetroVietnam
United Bank for Africa
Oriental Weavers
Dangote Flour Mills
Dangote Sugar Refinery

Top Geo. Allocation	
South Korea	23.97%
Mexico	22.96%
Indonesia	14.46%
Turkey	9.25%
Fund Info	
Fund Type	Open-End Fund
Asset Class	Equity
Strategy	Blend
Geo. Focus Region	International
Inception Date	01/26/11
Expense Ratio	2.15%

Assets   06/12/14   USD 1.38B

Morgan Stanley Investment Funds - Frontier Emerging Markets Equity Fund is an open-end fund incorporated in Luxembourg. The Fund's investment objective is to seek long-term capital appreciation, measured in USD, through investment primarily in a portfolio of equity securities in frontier emerging market countries.

Fund Info	
Fund Type	SICAV
Asset Class	Equity
Economic Association	Emerging Markets
Strategy	Blend
Geo. Focus Region	International
Inception Date	03/28/13
Front Load	5.75%
Current Mgmt Fee	2.40%
Expense Ratio	2.95%

Assets   06/12/14 USD 150.92M

Fund Name, Description, Holdings & Assets Under Management	Fund Details

Oppenheimer Developing Markets Fund is an open-end fund incorporated in the USA. The Fund's objective is capital appreciation. The Fund mainly invests in common stocks of issuers in emerging and developing markets throughout the world. Under normal market conditions, it will invest at least 80% in equity securities of issuers whose principal activities are in at least 3 developing markets.

Holdings Include:
Tullow Oil
Commercial International Bank, Egypt
Nigerian Breweries
Zenith Bank
Guaranty Trust Bank

Top Ind. Group Allocation

Internet	12.05%
Beverages	8.27%
Retail	7.98%
Oil & Gas	7.61%
Banks	6.72%
Food	6.22%

Top Geo. Allocation

China	15.63%
Brazil	12.95%
India	11.54%
U.K.	4.98%

Fund Info

Fund Type	Open-End Fund
Asset Class	Equity
Economic Association	Emerging Markets
Market Cap	Broad Market
Strategy	Growth
Geo. Focus Region	International
Inception Date	11/18/96
Front Load	5.75%
Min Investment	USD 1.00k
Current Mgmt Fee	.79%
Expense Ratio	1.35%

Assets   06/11/14   USD 42.62B

Parametric Emerging Markets Fund is an open-end fund incorporated in the USA. The objective is long-term capital appreciation. The Fund invests at least 80% of its net assets in equity securities of companies located in emerging market countries, including countries in Asia, Latin America, the Middle East, southern Europe, eastern Europe, Africa and Russia.

Holdings Include:
Commercial International Bank, Egypt
Safaricom
BRD Groupe – Société Générale
Banca Transilvania
OMV Petrom
East Africa Breweries
Empresa Nacional de Electricid
Eastern Tobacco
AngloGold Ashanti Juhayna Food

Top Ind. Group Allocation

Banks	18.07%
Telecommunications	9.93%
Oil & Gas	7.78%
Food	4.21%
Electric	3.96%
Holding Companies	3.37%

Top Geo. Allocation

China	6.86%
India	6.76%
South Africa	6.20%
Taiwan	6.16%

Fund Info

Fund Type	Open-End Fund
Asset Class	Equity
Economic Association	Emerging Markets
Market Cap	Broad Market
Strategy	Value
Geo. Focus Region	International
Inception Date	06/30/06
Current Mgmt Fee	.93%
Expense Ratio	1.38%

Assets   05/30/14   USD 4.70B

(Continued)

Fund Name, Description, Holdings & Assets Under Management	Fund Details

Schroder International Selection Fund - Frontier Markets Equity is an open-end fund incorporated in Luxembourg. The Fund's objective is to provide capital growth. The Fund invests in equity and equity-related securities of frontier market companies.

Holdings Include:
Guaranty Trust Bank Plc
Saudi Pharmaceutical
FBN Holdings Plc
PetroVietnam Gas
Saudi Basic Industries
Kenya Commercial Bank
Commercial Bank of Ceylon
Vietnam Dairy Products
John Keells Holding
Nigerian Breweries

Assets   05/30/14   USD 1.25B

Top Ind. Group Allocation	
Banks	40.15%
Oil &Gas	11.82%
Real Estate	10.78%
Holding Companies	8.48%
Telecommunications	5.60%
Chemicals	3.85%
Top Geo. Allocation	
U.A.E.	20.22%
Qatar	17.15%
Kuwait	14.31%
Nigeria	10.12%
Fund Info	
Fund Type	SICAV
Asset Class	Equity
Economic Association	Emerging Markets
Strategy	Blend
Geo. Focus Region	International
Inception Date	12/15/10
Front Load	5.26%
Min Investment	USD 1.00k
Min Subsequent	USD 1.00k
Current Mgmt Fee	1.50%
Performance Fee	15.00%
Expense Ratio	2.19%

Templeton Frontier Markets Fund is a SICAV incorporated in Luxembourg. The Fund's objective is long-term capital appreciation. The Fund will invest primarily in transferable equity securities of companies incorporated in Frontier Markets across the market capitalization spectrum.

Top Holdings (MHD)
Ooredoo QSC
Global Telecom Holding
United Bank Ltd/Pakistan
Industries Qatar QSC
First Gulf Bank PJSC
Zenith Bank plc
Telecom Argentina SA
Bank Muscat SAOG
Sonatel
KazMunaiGas Exploration

Assets   04/30/14   USD 2.15B

Top Ind. Group Allocation	
Banks	45.62%
Telecommunications	12.92%
Oil&Gas	7.98%
Mining	3.10%
Pharmaceuticals	3.00%
Chemicals	2.92%
Top Geo. Allocation	
U.K.	12.01%
Nigeria	9.52%
U.A.E.	9.51%
Qatar	8.30%
Fund Info	
Fund Type	SICAV
Asset Class	Equity
Economic Association	Emerging Markets
Market Cap	Broad Market
Strategy	Blend
Geo. Focus Region	International
Inception Date	10/14/08
Front Load	5.75%
Min Investment	USD 5.00k
Min Subsequent	USD 1.00k
Current Mgmt Fee	1.60%
Expense Ratio	2.58%

Fund Name, Description, Holdings & Assets Under Management	Fund Details

Wasatch Frontier Emerging Small Countries Fund is an open-end fund incorporated in the USA. The Fund's objective is long-term appreciation of capital. The Fund will invest at least 80% of its assets in the equity securities of companies that are tied economically to frontier markets and small emerging market countries.

Top Holdings:
Safaricom Ltd
Vietnam Dairy Products JSC
MTN Group Ltd
Universal Robina Corp
Nestlé Nigeria PLC
East African Breweries Ltd
Square Pharmaceuticals Ltd
Qatar National Bank
Nigerian Breweries PLC
Societe Des Brasseries du Maro

Assets   06/10/14   USD 1.29B

Top Ind. Group Allocation	
Food	22.44%
Banks	21.62%
Beverages	12.84%
Telecommunications	7.55%
Pharmaceuticals	4.42%
Building Materials	4.21%
Top Geo. Allocation	
Nigeria	11.20%
Kenya	9.01%
U.A.E.	7.52%
U.K.	6.20%
Fund Info	
Fund Type	Open-End Fund
Asset Class	Equity
Economic Association	Emerging Markets
Strategy	Blend
Geo. Focus Region	International
Inception Date	01/31/12
Min Investment	USD 2.00k
Early Withdrawal	2.00%
Min Subsequent	USD 100.00
Current Mgmt Fee	1.75%
Performance Fee	N.A.
Expense Ratio	2.25%

GLOBAL FRONTIER MARKET SMALL-CAP FUNDS

Fund Name, Description, Holdings & Assets Under Management	Fund Details

Aberdeen Global - Emerging Markets Smaller Companies Fund is an open-end investment fund incorporated in Luxembourg. The Fund's objective is to provide long-term total return. The Fund invests at least two-thirds of its assets in equities and equity-related securities of smaller companies with their registered office in an emerging market country.

Holdings Include:
BRD-Groupe Société Générale
East African Breweries
Guinness Nigeria

Top Ind. Group Allocation	
Retail	12.57%
Real Estate	8.72%
Food	7.83%
Banks	7.32%
Commercial Services	6.34%
Building Materials	5.64%
Top Geo. Allocation	
Brazil	13.41%
India	9.50%
South Africa	9.47%
Hong Kong	8.06%

(Continued)

Fund Name, Description, Holdings & Assets Under Management	Fund Details	

John Keells Holdings plc
Commercial Bank of Ceylon
Chevron Lubricants Lanka plc

Fund Info	
Fund Type	SICAV
Asset Class	Equity
Economic Association	Emerging Markets
Market Cap	Small-cap
Strategy	Blend
Geo. Focus Region	International
Inception Date	03/13/07
Front Load	5.00%
Min Investment	USD 1.50k
Min Subsequent	USD 1.50k
Current Mgmt Fee	1.75%

Assets	05/30/14	USD 2.17B

Expense Ratio	2.03%

Driehaus Emerging Markets Small Cap Growth Fund is an open-end fund incorporated in the USA. The Fund's objective is to maximize capital appreciation. The Fund uses a growth style of investment in equity securities of small cap emerging market companies.

Top Holdings:
CT Environmental Group Ltd
NagaCorp Ltd
Bank Al-Jazira
Taiwan Dollar
Jarir Marketing Co
Kaveri Seed Co Ltd
Coolpad Group Ltd
Saudi Airlines Catering Co
Matahari Department Store Tbk
SKS Microfinance Ltd

Top Ind. Group Allocation	
Retail	6.64%
Real Estate	6.56%
Banks	6.34%
Oil&Gas	6.33%
Oil&Gas Services	5.27%
Internet	3.84%
Top Geo. Allocation	
China	16.47%
Saudi Arabia	9.66%
India	8.18%
South Korea	6.18%
Fund Info	
Fund Type	Open-End Fund
Asset Class	Equity
Economic Association	Emerging Markets
Market Cap	Small-cap
Strategy	Growth
Geo. Focus Region	International
Inception Date	12/01/08
Min Investment	USD 10.00k
Early Withdrawal	2.00%
Min Subsequent	USD 2.00k
Current Mgmt Fee	1.50%

NAV	USD 13.56

Expense Ratio	1.85%

William Blair Emerging Markets Small Cap Growth Fund is an open-end fund incorporated in the USA. The Fund's objective is long-term capital appreciation. The Fund invests at least 80% of its net assets in equity securities of small capitalization emerging market companies.

Top Ind. Group Allocation	
Retail	11.23%
Banks	8.14%
Commercial S .	6.06%
Auto Parts&Equipment	5.46%
Lodging	4.92%
Apparel	3.97%

(Continued)

Fund Name, Description, Holdings & Assets Under Management	Fund Details	
Top Holdings:	Top Geo. Allocation	
Safaricom Ltd	India	16.84%
Kroton Educacional SA	China	11.82%
Coronation Fund Managers Ltd	Taiwan	8.33%
Hollysys Automation Technologies	South Korea	8.04%
King Slide Works Co Ltd	Fund Info	
Bank Millennium SA	Fund Type	Open-End Fund
IndusInd Bank Ltd	Asset Class	Equity
LPP SA	Economic Association	Emerging Markets
NagaCorp Ltd	Market Cap	Small-cap
Estacio Participacoes SA	Strategy	Growth
	Geo. Focus Region	International
	Inception Date	10/24/11
	Min Investment	USD 2.50k
	Early Withdrawal	2.00%
	Min Subsequent	USD 1.00k
	Current Mgmt Fee	1.10%
Assets USD 150.38M	Expense Ratio	1.65%

* * *

An alternative to mutual funds is to buy representative holdings across a country's overall stock market through exchange-traded funds. ETFs aim to provide the same returns as an index like the FTSE 100 or the S&P 500. They trade like regular shares on the major stock markets of the world. As they simply try to mimic an index, there's no need for expensive research, reducing the fees deducted. The downside is there's no way to weed out any individual stocks that might appear a bad bet or step up exposure to a favored company. ETFs currently exist for Nigeria, Vietnam, Argentina, Saudi Arabia, Romania and Egypt, as well as the overall MSCI Frontier Markets Index (Tables C9 and C10).

TABLE C9   ETFs: Exchange traded funds offer a way to buy a country's stock exchange without picking the individual shares.

Country	Security / Trading Platform	Issuer Description	Average Annual Return	Top 10 Index Holdings	
Romania Chapter 3	ETF BET Tradeville Bucharest Stock Exchange	Open-end ETF incorporated in Romania seeking to track the performance of the Bucharest Stock Exchange Trading (BET) Index by matching equity holdings	25.2% in first full year, 2013	Fondul Proprietatea SA/Fund	21.5%
				OMV Petrom SA	18.1%
				Banca Transilvania	15.5%
				Societatea Nationala de Gaze	15.4%
				BRD-Groupe Société Générale	8.9%
				Electrica SA	7.8%
				Transgaz SA Medias	5.8%
				Transelectrica SA	4.2%
				Societatea Nationala Nuclear	1.7%
				SC Bursa DE Valori Bucuresti	1.0%
Argentina Chapter 4	Global X FTSE Argentina 20 ETF New York Stock Exchange	ETF incorporated in the U.S. The fund seeks to track the performance of the FTSE Argentina 20 Index	-2.1% since inception in 2011	Tenaris SA	18.6%
				MercadoLibre Inc	16.5%
				YPF SA	9.6%
				Banco Macro SA	5.6%
				Grupo Financiero Galicia SA	5.4%
				Telecom Argentina SA	5.2%
				BBVA Banco Frances SA	3.9%
				Arcos Dorados Holdings Inc	3.3%
				Pampa Energia SA	3.0%
				Petrobras Argentina SA	2.8%
Vietnam Chapter 5	Market Vectors Vietnam ETF New York Stock Exchange	ETF incorporated in the U.S. aiming to replicate the price and yield performance of the Market Vectors Vietnam Index	-3.4% since inception in 2009	Masan Group Corp	8.8%
				Vingroup JSC	7.8%
				Bank for Foreign Trade	7.3%
				Saigon Thuong Tin	6.7%
				Gamuda Bhd	5.3%
				PetroVietnam Technical Serv	5.2%
				Minor International plc	5.0%
				Charoen Pokphand Foods	4.6%
				Bao Viet Holdings	4.4%
				Petrovietnam Fertilizer & Ch	4.2%

Country	Security / Trading Platform	Issuer Description	Average Annual Return	Top 10 Index Holdings	
Nigeria Chapter 6	Global X Nigeria Index ETF New York Stock Exchange	ETF incorporated in the U.S. seeking to provide investment results that correspond generally to the price and yield performance, before fees and expenses, of the Solactive Nigeria Index	N/A Inception mid 2013	Nigerian Breweries PLC	18.6%
				Guaranty Trust Bank PLC	11.0%
				Zenith Bank PLC	9.9%
				Nestlé Nigeria PLC	8.2%
				Ecobank Transnational	4.7%
				Guinness Nigeria PLC	4.0%
				Dangote Cement PLC	4.0%
				FBN Holdings Plc	3.6%
				Forte Oil PLC	3.5%
				Transnational Corp	3.5%
Egypt Chapter 7	Market Vectors Egypt Index ETF New York Stock Exchange	ETF incorporated in the U.S. with objective to replicate as closely as possible, before fees and expenses, the price and yield performance of the Market Vectors Egypt Index	-4.4% since inception in 2010	Commercial Int'l Bank	8.9%
				Global Telecom Holding	7.2%
				EFG-Hermes	7.1%
				Talaat Moustafa Group	6.9%
				Telecom Egypt	6.2%
				Six of October Development	5.4%
				Juhayna Food	5.1%
				ElSwedy Electric Co.	5.0%
				Egypt Kuwait Holding	4.9%
				Orascom Telecom Media	4.7%
Saudi Arabia Chapter 8	HSBC Amanah Saudi 20 ETF Saudi Arabia	Incorporated in Saudi Arabia, the Fund seeks to track the performance of the HSBC Amanah Saudi 20 Index, before excluding fees and expenses	20.7% since inception in 2011	No holdings reported	

(Continued)

Country	Security / Trading Platform	Issuer Description	Average Annual Return	Top 10 Index Holdings
Overall	iShares MSCI Frontier 100 ETF	Incorporated in the U.S., the ETF tracks the MSCI Frontier Markets 100 Index	22.2% in 2013, first full year	See below

Source: Data compiled by Bloomberg as of December 2014

TABLE C10   MSCI Frontier Markets Index

Company	Country
Grupo Financiero Galicia SA	Argentina
Telecom Argentina SA	Argentina
YPF SA	Argentina
BBVA Banco Frances SA	Argentina
Petrobras Argentina SA	Argentina
Banco Macro SA	Argentina
Aluminium Bahrain BSC	Bahrain
Bahrain Telecommunications Co BSC	Bahrain
Al-Salam Bank	Bahrain
Titas Gas Transmission & Distribution Co	Bangladesh
GrameenPhone Ltd	Bangladesh
Lafarge Surma Cement Ltd	Bangladesh
Square Pharmaceuticals Ltd	Bangladesh
Chimimport AD	Bulgaria
Sopharma AD/Sofia	Bulgaria
Hrvatski Telekom dd	Croatia
INA Industrija Nafte dd	Croatia
Adris Grupa dd	Croatia
Olympic Entertainment Group AS	Estonia

Company	Country
Tallink Group AS	Estonia
Jordan Phosphate Mines	Jordan
Jordan Telecommunications Co PSC	Jordan
Arab Bank plc	Jordan
KazMunaiGas Exploration Production JSC	Kazakhstan
KCell JSC	Kazakhstan
Halyk Savings Bank of Kazakhstan JSC	Kazakhstan
Kenya Commercial Bank Ltd	Kenya
East African Breweries Ltd	Kenya
Safaricom Ltd	Kenya
Equity Bank Ltd	Kenya
Co-operative Bank of Kenya Ltd/The	Kenya
Kuwait Projects Co Holding KSCP	Kuwait
Burgan Bank SAK	Kuwait
Mabanee Co KPSC	Kuwait
National Bank of Kuwait SAKP	Kuwait
Kuwait Finance House	Kuwait
Agility Public Warehousing Co KSC	Kuwait
Mobile Telecommunications Co KSC	Kuwait
Bank Audi SAL	Lebanon
Solidere	Lebanon
BLOM Bank SAL	Lebanon
Apranga PVA	Lithuania
TEO LT AB	Lithuania
State Bank of Mauritius Ltd	Mauritius
MCB Group Ltd	Mauritius
BMCE Bank	Morocco
Cie Generale Immobiliere	Morocco

(Continued)

Company	Country
Maroc Telecom	Morocco
Lafarge Ciments/Morocco	Morocco
Managem	Morocco
Attijariwafa Bank	Morocco
Wafa Assurance	Morocco
Douja Promotion Groupe Addoha SA	Morocco
Banque Centrale Populaire	Morocco
Zenith Bank PLC	Nigeria
FBN Holdings plc	Nigeria
United Bank for Africa plc	Nigeria
Union Bank of Nigeria plc	Nigeria
Guinness Nigeria plc	Nigeria
Forte Oil plc	Nigeria
Access Bank plc	Nigeria
Unilever Nigeria plc	Nigeria
Guaranty Trust Bank plc	Nigeria
Stanbic IBTC Holdings plc	Nigeria
Dangote Cement plc	Nigeria
Nestlé Nigeria plc	Nigeria
Lafarge Cement WAPCO Nigeria plc	Nigeria
SEPLAT Petroleum Development Co plc	Nigeria
PZ Cussons Nigeria plc	Nigeria
Flour Mills of Nigeria plc	Nigeria
Nigerian Breweries plc	Nigeria
Oman Cement Co	Oman
Bank Muscat SAOG	Oman
National Bank Of Oman SAOG	Oman

Company	Country
Bank Dhofar SAOG	Oman
Ooredoo	Oman
Oman Telecommunications Co SAOG	Oman
Ahli Bank SAOG	Oman
HSBC Bank Oman SAOG	Oman
Raysut Cement Co	Oman
Pakistan Telecommunication Co Ltd	Pakistan
United Bank Ltd/Pakistan	Pakistan
National Bank of Pakistan	Pakistan
MCB Bank Ltd	Pakistan
Pakistan State Oil Co Ltd	Pakistan
Fauji Fertilizer Co Ltd	Pakistan
Oil & Gas Development Co Ltd	Pakistan
Engro Corp Ltd/Pakistan	Pakistan
Lucky Cement Ltd	Pakistan
Pakistan Petroleum Ltd	Pakistan
Fatima Fertilizer Co Ltd	Pakistan
Pakistan Tobacco Co Ltd	Pakistan
Habib Bank Ltd	Pakistan
K-Electric Ltd	Pakistan
Pakistan Oilfields Ltd	Pakistan
BRD-Groupe Société Générale	Romania
ROMGAZ SA	Romania
Banca Transilvania	Romania
OMV Petrom SA	Romania
Electrica	Romania
Naftna Industrija Srbije Novi Sad	Serbia

(Continued)

Company	Country
AIK Banka AD	Serbia
Zavarovalnica Triglav dd	Slovenia
Petrol dd Ljubljana	Slovenia
Krka dd Novo mesto	Slovenia
Telekom Slovenije dd	Slovenia
Commercial Bank of Ceylon plc	Sri Lanka
Ceylon Tobacco Co plc	Sri Lanka
John Keells Holdings plc	Sri Lanka
Ecobank Transnational Inc	Togo
Banque International Arabe de Tunis	Tunisia
Banque de Tunisie	Tunisia
Ukrnafta OPJC	Ukraine
Motor Sich PJSC	Ukraine
Bank for Foreign Trade of Vietnam JSC	Vietnam
PetroVietnam Gas JSC	Vietnam
Petrovietnam Fertilizer & Chemicals JSC	Vietnam
HAGL JSC	Vietnam
Hoa Phat Group JSC	Vietnam
PetroVietnam Drilling and Well Services	Vietnam
Masan Group Corp	Vietnam
Bank for Investment and Development of Vietnam	Vietnam
Bao Viet Holdings	Vietnam
VietinBank	Vietnam
Saigon Thuong Tin Commercial JSB	Vietnam
Vingroup JSC	Vietnam
Kinh Do Corp	Vietnam

Source: Data compiled by Bloomberg as of December 2014. (*Function: MXFM Index MEMB GO*)

Endnotes

1. Anonymous (2014) Agent Orange, History. Available at: http://www.history.com/topics/vietnam-war/agent-orange.
2. A fully working laptop was being prepared for Samuel, courtesy of the assistance of Gary Everson of Whitstable Computer Repair and my late father-in-law Victor Brooker.
3. Nath, V., Culverhouse, S. (2011) *Frontier Markets Guidebook*, Exotix.
4. Anonymous (2013) The World Factbook, CIA. Available at: https://www.cia.gov/library/publications/the-world-factbook/fields/2079.html#ly.
5. Eckert, P. (2013) U.S. lifts more sanctions on Myanmar to support reforms, Reuters. Available at: http://www.reuters.com/article/2013/05/02/us-myanmar-usa-sanctions-idUSBRE9411AR20130502.
6. Bhalla, N. (2014) U.N. Chief says access not a must for Sri Lanka war crimes probe, Reuters. Available at: http://www.reuters.com/article/2014/08/11/us-srilanka-warcrimes-idUSKBN0GB11I20140811.
7. Allison, S. (2014) ICC should drop charges against Kenyatta – for now, *The Guardian*. Available at: http://www.theguardian.com/world/2014/jul/17/icc-uhuru-kenyatta-kenya.
8. El Deeb, S. (2014) Egypt sentences three Al-Jazeera reporters to seven years, AP. Available at: http://www.arabnews.com/news/591066.
9. Anonymous (2014) Marching forward, to the past, *The Economist*. Available at: http://www.economist.com/news/middle-east-and-africa/21605947-enigmatic-new-president-seems-be-harking-backwards-marching-forward?fsrc=email_to_a_friend.
10. Sloan, A. (2014) GCC divided over Egypt's aborted democracy, *Middle East Monitor*. Available at: https://www.middleeastmonitor.com/articles/middle-east/10132-gcc-divided-over-egypts-aborted-democracy.
11. Daraghmeh, M. (2014) Israel accepts Egypt's Gaza cease-fire proposal, AP. Available at: http://news.yahoo.com/israel-accepts-egypts-gaza-cease-fire-proposal-170641261.html.
12. Timu, A. (2014) Romania budget planning delays IMF review, Ponta says, Bloomberg News. Available at: http://www.bloomberg.com/news/2014-06-12/imf-postpones-romania-review-until-november-ponta-says.html.
13. Dullien, S. (2012) Reinventing Europe: Explaining the fiscal compact, European Council on Foreign Relations. Available at: http://www.ecfr.eu/content/entry/commentary_reinventing_europe_explaining_the_fiscal_compact.
14. Bronstein, H. (2014) Argentina won lottery with Vaca Muerta shale field – Chevron, Reuters. Available at: http://www.reuters.com/article/2014/05/22/chevron-argentina-idUSL1N0O824V20140522.
15. Hyde, D., Kerry, J. (2014) Remarks with Ghanaian President John Mahama and Millennium Challenge Corporation CEO Dana Hyde at the signing of

the Ghana Power Compact, All Africa. Available at: http://allafrica.com/stories/201408061462.html.

16. Seccombe, A. (2014) AngloGold Ashanti to retrench hundreds in Ghana, Business Day Live. Available at: http://www.bdlive.co.za/business/mining/2014/08/12/anglogold-ashanti-to-retrench-hundreds-in-ghana.

17. Anonymous (2014) AngloGold Ashanti to address Obuasi Mine's poor performance, CitiFM Online. Available at: http://www.citifmonline.com/2014/08/11/anglogold-ashanti-to-address-obuasi-mines-poor-performance/.

18. Anderson, M., McTernan, B. A. (2014) Ghana's cocoa farmers turn to smuggling as profits dwindle, *The Guardian*. Available at: http://www.theguardian.com/global-development/2014/aug/13/ghana-cocoa-farmers-smuggling-profits-dwindle.

19. Dontoh, E., Lima, M.S. (2014) Ghana soccer stars await $3 million plane before key match, Bloomberg News. Available at: http://www.bloomberg.com/news/2014-06-25/ghana-sends-plane-with-3-million-to-calm-world-cup-team-1-.html.

20. AbdAllah, A. (2014) Over 40,000 Arrests related to political turmoil since Morsi's Ouster: Wiki Thawra, *Egypt Daily News*. Available at: http://www.dailynewsegypt.com/2014/05/25/40000-arrests-related-political-turmoil-since-morsis-ouster-wiki-thawra/.

21. Anonymous (2014) Egypt: Rampant Torture, Arbitrary Arrests And Detentions Signal Catastrophic Decline In Human Rights One Year After Ousting Of Morsi, Amnesty International. Available at: http://www.amnesty.org/en/news/egypt-anniversary-morsi-ousting-2014-07-02.

22. Jones, S. (2013) General Al-Sisi's popularity soars after U.S. aid cut-off to Egypt, *The Daily Beast*. Available at: http://www.thedailybeast.com/articles/2013/10/10/general-al-sisi-s-popularity-soars-after-u-s-aid-cut-off-to-egypt.html.

23. Tomlinson, S. (2014) No, it's not Russia: Egypt comes top of Middle East-heavy list of countries that hate the U.S. the most, Mail Online. Available at: http://www.dailymail.co.uk/news/article-2708531/No-not-Russia-Egypt-comes-Middle-East-heavy-list-countries-hate-U-S-theyre-loved-Philippines.html#ixzz3AOjEcC00.

24. Anonymous (2014) Egyptian leader El-Sisi meets Putin on first foreign trip, RIA Novosti. Available at: http://en.ria.ru/world/20140213/187498184/Egyptian-Leader-El-Sisi-Meets-Putin-On-First-Foreign-Trip.html.

25. Anonymous (2014) Putin to Tackle Gaza Conflict, Food and Military Trade with Egypt's Sisi, RIA Novosti. Available at: http://en.ria.ru/russia/20140812/191929316/Putin-to-Tackle-Gaza-Conflict-Food-and-Military-Trade-with-Egypts-Sisi.html.

26. Anonymous (2014) El-Sisi, Putin stress close ties near arms deal, Ahram Online. Available at: http://www.worldaffairsjournal.org/content/el-sisi-putin-stress-close-ties-near-arms-deal.

27. Anonymous (2014) U.S. unlocks military aid to Egypt, backing President Sisi, BBC News. Available at: http://www.bbc.co.uk/news/world-middle-east-27961933.

28. Eccles, L. (2013) 'In January, the only thing left will be the goat': Romanian father-of-seven's boast as mayor says half the population of his villages are on their way to Britain for the higher salaries and generous benefits, *Daily Mail*. Available at: http://www.dailymail.co.uk/news/article-2498479/In-January-thing-left-goat-Romanian-father-sevens-boast-mayor-says-half-population-villages-way-Britain-higher-salaries-generous-benefits.html#ixzz3ASPDVSOX.

29. Chorley, M. (2013) 'We're importing a crime wave from Romania And Bulgaria': Tory MPs round on ministers as immigration curbs are lifted, *Daily Mail*. Available at: http://www.dailymail.co.uk/news/article-2526486/Were-importing-crime-wave-Romania-Bulgaria-Tory-MPs-round-ministers-immigration-curbs-lifted.html#ixzz3ASPyeQBy.

30. Hawley, C. (2012) A 'humiliating show trial' in Romania, Spiegel Online. Available at: http://www.spiegel.de/international/europe/eu-concerned-over-romanian-parliament-impeachment-of-president-basescu-a-843382.html.

31. Buckley, N., Fontanella-Khan, J. (2012) Romania President gets impeachment lifeline, *Financial Times*. Available at: http://www.ft.com/cms/s/0/f4beda04-caab-11e1-89be-00144feabdc0.html#axzz3ASRZvmrc.

32. Bernovici, A. (2013) PM Ponta: We propose budgetary discipline instead of austerity, Nine O'Clock. Available at: http://www.nineoclock.ro/pm-ponta-we-propose-budgetary-discipline-instead-of-austerity/.

33. Anonymous (2014) PM Ponta: It's proper time to cut social contributions, Agerpres. Available at: http://www.agerpres.ro/english/2014/07/22/pm-ponta-it-s-proper-time-to-cut-social-contributions-14-53-54.

34. Marinas, R. (2014) Romania's Electrica sets low-end share price in privatisation, Reuters. Available at: http://uk.reuters.com/article/2014/06/27/romania-electrica-idUKL6N0P84GB20140627.

35. Timu, A. (2014) Romania Electrica IPO oversubscribed two days before closing, Bloomberg News. Available at: http://www.bloomberg.com/news/2014-06-24/romania-electrica-ipo-oversubscribed-two-days-before-closing-1-.html.

36. Chirileasa, A. (2014) Romania's Fondul Proprietatea sells stake in Transelectrica for Eur 48.5 Mln, Romania insider. Available at: http://www.romania-insider.com/romanias-fondul-proprietatea-sells-stake-in-transelectrica-for-eur-48-5-mln/126949/.

37. Anonymous (2014) Fondul Proprietatea announces sale agreement for a 5% stake in Romgaz, Govnet. Available at: http://www.govnet.ro/Financial/Economics/Fondul-Proprietatea-announces-sale-agreement-for-a-5-percent-stake-in-Romgaz.

38. O'Brien,P.(2014)BeneaththestreetsofRomania'scapital,alivinghell,Channel4News.Available at: http://www.channel4.com/news/romania-tunnels-bucharest-orphans-photo.

39. Anonymous (2013) Total fertility rate: Countries compared, Nation Master. Available at: http://www.nationmaster.com/country-info/stats/People/Total-fertility-rate.

40. Henderson, A. (2013) Top 5: Countries with the fastest internet speeds in the world, Nomad Capitalist. Available at: http://nomadcapitalist.com/2013/12/01/top-5-countries-fastest-internet-speeds-world/.

41. Anonymous (2014) Cost of living, internet, broadband 6Mbps, uncapped data: Countries Compared, Nation Master. Available at: http://www.nationmaster.com/country-info/stats/Cost-of-living/Internet/Broadband-6Mbps%2C-uncapped-data.

42. Rajapaksa, M. (2014) UN flouts principles of justice – Sri Lankan President, Lankaweb. Available at: http://www.lankaweb.com/news/items/2014/08/09/un-flouts-principles-of-justice-sri-lankan-president/.

43. Glinski, N., Ondaatjie, A. (2014) Sri Lanka urges lower U.S. Human Rights focus as China gains, Bloomberg News. Available at: http://www.businessweek.com/news/2014-07-16/sri-lanka-urges-u-dot-s-dot-to-reduce-human-rights-focus-as-china-gains.

44. Anonymous (2012) UN Adopts resolution on Sri Lanka war crimes probe, BBC News Asia. Available at: http://www.bbc.co.uk/news/world-asia-17471300.

45. Anonymous (2013) UN: India to be world's most populous country by 2028, BBC News Asia. Available at: http://www.bbc.co.uk/news/world-asia-22907307.

46. Warner, G. (2013) Protesters call for justice in brutal gang rape in Kenya, NPR. Available at: http://www.npr.org/2013/10/31/242142611/protesters-call-for-justice-in-brutal-gang-rape-in-kenya.

47. Anonymous (2014) Kaimenyi reassures pupils on laptops project, Standard Digital. Available at: http://www.standardmedia.co.ke/m/?articleID=2000130449&story_title=Kaimenyi-reassures-pupils-on-laptops-project.

48. Limo, L. (2014) High Court stops fresh procurement of laptops following complaint by Olive Telecommunications, Standard Media. Available at: http://www.standardmedia.co.ke/?articleID=2000107332&story_title=court-halts-standard-one-laptop-project.

49. Gridneff, I. (2014) Kenya bids to revive tourism as al-Shabaab vows broader war, Bloomberg News. Available at: http://www.bloomberg.com/news/2014-05-22/kenya-bids-to-revive-ailing-tourism-as-al-shabaab-vows-wider-war.html.

50. Anonymous (2012) Innovation in Africa: Upwardly mobile, *The Economist*. Available at: http://www.economist.com/node/21560912.

51. Jamjoom, M. (2013) Saudi cleric warns driving could damage women's ovaries, CNN. Available at: http://edition.cnn.com/2013/09/29/world/meast/saudi-arabia-women-driving-cleric/.

52. Brown, S. (2014) "We are hostages": A Saudi princess reveals her life of hell. Available at: http://nypost.com/2014/04/19/a-saudi-arabian-princess-reveals-her-life-of-hell/

53. Robertson, C. (2014) Saudi Arabia – Best Macro Country In Frontier/Beyond Frontier To Open Up To Foreign Investors, Renaissance Capital.

54. Levitsky, S., Murillo, M.V. (2005) *Argentine Democracy: The Politics of Institutional Weakness*, Pennsylvania State University Press.

55. Saxton, J. (2003) Argentina's Economic Crisis: Causes and Cures, Joint Economic Committee U.S. Congress. Available at: http://www.hacer.org/pdf/Schuler.pdf.

56. Roming, S. (2014) Argentina's long history of economic booms and busts, *Wall Street Journal*. Available at: http://blogs.wsj.com/moneybeat/2014/07/30/argentinas-long-history-of-economic-booms-and-busts/.

57. Cancel, D., Gonzalez, P. (2014) Soros doubles YPF stake in Argentina's nascent shale boom, Bloomberg News. Available at: http://www.bloomberg.com/news/2014-08-14/soros-adds-to-ypf-trims-teva-exits-monster-in-quarter.html.

58. Hodal, K., Kaiman, J. (2014) At least 21 dead in Vietnam anti-China protests over oil rig, *The Guardian*. Available at: http://www.theguardian.com/world/2014/may/15/vietnam-anti-china-protests-oil-rig-dead-injured.

59. McCornac, D. C. (2011) Vietnam's relations with China: A delicate balancing act, China Research Center. Available at: http://www.chinacenter.net/vietnams-relations-with-china-a-delicate-balancing-act/.

60. Anonymous (2014) Vinamilk milk export hits record high, Dairy Vietnam. Available at: http://www.dairyvietnam.com/en/Dairy-in-Vietnam/Vinamilk-milk-export-hits-record-high.html.

61. Anonymous (2014) How the Vietnam war made female CEOs better than men, Bloomberg News. Available at: http://www.bloomberg.com/news/2014-03-30/how-the-vietnam-war-made-women-ceos-better-than-men.html.

62. Provost, C. (2013) Nigeria expected to have larger population than U.S. by 2050, *The Guardian*. Available at: http://www.theguardian.com/global-development/2013/jun/13/nigeria-larger-population-us-2050.

63. UN (2014) Major populations in 2100. Available at: http://image.guardian.co.uk/sys-files/Guardian/documents/2013/06/13/World_Populations_WEB.pdf.

64. Data from the National Bureau of Statistics during meeting with executives in January 2014.

TABLE C11 Stock listings chapter by chapter.

Country & Chapter	Company & Trading Platform	Description	Commentary from Chapter	Other Investor Comments	Investor Scores		Average Annual Return	Price-Earnings Ratio	Price-Book Ratio / NAV	Return on Equity	Gross Div. Yield	Market Value ($m)	Top Holders %
Kenya Chapter 1 Section 5	Safaricom Nairobi Stock Exchange	Kenya's biggest listed stock; No.1 provider of mobile services incl. M-Pesa mobile money	TCW's Rowley: Profit surged on M-Pesa success and alliance with banks. Expansion to media content for TVs, phones & tablets could spur new growth	Driehaus' Schwab: Near monopoly position, highly innovative. But competition is coming with banks talking up their own e-money platforms Deutsche's Taylor: Good growth, quality management	Anonymous Deutsche Driehaus Morgan Wells Average	2 2 3 2 5 2.8	36% since listed 2008	24.2	6.1	26.8%	3.4%	6129	Vodafone 39.9% State 35.0% Free float 25.1%
Kenya Chapter 1 Section 5	ARM Cement Nairobi Stock Exchange	Kenya's second biggest cement maker after Lafarge's Bamburi	TCW's Rowley: Good potential as Kenyan cement use increases faster than GDP	General comment: Daily trading volume is too low for many mutual funds to buy	Anonymous Driehaus Morgan Wells Average	3 5 6 3 4.25	48.1% since listed 1997	28.4	4.7	18.0%	0.7%	472	Amanat 27.8% Paunrana 18.1% Free float 48.4%
Myanmar Chapter 2 Section 4	Yoma Strategic Singapore Exchange	Biggest listed Myanmar business. Property, transport, autos, farming	Driehaus' Schwab: Go-to proxy for the country as the only liquid stock that's a pure play on Burma	Deutsche's Taylor: Great access to Myanmar. Scarcity value	Driehaus Deutsche Morgan Wells Average	5 3 5 5 4.5	166% from 2011, when reforms paved way for sanctions easing	37.0	2.2	4.5%	N/A	703	SergePun 37.3% Aberdeen 7.1% Free float 62.1%

Country & Chapter	Company & Trading Platform	Description	Commentary from Chapter	Other Investor Comments	Investor Scores	Average Annual Return	Price-Earnings Ratio	Price-Book Ratio / NAV	Return on Equity	Gross Div. Yield	Market Value ($m)	Top Holders %
Romania Chapter 3 Section 2	Fondul Proprietatea Bucharest Stock Exchange	Romania's restitution fund has become the country's most traded stock & the world's largest closed-end investment fund	Raiffeisen's Szalkai: It's a good way of getting stakes in the biggest state-owned companies albeit very biased to energy companies	Driehaus' Schwab: Given the stewardship of the fund, Fondul is a pretty clean way of gaining exposure to the reform environment of Romania Deutsche's Taylor: Macro liquid play on Romania	Deutsche 5 Driehaus 3 Morgan 7 Wells 5 Average 5	40% since listed 2011	N/A	24% discount to NAV	N/A	5.4%	3530	Manchester Securities 15.4% Baillie Gifford 1.4% ING Int'l 0.7%
Romania Chapter 3 Section 3	BRD-Groupe Bucharest Stock Exchange	Romania's second-largest bank. Nearly 1/4 of debt was non-performing at height of banking crisis	Raiffeisen's Szalkai: BRD was in big trouble with its NPLs. This has been reflected in its cheaper share price	Deutsche's Taylor: Best quality bank in Romania with SG management	Driehaus 5 Deutsche 4 Morgan 3 Templeton 4 Wells 4 Average 4	34.5% since listed 2001	N/A	1.1	-7.0%	N/A	1595	Societe Generale 60.2% SIF3 4.6% Free float 39.8%

(Continued)

Country & Chapter	Company & Trading Platform	Description	Commentary from Chapter	Other Investor Comments	Investor Scores	Average Annual Return	Price-Earnings Ratio	Price-Book Ratio / NAV	Return on Equity	Gross Div. Yield	Market Value ($m)	Top Holders %
Romania Chapter 3 Sections 2 & 5	OMV Petrom Bucharest Stock Exchange	Romania's largest oil producer	Raiffeisen's Szalkai: OMV discovered with ExxonMobil 1.5 to 3 trillion cubic feet of gas in the Black Sea, five times Romania's annual gas consumption	Fondul Proprietatea: Largest holding	Deutsche 6 Morgan 3 Templeton 4 Wells 3 Average 4	39.1% since listed 2001	6.6	0.9	13.5%	7.4%	6642	OMV AG 51.0% State 20.6% Fondul Proprietatea 19.0% Free float 28.4%
Romania Chapter 3 Sections 2 & 5	Romgaz Bucharest Stock Exchange	Romania's largest gas producer	Raiffeisen's Szalkai: Dividends are key. If I can't sell because it's too illiquid at least I'm getting a higher return on dividends	Deutsche's Taylor: Regulation is a headwind	Deutsche 6 Driehaus 3 Morgan 4 Wells 3 Average 4	N/A Listed 2013	13.1%	1.4	10.7	7.6%	3676	State 70.0% Fondul Proprietatea 10.0% Free float 30.0%

Country & Chapter	Company & Trading Platform	Description	Commentary from Chapter	Other Investor Comments	Investor Scores	Average Annual Return	Price-Earnings Ratio	Price-Book Ratio / NAV	Return on Equity	Gross Div. Yield	Market Value ($m)	Top Holders %
Romania Chapter 3 Section 2 & 5	Transelectrica Bucharest Stock Exchange	Romania's power grid operator	Fondul Proprietatea CEO Grzegorz Konieczny: If all goes to plan with phantom share options, managers will be checking the stock and promoting the company	N/A	Morgan Wells 9 3 Average 6	-0.6% since listed 2006	10.2	0.8	8.1%	7.7%	592	State 58.7% Fondul Proprietatea 13.5% Free float 41.3%
Romania Chapter 3 Section 4	New Europe Property Investments Johannesburg Stock Exchange	Developer of mostly Romanian shopping malls & office blocks	Raiffeisen's Szalkai: There are no consumer stocks in Bucharest, so that makes NEPI interesting for their shopping malls	Driehaus's Schwab: Good medium term strategy. Property/retail is the best way to tap the aspirational brands/consumers	Driehaus Morgan Wells 3 9 6 Average 6	35.2% since shares issued 2009	N/A	~2 (based on co. data)	N/A	4.35%	1.840	Resilient Property 9.6% Fortress Income 7.6%

(Continued)

Country & Chapter	Company & Trading Platform	Description	Commentary from Chapter	Other Investor Comments	Investor Scores	Average Annual Return	Price-Earnings Ratio	Price-Book Ratio / NAV	Return on Equity	Gross Div. Yield	Market Value ($m)	Top Holders %
Argentina Chapter 4 Section 3	Edenor Buenos Aires Stock Exchange	Distributes & sells electricity in north-east of greater Buenos Aires	Adelante's Adams: Trading price had anticipated complete demise. Then suddenly the government changed course	Deutsche's Taylor: Argentina macro play Driehaus's Schwab: Not a big fan of regulated utilities	Deutsche 6 Driehaus 8 Morgan 9 Wells 3 Average 6.5	40.7% since offering 2007	N/A	N/A	N/A	N/A	795	Admin Nacional Segur 55.0% Pampa Energia SA 4.4% Free float 38.5%
Argentina Chapter 4 Section 1,3,4	YPF Sociedad Anonima New York Stock Exchange	Biggest Argentine company; oil producer exploring world's 2nd largest deposits of shale gas and 4th largest of shale oil	Adelante's Adams: Policy shift of 2013 was positive esp. the resolution of the Repsol issue with YPF	Deutsche's Taylor: Interesting re-rating story Morgan Stanley: Among top 10 holdings in Frontier Emerging Markets Fund	Deutsche 3 Morgan 1 Wells 2 Average 2	19.9% from 2002, after Argentine default	N/A	N/A	N/A	0.4%	13,154	Grupo Financiero 5.7% Mason Capital 4.0% Lazard 4.0%

Country & Chapter	Company & Trading Platform	Description	Commentary from Chapter	Other Investor Comments	Investor Scores	Average Annual Return	Price-Earnings Ratio	Price-Book Ratio / NAV	Return on Equity	Gross Div. Yield	Market Value ($m)	Top Holders %
Vietnam Chapter 5 Section 3	Imexpharm Ho Chi Minh Stock Exchange	Drugmaker	Templeton's Mobius: In a global context this company is very cheap	Driehaus's Schwab: Long-term potential, however need to see more private sector involvement for drugs business to work. In meantime it will rely on state	Driehaus 7, Morgan 5, Templeton 3, Wells 2, Average 4.25	3.1% since listing 2006	14.9	1.38	8.4%	3.9%	50	Vinapharm 27.4% Franklin Resources 16.4% Free float 53.8%
Vietnam Chapter 5 Section 4	Binh Minh Plastics Ho Chi Minh Stock Exchange	Pipes producer	Templeton's Mobius: Usually this kind of plastics manufacturing isn't high-margin, so this is unusual	N/A	Morgan 9, Templeton 3, Wells 3, Average 5	49.1% since listing 2006	8.4	1.8	23.2%	3.0%	142	State Capital & Invest 29.5% Free float 31.0%

(Continued)

Country & Chapter	Company & Trading Platform	Description	Commentary from Chapter	Other Investor Comments	Investor Scores	Average Annual Return	Price-Earnings Ratio	Price-Book Ratio / NAV	Return on Equity	Gross Div. Yield	Market Value ($m)	Top Holders %
Vietnam Chapter 5 Section 5	Vinamilk Ho Chi Minh Stock Exchange	Vietnam's biggest milk producer	Templeton's Mobius: Most impressive was the UHT unit, operated by only 4 people, everything was automated. We'd love to get more of the stock. It sells at a premium	Deutsche's Taylor: Great consumer story. Driehaus' Schwab: Good company with strategic positioning. Also further along in being managed for minorities shareholder interests. It does have binary risk exposure to chemicals in milk issues	Deutsche 1 Driehaus 2 Morgan 3 Templeton 3 Wells 7 Average 3.2	34.4% since listing 2006	17.4	5.5	33.2%	2.0%	4641	State Capital & Invest 37.6% Fraser & Neave 11.0% Free float 57.5%
Vietnam Chapter 5 Section 6	Vingroup Ho Chi Minh Stock Exchange	Vietnam's largest property developer & mall operator	Templeton's Mobius: These luxury stores and malls represent a big, big change from what we saw before	N/A	Driehaus 4 Morgan 2 Wells 4 Average 3.33	27.4% since listing 2007	16.7	3.7	20.9%	3.0%	3293	Nhat Vuong Pham 29.1% Vietnam Inv 12.4% Free float 49.6%

Country & Chapter	Company & Trading Platform	Description	Commentary from Chapter	Other Investor Comments	Investor Scores	Average Annual Return	Price-Earnings Ratio	Price-Book Ratio / NAV	Return on Equity	Gross Div. Yield	Market Value ($m)	Top Holders %
Nigeria Chapter 6 Section 2, 3	Dangote Cement Nigerian Stock Exchange	Nigeria's biggest company; Africa's No.1 cement producer	Lamido Sanusi: We've seen with Dangote proof of what can be done, from being a trader to cement, sugar, refineries, fertilizer	Driehaus's Schwab: Size and scale advantage, charismatic owner, but also increasing risk of him being an "empire builder" and destroying shareholder value	Anonymous 6 Driehaus 3 Morgan 1 Wells 7 Average 4.25	30.2% since listing 2010	16.5	5.4	34.3%	3.9%	17,160	Dangote Industries 92.8% Aliko Dangote 0.2% Free float 7.0%
Nigeria Chapter 6 Section 2, 3	Dangote Sugar Nigerian Stock Exchange	Nigeria's biggest sugar producer	Dangote's Devakumar Edwin: We were known as the sugar kings, importing all Nigeria's sugar requirement before expanding	Deutsche's Taylor: Volatile earnings history	Anonymous 6 Deutsche 6 Driehaus 4 Morgan 6 Wells 7 Average 5.8	0.5% since listing 2007	8.2	N/A	N/A	8.6%	468	Dangote Industries 67.7% Dangote Aliko 5.4% Free float 26.8%

(Continued)

Country & Chapter	Company & Trading Platform	Description	Commentary from Chapter	Other Investor Comments	Investor Scores	Average Annual Return	Price-Earnings Ratio	Price-Book Ratio / NAV	Return on Equity	Gross Div. Yield	Market Value ($m)	Top Holders %
Nigeria Chapter 6 Section 2	Guaranty Trust Bank London Stock Exchange	Nigeria's biggest bank by market value	Aberdeen's Daly: Nigerian banks are very well capitalized after Sanusi's reforms. GTB and FBN have the highest capital adequacy ratios, with GTB at 24–25%	Deutsche's Taylor: Core Nigerian bank, good growth profile Driehaus's Schwab: Very well managed bank with an eye toward governance and shareholder returns. Strong deposit and lending franchise	Anonymous 6 Deutsche 3 Driehaus 1 Morgan 2 Templeton 2 Wells 5 Average 3.17	23.3% since listing 2007	N/A	N/A	N/A	2.2%	4120	FMR 1.5% Fiedelity 1.2% BankInvest 0.4%
Nigeria Chapter 6 Section 2	FBN Holdings Nigerian Stock Exchange	Nigerian lender	See above	Deutsche's Taylor: Good growth profile	Anonymous 7 Deutsche 3 Driehaus 4 Morgan 3 Templeton 2 Wells 4 Average 3.83	24.8% since data starts 2002	4.9	0.7	14.4%	11.1%	1817	Franklin Resources 2.8% Fiedelity 1.5% Free float 98.4%

Country & Chapter	Company & Trading Platform	Description	Commentary from Chapter	Other Investor Comments	Investor Scores	Average Annual Return	Price-Earnings Ratio	Price-Book Ratio / NAV	Return on Equity	Gross Div. Yield	Market Value ($m)	Top Holders %
Egypt Chapter 7 Section 2	Eastern Tobacco Cairo Stock Exchange	Mideast's biggest tobacco manufacturer	Baillie Gifford's Stobart: Cash flow should increase at a faster pace than sales and allow healthy growth in the dividend	Deutsche's Taylor: Good dividend, tough market, done well Driehaus's Schwab: Tobacco is always a great business. Strong potential for share buyback and inelastic demand. Competition not an issue for now	Deutsche 6 Driehaus 2 Morgan 7 Wells 5 Average 5	18.4% from 2005, year of share offering	8.1	1.9	25.1%	4.9%	1225	Chemical Industries 55.0% Investec Africa 5.0% Free float 44.1%
Egypt Chapter 7 Section 2	Juhayna Food Industries Cairo Stock Exchange	Egypt's biggest dairy and fruit juice producer	Baillie Gifford's Stobart: Juhayna has suffered from raw material cost pressures, but long run this is likely to be a leading consumer goods company	Deutsche's Taylor: Great consumer story Driehaus's Schwab: Well-run franchise but seeing increasing risk from input costs and also growing competition	Anonymous 6 Deutsche 1 Driehaus 5 Morgan 7 Wells 6 Average 5	55.1% since IPO in 2010	54.6	3.6	7.1%	N/A	1122	Pharaoh Invest 51.0% Aberdeen 1.9% Free float 47.9%

(Continued)

Country & Chapter	Company & Trading Platform	Description	Commentary from Chapter	Other Investor Comments	Investor Scores	Average Annual Return	Price-Earnings Ratio	Price-Book Ratio / NAV	Return on Equity	Gross Div. Yield	Market Value ($m)	Top Holders %
Egypt Chapter 7 Section 3	Egyptian Resorts Co. Cairo Stock Exchange	Developer building a new town in Red Sea resort of Sahl Hasheesh	Baillie Gifford's Stobart: This is a volatile business with significant uncertainty and where land sales account for half of the revenue base	Deutsche's Taylor: Expensive and illiquid	Deutsche 8 Morgan 8 Wells 3 Average 6.33	93.2% since data starts 2003	N/A	1.7	-7%	N/A	180	Kato Investment 11.9% Rowad Touristic 10.0% Free float 52.0%
Egypt Chapter 7 Section 4	Ghabbour Auto Cairo Stock Exchange	North Africa's largest listed automaker	Baillie Gifford's Stobart: Given the low level of penetration in the country (30 cars per 1000 people), the market should grow for many years	Deutsche's Taylor: Great structural story when Egypt stabilizes. Driehaus's Schwab: Cyclical business with competition risk however they have executed well and auto distribution is a good business in these countries	Deutsche 3 Driehaus 4 Morgan 4 Wells 3 Average 3.5	10.7% since IPO in 2007	22.1	2.0	9.0%	N/A	584	Ghabbour Raouf Kamal 20.6% Ghabbour Nader Raouf 12.9% Free float 37.9%

Country & Chapter	Company & Trading Platform	Description	Commentary from Chapter	Other Investor Comments	Investor Scores	Average Annual Return	Price-Earnings Ratio	Price-Book Ratio / NAV	Return on Equity	Gross Div. Yield	Market Value ($m)	Top Holders %
Egypt Chapter 7 Section 4	Citadel Capital Cairo Stock Exchange	Spans region in cement, transport, mining, agriculture, now building oil refinery	Baillie Gifford's Stobart: Hope will reap rewards one day, but a lot of things outside Citadel's control need to happen before they do	Deutsche's Taylor: Well managed long term story	Deutsche 5 Driehaus 4 Morgan 7 Wells 4 Average 5	-5.8% since IPO in 2009	N/A	0.7	-14.9%	N/A	909	Citadel 20.5% Abd Allah Soliman 11.0% Free float 66.7%
Egypt Chapter 7 Section 4	Commercial Int'l Bank (CIB) Cairo Stock Exchange	Egypt's biggest private sector bank	Baillie Gifford's Stobart: With stability and a growing economy, confidence should improve, generating greater demand for credit and boosting CIB's profits	Deutsche's Taylor: Top Egyptian bank - well managed Driehaus's Schwab: Very well run bank, strong franchise, good governance	Anonymous 3 Deutsche 1 Driehaus 1 Morgan 2 Wells 5 Average 2.4	26.6% since IPO in 1996	13.0	3.3	27.5%	2.0%	6302	Oppenheimer 4.5% Wentworth Insurance 4.4%

(Continued)

Country & Chapter	Company & Trading Platform	Description	Commentary from Chapter	Other Investor Comments	Investor Scores	Average Annual Return	Price-Earnings Ratio	Price-Book Ratio / NAV	Return on Equity	Gross Div. Yield	Market Value ($m)	Top Holders %
Egypt Chapter 7 Section 4	EFG Hermes Cairo Stock Exchange	Leading Egyptian investment bank	Baillie Gifford's Stobart: Highly operationally geared play on expansion in financial activity in the MENA region	Deutsche's Taylor: Cyclical GCC exposure. Driehaus's Schwab: Well managed bank which is getting its house in order. However, the business is more cyclical as they focus on investment bank, so prefer CIB	Deutsche 4, Driehaus 5, Morgan 4, Wells 4, Average 4.25	4.2% from 2009, year of share offering	N/A	1.19	-1.7%	N/A	1531	DF EFG 11.7% Rahman Abdel 7.7% Free float 72.9%
Saudi Arabia Chapter 8 Section 2	Jarir Saudi Arabian Stock Exchange	Biggest Saudi retailer of books, smart phones, tablets, laptops	Deutsche's Taylor: Retail companies are a good bet and Jarir seems like a core holding. The Saudization process & employing women can only help boost consumer spending	Driehaus's Schwab: Good business and like the management, although they are heavily reliant on electronics and will face a risk from e-commerce one day (similar to Best Buy)	Anonymous 5, Deutsche 1, Driehaus 4, Morgan 3, Wells 6, Average 3.8	29.1% since data starts in 2003	23.9	12.7	56.4%	3.9%	4455	Al Aqeel Nasser 9.0% Al-Aqeel Abdulsalama 9.0% Free float 54.2%

Country & Chapter	Company & Trading Platform	Description	Commentary from Chapter	Other Investor Comments	Investor Scores	Average Annual Return	Price-Earnings Ratio	Price-Book Ratio / NAV	Return on Equity	Gross Div. Yield	Market Value ($m)	Top Holders %
Saudi Arabia Chapter 8 Section 3	Almarai Saudi Arabian Stock Exchange	World's largest integrated dairy foods company	Deutsche's Taylor: Well managed but prices are regulated. May surprise on the upside once its problems on poultry are resolved	Driehaus's Schwab: Good holders, good product lineup and above average governance. Well positioned in segments to tap the consumer in Saudi	Anonymous 4, Deutsche 3, Driehaus 3, Morgan 4, Wells 8, Average 4.4	12.3% since data starts in 2005	27.8	4.1	15.8%	1.4%	11,740	Savola Group 36.5% Al-Saud Sultan Moham 28.6% Free float 26.5%
Sri Lanka Chapter 9 Section 4	Cargills Colombo Stock Exchange	Sri Lanka's biggest retailer; businesses span beer to broking	Cargills Deputy Chairman Ranjit Page: Building a banking network that uses technology and regional presence to bring financial services to a wider socio-economic group	N/A	Driehaus 4, Morgan 5, Wells 7, Average 5.33	73.2% from 2009, year civil war ended	N/A	2.9	2.4%	1.3%	264	CT Holdings 70.0% Page Valentine 6.4% Free float 11.7%

(Continued)

Country & Chapter	Company & Trading Platform	Description	Commentary from Chapter	Other Investor Comments	Investor Scores	Average Annual Return	Price-Earnings Ratio	Price-Book Ratio / NAV	Return on Equity	Gross Div. Yield	Market Value ($m)	Top Holders %
Sri Lanka Chapter 9 Section 4	John Keells Colombo Stock Exchange	Largest Sri Lanka listed company; businesses include Cinnamon hotel group, supermarkets, ports, bunkering	Morgan's Drinkall: Remains a core holding because of the exposure to a lot of the good growth areas in the economy. About 1.8% of frontier fund is in John Keells	Driehaus's Schwab: Company has some upfront investments to make as it shifts strategy, but still a very transparent western style of management and the only liquid access to Sri Lanka as well for most investors	Driehaus 1 Morgan 2 Wells 8 Average 3.66	65.7% from 2009, year civil war ended	18.5	1.9	11.7%	1.5%	1824	Captain SE 13.9% Broga Hill 10.5% Free float 59.4%

Country & Chapter	Company & Trading Platform	Description	Commentary from Chapter	Other Investor Comments	Investor Scores	Average Annual Return	Price-Earnings Ratio	Price-Book Ratio / NAV	Return on Equity	Gross Div. Yield	Market Value ($m)	Top Holders %
Sri Lanka Chapter 9 Section 4	Aitken Spence Colombo Stock Exchange	Largest inbound travel operator through 50:50 joint venture with TUI Travel	Morgan's Drinkall: Almost purely tourism, catering to higher-end. Tourist numbers are really nothing yet – there is a lot of potential	Driehaus's Schwab: Joint venture with TUI is key. Story will take some time to play out as outbound travel is still in early stages – monitor the development of internet platform and potential competition from internet players	Driehaus 4 Morgan 3 Wells 5 Average 4	74.8% from 2009, year civil war ended	10.8	1.3	12.4%	2.0%	309	Melstacorp 39.8% Aberdeen 16.9% Free float 32.1%
Sri Lanka Chapter 9 Section 4	Chevron Lubricants Lanka Colombo Stock Exchange	Manufactures and sells petroleum-based lubricants	Morgan's Drinkall: Push into Bangladesh could drive dividend yield sharply higher	Driehaus's Schwab: Good steady business in Sri Lanka	Driehaus 3 Morgan 8 Wells 4 Average 5	53.1% from 2009, year civil war ended	14.8	6.9	49.2%	5.6%	250	Chevron Ceylon 51.0% Aberdeen 24.6% Free float 40.4%

(Continued)

Country & Chapter	Company & Trading Platform	Description	Commentary from Chapter	Other Investor Comments	Investor Scores	Average Annual Return	Price-Earnings Ratio	Price-Book Ratio / NAV	Return on Equity	Gross Div. Yield	Market Value ($m)	Top Holders %
Sri Lanka Chapter 9 Section 3	Commercial Bank Ceylon Colombo Stock Exchange	Sri Lanka's biggest non-state bank	Morgan's Drinkall: Commercial remains the standout among banks, with the highest return on equity and little exposure to pawning loans	Driehaus's Schwab: Well-run bank with the right platform for the long term	Driehaus 2, Morgan 2, Templeton 8, Wells 5, Average 4.25	58.2% from 2009, 5 year civil war ended	12.2	2.2	17.8%	2.8%	1029	DFCC Bank 14.8% Franklin Resources 13.6% Free float 75.7%
Ghana Chapter 10 Section 2	Enterprise Group Ghana Stock Exchange	Ghana's second biggest listed insurer	Wells' Irwin: It looks like a good way to get exposure to the economy as demand for insurance will increase as incomes grow	N/A	Morgan 4, Wells 8, Average 6	70.1% since data starts 1995	5.6	2.8	36.9%	13.0%	65.0	Ventures & Acquisition 41.1% ELAC 8.0% Free float 38.5%

Country & Chapter	Company & Trading Platform	Description	Commentary from Chapter	Other Investor Comments	Investor Scores	Average Annual Return	Price-Earnings Ratio	Price-Book Ratio / NAV	Return on Equity	Gross Div. Yield	Market Value ($m)	Top Holders %
Ghana Chapter 10 Section 3	AngloGold Ashanti	Ghana's mines contribute a third of the company's non-South African gold	Wells' Irwin: Restructuring its Obuasi mine should add value. If it takes longer than expected, or is more expensive, it would be negative for the share price	Driehaus's Schwab: Not our preferred business in frontier	Anonymous 7, Driehaus 7, Morgan 8, Wells 4, Average 6.5	-3.6% from 2004, year of Anglo-Gold merger with Ashanti	N/A	1.2	-5.8%	N/A	3617	Gov't Emp Pension 7.6% State St Custodian 6.4% Free float 87.3%

Source: Data compiled by Bloomberg as of December 2014
Annual return is in the currency of the securities, for the period cited through 2013.

TABLE C12 Bond listings chapter by chapter.

Country & Chapter	Security & Trading Platform	Description	Key Commentary from Chapter	Other investor comments	Investor Scores	Maturity / Amount Outstanding	Average Annual Price Change	Coupon/ Interest	Yield
Kenya Chapter 1 Section 5	Sovereign Eurobonds Euroclear/ Clearstream	Sovereign Dollars	TCW's Rowley: Kenya's long-anticipated Eurobond was more than four times oversubscribed. With such strong demand, officials could have tightened pricing a bit further, but it would have left a bad taste if they tried to squeeze all the value out	N/A	Adelante 10 Aberdeen 3 Anonymous 2 Wells 3 Average 4.5	2019 + 2024 Largest is 2024 maturity with $2 billion	N/A	6.875%	5.9%
Kenya Chapter 1 Section 5	Infrastructure Bonds Nairobi Securities Exchange	Sovereign Local Currency	TCW's Rowley: Key element is they're tax-free for diaspora & institutional investors, who otherwise would pay 15% withholding tax. This makes them very oversubscribed	N/A	Adelante 10 Aberdeen 3 Anonymous 2 Wells 3 Average 4.5	2018 - 2025 Biggest of the 6 bonds matures 2025 with 36.9b shillings ($410m) outstanding	N/A	12.5% on 2021 bond	11.7% on 2021 bond

Country & Chapter	Security & Trading Platform	Description	Key Commentary from Chapter	Other investor comments	Investor Scores	Maturity / Amount Outstanding	Average Annual Price Change	Coupon/ Interest	Yield
Romania Chapter 3 Section 2	Sovereign Eurobonds Euroclear/ Clearstream	Sovereign Dollars/ Euros	IMF resident representative Guillermo Tolosa: Vulnerabilities include large financing needs and short maturity debt. Helping is the fiscal compact to cut budget deficit below 3% of GDP	Adelante's Adams: Good but low yield	Adelante 8 Anonymous 3 Wells 9 Average 6.66	2015–2044 Most traded of the bonds matures 2024 with $1.5b outstanding	6.7% on bond due 2022 issued in 2012	6.75%	3.5%
Argentina Chapter 4 Section 2	Aeropuertos Argentina 2000 corporate bonds EuroMTF/ Frankfurt/ Luxembourg	Corporate Dollars	Adelante's Adams: Eurnekian is a big picture ideas person – a tunnel through the mountain to Chile to get access to ports on the Pacific. At time I thought it was pretty crack pot, but it makes sense	N/A	Aberdeen 2 Adelante 4 Anonymous 5 Wells 7 Average 4.5	2020 $300m	-1% since issued in 2010	10.75%	8.6%

(Continued)

Country & Chapter	Security & Trading Platform	Description	Key Commentary from Chapter	Other investor comments	Investor Scores	Maturity / Amount Outstanding	Average Annual Price Change	Coupon/ Interest	Yield
Argentina Chapter 4 Section 4	Province of Buenos Aires Bonds Euroclear/ Clearstream	Municipal Dollars/ Euros	Adelante's Adams: More market-friendly policies and a strengthening economy will drive the yield down toward the level of the federal government.	N/A	Aberdeen 2, Adelante 2, Anonymous 6, Wells 8, Average 4.5	2015–2035 Among the most traded of the bonds matures 2015 with $1.05b outstanding	-1.6% on bonds due 2015 since issued in 2010	11.75%	14.3%
Argentina Chapter 4 Section 4	Argentine Republic Euroclear/ Clearstream	Sovereign Euros	Adelante's Adams: The yield is higher on bonds in euros than on the same debt in dollars because the debt in euros isn't included in the benchmark JPMorgan indexes	N/A	Aberdeen 2, Adelante 1, Anonymous 8, Wells 9, Average 5	2033 EU2.3b	12.0%	7.82%	9.6%
Vietnam Chapter 5 Section 6	Socialist Republic of Vietnam Singapore Exchange/ Stuttgart	Sovereign Dollars	Pham Nhat Vuong, Vietnam's only billionaire: Vietnam is just reaching a "golden age" when its young population is starting to enter the workforce and spending money. Half of the population is under 30	Adelante's Adams: Probably pretty expensive, macro not so good	Aberdeen 6, Adelante 9, Anonymous 5, Wells 6, Average 6.5	2016–2028 Among the most traded of the bonds matures 2020 with $1b outstanding	2.4% on bonds due 2020 since issued in 2010	6.75%	4.0%

Country & Chapter	Security & Trading Platform	Description	Key Commentary from Chapter	Other investor comments	Investor Scores	Maturity / Amount Outstanding	Average Annual Price Change	Coupon/ Interest	Yield
Nigeria Chapter 6 Section 2,3	Republic of Nigeria Euroclear/ Clearstream	Sovereign Dollars	Aberdeen's Daly: The one country in Africa that may be investment grade within a decade. Now it looks like single A speculative grade based on debt, current account surplus, reserves. Improvement could boost the rating and bonds	Adelante's Adams: Good but expensive	Aberdeen 1 Adelante 6 Anonymous 3 Wells 4 Average 3.5	2018–2023 Longest dated matures 2023 with $500m outstanding	2.2% on bonds due 2021 issued in 2011	6.75%	5.5%
Nigeria Chapter 6 Section 2	Federal Government of Nigeria Euroclear/ Clearstream	Sovereign Local currency	Aberdeen's Daly: Opted for the shorter maturity than the 2022s as a more defensive play because the FGNs are more sensitive to local politics than the dollar Eurobonds	Adelante's Adams: Very interesting as high carry, stable currency	Aberdeen 1 Adelante 3 Anonymous 1 Wells 4 Average 2.25	2017	-4.8% since issued in 2012	15.1%	14.0%
Nigeria Chapter 6 Section 2	Guaranty Trust Bank Euroclear/ Clearstream	Corporate Dollars	Aberdeen's Daly: Nigerian banks offer some attractive yields. They are very well capitalized after Sanusi's reforms. GTB and FBN have the highest capital adequacy ratios, with GTB at 24–25%	N/A	Aberdeen 1 Anonymous 3 Wells 3 Average 2.33	2018 $400m	N/A Issued late 2013	6%	6.7%

(Continued)

Country & Chapter	Security & Trading Platform	Description	Key Commentary from Chapter	Other investor comments	Investor Scores	Maturity / Amount Outstanding	Average Annual Price Change	Coupon/ Interest	Yield
Nigeria Chapter 6 Section 2	FBN Finance Euroclear/ Clearstream	Corporate Dollars	See above	N/A	Aberdeen 1 Anonymous 8 Wells 3 Average 4	2020 $300m	N/A Issued mid 2013	8.25%	9.1%
Egypt Chapter 7	Arab Republic of Egypt Euroclear/ Clearstream	Sovereign Dollars	Baillie Gifford's Stobart: The economic problems aren't new – distorting subsidies, fiscal & current account deficits, made worse by collapse in tourism. Positives – sizeable and young population, wages are low, and Saudi, UAE, Kuwait are underwriting the government for now	Adelante's Adams: Very volatile	Aberdeen 5 Adelante 5 Anonymous 5 Wells 4 Average 4.75	2016–2040 Among the larger bonds is a $1 billion issue due in 2020	-2.25% since issued in 2010	5.75%	4.1%

Country & Chapter	Security & Trading Platform	Description	Key Commentary from Chapter	Other investor comments	Investor Scores	Maturity / Amount Outstanding	Average Annual Price Change	Coupon/ Interest	Yield
Sri Lanka Chapter 9	Republic of Sri Lanka	Sovereign Dollars	Morgan Stanley's Drinkall: Post-conflict countries should be able to achieve growth above 8% a year, assuming they have slack in their labor markets and the economy isn't running at close to full capacity. The Sri Lankan economy doesn't have that slack, so growth rates at 7% plus tend to fuel inflation, leading to higher interest rates and a slowdown in growth	N/A	Aberdeen 4 Adelante 6 Anonymous 2 Wells 5 Average 4.25	2015 - 2022 Longest dated matures 2022 with $1b outstanding	-12.4% in 2013 after issue in 2012	5.875%	5.2%
Ghana Chapter 10	Republic of Ghana	Sovereign Dollars	Wells Capital's Irwin: Ghana has fairly shallow capital markets. However, banks are well run, the Ghana Stock Exchange is efficient and the country has access to global debt markets	Adelante's Adams: Not good as budget deficit is out of control	Aberdeen 7 Adelante 7 Anonymous 3 Wells 3 Average 5	2017 - $750 2023 - $1b 2026 - $1b	6.7% on 2017 bond since issued in 2007	2017: 8.5% 2023: 7.875%	2017: 6.3% 2023: 8.0%

Source: Data compiled by Bloomberg as of December 2014

TABLE C13 Investment pipeline.

Country	Security / Trading Platform	Issuer Description	Issuer Comments	Fund Manager Comments
Kenya Chapter 1 Section 5	ARM Cement Inaugural corporate Eurobond	Kenya's second biggest cement maker after Lafarge's Bamburi	Managing Director Pradeep Paunrana: ARM Cement plans to sell \$300 million of Eurobonds to boost capacity. "The faster we develop the credit markets, the faster we can build capacity"	TCW's Brett Rowley: Good potential as Kenyan cement use increases faster than GDP
Myanmar Chapter 2 Section 5	Yangon Stock Exchange	Plans for opening stock exchange following easing of trade sanctions	Deputy Finance Minister Maung Maung Thein: Exchange opening in 2015 capitalized initially with 32 billion kyats (\$33 million). Three or four companies are to list shares immediately including Asia Green Development Bank, a Yangon-based lender with 29 branches. Government local-currency bonds to move across from the securities exchange	Driehaus's Schwab: It seems like real trading on the exchange is a few years out but we'll be watching so we're ready to jump in
Romania Chapter 3 Section 5	Hidroelectrica Bucharest Stock Exchange	Hydropower provider in technical insolvency since 2012, a process engineered to get rid of unprofitable contracts. IPO planned once insolvency concludes	Romania may sell Hidroelectrica shares in the second half of 2015, said Energy Minister Rezvan Nicolesu (Bloomberg, September 2014)	Raiffeisen's Szalkai: This is Europe's 2nd largest water utility. It's the jewel of the jewels. It's clean energy. At the end of the day, which energy source has a future? I'm excited
Argentina Chapter 4 Section 2	Corporacion America NY Stock Exchange	World's biggest private airports operator by number of licenses; most diversified holding company in Argentina. Seeking to build tunnel through the Andes	Corporacion America founder Eduardo Eurnekian plans to issue shares in his energy, airports and technology businesses on the New York Stock Exchange. The value could be anywhere from \$15 billion	Adelante's Adams: Eurnekian's big message was there's change afoot, that Argentina's turn is coming around again. Now is the time to ramp up business

Note: Stocks and bonds investors are expecting to be sold on the capital markets in the coming months or years.

Acknowledgments

M y journey began with a question: Where's the best place in the world to invest?

Given my job, it's something friends and family would often ask and, despite having penned countless articles speculating on which countries might be the next to bounce or bomb, I could never provide a satisfying answer. Most news and research is focused on what might happen in the coming days, hours or minutes rather than years or decades. I'm indebted to those who asked the question and the ten investors who led me to an answer.

Having a journalist traipsing along, earwigging and butting in on sensitive conversations with ministers and executives, isn't every money manager's cup of tea. Life on the road for most amounts to an exhausting series of meetings crammed into short pockets before heading to the next country to do it all again. Traveling with Mark Mobius – and trying to keep up with the 78-year-old's frenetic run of factory tours, gym workouts and evening engagements – was truly a privilege. I'm grateful to Julian Adams for his meticulous note taking when I was called away from Argentina as my father-in-law fell ill, and to Kevin Daly and Derrick Irwin for gracefully re-arranging high-level meetings in Nigeria and Ghana to postpone our trip. I was suitably impressed by Brett Rowley's determination to press ahead with our Kenya plans in the face of terrorist attacks and Andrew Stobart's unwavering resolve to visit Egypt in what turned out to be one of the country's worst weeks of violence. Howie Schwab, the only fund manager of the group still half Mobius's age, who went from honeymooning in a Kenyan elephant camp to join me in Myanmar, boosted my confidence early on in the project as the first committed sign up. Tim Drinkall was great company in Sri Lanka (until he tore ahead of me on our jog around town) and Andras Szalkai and Sean Taylor were the fountains of local knowledge I needed to make sense of Romania and Saudi Arabia's markets.

The deep insights, wide connections and engrained skepticism of Bloomberg journalists helped me get a warts-and-all picture in each country. My thanks to Paul Richardson, Eric Ombok, David Malingha Doya and Sarah McGregor in Nairobi; to Kyaw Thu in Myanmar, whose constant translations and interviews with religious leaders were invaluable to that chapter; and to Daniel Cancel in Argentina, who jumped in with both feet when I had to leave in a hurry. I'm hoping the careful proofreading by Romanian reporters Andra Timu and Irina Savu at least might have helped send Irina's baby to sleep. My evening driven around Saigon by a near-blind motorcyclist made Jason Folkmanis's birthday unforgettable, while in Hanoi, Oanh Ha pulled from her rolodex the communist nation's only billionaire. Blonde-haired Chris Kay, in full African robes and speaking fluent Pidgin, was my uniquely qualified guide to Naija. With Anusha Ondaatjie's help I found some of the most beautiful and tragic corners of the world in Sri Lanka, before Andres Martinez chilled a weary traveler in Ghana.

None of this would have been possible without the support of the managers at Bloomberg News, from Editor-in-Chief Emeritus Matt Winkler and his deputy Reto Gregori – who only once intervened after my "Egyptian adventure" to suggest a little more "visibility" on my travel plans – to Ken Kohn, who gave me the right connections to get the project off the ground. I'm grateful to Laura Zelenko, Justin Carrigan, Heather Harris and Mark Gilbert for smoothing my transition from the newsroom and back again. The crew of Bloomberg TV Africa steered by Ijeoma Ndukwe and Karin Johansson recorded my travels through Nigeria, Ghana and Kenya with the help of Kelly Wainaina and Gabriel Rotich of A24 Media, and Eddie Saade. Bloomberg's travel bookers including Claire Devin, Jason Coggles, Jacqueline Docherty and Rafael Rosario pulled off a seemingly impossible list of visa applications and constantly evolving schedule of connecting flights, while Riaan Crous and Sven Christen in the data department pored over spreadsheets for the fund rankings and tables.

Bloomberg's commissioning editor Stephen Isaacs and Wiley's Werner Coetzee, Jennie Kitchin, Tessa Allen and Abirami Srikandan provided the constant support and guidance needed by this first-time author. The editing process was invaluably assisted by Jerome Booth, whose success in building the fund management company Ashmore with Mark Coombs and his own book *Emerging Markets in an Upside Down World* made him my chosen expert to review a decidedly inferior first draft. I was incredibly honored that between transforming Nigeria's economy and expanding his business around the world, Aliko Dangote found the time to absorb and provide feedback for this book. Matthew May at C21 built me the www.frontierfunds.org website as the most wonderful surprise. This will become a reference point for updates, perspectives and any clarifications or corrections.

Finally, there's the domestic support team. Life doesn't stand still even for a book to be written. To my wife Jules, who I heard only once or maybe twice muttering about "that confounded book" while rescuing me from police and tweeting my scrapes; to Stanley, Ruth, Josh, Sydney, Che, Melanie, Stuart, Andrea, Rob, Elliott and all the rest of my clan who put up with a physically or mentally absent husband, son, father, brother and friend through an emotional year, a hundred thousand words couldn't sum up my love and appreciation.

While a handful of names of the locals featured in this book were changed for their protection, most were adamant they needed to be on record to provide a true portrayal of their lives. From Gbenga to Mwalimu Mati fighting their corners against corruption, to Samuel Pelumi studying to combat poverty and disease, to Prem facing down threats to see another *Rising Sun* – these people provide reasons beyond money to invest at the frontier.

Index

MSCI Frontier Markets Index,
  249–50, 259, 350–4
Mu, Aye Aye, 69–70, 71
Mubarak, Hosni, 200, 204, 224
Mudavadi, Musalia, 20, 22–3, 329
Muslim-Bhuddhist conflict, Myanmar,
  70–1, 73, 74–7
Muslim Brotherhood, 200, 201, 202,
  321, 326, 326
Myanmar, 45–78, 324–5
  Buddhism, 73–6
  Burst Networks CEO, 63–5
  ethnic conflict, 46–7, 70–1, 74–7
  military connections, 62
  Schwab's analysis, 53, 58–60, 65, 77
  Yoma and City Mart, 55–60

Nairobi
  airport rebuild, 17–18
  All-Share Index, 30, 31
  railway to Mombasa, 14, 39, 264
  Westgate mall siege, 13, 18, 23, 24,
    30, 37
nascent consumerism, 59
National League for Democracy (NLD),
  Myanmar, 50, 51, 52, 403
national parks, Kenya, 13, 15, 21, 401
NBFI debt, Sri Lanka, 268
Ndung'u, Njuguna, 29–30, 32–3,
  35, 37
NEPI (New Europe Property Invest-
  ment), 94, 95–7
nepotism, 19–20, 61, 138, 257
net profit margin, 150
Ne Win, Burmese dictator, 47, 50–1
Newmont Mining Corp., 307, 308
Nigeria, 169–97, 333–7
  Boko Haram, 178, 181, 186, 334
  Daly's analysis, 186, 196–7
  equities, 189
  ETFs, 190, 348
  oil refining, 192–7
  oil revenue theft, 181–3

+233 nightclub, Ghana, 299
Nollywood, 195, 322
Nuclearelectrica, 85, 101, 102, 104, 107

Obama, Barack, 29, 50, 296
obesity, Egypt, 205–6
Obuasi mine, Ghana, 304, 305,
  306–7, 308
Odinga, Raila, 12, 20, 23, 24, 25
oil production/refining
  Argentina, 126–30
  Nigeria, 181–2, 192–3
oil revenue disappearance, Nigeria,
  181–3
Okonjo-Iweala, Ngozi, 182, 194, 195
OMV Petrom, Romania, 85, 86, 101,
  103, 107, 338, 362
O'Neill, Jim, praise for Sanusi, 182–3
Oo, Tin, NLD, Myanmar, 47, 50,
  51–2, 318
Oppenheimer Developing Markets
  Fund, 343
OTC drug sales, Imexpharm, 153–5
Oueijan, Habib, 249–50, 331

pagodas, Myanmar, 46, 47, 48, 66,
  74, 324
Parametric Emerging Markets Fund,
  343
passenger car demand, 209
Paunrana, Pradeep, ARM Cement,
  39–40
pawning loans, 267–70, 271
People's Democratic Party (PDP), 184,
  186, 187
pharmaceuticals, Vietnam, 152–8
plastics, 159–63
p-notes, Saudi Arabia, 248–9
police
  Egypt, 223–8
  Ghana, 296–7
  Nigeria, 171–2
  Saudi Arabia, 232, 234–5, 236, 411